Screen Histories

A *Screen* Reader

Screen Histories
A *Screen* Reader

Edited by
ANNETTE KUHN
and **JACKIE STACEY**

CLARENDON PRESS · OXFORD

Oxford University Press, Great Clarendon Street, Oxford OX2 6DP

Oxford New York
Athens Auckland Bangkok Bogotá Buenos Aires Calcutta
Cape Town Chennai Dar es Salaam Delhi Florence Hong Kong Istanbul
Karachi Kuala Lumpur Madrid Melbourne Mexico City Mumbai
Nairobi Paris São Paolo Singapore Taipei Tokyo Toronto Warsaw
and associated companies in
Berlin Ibadan

Oxford is a registered trade mark of Oxford University Press

Published in the United States
by Oxford University Press Inc., New York

British Library Cataloguing in Publication Data

Data available

Library of Congress Cataloging in Publication Data

Screen histories : a reader / edited by Annette Kuhn and Jackie Stacey.
A collection of articles published in Screen over the past twenty years.
1. Motion pictures.   I. Kuhn, Annette.   II. Stacey, Jackie.
III. Screen (London, England)
PN1994.S425   1998   791.43'09—dc21   98-38145
ISNB 0–19–815946–3
ISBN 0–19–815949–8 (pbk.)

1 3 5 7 9 10 8 6 4 2

Typeset by Graphicraft Limited, Hong Kong
Printed in Great Britain
on acid-free paper by
Bookcraft Ltd,
Midsomer Norton, Somerset

Contents

Screen Histories: An Introduction

ANNETTE KUHN AND JACKIE STACEY

In the twenty-five or thirty years since it began to emerge as a discipline in its own right, screen studies has rarely been free of controversy. Among the more common complaints is that an overwhelming obsession with theory has been detrimental to the status and development of scholarly work on the history of cinema. In Britain, film history has been described as the poor relation of film studies, having taken a back seat during the reign of 'high theory'; while in the USA until relatively recently scholars were wary of historical research and 'all cool graduate students were analysing [film] texts'. Indeed, Stephen Bottomore, an independent film historian, goes so far as to claim that in Britain cinema history has been marginalized within the academy to such a degree that its production has been left entirely to the famous 'British amateur'.[1] 'It is difficult', he contends, 'to think of any other country where "amateurs" have played such a prominent role in film history': elsewhere, he says cinema history is the province of academics and workers in film institutes and film archives. But in Britain, 'a kind of cinema studies "apartheid" exists, wherein history and academia remain separated, and the amateur film historian and the academic scarcely communicate'.[2]

Such a state of affairs is regrettable, not simply because of the limits it imposes upon the discipline of film studies itself, but also because of its impact on the range and the quality of those screen histories which *are* undertaken. For example, Bottomore complains that many of the independently written local histories of British cinema lack scholarly address, the reason for this being that they are produced in the isolation induced by the 'two cultures' of British film studies. Furthermore Britain, unlike other countries (France, for example) has no scholarly journal devoted exclusively to the history of cinema, and the absence

1 Robert Allen, 'From exhibition to reception', *Screen,* vol. 31, no. 4 (1990), p. 347 (reprinted in this volume, Chapter 1); Stephen Bottomore, 'Film history in Britain', *Viewfinder,* no. 27 (1996), p. 10.

2 Ibid.

3   Ibid.

of funding for national cinema history projects has meant a lack of direction, policy, and breadth of work in this field.[3] Although Bottomore's concern is cinema, the same is arguably true of the historical study of television, which has been subordinated within the academy to sociological and social-psychological studies of contemporary programming, audiences, and impacts.

While some of these criticisms may be overstated (a number of social and political historians in British universities have made important contributions in this area, and the *Historical Journal of Radio, Film and Television*, now based in the USA, was founded in Britain), they do raise crucial questions concerning the lack of funding and the paucity of institutional support for historical research of this kind in Britain; and it might well be that the protracted development of the historical dimensions of the study of film and television is in some measure attributable to the absence of such support. It is certainly the case that these areas have been slow to attract attention and gain momentum. However, despite the unevenness of their disciplinary status in Britain and beyond, histories of film and of television have been and continue to be written. As this collection itself demonstrates, *Screen* for one has been publishing work in history and historiography for over two decades. Since the journal's move to Glasgow in 1989 this emphasis has intensified, and the selection of work included here highlights the increasing centrality of historical research to developments within screen studies: between 1990 and 1997, *Screen* published more than twenty articles on the history of film and television.[4]

4   See Appendix for details. The cut-off date for inclusion in this collection is the end of vol. 35 (1994).

Bringing together some of this work in one volume not only makes some excellent scholarship more widely available, but also marks *Screen*'s contribution to an ever-expanding body of work in film and television history. We would contend, therefore, not only that Bottomore's claims about the dearth of academic screen history are increasingly unfounded, but also that the theory/history binary implicit in his claims is rapidly breaking down. This is not to deny the historical significance of such a dichotomy; for of course *Screen,* with its influential work of the 1970s on ideology, subjectivity, and textuality, has in the past been rather more readily associated with 'theory' than with 'history'. 'Screen Theory', indeed, has become shorthand for a set of theoretical debates characterized by engagement with particular versions of semiotics and psychoanalysis, influenced by Althusserian philosophy, and assuming a highly critical stance towards 'historicism'. But the theory/history dichotomy can only lead to damaging divisions and reifications within the discipline, and we should be wary of perpetuating it. Alison Butler is surely correct in her assertion that 'it is as artificial to separate theory from history as it is to sever cinema from the world'.[5] Challenging film studies to establish a dialogue, if not a convergence, between the two, Butler urges us to resist a tendency to attribute coherence and autonomy to either approach. While acknowledging that the tensions within film studies produced by the theory/history dualism are part of the discipline's intellectual history,

5   Alison Butler, 'New film histories and the politics of location', *Screen,* vol. 33, no. 4 (1992), p. 426.

our introduction to this volume is offered in the spirit of Butler's bid for dialogue. The remarks which follow are offered not only as an introduction to the 'screen histories' in this collection, but also as an account of the shifting, and sometimes conflicting, agendas which motivate their reproduction here and now.

In its spring 1976 issue, *Screen* published an article on the coming of sound to Hollywood cinema in the late 1920s. Through reference to hitherto unexploited historical source materials, Douglas Gomery succeeded in upturning the then received wisdom that it was the impending bankruptcy of Warner Bros which led the studio to pioneer its innovations in film sound technology. As its title—'Writing the history of the American film industry: Warner Bros and sound' —suggests, Gomery's essay not only presented fresh historical information but also, and perhaps more importantly, constituted a manifesto for a bold new approach to the historiography of cinema, for what the author calls a 'revisionist film history': 'we must not simply trust the old bibliographies or faulty recollections, but go out and seek the evidence wherever it may be'.[6]

6 J. Douglas Gomery, 'Writing the history of the American film industry: Warner Bros and sound', *Screen*, vol. 17, no. 1 (1976), pp. 40–53. Gomery's essay is reprinted in this volume, minus its original introductory remarks—from which this quotation is taken (p. 40)—as Chapter 9.

7 Ibid., p. 53.

If this statement heralded a revolution in the historiography of cinema, however, the modesty of its tone ran somewhat counter to the current of heroic theory then coursing with fervid energy through the pages of *Screen*. While it would be an overstatement to suggest that Gomery's call for primary research and scholarly rigour ('We must create our own first principles, and methods. We must examine the accepted notions of bias and cause, and begin to search out new sources or primary data')[7] fell on deaf ears, *Screen*'s engagement with the new film history was perhaps at this point tangential to its preoccupations with film language and with the ideological practices of cinema. While such concerns did not necessarily preclude attention to the history of cinema and its institutional practices, they did mean that any such considerations were in effect subsumed to the journal's theoretical–political agenda: and indeed, *Screen*'s early contributions to debates on the history of cinema were made under the sway of Jean-Louis Comolli and Paul Narboni's *Cahiers du Cinema* work (translated in *Screen* in 1971) on the interrelations of ideology and film technologies.[8]

8 Jean-Louis Comolli and Paul Narboni, 'Cinema/ideology/criticism', *Screen*, vol. 12, no. 1 (1971), pp. 27–35.

9 Patrick L. Ogle, 'Technological and aesthetic influences upon the development of deep focus cinematography in the United States', *Screen*, vol. 13, no. 1 (1972), pp. 45–72; commentary by Christopher Williams, ibid., pp. 73–6; Peter Baxter, 'On the history and ideology of film lighting', *Screen*, vol. 16, no. 3 (1975), 83–106.

In the following year, *Screen* published a substantial piece of primary historical research by Patrick Ogle on developments in deep focus cinematography in the USA: appended to this was a commentary and critique by Christopher Williams, an editorial board member, which situated Ogle's discussion within the terms of Comolli's arguments and called for attention to be given to questions of 'Ideology and Economy'. In 1975, film lighting was accorded similar Comollian treatment by Peter Baxter.[9] The significance of the fact that *Screen*'s earliest forays into the 'new' film history were all histories of technology (of deep focus cinematography, lighting, and sound) is that they were prompted precisely by the interest in the ideological implication of cinematographic technology which at that time formed part of the journal's overall theoretical agenda.

If *Screen*'s 1970s project in some respects demanded that attention be given at least to these aspects of the history of cinema, it also militated against certain approaches to historical scholarship. This contradiction emerged most forcefully not in the pages of *Screen* but in a seminar series organized by one of the journal's editorial board members, Claire Johnston, in connection with the 1977 Edinburgh Film Festival. In the publication accompanying the seminars, Geoffrey Nowell-Smith drew attention to doubts which were at the time being cast upon the validity of historical inquiry, and pointed out that this new

> loss of confidence in traditional historiographic procedures and the turn towards non-historical modes of theorisation has produced a severe hiatus in the study of the cinema. No one now accepts accounts of film history . . . which pass blandly from one 'fact' to another . . . And yet no one knows how to do better, except at a cost of a sceptical unwillingness to do anything.[10]

10 Geoffrey Nowell-Smith, 'On the writing of the history of the cinema: some problems', *Edinburgh '77 Magazine: History/Production/Memory* (Edinburgh: Edinburgh Film Festival, 1977), p. 10. However, this publication did include, though rather uneasily, some screen history: see, for example, Annette Kuhn, ' "Independent" filmmaking and the State in the 1930s', ibid., pp. 44–55.

For a time, *Screen* itself appears to have fallen prey to this unwillingness: following the publication of Gomery's 1976 article, no work of film history appeared in the journal until Jeanne Allen's study of copyright protection in early cinema (reprinted here as Chapter 7) was published in the summer of 1980.

During the years of ascendance of 'high theory', the difficulty highlighted by Nowell-Smith persisted, and work in film history was always at risk of being scare-labelled 'empiricist' or 'historicist'. But the new film history, while always advocating empirical research, was never empiric*ist*: this indeed was a central tenet of its revisionism. Since the two terms—empirical and empiricist—are frequently confused, it is perhaps worth clarifying the distinction: 'Empiricism names a philosophical tradition that places primary emphasis upon experience in explaining how humans acquire knowledge. . . . An empirical inquiry is one which seeks answers to its questions from evidence outside the mind of the inquirer'.[11]

11 David Bordwell, 'Contemporary film studies and the vicissitudes of Grand Theory', in David Bordwell and Noel Carroll (eds.), *Post Theory: Reconstructing Film Studies* (Madison, WI: University of Wisconsin Press, 1996), p. 34, note 63.

A further, and related, defining feature of the new film history was its refusal to countenance the theory/history division: indeed in his 1976 article, Gomery had voiced a commitment to theory alongside his concern with historical methods and sources ('the problem is not the non-existence of data, it is one of theory and methodology').[12] It might be added that one of the more positive aspects of the Althusserian legacy is a self-critical and reflexive attitude towards scholarly activity. From the beginning, the new film history adopted an open and questioning approach to its own methodologies; and to some extent also to the purposes of historical inquiry. What is film history for? What are its uses?

12 Gomery, 'Writing the history of the American film industry', p. 40.

As Gomery pointed out, historians of the US film industry had hitherto failed to follow even the most fundamental principles of the historian's craft. Standard film histories relied for evidence on hearsay and anecdote, primary sources were ignored, and footnotes were few

13 Barbara Klinger, 'Film history terminable and interminable: recovering the past in reception studies', *Screen*, vol. 38, no. 2 (1997), p. 111. See also Thomas Elsaesser, 'The new film history', *Sight and Sound*, vol. 55, no. 4 (1986), pp. 246–51.

and far between. The most urgent task for a new film history, then, was simply to 'displace secondary and anecdotal forms of history with primary documentation, archival research and other historiographical tools of evidence and verification'.[13] But what counts as admissible evidence, and how should it be used? This, of course, raises the question of what film history is, or ought to be, *about*: questions concerning source materials, in other words, lead straight back to questions about objects and purposes of inquiry.

By the mid-1980s, the new film history had begun to establish itself in those interstices of the US academy inhabited by cinema studies, and to attract attention elsewhere via scholarly journals, conferences, and other events and publications. Robert Allen and Douglas Gomery's *Film History*, the first book-length work of revisionist film history, appeared in 1985. It combined discussion of the new film history's objectives, objects, and methodologies with case studies in four types of film history: aesthetic, technological, economic, and social. In 1983, the Paris-based journal *Iris* was founded, devoting many of its early issues to theoretical and methodological considerations of, as well as to examples of work in, the new film history, largely by scholars working in the USA and in France.[14] In 1986, US scholar Janet Staiger published a ground-breaking essay on *Foolish Wives* (Erich von Stroheim, 1922) which aimed to shed light on the nature of the relationship between film texts and spectators or audiences, and on how to think and research this relationship—the question of the film reception—historically. *Screen*'s contribution to the debate consisted of a report on a conference held in France on new approaches in film history.[15] What all of these initiatives share is a self-reflexive approach to methodology, and a quest to integrate theory with history—the very hallmarks of the new film history.

14 Robert C. Allen and Douglas Gomery, *Film History: Theory and Practice* (New York: Alfred A. Knopf, 1985); Kristin Thompson, 'Cinematic specificity in film criticism and history', *Iris*, vol. 1, no. 1 (1983), pp. 39–49.

15 Janet Staiger, ' "The handmaiden of villainy": methods and problems in studying the historical reception of a film', *Wide Angle*, vol. 8, no. 1 (1986), pp. 20–7, reprinted in Staiger's *Interpreting Films: Studies in the Historical Reception of American Cinema* (Princeton, NJ: Princeton University Press, 1992); Ginette Vincendeau, 'New approaches to film history', *Screen*, vol. 26, no. 8 (1985), 70–3.

16 Examples of this work appear in Thomas Elsaesser (ed.), *Early Cinema: Space, Frame, Narrative* (London: British Film Institute, 1990). See also Rod Stoneman, 'Early cinema', *Screen*, vol. 23, no. 2 (1982), pp. 2–3; Thompson, 'Cinematic specificity in film criticism and history'.

In terms of objects of study and source materials, the new film history exhibits two broad tendencies. A strand of work on early cinema, pioneered among others by André Gaudreault, Ben Brewster, and Barry Salt, concerns itself with developments in film form in the years preceding the rise in the late 1910s of classical cinema:[16] this influential tendency, represented by the contributions in Part IV of this volume, appears to have no counterpart in the historical study of television. For this work, both the object of study and also its principal evidentiary source lie in films themselves; and the main challenge it faces is the availability of source materials. The vast majority of films produced during cinema's earliest years have been lost, and the preservation of those which survive is a costly business. Besides which, access even to these can present great difficulties. The work of these 'textual historians' consequently goes hand in hand with the archiving, preservation and making accessibile of early films; a necessity and a conjunction most famously apparent in the festival of silent cinema held in Pordenone, Italy each year since 1981.

Other tendencies within revisionist film history follow the lead taken by scholars like Gomery in concerning themselves with matters outside the film text itself. The objects of such histories range widely, from the organization of the film industry as a set of institutions and practices of production, distribution, and exhibition, through developments in cinematographic technologies, to cinema's broader social and cultural contexts.[17] Source materials vary accordingly. For his study of Warner Bros and the coming of sound—an example of economic film history— Gomery consulted film industry trade periodicals of the late 1920s and transcripts of court cases concerning patents for new cinema sound equipment. Source materials for economic and social histories of cinema recommended by Gomery and Allen in *Film History* include city and business directories, local newspapers, the film trade press, local public records, and photographs.

17 For a recent overview, see Klinger, 'Film history terminable and interminable'.

Contributions to the present volume draw upon sources as diverse as box-office data and cinema-goers' memories for the historical studies of film reception in Part I; reformers' reports on prostitution, popular magazines, and records of the birth control movement for the social histories of cinema in Part II; and patent and copyright law, the records of individual film studios and of industry-wide bodies such as the Production Code Administration for the institutional histories in Part III. Reception histories, social histories, and institutional histories of cinema all have counterparts in the historical study of television; though it is incontestable that revisionist television history—if such a body of work is identifiable—is markedly underdeveloped by comparison with the new film history. The undeniably minimal representation in this volume of such work (Chapter 8) serves to highlight this regrettable state of affairs.

It must be acknowledged that the substance of any historical account is bound to be informed by the source materials deployed in its production; and indeed that conversely some forms of historical research may be frustrated by the limitations, or even the non-existence, of relevant source materials. In historical studies of cinema in Britain, certainly, where primary materials on and around the film industry are for a variety of reasons much more limited in both quantity and accessibility than in the USA, the historian's attention has been more readily directed at cinema's political, social, and cultural contexts than at the film industry itself. In this regard, differences of approach between British and US historians of film reception are of particular import: the deployment of cultural studies-style methods in historical ethnographies of film reception by British scholars Helen Taylor and Jackie Stacey, for example, stand in marked contrast to their US counterparts' focus on film industry discourses and intertexts.[18]

18 Helen Taylor, *Scarlett's Women: 'Gone With the Wind' and its Female Fans* (London: Virago Press, 1989); Jackie Stacey, *Star Gazing: Hollywood Cinema and Female Spectatorship* (London: Routledge, 1994), and Chapter 2 in this volume. For ' "The handmaiden of villainy" ', Janet Staiger draws upon contemporary reviews of *Foolish Wives*.

19 Allen and Gomery, *Film History*, p. 104.

The authors of *Film History* remain agnostic about the role of films as evidence in forms of historical scholarship other than that variant of aesthetic film history which attends to the 'history of film as signifying practices'.[19] Nevertheless, the question of the relationship between film texts and their social, cultural, and industrial contexts has emerged as crucial for revisionist film history; and this development has far-reaching implications. For example, social historians of cinema who wish to address film texts in their work without recourse to formalism or to determinism are faced with potentially daunting theoretical and methodological challenges. Even film histories which make conscious efforts to avoid determinism may appear to privilege social, historical, or industrial contexts over film texts—or vice versa—if only because of the difficulties of weaving together in a single historical account the disparate strands of a complex historical narrative.[20]

The challenge becomes all the more pressing as social historians of cinema turn their attention to the historical reception of films. Before the rise of the new film history, work on the history of cinema tended to remain focused on the film and its production: 'as recently as 1975 . . . film history still was almost universally taken to mean the history of films'.[21] Making the case for broadening the remit of cinema history to include audiences and exhibition, Robert Allen argues that in the 1970s 'film history [was] . . . written as if films had no audiences or were seen by everyone in the same way, or as if however they were viewed and by whomever, the history of "films" was distinct from and privileged over the history of their being taken up by the billions of people who have watched them since 1894'.[22] In similar vein, Geoffrey Nowell-Smith has argued that what is needed—and 'what is so hard to supply'—is not so much a history of the texts produced by the media of the twentieth century as a 'history of subjectivities'; to this end, he suggests, 'reception studies need to be supplemented by theories of fantasy on the one hand and of the relation between images and their referents on the other'.[23] Such an undertaking would require an imbrication of historical and theoretical approaches, demonstrating precisely their mutual dependence rather than their incompatibility.

But the project of reuniting film theory and film history raises complex questions: what, for example, is the place of the film text in historical reception studies which use the memories of cinema-goers as their source materials? Our own experience as cultural historians suggests that in cinema memory films either accrue layers of meaning coloured by informants' subsequent life stories so that memories then become objects of interpretation in their own right; or else that films actually disappear beneath the weight of memory. Similar questions face historical studies of television, although in rather different and as yet largely unexplored ways.[24] While such difficulties certainly do not render the enterprise of revisionist film history too troublesome to contemplate, they do demand ongoing reconsideration of its objects, its objectives, and its uses.

If the 1990s have seen an expansion in the breadth and depth of historical research in screen studies, it is perhaps worth pausing to consider the significance and the broader intellectual context of this invigorated concern with historical agendas. For what might be referred to as the 'historical turn' within film and television studies is not an isolated phenomenon. We conclude, therefore, with some reflections on the historical conjuncture within which this collection of work on screen

20 See, for example, Annette Kuhn, *Cinema, Censorship and Sexuality 1909–1925* (London: Routledge, 1988), chapter 1. See also Patrice Petro, 'Feminism and film history', *Camera Obscura*, no. 22 (1990), pp. 9–26.

21 Allen, 'From exhibition to reception', p. 347.

22 Ibid., p. 348.

23 Geoffrey Nowell-Smith, 'On history and the cinema', *Screen*, vol. 31, no. 2 (1990), pp. 170–1.

24 Stacey, *Star Gazing*, chapter 4; Annette Kuhn, 'Memory and textuality', in Susannah Radstone (ed.), *Memory and Method* (London: Berg, forthcoming). For television, see Lynn Spigel, 'From the dark ages to the golden age: women's memories and TV returns', *Screen*, vol. 36, no. 1 (1995), pp. 16–33.

histories has been assembled, and offer some speculations on the directions such work might take in the future.

While having its own inflections and agendas, the proliferation of screen histories in the past decade is perhaps attributable in some measure to a move within all areas of cultural analysis towards an increased attention to historical specificity. This might be seen as part of a more general concern with locatedness and situatedness in social and cultural theory, in which 'history' has assumed the status of privileged signifier in various areas of scholarship. In this regard, two influences may be signalled, both of which have been identified with the 'post-modernization' of culture and of knowledge. First, the widening of interdisciplinary activity in many academic institutions has facilitated a 'borrowing' of theories and methodologies across intellectual traditions: 'historical approaches' have consequently had considerable impact on research in departments of sociology, cultural studies, and literature, as well as in screen studies. Secondly, the breakdown of theoretical universalisms has led to a deeper focus on historicity. While uneven and contested, this historical turn is nevertheless part of a more general desire to locate some of the grand narratives of structuralism, semiotics, and psychoanalysis within specific historical conjunctures.

However, there are larger issues still at stake in the rise of history within screen studies. In particular, we might point to the impact of the millennium on intellectual agendas and consider its significance in the increased sense of urgency about the nature and purpose of film and television (and other) histories. For, as the end of the twentieth century generates innumerable opportunities for reflection, contemplation, nostalgia, and speculation, scholars and intellectuals in all disciplines respond to pressures to encapsulate the 'spirit of the age'. Since the history of the cinema is the history of the twentieth century, the significance of this millennialism is especially potent within film studies. Geoffrey Nowell-Smith reminds us that: 'In their activities along the boundary of fact and fiction, reality and pleasure, actual and imagined, cinema first, and then television, have established themselves as the principal repository of the social imaginary of the twentieth century.'[25] The millennial context of the 'historical turn' within screen studies thus provides opportunity for careful reflection both upon the place of these media within contemporary cultures and also upon the kinds of history-making in which scholars in the field should be engaged. In attempting to broaden the remit of film and television history, we might consider what kinds of inclusiveness are desirable and where the boundaries around the discipline now lie, given the expanding horizon of research required to address the complexities of the place of cinema and of television (as well as of other media) in contemporary social life.

Such an inclusive historical project promises to locate media texts and situate them within the cultural practices which inform their significance. Indeed, in this sense screen histories would seem to fall very much within the remit of that more located and situated study

25 Nowell-Smith, 'On history and the cinema', p. 165.

demanded by scholars engaged in the critical and theoretical debates of the 1990s. Much feminist research, for example, has moved towards a more temporally and spatially located consideration of the meanings ascribed to the category 'woman'; and the impact of cultural studies work on a number of disciplines might arguably be seen in terms of its insistence precisely upon *situating* the cultural objects, texts, industries, or subjectivities under scrutiny.

However, the assumption that historical work necessarily addresses spatial as well as temporal specificity is not always borne out in the practice of research. Responding to examples of 'revisionist film history' which focus upon the history of modes of production without sufficient attention to *where* cinema history 'takes place', Alison Butler argues that: 'if the manifest material of cinema histories is time, its other major determinant is place'.[26] Butler goes on to caution against the problems this kind of approach might generate:

26 Butler, 'New film histories', p. 414.

> the less film historians acknowledge their place, the more their work will be invaded by its concerns. The limit case of this will be those histories which assume the universality of either their object or their approach. These histories, produced in the West, will tend strongly to imperialism of one kind or another. In order to confront problems of periodization, we will need to examine our cultural-historical categories carefully, and to ask how they have functioned to temporalize spatial dominance.[27]

27 Ibid., p. 425.

As Butler makes clear, it is not simply that screen histories need to integrate a consideration of 'place', but that such a consideration of locatedness requires an analysis of the power relations of colonialism and of the dynamics of global cultures more generally. One of the central tensions in the writing of screen histories then is inevitably that between the general and the particular. Butler's reservations about the politics of certain kinds of revisionist history highlight the complexities embedded within this tension: whereas we might expect historical research to pay attention to 'the politics of location', there may well be ways in which it can reproduce many of the problems of its less-rooted counterparts in the field, such as semiotics or psychoanalysis. According to Butler, however, scepticism about large-scale generalizations is no protection against the occlusions of 'universalist' film theory. While we tend to think of the historical as adding the necessary attention to details, Butler's intervention reminds us that critical self-reflection and rigorous theoretical interrogation of our terms of history-making continue to be of paramount importance. Our own investments in the kinds of histories we are engaged in producing thus need to be made explicit. Furthermore, Butler suggests, we need to recognize that 'histories, as Walter Benjamin pointed out, are discourses of legitimation inextricably connected to the present and the future'.[28] Thus, we might remind ourselves that rather than being simply 'about the past' in any straightforward way, screen histories are of necessity concerned with past–present relations with a view to the future.

28 Ibid., p. 413.

To write of 'screen histories' then is to contemplate a multiplicity of connections between the screen and history, rather than simply offering a history of the screen—be it cinema, television, or even computer screen. But the changing technologies and contexts of exhibition and reception in the latter part of the twentieth century produce new challenges for screen historians: it becomes increasingly difficult, for example, to keep cinema and television separate as objects of study. For if, as Geoffrey Nowell-Smith claims, 'cinema no longer happens in the cinemas', how is the ever-expanding remit of screen history to address these shifting boundaries? In the endless recycling of cinema images on television and video, for example, what is the impact of the removal of the original viewing conditions on contemporary consumption of images produced in the past? The sheer number and random combinations of films shown in domestic settings profoundly change the meaning of cinema and television:

> What is particularly lacking . . . amid the abundance, is any sense of history. Sixty years of film history—plus the occasional dip into the silent period—parades in front of our eyes without any indication of where it has been dredged up from, or that it is history at all. . . . In this two-dimensional space, whose only temporality is that of schedules, differences are obliterated: differences of kind, in the sense that movies, music, reportage all appear there as 'something on TV'; and differences of historical time, which are endlessly referred to but continually elude representation. Somehow it is necessary to restore the dimensions which have been lost.[29]

29 Nowell-Smith, 'On history and the cinema', pp. 167–8.

We have touched upon some reasons for the increased importance of screen histories within film and television studies. The broader influences of academic shifts and tendencies no doubt play their part and account for the place of these histories within more general trends towards specificity, locatedness, and acknowledgement of the importance of differences. However, we are not suggesting that the discipline is merely caught up in a more general wave of history-making sweeping academia; but rather that there are subject-specific agendas at stake here as well. The rapid and radical transformation of the meanings of film, television, and other screen imaging technologies in the twentieth century call, both inside and outside the academy, for a scholarly account of these changes and an informed sense of their histories.

Part I Reception Histories

1 From Exhibition to Reception: Reflections on the Audience in Film History

ROBERT C. ALLEN

As recently as 1975, when I taught my first film history class, film history still was almost universally taken to mean the history of films. Not all films, of course, just those films a teacher could nominate with a straight face as 'art' in defending his or her course to a colleague in art history or literature. Ironically, the first film 'theory' that French, then British, and finally American scholars took up in opposition to this cinematic New Criticism—the 'auteur theory'—merely bolstered the historiographic notion that film history was to be studied as a succession of texts. The corpus of film history—especially American film history—was certainly modified as a result of auteurism, but the idea that film history rested upon the interpretation of a body of texts remained unchallenged. Any hopes of dethroning the text in film studies and textual interpretation in film history were dashed in the mid-1970s as auteurism was succeeded by structuralism, semiotics, and Lacthusserianism. Film history was to take a very back seat indeed during the reign of high theory, which is not surprising given its resolutely ahistorical and thoroughly conventionalist underpinnings. All the cool graduate students were analysing texts. Anyone interested in questions of history was clearly not with the programme; and anyone interested in non-cinetextual historical questions—economic structures, the relationship between cinema and other forms of popular entertainment, technology, the organization of labour, or what might have gone on the billions of times the texts of film history were 'read' by viewers—was also a damned empiricist!

And yet as I prepared that first set of film history lectures, issues of context not textual interpretation troubled and fascinated me most—a fascination, I must admit, that owed more to intellectual perversity than prescience. Specifically, I was struck by how little the audience or even exhibition featured in the received film history we all learned in film courses or read about in survey accounts. Except for the legendary viewers who dived under their seats at the sight of Lumiere's train coming into the station; the countless immigrants to the USA who, we are told, learned American values in the sawdust-floored nickelodeons of the lower East Side; and those who, to a person it would seem, applauded Al Jolson's 'You ain't seen nothin' yet' in 1927,[1] film history had been written as if films had no audiences or were seen by everyone and in the same way, or as if however they were viewed and by whomever, the history of 'films' was distinct from and privileged over the history of their being taken up by the billions of people who have watched them since 1894.

Furthermore, a good deal of what had been written about film audiences was supported (if at all) by the flimsiest of evidence and yet was couched in terms of unqualified generalization. In one of my early lectures I got to the point in American film history when films had been successfully introduced as vaudeville acts (1896). But quickly thereafter (1897), as I had read in all the standard histories, audiences became so disenchanted with the movies that theatre managers began to use them as 'chasers'—acts so unpopular that they drove the audience from the theatre. The words stuck in my throat. I could not 'profess' this moment of film history. As a result, I was driven back to more contemporaneous sources and to a wider consideration of the contexts within which early films were received. I shall not belabour the 'chaser' issue further here, except to say that nearly fifteen years later I am far from convinced that films universally sank into a trough of audience disdain during this period nor that vaudeville managers routinely used movies they knew their audiences did not want to see to clear the house.[2]

Over the past fifteen years, a number of scholars in the USA and elsewhere have added exhibition at least to the agenda of film history, demonstrating, among other things, how important exhibition was as an historical determinant in the development of the film industry in the USA. In the process, they have also suggested something of our appalling ignorance of the most basic facts of exhibition history: differences in exhibition practices between cities and towns, the likely audiences for the tens of thousands of exhibition venues across the USA and over time, and the complexities of the relationship between movie-going and other social practices. Today I would hope that no film scholar would write a serious film history with the near total elision of the audience that characterized such works fifteen years ago, and I would similarly hope (although I know in fact they are) that film history classes would not be taught without some minimal attention being given to the conditions under which viewers actually saw films.

1 Indeed, in their rush to celebrate sound technology, historians of American cinema have ignored the fact that there was serious audience resistance to the introduction of the talkies in the late 1920s in some parts of the USA. As late as January 1929, for example, a survey of movie-goers in Syracuse, New York, found that only 50% preferred talkies to silents, and only 7% favoured elimination of silent films. See Henry Jenkins III, 'Shall we make It for New York or for distribution? Eddie Cantor, *Whoopee*, and regional resistance to the talkies', *Cinema Journal*, vol. 29, no. 3 (1988), pp. 32–52.

2 I laid out my arguments against the 'chaser theory' in 'Contra the chaser theory', *Wide Angle*, 3 (1979), pp. 4–11. See also my exchange with Charles Musser on the subject in *Studies in Visual Communication*, 10 (1984), pp. 24–52.

3 Philip Corrigan, 'Film entertainment as ideology and pleasure: a preliminary approach to a history of audiences', in James Curran and Vincent Porter (eds.), *British Cinema History*, (London: British Film Institute, 1983), pp. 24–35.

In 1983 Philip Corrigan declared the history of film audiences to be 'still almost completely undeveloped, even unconsidered'. He argued that the problem of the audience in film history could usefully be recast within the rubric of cultural studies.[3] What I would like to propose here is taking Corrigan's reconsideration of the audience in film history a step further: namely, the enlarging of the notion of exhibition and the audience to encompass a more general historical concern with reception—a move implied in the work of a growing number of film scholars. I am using the term reception here to mean the most inclusive category of issues surrounding the confrontation between the semiotic and the social. Reception thus conceived would have at least four overlapping but theoretically and methodologically distinct components.

Exhibition designates the institutional and economic dimensions of reception—that is, the nature of the institutional apparatus under whose auspices and for whose benefit films are shown; the relationship between exhibition as that term has been used within the industry and other segments of the film business; and the location and physical nature of the sites of exhibition.

Although no study has systematically charted the nature and historical development of exhibition in the USA, a number of individual studies have suggested something of the previously unacknowledged variety of exhibition practices, particularly during the first two decades of the commercial exploitation of the movies. The first thing these studies are discovering is that New York City—the place from which many of our generalizations about movie-going across the country are taken—is probably *sui generis* with respect to exhibition. As soon as we look at cities in other parts of the country, smaller cities without large immigrant populations, and small towns and villages, a very different exhibition picture emerges.

For example, concentration on early movie-going as an urban phenomenon has obscured the fact that during the first decade of the movies' commercial growth, 71 per cent of the population of the USA lived in rural areas or small towns. The first audiences for the movies in these areas were not to be found in vaudeville theatres (the towns were too small to support them) or store-front movie theatres (which, if they came at all, came later), but in tents, amusement parks, the local opera house, YMCA hall, public library basement—wherever an itinerant showman could set up his (or her?—were there any female itinerant exhibitors?) projector. Edward Lowry has suggested that one consequence of small communities' reliance upon itinerant showmen was that their audiences attached much more importance to the exhibitor—who, after all, was the present, human agent of their film-going pleasure—than to the producers of the films he showed.

For years, travelling exhibitors provided the only opportunities for movie-going to millions of Americans. The dispatching of Lumiere

4 On itinerant film exhibition in the USA, see Edward Lowry, 'Edwin J. Hadley: traveling film exhibitor', *Journal of the University Film Association*, 28 (1976), pp. 5–12; Burnes St. Patrick Hollyman, 'The first Picture Shows: Austin, Texas (1894–1913)', *Journal of the University Film Association*, 29 (1977), pp. 9–22; David O. Thomas, 'From page to screen in smalltown America: early motion picture exhibition in Winona, Minnesota', *Journal of the University Film Association*, 33, no. 3 (1981), pp. 3–14; Calvin Pryluck, 'The itinerant movie show and the development of the film industry', *Journal of the University Film Association*, 35 (1983), pp. 11–22; Mark E. Swartz, 'Motion pictures on the move', *Journal of American Culture*, 9 (1986), pp. 1–8.

5 I discuss early exhibition in Durham, North Carolina, in *Film History: Theory and Practice* (New York: Alfred A. Knopf, 1985), pp. 202–7. On the role of amusement parks in early exhibition, see Lauren Rabinowitz, 'Temptations of pleasure: cinema, sexuality, and the turn-of-the-century amusement park', *Camera Obscura*, forthcoming; Greg Waller, 'Situating motion pictures in the pre-Nickelodeon period: Lexington, Kentucky 1897–1906', paper presented at the 1989 Conference of the Society for Cinema Studies; and Charlotte Herzog, 'The archaeology of cinema architecture: the origins of the movie theater', *Quarterly Review of Film Studies*, 9, no. 1 (1984), pp. 11–32.

6 Some interesting work *is* being done on 'amateur' film-making practices, particularly that by Patricia R. Zimmerman. See, for example, 'Hollywood, home movies, and common sense: amateur film as aesthetic dissemination and social control, 1950–62', *Cinema Journal*, vol. 27, no. 4 (1988), pp. 23–44; and 'Trading down: amateur film technology in fifties America', *Screen*, vol. 29, no. 2 (1988), pp. 40–51.

'operators' around the world in 1896 has left the impression that exposure to motion pictures, at least in the West, was universal and simultaneous. However, the more we learn about US exhibition patterns, the more aware we become of just how long it took the movies to reach some parts of the country. Although we know that films were shown in some remote locations (Klondike mining camps in 1898, for example), one itinerant showman claimed to have given the first movie exhibition in Arizona during the 1911–12 season. Furthermore, although many travelling exhibitors ceased operation with the spread of permanent exhibition in the 1910s, there were still itinerant showmen on the road as late as 1947. One showman, who worked the small towns of North and South Carolina, Virginia, and Georgia, recalled that one of his best customers was a woman who had never seen the movies until he set up his tent in her village for the first time in the mid-1930s.[4]

For some time now my graduate students and I have been charting exhibition patterns in cities and towns throughout North Carolina between 1896 and 1915. Without exception, the exhibition situation contrasts sharply with that in New York. Permanent exhibition, for example, was not established even in the largest North Carolina city until 1906. The first permanent theatres were not located in working-class ghettos but invariably in the centre of the downtown business district. Most of these theatres attempted to attract a middle-class clientele from the outset. In some cases itinerant showmen were the first to bring movies to the community, but more often than not in the case of large towns, the first sustained exhibition programmes took place in amusement parks, which were constructed at the end of streetcar lines to encourage ridership. My favourite example is the mountain community of Asheville, NC where, in the summer of 1902, movies were projected on a screen erected on an island in the middle of a lake. Many Ashevillians saw their first movie from the stern of a canoe.[5]

The history of non-commercial exhibition has hardly even been considered and has certainly not been written about, despite the fact that film projectors have been marketed for home use since the 1890s, and in 1948—well before the popularity of Super-8 and half-inch video—more than one million American households owned movie cameras.[6] We have also yet to explore the history of the use of movies in schools—another important non-commercial site of filmic reception.

Obviously, at the most basic level the *audience* designates the 'who' of reception. The direct study of contemporary audiences is already fraught with enormous theoretical and methodological problems, which are, of course, multiplied greatly when questions of audience are cast in the past tense. Although some contemporaneous and 'independently' collected data on American movie audiences is available to scholars (the Gallup Poll surveys of audience movie preferences in the 1940s, for example), we know much less in gross demographic terms about the audiences for movies than we do about the historical audiences for broadcasting. In large measure this is because, as Motion Picture Association of America

7 Bruce Austin, *The Film Audience: An International Bibliography of Research* (Metuchen, NJ: Scarecrow Press, 1983), pp. xx, xxii.

President Eric Johnson noted in 1946, the Hollywood film industry knew less about itself than any other American industry. As an industry executive characterized market research in Hollywood a few years later, 'We stand in the dark and throw a rock and [if] we hear a crash, [we assume] we've hit the greenhouse'.[7] But leaving the practicalities of historical audience research aside for a moment, the study of historical audiences for the movies should include, as a beginning, an attempt to determine the size and constitution of the audiences for various films; and the relationship of movie-going patterns to race, gender, class, ethnicity, and other variables.

To give another American example from the early period: although immigrants in New York City did go to nickelodeons between 1906 and 1912, not all immigrant groups were equally attracted to the movies. Jewish immigrants frequently went to the movie theatres that sprang up on the Lower East Side after 1905, but relatively fewer Italian immigrants, who lived in large numbers in an adjacent neighbourhood, went. Why? The best answer I can come up with is that Jews came to the USA to stay and they came as families. Eighty-five per cent of Italian migration to the USA between 1885 and 1915 was of single men between the ages of 18 and 35 who came to New York to dig the subways or build the Brooklyn Bridge. Then the vast majority returned to Italy. For many in this group the movies were an irrelevant extravagance.

8 On immigrant audiences for early movies see my 'Motion picture exhibition in Manhattan: beyond the Nickelodeon', *Cinema Journal*, 18 (1979), pp. 2–15, and Judith Mayne, 'Immigrants and spectators', *Wide Angle*, vol. 52, no. 2 (1982), pp. 32–41. As Pryluck ('The itinerant movie show', p. 17) has pointed out, in 1900 immigrants constituted only 7.7% of the rural population of the USA, which itself represented 71% of the total population.

9 Janice Radway, *Reading the Romance: Women, Patriarchy, and Popular Literature* (Chapel Hill, NC: University of North Carolina Press, 1985).

We have just begun to uncover the history of black exhibition in the USA. In the south blacks were barred from 'white' theatres until the 1960s or were forced to sit in restricted areas of the auditorium. By 1915 however, the black ghettoes of a number of southern cities featured black theatres which served as important cultural centres for the community and provided an outlet for black films.[8]

Within the category of audience, I am also talking about the social meanings attached to movie-going, in the same way that Janice Radway talks about the social meanings of reading romantic novels.[9] Obviously, the social meaning ascribed to the viewing of a European art film at the Lincoln Center or the National Film Theatre is different from being part of the audience for *Debbie Does Dallas* a few blocks away on Times Square or in Soho.

10 Ien Ang, *Desperately Seeking the Audience* (London: Routledge, 1991).

As Ien Ang's *Desperately Seeking the Audience* makes abundantly clear with respect to the television audience, 'audience' is as much a discursive as a social phenomenon.[10] Individuals are not only solicited but constructed as audience members through industry attempts at marketing research, advertising, promotions, the decor of movie theatres, and so on. The discourse constructs some audience groups more precisely and differently than others. Diane Waldman, for example, has argued that women film-goers have been 'pursued' through advertising, publicity stunts, and other promotional devices 'to a degree disproportionate with their actual representation in the filmgoing audience'. Other groups—blacks and other identifiably non-WASP ethnic groups, for example—have for the most part been omitted from Hollywood's construction of 'the audience' for films.

Mary Beth Haralovich's extensive work on Hollywood advertising has examined both the industry's self-representational strategies as well as those for interpellating viewers.[11] We need to ask whom the industry and their agents have thought they were talking about when they talked about 'the audience'. What presumptions lie behind not only advertising and promotion, but also studio pronouncements and internal discourse regarding 'popularity', 'box office', and films that 'work' with particular audiences?

Performance is the immediate social, sensory, performative context of reception. We tend to talk of films being 'screened' as if the only thing going on in a movie theatre were light being bounced off a reflective surface. Obviously, at a number of levels there is much more going on during a film viewing situation than that. Again, we have only begun to chart the enormous variety of cinema performance and changes over time. A look at what I am calling performance serves to remind us that film has been merely one component of reception. Given the rather phenomenologically impoverished nature of commercial film viewing in the USA and the UK at present, it is easy to overlook the fact that in the 1920s in America, for example, many viewers were not particularly interested in what feature film was playing. They were attracted to the theatre by the theatre itself, with its sometimes bizarre architectural and design allusions to exotic cultures, its capacious public spaces, its air conditioning in the summer, and its auditorium, which may have been decorated to resemble the exterior of a Moorish palace at night—complete with heavenly dome and twinkling stars. Regardless of what feature the theatre chain had secured from the distributor that week, there was sure to be a newsreel, a comedy short, a programme of music by pit orchestra or on the mighty Wurlitzer, and, in many theatres, elaborate stage shows. Trade papers from the 1920s (*Moving Picture World* in particular) provided smaller exhibitors with suggestions for lobby displays, promotional tie-ins, and publicity stunts, as well as stage shows to complement particular films or genres of films.

In a fascinating paper, Mary Carbine has pointed out the role of black movie theatres on the south side of Chicago as providing a venue for jazz and blues.[12] Louis Armstrong, Fats Waller, Erskine Tate, Earl Hines, and other legendary black musicians provided musical accompaniment for mainstream Hollywood films. Advertisements in black newspapers featured the pit orchestra much more prominently than the film. At times, the jazz bands provided not so much accompaniment to the film as counterpoint. A critic complained that 'Race orchestras discolor the atmosphere that should prevail in the picture house by not characterizing the photoplay. . . . During a death scene flashed on the screen, you are likely to hear the orchestra jazzing away on "Clap Hands, Here Comes Charlie" '.

I am borrowing the term *activation* from reception theory in literature to denote how particular audience groups make or do not make sense,

11 Diane Waldman, 'From midnight shows to marriage vows: women, exploitation, and exhibition', *Wide Angle*, vol. 6, no. 2 (1984), pp. 40–49: Mary Beth Haralovich, 'Mandates of good taste: the self-regulation of film advertising in the theatres', *Wide Angle*, vol. 6, no. 2 (1984), pp. 50–57; 'Film history and social history: reproducing social relationships', *Wide Angle*, vol. 8, no. 2 (1986), pp. 4–14, and 'Advertising heterosexuality', *Screen*, vol. 23, no. 2 (1982), pp. 50–60.

12 Mary Carbine, 'The finest outside the loop: motion picture exhibition in Chicago's black metropolis', *Camera Obscura*, no. 23 (1990), pp. 9–41.

13 Janet Staiger, 'The handmaiden of villainy: methods and problems in studying the historical reception of a film', *Wide Angle*, vol. 8, no. 1 (1986), pp. 19–27.

14 On the relationship between realism (as a position within the philosophy of science) and film study, see Terry Lovell, *Pictures of Reality* (London: BFI, 1980).

15 Tony Bennett and Janet Woollacott, *Bond and Beyond: The Political Career of a Popular Hero* (London: Macmillan, 1987), p. 45. Michael Budd provides a useful model for analysing the critical discourse produced in response to a given film. See '*The cabinet of Dr. Caligari*: conditions of reception', *Cine Tracts*, 12 (1981), pp. 41–9.

relevance, and pleasure out of particular moments of reception. Again, this is obviously difficult to determine with regard to contemporary reception and even more so with regard to reception in the past, as Janet Staiger has pointed out.[13]

It is important to note that I am not talking here of individual activations of filmic texts. In the first place, except for critical discourse we have little evidence of this, and even if we did they would have little relevance except where they represented a more generalizable appropriation of the text. Rather we are trying to locate what realists would call the 'generative mechanisms' that operate variably and with uneven force in producing the myriad readings of individual texts among viewers and over time.[14] Thus, charting the location of theatres in cities, hamlets, and villages, or unearthing box-office records for a particular film, or reconstructing the critical discourse surrounding a given filmic text has relevance for the history of filmic reception not in itself but only in relation to what these data might suggest about the underlying structures of reception, their interaction, variability, modification over time, or resistance to change. I would argue that without the realist notion of generative mechanisms or underlying structures, the historical study of filmic reception becomes either an empiricist fool's errand (in which the scholar is guided by a misplaced faith that by collecting all the available data, he or she can arrive at the truth of the history of film viewing) or merely a game.

It is here that work on film viewing (both historical and contemporary) touches upon and may benefit from reader-oriented theoretical and critical work being undertaken in literature, cultural studies, and media studies. Clearly, for example, what viewers have 'made' of films has involved the mobilization of a number of sets of abilities and competences, ranging from the perceptual to the cognitive, and from the affective to the cultural. Some levels, obviously, would seem to yield to historical investigation more easily than others. Although it is difficult and the knowledge yielded enormously speculative, we can attempt to contextualize historical activations of filmic texts by taking a stab (and that is all it is) at the cultural repertoires audiences might have brought with them to the theatre. Or, to use Bennett and Woollacott's terminology, we might attempt to examine a given film's *intertextuality*: 'the social organisation of the relations between texts within specific conditions of reading.'[15]

To give but one example of a vexing historical problem requiring both textual and intertextual analysis, let me raise the small matter of the relationship between patterns of style and narration in early cinema and how audiences made sense and pleasure out of their engagements with these texts. Numerous early narrative films (1900–5) cannot be 'read' smoothly by contemporary viewers according to the conventions of classical narrative. They contain repeated action, 'unexplained' ellipses, or other features that to us mark them as primitive or their surviving prints as possible victims of some sort of mutilation. Are there inter-titles missing from existing prints? Were screenings of these films accompanied by an interlocutor, who provided the missing narrational links? Were audiences in 1900 similarly perplexed by these story-telling strategies? A closer look at the intertextual contexts of the reception of these films helps account for their textual structures. In his analysis of *Life of an American Fireman* (Edwin S. Porter, 1903) Charles Musser suggests that its repeated narrative action draws upon what would have been well known and understood conventions of magic lantern shows.[16] Patrick Loughney, an archivist at the Library of Congress, has discovered that many early filmic narratives reference popular stage productions mounted just before or at the same time as the film's release. Thus some of the 'missing' narrative information in some early narratives might have been supplied by the audience, in the form of their knowledge of the theatrical text which was being referenced by the film.

16 Charles Musser, 'The early cinema of Edwin S. Porter', *Cinema Journal*, 19 (1979), pp. 1–35.

Let me end by indicating two additional reasons why the historical study of reception might be of more than antiquarian interest. The first is pedagogic. In my film history classes I sometimes have students conduct a study of exhibition in their home towns. They use old newspapers, city directories, fire insurance maps, municipal ordinances, interviews with their grandparents, and surviving architecture to uncover something about their community that they did not know. This kind of assignment can have several effects. First, it helps to break down what students all too frequently perceive as the barrier that exists between producers of knowledge (someone else) and themselves. A student can be wonderfully empowered by becoming the world's leading expert on the history of film exhibition in Shelby, NC. Secondly, students learn something about the way history is conducted and written: the process of question-framing, collection of evidence, the exercise of historical judgement, and so on. Thirdly, they frequently learn what has been written *out* of the history of their community and region. Invariably, black audiences and theatres have left only the faintest historical traces, and yet when students talk with people who attended black theatres in the 1920s and 1930s, they find how important they were to the cultural life of the black community. And fourthly, I can honestly tell my students that the work they are doing is not a mere exercise—each study helps us better to understand the complexities and variety of filmic reception.

Although I have concentrated in this article on the history of filmic reception in the USA—where my own work has been located—the historical study of reception may help to open up film history for parts of the world we have too often seen as having no film history. When Roy Armes was writing *Third World Filmmaking and the West*, he told me he was struck by the fact that for the most part film history of the Third World has meant film production history. It is as if, he said, film history erupts in Bolivia or Chile or Senegal only when there is a notable (usually notable in terms of Western notions of aesthetic worth) director or film movement in evidence in that country. The rest of the time, these countries are written about as if film is not a part of their cultures. But, of course, in many cases indigenous film movements are historical anomalies in the course of a larger history of filmic reception, as millions and millions of people continue to watch films—films made on the other side of the world for very different audiences. One of the challenges for film history is to write back in this enormous and enormously important history.

In short, what I am calling for is the study of the historical conditions of filmic reception, a study which may lead us to a better understanding of the mechanisms of reception: of how these mechanisms are formed, sustained, change, and vary. In effect, we need to ask: what generalizable forces help to account for the unstudiable and, for any individual investigator, incomprehensibly numerous and diverse instances of reception which have occurred since 1895 and which continue as you read this?

2

Hollywood Memories

JACKIE STACEY

1 For a comprehensive debate about the multiple meanings of the category 'the female spectator', see *Camera Obscura*, nos. 20–1 (1989).

2 Helen Taylor, *Scarlett's Women: 'Gone With The Wind' and its Female Fans* (London: Virago, 1989); Jacqueline Bobo, '*The Color Purple: Black Women as Cultural Readers*', in E. Deidre Pribram (ed.), *Female Spectators: Looking at Film and Television* (London: Verso, 1988); Angela Partington, 'Consumption practices as the production and articulation of differences: rethinking working-class femininity in 1950s Britain' (unpublished Ph.D.: University of Birmingham, 1990); Janet Thumim, *Celluloid Sisters: Women and Popular Cinema* (London: Macmillan, 1992); Annette Kuhn, 'Researching popular film fan culture in 1930s Britain', in *Historical Studies of Film Reception* (Oslo: Norwegian Universities Press, 1994).

3 'Historical Methodologies' was the title of the opening plenary panel at the Screen Studies Conference 1993, at which an earlier version of this essay was presented. For discussions of this subject within film studies, see Janet Staiger, *Interpreting Films: Studies in the Historical Reception of American Cinema* (Princeton, NJ: Princeton University Press, 1992); and Thumim, *Celluloid Sisters*.

The absence of 'woman' from Hollywood cinema has been a central concern within feminist film criticism for many years now; and I want to continue the investigation of this case of 'the missing woman'. My struggle, however, is not with the absence of certain screen images, but with the absence of the audience from both cinema history and feminist film criticism. The missing woman in the context of this article, then, is that slippery category 'the female spectator'.[1] How can we go about trying to trace this missing woman, and what methodological issues might such a search raise? After twenty years of feminist film theories preoccupied mainly with textual spectatorship, there is now an increasing interest in actual cinema audiences. Work by women such as Helen Taylor, Jacqueline Bobo, Angela Partington, Janet Thumim, and Annette Kuhn has begun to investigate how texts might be read by particular audiences at particular times.[2]

My interest in questions of historical methodology[3] arises out of my own research with the memories of a particular group of female spectators of 1940s and 1950s Hollywood cinema. The women whose memories are used in this study are all white British women, mostly in their sixties and seventies (though ranging in age from 40 plus to over 90), and are readers of the two leading women's magazines *Woman's Weekly* and *Woman's Realm*, through which I initially contacted them. The focus of this research is the relationships between female film stars of this period and their female spectators. Letters and questionnaires from over 350 women containing their memories of favourite Hollywood stars form the basis of the study, though I also draw on other historical sources in the longer version of this study.[4] My concern here is with how female spectators' memories might be used as a source for historical studies of cinema and the methodological issues raised by their use.

4   Jackie Stacey, *Star Gazing: Hollywood Cinema and Female Spectatorship* (London: Routledge, 1994).

5   Valerie Walkerdine, 'Video replay: families, films and fantasy', in Victor Burgin, James Donald, and Cora Kaplan (eds.), *Formations of Fantasy* (London: Methuen, 1986), p. 171.

The focus is obviously on *past* cinema audiences, though many of the methodological issues raised pertain to all kinds of audience research. For just as we cannot view history as a straightforward retrieval of past time, neither can audience research ever capture that 'pure' moment of reception, what Valerie Walkerdine has called the 'magic convergence'.[5] The methodological complexities of audience research are merely amplified when we begin to investigate audiences from previous decades. After all, in one sense, the 'audiences' of the 1940s and the 1950s no longer exist: that originary moment of spectatorship is lost and can never be recaptured. However, the fact that audiences' accounts of their experiences are inevitably retrospective representations is a methodological issue for any 'ethnographic' audience research. A critical analysis of the forms and processes of memory, then, is pertinent to all ethnographic studies of audiences. However, in historical research, the length of the gap between the events and their recollection (in my own research, some forty or fifty years) highlights especially sharply the question of processes of memory formation.

The memories produced by these female spectators in the letters and questionnaires they sent me are structured through certain codes and conventions. Like other kinds of texts, these memories present an identifiable set of generic features. In this part of my article, I want to discuss briefly two of these genres of memory formation, before going on to analyse the dialogic exchange through which they are produced.

The first genre I call *iconic memory*. Memories of 1940s and 1950s Hollywood frequently take the form of a particular 'frozen moment', a moment removed from its temporal context and captured as 'pure image': be it of Bette Davis's flashing eyes, Rita Hayworth's flowing hair, or Doris Day's 'fun' outfits. A memory of 'love at first sight' is typical of this genre. Here religious signifiers articulate the special status of the star and the intensity of this moment:

> I'll never forget the first time I saw her, it was in *My Gal Sal* in 1942, and her name was Rita Hayworth. I couldn't take my eyes off her, she was the most perfect woman I had ever seen. The old cliché of 'screen goddess' was used about many stars, but those are truly the only words that define that divine creature. . . . I was stunned and amazed that any human being could be that lovely. (Violette Holland)

Iconic memories are not only produced as memories of the stars: they can also be spectators' memories of themselves in such 'frozen moments': 'Our favourite cinema was the Ritz—with its deep pile carpet and double sweeping staircase. Coming down one always felt like a Hollywood heroine descending into the ballroom' (anon.).

The frequent recurrence of this form of memory might be explained by the centrality of the idea of 'image' in the definition of 'successful' femininity in patriarchal culture. Given the extent to which female stars function in Hollywood cinema through their status as objects of visual

6   Laura Mulvey, *Visual and Other Pleasures* (London and Basingstoke: Macmillan, 1989).

pleasure, it is hardly surprising that iconic memory features so centrally in these accounts.[6]

The second genre of memory which occurs most frequently is *narrative memory*. Narrative memories present temporally located sequential stories of cinema-going in the 1940s and 1950s. As well as remembering particular narratives featuring their favourite screen idols, these spectators also recreate their own relationships to the stars through narrative forms of memory. These memories of Hollywood stars are often specific forms of self-narrativization in relation to cultural ideals of femininity. These spectators construct themselves as heroines of their remembered narratives, which in turn deal with their own cinema heroines of that time. Memories of Hollywood stars are thus represented through the narrative structures which connect the self to the ideal. This next memory reworks the conventions of the romance narrative, for example, giving a homoerotic charge to the pleasures of female spectatorship:

> In the late 1930s, when I was about nine or ten, I began to be aware of a young girl's face appearing in magazines and newspapers. I was fascinated. The large eyes, full mouth, sometimes the wonderful smile, showing the slightly prominent but perfect teeth. I feel rather irritated that I don't recall the moment when I realised that the face belonged to a lovely singing voice beginning to be heard on the radio record programmes. . . . The face and the voice belonged to Deanna Durbin. . . . In the 1940s at the age of twelve I was evacuated from my house in South London to Looe in Cornwall, and it was there I was first taken to the pictures for a special treat. There at last I saw her. The film, a sequel to her first, was *Three Smart Girls Grow Up*. The effect she had on me can only be described as electrifying. I had never felt such a surge of adoration before. . . . My feeling for her was no passing fancy. . . . (Patricia Robinson)

7   Jackie Stacey, entry on 'Romance', in Annette Kuhn (ed.), *The Women's Companion to International Film* (London: Virago, 1990), pp. 345–6; and Jackie Stacey and Lynne Pearce, 'The heart of the matter', in Lynne Pearce and Jackie Stacey (eds.), *Romance Revisited* (London: Lawrence and Wishart, 1994).

The structure of this first 'meeting' or, rather, first sighting is built around a series of enigmas, or absences, typical of the romance genre:[7] the anonymous face whose details are 'unforgettable', the voice on the radio, the lost moment when face and voice are matched together, and the gradual buildup to the culmination when 'there at last I saw her'. The star's screen appearance signifies closure, and yet, true to generic conventions, this moment of ending simultaneously suggests the beginning of a lifetime's devotion.

Several memories combine narrative and iconic elements. These two genres frequently construct each other: iconic memories may be of a narrative image from a particular film, for example; and many of the iconic memories, such as the fantasy of being a Hollywood heroine descending the cinema staircase, are also narrativized. Visual display is the common current running through many of these memory formations. Significantly, each of the processes of memory formation and selection I have discussed so far replicates, and is replicated by, distinguishing features of Hollywood cinema. Popular memories of Hollywood cinema in these accounts thus take cinematic forms. Memories are typically constructed through key icons, significant moments, narrative structures, and heroic subject positions. These examples demonstrate how the past is produced in the present through visual and narrative conventions replicating their historical object: cinema.

> . . . the life of any text—case history or otherwise—is not generated by itself, but through the act of being read.[8]

> . . . the intervention of the historian . . . is of crucial significance . . . as a catalyst for whole process of structured remembrance.[9]

Having identified some of the formations of memory in my study, I want now to consider the role of the research process, and indeed the researcher, in their production. I would suggest that this type of audience research involves 'a dialogic exchange' in which the fantasies researcher and respondents have about each other have a determining effect on the accounts produced. The 'imagined reader' structures the forms of memory offered and, to a greater or lesser extent, is present within the texts themselves. Integral to an understanding of the textuality of these memories, then, is a recognition of the dialogic nature of textual production. Here, audience researchers might usefully draw upon insights from dialogic theory which emphasize the ways in which texts are always produced *for readers*; indeed the imagined reader can be seen as written into particular textual modes of address.[10] This process might be summed up in what Lynne Pearce has recently identified as Voloshinov's most eloquent expression of addressivity:

> Orientation of the word toward the addressee has an extremely high significance. In point of fact, *word is a two-sided act*. It is determined equally by *whose* word it is and *for whom* it is meant. As word, it is precisely *the product of the reciprocal relationship between speaker and listener, addresser and addressee*. Each and every word expresses 'one' in relation to the 'other'. I give myself verbal shape from another's point of view of the community to which I belong. A word is a bridge thrown between myself and another. If one end of the bridge belongs to me, then the other depends on my addressee. A word is a territory shared by both addresser and addressee, by the speaker and his [*sic*] interlocutor. (Voloshinov's emphasis)[11]

In her comprehensive account of dialogic theory, Lynne Pearce outlines the significance of Bakhtin's work on the role of the addressee in characterizing various 'speech genres' in which the relationship between speaker and addressee is of crucial significance in understanding meaning:

> An essential (constitutive) marker of the utterance is its quality of being directed to someone, its *addressivity*. . . . Both the composition and, particularly, the style of the utterance depend on those to whom the utterance is addressed, how the speaker (or writer) senses and imagines his addressee, and the force of their effect on the utterance.

8 'Review discussion: *In Search of a Past*: a dialogue with Ronald Fraser', *History Workshop Journal*, no. 20 (1985), pp. 175–88 (p. 182).

9 Popular Memory Group, 'Popular memory: theory, politics, method', in Centre for Contemporary Cultural Studies, *Making Histories* (London: Hutchinson, 1982), p. 243.

10 For a discussion of memory forms in oral history, see Luisa Passerini, *Fascism in Popular Memory: The Cultural Experience of the Turin Working Class*, trans. Robert Lumley and Jude Bloomfield (Cambridge: Cambridge University Press, 1987).

11 V. N. Voloshinov, quoted in Lynne Pearce, *Reading Dialogics* (London: Edward Arnold, 1994), p. 43. I am indebted to Lynne Pearce for my understanding and use of dialogic theory in this section.

Each speech genre in each area of speech communication has its own typical conception of the addressee, and this defines it as a genre. (Voloshinov's emphasis)[12]

12 M. Bakhtin, quoted in ibid., p. 74.

Although this theory is derived from speech communication, it has been widely developed in relation to written texts.[13] Dialogic theory then highlights the subjective, yet social, relations of textual production: the role of the imagined reader in meaning production. It is important here to approach the text as a dialogic form in which the addressee is part of its structure and mode of communication. In audience research the relationship between the academic researcher and interviewees or respondents necessarily shapes which accounts are told and which are not, and indeed how they are told. This mutual (though, importantly, not equal) relationship has been paralleled with that between analyst and analysand in psychoanalysis.[14] For audience research such as this, a more textual model of exchange and interpretation might be appropriate: in either case, though, audiences and researchers may be seen as in a dialogic relationship—one in which the imagined other proves integral to the forms of knowledge produced. Dialogic theories of the reader imagined through the function of addressivity might be used to investigate this textual relationship between audiences and researchers. This model would operate in any kind of audience–researcher exchange. However, in retrospective representations of the past, it functions as a way for respondents to reconstruct their pasts in the present for another who is outside their worlds, but also (and as we shall see, importantly) outside their generation. Here, as work on popular memory has highlighted, the 'centrality of generation . . . [is] a fundamental impulse to remember'.[15] Thus, in this dialogic exchange, some of the processes of memory formation become visible as respondents negotiate their constructions of the past in relation to an imagined reader in the present.

13 See, for example, Pearce's own textual readings in this light, ibid.

14 For a discussion of the uses of psychoanalysis in oral history, see Karl Figlio, 'Oral history and the unconscious', *History Workshop Journal*, no. 26 (1988), pp. 120–32; T. G. Ashplant, 'Psychoanalysis in historical writing', *History Workshop Journal*, no. 26 (1988), pp. 102–19; and responding to this work, Jacqueline Rose, 'A comment', *History Workshop Journal*, no. 28 (1989), pp. 149–54.

15 Popular Memory Group, 'Popular memory', p. 246.

Dialogic practices of writing are integral both to my initial invitations to produce a remembered past, which posit an imagined addressee, and also, in turn, to the written responses I received—which embody the projection of an imagined reader: the researcher. In my first communication with respondents, I imagined female fans who had stories to tell about their relationships to Hollywood stars of the past. My advertisement addressed them directly using the second person: 'Were you a keen cinemagoer of the 1940s and 1950s?' The ways in which I requested information encouraged women to use narrative forms to construct their memories. My request for letters from women who were keen cinema-goers in the 1940s and 1950s invited retrospective self-narrativizations in the retelling of past events so characteristic of the conventions of letter-writing more generally. Even in the follow-up questionnaire, a less personal mode of communication, and one associated with 'scientific' information-giving rather than with storytelling, the kinds of questions I asked inevitably produced, or at least delimited, the forms of responses. I invited a kind of narrativization of the past, for example, when I asked respondents to 'describe a

16 For the full questionnaire see Stacey, *Star Gazing*, pp. 245–51.

favourite cinema experience of the 1940s/1950s'. Finally, I allowed maximum space for the central question in the questionnaire in which respondents were asked to 'write about your favourite star from the 1940s and then the 1950s, explaining what you liked about them and what they meant to you: what made these stars more appealing than others?'[16] This clearly requested narrativizations of the past and invited a commentary on respondents' own tastes and preferences.

Similarly, respondents signal my presence in their imaginations through a number of textual enunciations. Some use my name to effect a personal mode of address in order to emphasize a specific feeling: 'Oh Jackie, what lovely memories are being recalled—I do hope you are going to ask for lots more information as a trip down memory lane of this nature is most enjoyable' (Barbara Forshaw). This example is taken from a letter; the use of my name suggests a familiarity which easily accompanies the letter form, but is normally absent from the relationship of researcher and researched. It also adds a note of authenticity to the exchange which is lacking in more formal types of address, suggesting a personal sharing of experiences 'between friends'. The depth of the emotion felt about the research project is given wistful exclamation here in the 'oh' as well as in the use of my name. My role in this dialogic exchange is thus included in the text itself as this respondent pauses to reflect upon the pleasures of remembering the 'Golden Age of Hollywood'. My obviously 'younger' generation name, in contrast to many of the respondents' names (such as 'Vera', 'Mabel', or 'Betty') which connote a very different generation, placed me outside the experience of 'Hollywood at its best': this produced a further imperative to convey to me the importance of Hollywood stars in their lives at that time, the significance of changes in the cinema since then, and the depth of the loss they mourn. Several respondents used stereotyped or cliched language to describe Hollywood stars of this era: 'stars of yesteryear', 'screen goddesses', and 'a trip down memory lane'. These and many other similar examples construct a special relationship to the past (through a direct knowledge of it, and use of dated language about it) for an imagined reader of a different generation.

In the role of 'invisible other' outside the memories, yet as the person for whom they are being produced, my position might be seen as equivalent to Bakhtin's 'superaddressee': 'the hypothetical presence who fully comprehends the speaker's words and hence allows his or her utterance to be made despite doubt about whether the "actual" addressee will understand and/or respond'.[17] As 'superaddressee' the researcher (by requesting them and then reading them) brings these memories into being, as it were. However, an ambivalence towards my role in this respect is also articulated; there is a feared mismatch between the ideal reader's and my actual position, for many respondents expressed anxiety about my not understanding the full significance of these memories (because I had not been there). The question of power imbalances between researcher and researched is central here. Straddling the roles of superaddressee and imagined addressee, I am expected to exercise

17 Pearce, *Reading Dialogics*, p. 76.

authority over these memories (by representing them for publication, for example)—and indeed, this authority is seen in turn to 'authorize' these memories. However, my relationship to the material is also constantly under negotiation within the texts, as respondents establish their own authority about the Hollywood stars of the past over and above my own, and try to ensure that I make the correct readings of their memories.

In offering narrative accounts of the past, many respondents tell their stories and then add their own reflections upon them, as if anticipating the reader's response. This 'anticipatory mode' functions as a mediating voice which moves between the subject positions of 'self' and 'imagined other', producing a particular type of dialogicality in which reflexivity foregrounds the role of the addressee. The 'love at first sight' story about Deanna Durbin quoted above, for instance, ends with a shift of register in which the respondent comments directly on a possible (and within contemporary critical debates, virtually inevitable) interpretation of her love of Deanna Durbin. Continuing directly from the quotation above, she writes:

> I might just add that the members of our society [the Deanna Durbin Society] seem to be about equal in number male and female. I think perhaps it would be considered a bit of a giggle today, if a large number of women confessed to feeling love for a girl. Nobody seemed to question it then. Just in case: I have been married since 1948! Have two sons and a daughter, one grandchild.
> (Patricia Robinson)

In writing about her devotion to a star of the same sex, this respondent feels the need to guard against possible interpretations of homoeroticism in this charged connection. Heterosexuality and reproduction are thus invoked to counter such speculations: a grandchild is even mentioned as if to stress the 'purity' and 'normality' not just of the respondent's desires, but also the next generation's. In the retelling, then, the presence of a (younger) imagined reader produces an anxiety about the story's significance today which needs to be defended against. A contrast is constructed between the 'innocence' of such an attachment in the past, and the embarrassment of 'confessing' it in today's culture in which homosexual interpretations might be more freely applied to such a declaration. Externalizing this memory of the 1930s and 1940s for a researcher in the 1980s, this respondent is brought up against a clash between present knowledge and past self: the former suggesting a different interpretation of the latter. If such a reading has occurred to the respondent's present self, she (quite correctly) anticipates its coincidence with my response to her story. Appealing against today's sexualization of such desires, she articulates concern that her memory may be spoiled or 'corrupted' by such discourses. Thus the reflection upon the account is produced in direct dialogue with the addressee, whose different values, or indeed desires, are imagined and incorporated into the account, and function to mediate between past and present discourses of sexuality and fandom.

An even more explicit extension of this anticipatory mode of addressivity occurs in the following example. Here, another respondent's account seems to be in dialogue not only with me, but also with herself, or rather with a version of her 'former selves'. Initially, an account is offered of how female stars functioned as role models for new fashions: 'We were quick to notice any change in fashion and whether it had arrived this side of the Atlantic. We were pleased to see younger stars without gloves and hats—we soon copied them'. However, this is followed by a self-conscious autocritique of the cultural construction of such feminine desirability:

In retrospect, it's easy to see Hollywood stars for what they really were. This was pretty packaged commodities . . . the property of a particular studio. At the time I did most of my filmgoing, while I was always aware that stars were really too good to be true, I fell as completely under the spell of the Hollywood 'Dream Factory' as any other girl of my age. . . . Looking back, I can see much of what I took as authenticity was really technical skill. . . . Later on I realised just how much money and expertise went into creating the 'natural' beauties the female stars appeared to be. (Kathleen Lucas)

Throughout a long and very detailed reflection in answer to the central question about the appeal of particular stars in the 1940s and 1950s, this respondent shifts between a past self who was 'under the spell of Hollywood' and a present 'critical' self, producing an important contrast which might be seen to be in dialogue, as it were, with the reader/researcher. This example is exceptional rather than typical, and its particular form of dialogicality is due in part to the respondent's experience of similar research with the Mass-Observation Archive at Sussex University, to which she herself draws my attention in a covering letter. The self-commentary is offered here in response to an expected, even previously experienced, authoritative interpretation which might be imposed on these memories: the feminist critique is thus successfully anticipated and given voice in dialogue with the imagined researcher reading this account. As part of the same account she writes: 'Make-up artists were clever enough not to show the female stars as too artificial. The servicemen didn't want to see anything but a parade of glamour queens, so the make-up men aimed for a naturally perfect, or perfectly natural look'. Drawing attention to the power imbalances between researcher and researched, she correctly anticipates certain contemporary feminist critiques of stardom, glamour, and 'the male gaze', and yet insists upon the pleasures for female spectators nevertheless: 'Really we were conned, but in the nicest possible way', she concludes.

Both these accounts might be seen as examples of what Bakhtin calls 'double-voiced discourse': this includes all speech 'which not only refers to something in the world but which also refers to another speech act by another addressee'.[18] The most obvious types of double-voiced discourse operating in these examples are what Bakhtin calls 'hidden

18 David Lodge, quoted in ibid., p. 51.

19 Pearce, ibid., p. 53.

dialogue' or 'hidden polemic' in which the narrator actively engages with an 'interlocutor not named in the text, but whose presence may be inferred'.[19] This inferred other outside the text may be a discourse as well as a known, or unknown, subject. In the case of hidden polemic, the inferred subject or discourse is seen as potentially antagonistic or hostile, which is not the case in hidden dialogue. Both the above examples present interesting dialogues with inferred others: each might be characterized as in dialogue with a discourse via my imagined subject position. Interestingly, despite never having met me, each narrator anticipates my concern with contemporary discourses of sexuality. In the Deanna Durbin example, for instance, the respondent both positions herself as the imagined reader of her own account, and comments upon the nature of her passion for this female star, while simultaneously defending against my also making such a comment and so constructing her desires within what she would consider a 'perverse' reading of her memories.

Similarly, in the last example, the respondent both produces an account of the 'mindless escapism of Hollywood of the past'; and yet, not wanting to be constructed as naive, also draws attention to the critique of such pleasures. In this case, the hidden polemic is not only with a potential feminist critique of Hollywood cinema, but also with a form of 'high culture' scorn for popular pleasures: her own ambivalence articulates precisely the complexity of the relationship between these two discourses. To offer one final example from this same account, which illustrates this exchange perfectly:

> Everything was rationed and shabby, then along came the glamour and expertise of Hollywood and we soaked it up like a sponge. It 'took people out of themselves' and transported them to a plane where they didn't need to think or worry. All they had to do was sit and stare. And the top Hollywood studios knew exactly what people wanted to see and they gave it to them. In a word, people needed 'escapism'. (Kathleen Lucas)

The repeated use of inverted commas, and the third, as well as the first person plural, produce a critical distance from the experience (this is something other people felt) while also including herself in it. The earlier reference to Hollywood as a 'Dream Factory' further reinforces this distance by invoking (knowingly?) a well-known sociological study of the American film industry.[20]

20 Hortense Powdermaker, *Hollywood, the Dream Factory* (Boston, Mass.: Little Brown, 1950).

Thus, a contrast and mediation between past and present selves represented in these accounts is constructed through forms of dialogue with the researcher: it is, in part, my imagined presence in their texts which facilitates respondents' commentary and reflection upon their 'past selves' from the point of view of their present knowledges. In both the above examples, this anticipatory mode of addressivity not only incorporates me into the text as an imagined reader from another generation, but my anticipated construction of respondents' own identity is also projected into the text. Thus, not only is there a dialogue here between self and imagined other, but what might more accurately be described as a 'trialogic' relationship between self, imagined other, and imagined other's fantasy of the self: in other words, the respondents, their projection of me, and, finally completing this 'trialogic circuit', how they imagine my reading of their texts will in turn produce a version of their identities. Indeed this 'third person presence' might be seen to characterize certain '*dynamics* of the dialogic context' if, as Pearce suggests, 'dialogues can be between more than two persons'.[21]

21 Pearce, *Reading Dialogics*, pp. 202–3.

One of the 'inferred presences' of these hidden polemics is an evaluative discourse about popular culture and female pleasure in it. These negotiations of the researcher's anticipated responses, then, highlight particularly sharply the question of the value placed on female pleasures in these forms of popular culture: how should my 'invitation to remember' such pleasures be received—as a promise of their validation or as a threat of their condemnation? Either way, an anxiety about this question is clearly present in many of the responses I received, since, after all, I have the power to interpret and comment upon these texts and to represent them to (another) public. Kathleen Lucas is unusual in offering an autocritique of 'female fandom', but typical in so far as her memories are produced in relation to the *idea* of a judgement of such pleasures. For many respondents, my anticipated response is assumed to be an acknowledgment of the importance of their memories through their inclusion in 'cinema history', contradicting the usual derision they receive within patriarchal culture. Indeed, many offer accounts of how such attachments have been trivialized and not considered suitable for a 'mature' woman. Commenting on her brother's response to her collection of photographs of British and Hollywood stars, one woman writes:

> I had pictures of Patricia Roc, Margaret Lockwood, Petula Clarke, Jeanette McDonald, Dulcie Gray and my favourite, best loved of all—Margaret O'Brien! We used to send for photographs to MGM and RKO. . . . I'm afraid my brother cleared all 'that sort of rubbish' (his words, not mine) from my late mother's house before I was able to get there. (Cynthia Mulliner)

This respondent is keen to distance herself from the masculine trivialization of her much-loved collection by highlighting the gulf between his use of derisive language and her attachment to her belongings. Furthermore, her sense of regret is emphasized in the final phrase, 'before I was able to get there', suggesting the possibility of retrieval had the timing been different.

For others, the loss of such valued collections is attributed to World War II, *the* key event associated with loss during this period:

> I had a wonderful collection of personally autographed photos, mostly with my name written on them. Unfortunately, they went when my home was bombed during the war and I have been sad about this ever since. No personal loss has had so much effect on me as the loss of this collection (started when I was a schoolgirl). (Mrs M. Caplin)

I wish I still had some of my magazines. My copies of *Photoplay* were immaculate—they were *never* loaned to *anybody*. I kept most of them for years, but unfortunately when the war came, they were discarded during my absence in the forces—much to my rage and frustration. (Mrs J. Kemp, emphasis in original)

The most common explanation for change in spectators' attachments to the cinema at this time, however, is marriage—which marked the end of many female spectators' devotion to female stars. These accounts represent a shift in acceptability of such feelings for Hollywood stars:

It amazes me to think of what choice of Picture Houses we had. I can remember at least twelve. You could go every night and see a different picture. And they were always full, with queues outside. We spent most of our Bank Holiday afternoons queuing to see Doris Day. But after I was married, we were rationed to once a week. (Jean Shepherd)

At the time (1945) there was a film magazine called *Picturegoer* and I loved this book, but it was also a time of shortages, so one could only get this magazine from under the counter and also if you were a regular customer of that particular shop. When I discovered I could obtain this item I used to cycle like crazy from my work in the dinner time, just to obtain this film star book. I drove my poor Mum potty with all the cuttings plastered all over my bedroom walls and my masses of scrapbooks. I even dreamed of being an usherette. . . . I stopped going to the pictures after I was married and had a family. (Mrs M. Russell)

In a few examples, mothers are blamed for not recognizing the significance of such collections (though perhaps they were thrown away precisely because such significance seemed inappropriate):

I left home in 1953 on marriage and lived in a minute flat in London. By the time we could afford more space, my mother had dumped the things she thought a married woman didn't need. I found it hard to forgive her. (anon.)

All these stories point to respondents' feelings of a previous lack of recognition of the importance of film stars in their lives. Anger, betrayal, and regret are expressed at the discrepancy between female spectators' high valuation of these photos and scrapbooks and other people's ridicule of them. Furthermore, marriage functions as a key boundary between 'girlhood' in which such attachments might be permissible and 'adulthood' in which such devotions might conflict with more 'appropriate' ones: 'When the time came to distinguish between "Childhood" and "Growing-Up", I must have destroyed as many as fifty books full' (Avril Feltham). This construction of attachments to Hollywood stars of the same sex as immature, naive, foolish, or even perverse, draws on a number of discourses of femininity and feminine sexuality in which the adoption of a man as the central love object signifies heterosexual maturity. In all these accounts, respondents articulate an ambivalent desire for recognition of the significance of these same-sex attachments as more than simply schoolgirl crushes or regressive narcissism, while simultaneously guarding against my criticism of their Hollywood passions: this they half-expect because they are so familiar with contempt from external critics, be these family, friends, husbands, or researchers. Thus, running throughout many of these accounts is a dialogue with the imagined reader about the validity of indulging in such reminiscences of these 'silly' feminine pleasures.[22] Indeed, many express their own anxieties about the worth of their memories for cinema history, echoing the remembered questionability of their validity as a cultural experience at the time: several accounts finish with comments such as 'I can't imagine this is of much use to you' or 'I hope I have been of some help' and 'I can't see that my ramblings will be of great significance'.

22 Taylor, *Scarlett's Women*, p. 204.

Some respondents, however, took my research request for their memories to be a guarantee of recognition of previously low-status or stigmatized feelings about female stars. For example, an account of a previously discredited attachment to Doris Day implies a welcome contrast between past ridicule and my anticipated response. The direct address ('I wanted to write and tell you') suggests a sharing of a confidence with the expectation of an understanding reader:

> I wanted to write and tell you of my devotion to Doris Day. I thought she was fantastic, and joined her fan club, collected all the photos and info I could. I saw *Calamity Jane* 45 times in a fortnight and still watch all her films avidly. My sisters all thought I was mad going silly on a woman, but I just thought she was wonderful. . . . My sisters were all mad about Elvis, but my devotion was to Doris Day. (Veronica Mills)

The contrast to her sisters' attachments to Elvis, the epitome of smouldering heterosexual masculinity, suggests the unacceptability of the homoerotic connotations of this respondent's devotion. Previously dismissed as immature and trivial (she was considered 'mad' to be going 'silly' on a woman), these feelings towards a female star have not been recognized as significant since they lack the seriousness of mature heterosexual love. The dialogicality of this text is not just in relation to my position as imagined reader, then, but also in a 'hidden polemic' with her sisters; contesting her sisters' definition of her attachment to Doris Day as 'mad', the narrator defines it instead as 'devotion' and uses the (interestingly ambiguous) former term to refer to their love of Elvis.

These memories of cinematic spectatorship are thus constructed through forms of private storytelling which are given public recognition in the research process. Like many confessional acts, although utilizing so-called private forms, they are nevertheless written for another: for a kind of public consumption, first by me, the researcher; and secondly, once in print, by a wider audience. Indeed, perhaps the desire for recognition or validation of these previously low-status feelings is one reason why some of these female spectators offered their memories in a rather confessional mode. The disclosure of secret loves, private collections, and lifetime devotions suggests that for some respondents the research process might function as a kind of 'secular confessional'. Perhaps my initial invitation to remember feelings towards female stars of the past belongs to a more general cultural imperative which encourages 'confession'. As Foucault has pointed out:

> We have become a singularly confessing society. The confession has spread far and wide. It plays a part in justice, medicine, education, family relationships, and love relations, in most ordinary affairs of everyday life, and in the most solemn rites; one confesses one's crimes, one's sins, one's thoughts and desires, one's illnesses and troubles; one goes about telling whatever is most difficult to tell. One confesses in public and in private, to one's parents, one's educators, one's doctor, to those one loves; one admits to oneself, in pleasure and in pain, the things people write books about.[23]

23 Michel Foucault, *The History of Sexuality: An Introduction*, trans. Robert Hurley (Harmondsworth: Penguin, 1981), p. 59.

In describing some of these accounts as confessional, I do not mean to criticize the self-disclosures offered in this research process, but rather to comment on one particular form of articulation in the dialogic exchange between researcher and researched. As Rita Felski has pointed out, the use of the term 'confession' has sometimes 'acquired slightly dismissive overtones in recent years'; however, for her, the confessional text is simply a subgenre of women's autobiography which 'makes public that which has been private'.[24] In the context of this research the making public of that which has been private is effected through producing written memories for someone else, someone invested with a certain amount of power and credibility. As a 'researcher', my academic status might in turn invest these memories with a weight and importance they are felt to lack. Confession might be understood here as a form of dialogics, for confession hinges on the idea of an addressee. According to Foucault we always confess to someone else, usually someone who represents authority:

24 Rita Felski, *Beyond Feminist Aesthetics: Feminist Literature and Social Change* (London: Hutchinson Radius, 1989), pp. 87–8.

> The confession is a ritual of discourse in which the speaking subject is also the subject of the statement; it is also a ritual that unfolds within a power relationship, for one does not confess without the presence (or virtual presence) of a partner who is not simply the interlocutor but the authority who requires the confession, prescribes and appreciates it and intervenes in order to judge, punish, forgive, console, and reconcile; a ritual in which truth is corroborated by the obstacles and resistances it has to surmount in order to be formulated; and finally, a ritual in which the expression alone, independently of its external consequences, produces intrinsic modifications in the person who articulates it: it exonerates, redeems, and purifies him [*sic*]; it unburdens him of his wrongs, liberates him and promises him salvation.[25]

25 Foucault, *History of Sexuality*, p. 62. I am grateful to Hilary Hinds for drawing my attention to these passages on confession.

The invitation to tell one's story to a researcher may offer the promise of being heard, recognized, and taken seriously. What makes this study particularly appealing as a 'confessional opportunity' is the way in which the act of confession itself elevates the material into significance. It thus offers the chance to (re)gain the (lost) status of certain emotions from the past. For what surfaces repeatedly in these narratives is the desire to recapture past pleasures which were either 'laughable' to begin with (as in the Doris Day example), or which have since lost their status (with marriage or maturity). The subsequent discrediting of attachments to female stars, then, seems to cast doubt on their original validity. In addition to changes in the film industry and the star system through which stars are perceived to have lost their earlier idol status, life history changes also mean the loss of status of earlier attachments to stars. These are combined in the desire to return to past moments and revalue them through the external recognition anticipated in the research process. This dialogical exchange thus promises an imagined transformation in the cultural status of emotional connections to Hollywood stars, resolving the discrepancy between respondents' own valuation, and others' trivialization, of these feminine popular pleasures.

For memory is, by definition, a term which directs our attention not to the past but to the past–present relation.[26]

Memory alone cannot resurrect past time, because it is memory itself that shapes it, long after historical time has passed.[27]

The dialogic analysis in the previous section highlights especially sharply the processes of memory in reworking past identities in relation to the present, and vice versa. Through these multiple dialogues, respondents are able to shift between past and present identities in their imaginations, and use my inferred presence to facilitate such temporal shifts. The dialogic exchanges function to produce both a dialogue with an imagined reader in the present, and also numerous other dialogues with discourses and interlocutors from the remembered past. These, it is argued, can only be understood in terms of 'the way in which popular memories are constructed and reconstructed as part of a *contemporary* consciousness'.[28] Popular memory theory therefore stresses the significance of the present as the standpoint from which remembered accounts are produced.

Why, then, do certain memories figure repeatedly in some people's accounts of the past, and how do such memories function as touchstones in their self-narrativizations? Certain memories, it has been suggested, have a particular function in processes of identity formation. Memories in which we have an enduring and recurring personal investment in terms of our identities have been called *treasured memories*.[29] Many respondents in my research wrote of such treasured memories and of their continuing significance: 'I have memories I shall always treasure. Other things in life take over, visiting the cinema is nil these days, but I shall always remember my favourite films and those wonderful stars

26 Popular Memory Group, 'Popular memory', p. 211.

27 Carolyn Steedman, *Landscape for a Good Woman: A Story of Two Lives* (London: Virago, 1986), p. 29.

28 Popular Memory Group, 'Popular memory', p. 219.

29 Popular Memory Group, unpublished papers on popular memory (University of Birmingham: Centre for Contemporary Cultural Studies, n.d.).

of yesteryear' (Mrs B. Morgan). Such treasured memories might be likened to a valued personal possession: an object of vast sentimental significance to the self, but a worthless trinket to others; that is, until the audience researcher revalues it, as it were. Here memories of Hollywood stars are a kind of personal cinema memorabilia. These fantasy objects are not only treasured by respondents, but also anticipated to be valuable proof of their own credentials as cinema historians:

> The major film stars of my major film-going period made a big impact on me. I can see a short clip from a film and know instantly whether I've seen it before or not—and as like or not, be able to add—'then she moves off down the staircase' or 'the next dress she appears in is white with puffy net sleeves'. (M. Palin)

30 Ibid., p. 26.

Indeed, it has been argued that treasured memories are particularly significant in conserving a fantasy of a past self and thereby guarding against loss.[30] Treasured memories may thus signify past selves or imagined selves which have also become important retrospectively. The notion of the treasured memory also suggests a place which can be regularly revisited. One woman writes:

> My grandfather's boss was kind enough to, every Christmas of my childhood, give me a present of a film annual. I enjoyed them then, but never dreamt what a treasure trove they'd prove to be. Now in my 50's, I pore over them from time to time and it's like opening Pandora's Box [sic]. Stars of yesteryear, long forgotten. Films I saw, but had forgotten all about. Hollywood at its height, the glitz and glamour. . . . (Barbara McWinter)

31 Ibid., p. 161.

How might these treasured memories be understood as investments in particular versions of the past? One explanation might be that these memories represent particular 'transformative moments' in the spectator's life history.[31] Such moments are especially pertinent to the film star–spectator relationship because Hollywood stars embody cultural ideals of femininity and represent to spectators the possibility of transforming the self. Indeed, many memories pinpoint the role of Hollywood stars in the changes in spectators' own identities. This is partly due to the power of the discourse of transformation in the feminine life history, in which adolescence prefigures a fundamental change. Many respondents' memories are of a transitional period: their 'teenage' years, in which change and self-transformation were central to their desires and aspirations; and cinema is remembered as a transitional space in which the fantasy of possible futures is played out.

> The moment I took my seat it was a different world, plush and exciting, the world outside was forgotten. I felt grown up and sophisticated. (Betty Cruse)

It has been suggested that the pleasure of such memories derives from the ways they work as 'personal utopias', offering escape from the present. This is particularly pertinent with regard to spectators'

32 Richard Dyer, 'Entertainment and utopia', in Bill Nichols (ed.), *Movies and Methods*, ii (Berkeley: University of California Press, 1985), pp. 220–32; see also Stacey, *Star Gazing*, pp. 80–125.

33 Popular Memory Group, unpublished papers, p. 30.

34 Stacey, *Star Gazing*, pp. 212–17.

35 Steedman, *Landscape for a Good Woman*.

36 Graham Dawson and Bob West, 'Our finest hour?: the popular memory of World War II and the struggle over national identity', in Geoff Hurd (ed.), *National Fictions: World War Two in British Films and Television* (London: British Film Institute, 1984), pp. 10–11.

37 Popular Memory Group, 'Popular memory', p. 243.

memories of Hollywood stars, who seem to offer the most utopian fantasies to *female* spectators.[32] In this context, femininity itself might be seen as the ultimate utopian identity: an impossible ideal, predicated upon loss through its very embodiment in the *visual* image. The kinds of personal utopias produced depend upon past expectations and the extent to which these expectations have been met: some memories, in other words, retain a central emotional importance because of frustrations, disappointments, and unfulfilled hopes. Furthermore, certain memories perhaps assume especial significance because they are 'stories of unfinished business'.[33] The degree of emotional investment in a memory may have to do with the extent to which the narrativization of a past self represents an aspect of identity with continuing significance in the present. Indeed, femininity might itself be regarded as 'unfinished business', since its production is quite literally never-ending.

Female spectators' youthful expectations and subsequent experiences of romance, motherhood, or paid work, for example, may shape their reconstructions of past attachments to Hollywood ideals of femininity. Given the 'impossibility of femininity', such feelings may be especially pertinent to an understanding of these memories.[34] Feminine ideals are unrealizable, not only because of the fragility of the image, but also because they are often fundamentally contradictory (as, for example, ideals of motherhood and of sexual desirability). Furthermore, as Carolyn Steedman has shown, material constraints in certain periods in women's lives may shape investments in particular memories. This is especially pertinent in the context of 1950s consumerism and the 'age of affluence'.[35] Memories of Hollywood stars, as retrospective constructions of past time in which feminine identity still seemed realizable in the future, may have particular significance for female spectators as representations of a fantasy self never realized.

> These occasions offer opportunities to *reassess* the past, in the light of subsequent experience and new information, in both personal terms ('when I was') and a past–present relation, and involve a constant process of reworking and transforming remembered experience.[36]

Dialogic negotiations between past and present discourses and subjects are far from neutral. They are often shot through with wistful longing for remembered times, and with desire to recapture a lost sense of possibility: such memories, in other words, are deeply nostalgic. A yearning for an irretrievable lost time characterizes many of the memories in my study. The invitation to produce a remembered past promises the pleasure of an imagined retrieval, but simultaneously reminds respondents of the impossibility of reliving that past. In producing memories, 'people do *relive* certain past events imaginarily, often with peculiar vividness. This may be especially the case for those (for example, the elderly) who have been forced into a marginal position in the economic, cultural and social life of a society, and, fearful of absolute oblivion, have little to lose but their memories'.[37]

A typical version of the remembered past constructed in many of these Hollywood memories might be understood in relation to what Graham Dawson has referred to as a kind of 'mythic past': 'myth is always in the process of being alluded to, recycled, even controverted . . . yet there is never a moment when it appears *as itself* in pure form'.[38] In this respect, nostalgic yearnings for a lost Hollywood and for the 'truly great' stars of the 'Silver Screen' reinforce its mythic status during a 'Golden Age' of cinema which can never be recaptured. The 'genuine' star system is marked off from what came after, the demise of the studio era of Hollywood, in a remembered past in which stars were distant and still functioned as impossible ideals: 'I think in those eras we were more inclined to put stars on a pedestal. They were so far removed from everyday life, they were magical. These days are so ordinary —the magic has gone. Hollywood will never be the same again!' (Kathleen Sines).

This nostalgic pleasure of remembering Hollywood stars of the past has a particular appeal for female spectators because of the ways it connects with cultural constructions of femininity. Feminists using psychoanalytic theory have argued that nostalgia does indeed have a particular gendered appeal and that this is attributable to the significance of early feelings and beliefs about loss in relation to sexual difference.[39] However, the gendering of nostalgic desire in these memories hinges on the extent to which femininity is constructed in patriarchal culture as an unattainable visual image of desirability. To present oneself to the world for approval in terms of visible physical attractiveness is the fundamental and the ultimate demand made of femininity. Few women ever overcome the sense of mismatch between self-image and the feminine ideals of physical appearance. Feminine ideals are youthful ones and, being ephemeral, contain loss even in their rare attainment. The sense of loss evoked by nostalgic desire in these memories is partly bound up with the predication of femininity-as-image upon loss. The feelings of loss, often experienced in the gap between self-image and the currently fashionable ideal image, are deepened and extended as the ideal becomes ever-increasingly an impossibility. For these female spectators, then, nostalgic desire may be bound up with a particular sense of loss rooted in the unattainability of feminine ideals: perhaps it is its particular designation of femininity as image which gives cinematic nostalgia such potency.

Nostalgia is articulated here in relation to several 'lost objects': for a Hollywood of the past when cinema meant so much more than it does today; for a time when star status kept femininity a distant ideal image on the screen; for a former self—younger, more glamorous—who still maintained a fantasy connection to such ideals; for a past in which the future seemed to offer a promise of fulfilment. Nostalgia here is expressed as a yearning for a past in which the remembered self yearned for the future. The missing woman of cinema history and feminist film criticism has multiple references here: she is lost in history; lost in the demise of Hollywood and the star system; lost in the inevitable failure of

38 Graham Dawson, 'History-writing on World War II', in Hurd, *National Fictions*.

39 For an account of the psychoanalytic arguments about gender and nostalgia, see Susannah Radstone, 'Remembering Medea: the uses of nostalgia', *Critical Quarterly*, vol. 35, no. 3 (1993), pp. 54–63; 'Remembering ourselves: memory, writing and the female self', in Penny Florence and Deidre Reynolds (eds.), *Feminist Subjects, Multi-Media: New Approaches to Criticism and Creativity* (Manchester: Manchester University Press, 1995).

femininity as desirable image; lost in personal narratives in which youth and feminine ideals no longer offer a promise of fulfilment. This sense of loss is bound up with femininity's cultural construction as an unattainable visual image of desirability, an image which is youthful and so doomed to transience. Memories of Hollywood stars in the 1940s and 1950s evoke nostalgic desire for a lost past, for imagined former identities, and for a time 'when stars were really stars'. Remembering these stars is an acknowledgement of the loss of that time, and yet also a way of guarding against complete loss by recreating the feeling of a past in which the future still held out promise.

3 The 'Popular', Cash, and Culture in the Postwar British Cinema Industry

JANET THUMIM

In 1946 the 'Biggest Box Office Attraction' in the UK, according to *Kinematograph Weekly*'s (*KW*) annual review, was *The Wicked Lady*. It was also the 'Best British Film', featuring two of the 'Most Popular and Consistent Stars', James Mason and Margaret Lockwood; it had one of the 'Best British Directors', Leslie Arliss; and was made by the 'Most Successful Studio', Gainsborough. What does this string of superlatives tell us, though, about the film or its audience? Josh Billings, in his introduction to *KW*'s review, had no doubts about the solidity of the film's value:

> their success was no fluke. They had the stars, the stories and the necessary production glamour and not even an indifferent Press could halt so persistent and shrewd a box-office combination.[1]

In *Tribune*, the 'indifferent press', in the form of Simon Harcourt-Smith reviewing the same film, clearly operated according to a quite different set of values:

> This, on the whole, is a time when the new films can claim no privilege as works of art. . . .
>   *The Wicked Lady* arouses in me a nausea out of all proportion to the subject. . . .
>   Six months hence one of my friends in the industry will announce that this portentous piece of shabbiness has broken all records in, let us say, Middlesbrough. My argument will, however, remain valid.[2]

1 *Kinematograph Weekly* (*KW*), 19 December 1946, p. 46. This is a shortened version of the article originally published in *Screen*, vol. 32, no. 3 (1991), pp. 245–71.

2 *Tribune*, 23 November 1945.

Now this film was the box-office hit of 1946, and thus in quantitative terms an immense popular success. This very popular object, however, gave rise to Harcourt-Smith's admittedly disproportionate nausea: it was not well liked by him. His choice of the term 'nausea' indeed suggests such extreme revulsion that we might well wonder what it was about the film that so disturbed him. It is hard to believe, as he claimed elsewhere in his review, that it was simply a question of his historical sensibilities being offended. The most interesting question about the contemporary popularity of this film—what was it about 'this portentous piece of shabbiness' that was so well liked?—is one that Harcourt-Smith was incapable of answering, simply because it had not occurred to him that it was worth asking. For the cultural historian it is the very success of this film which provokes questions about its content: what pleasures did it offer, what widespread desires did it satisfy, in short, how was it *used* by its audiences? In other words the ascertainable fact of *The Wicked Lady*'s popularity in quantitative terms makes it an ideal candidate for an exploration of the qualitative aspects of popularity: despite Harcourt-Smith's nausea, large numbers of people chose to view this film: why *this* film?

The study of popular culture in any given period offers insights into both the conditions of social formation and also the language and attitudes of the various social groups competing with each other for dominance—in hegemonic struggle—at the time. This essay is concerned with the qualifications which must be borne in mind while engaging in such an exploration of cinema popular in Britain in the immediate postwar period (between 1945 and 1960). There are complex problems to be faced in the course of such an exploration of the discursive field within which meanings were produced by the industry, the critics, and the audience. Though all three groups both contributed to and drew upon this discursive field, it is no simple matter to discover the details of specific interventions. My concern here is to map some points in the field, to draw attention to tendencies rather than attempt categorical assertions about the substantive interactions of these interrelated historical groups. My remarks are therefore necessarily general—and this may be their weakness: their strength rests on the systematic methods used to generate a sample of films for analysis[3] and on a scrupulous insistence on the correlation of data from disparate sources as the foundation for any proposition.

A notable feature of popular cinema during this period, for example, is the striking change in the typical heroine: the transgressive adult woman portrayed by Margaret Lockwood in *The Wicked Lady* gave way by 1964 to the troubled child–woman played by Tippi Hedren in *Marnie*. But can this observation offer any insights about the evolution of gender politics in the postwar period, and how can we understand these representations to have been read by their contemporary audiences? Not only were the internal features, as it were, of popular films, subject to change: the context of the cinematic institution itself

3 The annual assessments of 'popularity' published by three different sources—the British fan magazine *Picturegoer*, the British trade paper *KW*, the American trade paper *Motion Picture Herald*—were correlated; only films which appeared in two or more out of six possible citation categories being considered 'popular' for the purpose of my sample. See Table 3.1 for a full list of these titles.

TABLE 3.1. Most Popular Films at the British Box Office, 1945–1960

1945	*Madonna of the Seven Moons* (UK) 5*		I Remember Mama (USA) 2
	Mr Skeffington (USA) 4		Homecoming (UK) 2
	The Seventh Veil (UK) 5		It Always Rains on Sunday (UK) 3
	Henry V (UK) 2		Road to Rio (USA) 2
	The Way to the Stars (UK) 2		An Ideal Husband (UK) 2
	A Song to Remember (USA) 2		Green Dolphin Street (USA) 2
	Valley of Decision (USA) 3		Forever Amber (USA) 2
	The Affairs of Susan (USA) 3		Life With Father (USA) 3
	I Live in Grosvenor Square (UK) 2		The Weaker Sex (UK) 2
	Old Acquaintance (USA) 2		If Winter Comes (USA) 2
	Frenchman's Creek (USA) 2	1949	Maytime in Mayfair (UK) 5
	Mrs Parkington (USA) 2		Johnny Belinda (USA) 3
	Here Come the Waves (USA) 2		Whispering Smith (USA) 2
	They Were Sisters (UK) 3		Jolson Sings Again (USA) 3
	Perfect Strangers (UK) 2		Scott of the Antarctic (UK) 3
	Conflict (USA) 2		Red River (USA) 2
	Duffy's Tavern (USA) 2		Madness of the Heart (UK) 2
	A Place of One's Own (UK) 2		Adam and Evelyne (UK) 2
1946	*The Wicked Lady* (UK) 5		The Secret Life of Walter Mitty (USA) 2
	The Corn is Green (USA) 4		Paleface (USA) 2
	Piccadilly Incident (UK) 4		The Blue Lagoon (UK) 2
	Caesar and Cleopatra (UK) 4		Easter Parade (USA) 3
	Brief Encounter (UK) 4		The Barkleys of Broadway (USA) 2
	Spellbound (USA) 3		Three Came Home (USA) 2
	The Captive Heart (UK) 2		The Forsyte Saga (USA) 2
	The Bells of St Mary's (USA) 3	1950	*Odette* (UK) 5
	Mildred Pierce (USA) 2		*Annie Get Your Gun* (USA) 5
	Leave Her to Heaven (USA) 2		Father of the Bride (USA) 3
	Road to Utopia (USA) 3		Sunset Boulevard (USA) 2
	Kitty (USA) 2		Morning Departure (UK) 2
	Caravan (UK) 2		The Wooden Horse (UK) 3
	Blue Dahlia (USA) 2		Samson and Delilah (USA) 4
	Bedelia (UK) 2		Pandora and the Flying Dutchman (UK) 2
	O. S. S. (USA) 2		*All About Eve* (USA) 4
1947	Great Expectations (UK) 5		The Blue Lamp (UK) 2
	Odd Man Out (UK) 4		The Happiest Days of Your Life (UK) 2
	The Courtneys of Curzon Street (UK) 4		Treasure Island (UK) 2
	The Jolson Story (USA) 3		Fancy Pants (USA) 2
	Deception (USA) 2	1951	The Lavender Hill Mob (UK) 2
	They Made Me a Fugitive (UK) 2		*The Great Caruso* (USA) 4
	The Razor's Edge (USA) 2		*Born Yesterday* (USA) 2
	Frieda (UK) 3		*The Browning Version* (UK) 2
	Black Narcissus (UK) 3		No Highway (UK) 2
	Duel in the Sun (USA) 2		The Lady with the Lamp (UK) 2
	So Well Remembered (UK) 2		Encore (UK) 2
	October Man (UK) 2		Detective Story (USA) 2
	The Upturned Glass (UK) 2		Captain Horatio Hornblower (UK) 4
	Two Mrs Carrolls (USA) 2		White Corridors (UK) 2
1948	Spring in Park Lane (UK) 5		Laughter in Paradise (UK) 2
	Oliver Twist (UK) 5		Worm's Eye View (UK) 2
	The Red Shoes (UK) 5		Cinderella (USA) 2
	Miranda (UK) 5		King Solomon's Mines (USA) 2
	Hamlet (UK) 4		The Mudlark (UK) 2
	The Winslow Boy (UK) 2		Scrooge (UK) 2
	My Brother Jonathan (UK) 2	1952	The African Queen (UK) 4
	The Fallen Idol (UK) 2		The Sound Barrier (UK) 4
	Saigon (USA) 2		
	The Best Years of our Lives (USA) 3		

TABLE 3.1. (Cont'd)

Year	Film	Year	Film
	The Greatest Show on Earth (USA) 3		White Christmas (USA) 2
	The Planter's Wife (UK) 3		One Good Turn (UK) 2
	A Streetcar Named Desire (USA) 2		Raising a Riot (UK) 2
	Where No Vultures Fly (UK) 2		20,000 Leagues Under the Sea (USA) 2
	The Quiet Man (USA) 2	1956	*Reach for the Sky* (UK) 5
	Ivanhoe (UK) 2		The King and I (USA) 4
	Angels One Five (UK) 2		The Man with the Golden Arm (USA) 2
	Reluctant Heroes (UK) 2		*Rebel Without a Cause* (USA) 2
	Mandy (UK) 3		It's Great to be Young (UK) 3
1953	The Cruel Sea (UK) 4		Guys and Dolls (USA) 3
	Shane (USA) 2		A Town Like Alice (UK) 2
	Roman Holiday (USA) 2		The Man Who knew Too Much (USA) 2
	Moulin Rouge (UK) 3		The Rose Tattoo (USA) 2
	Quo Vadis (USA) 2		Picnic (USA) 2
	Limelight (USA) 2		Trapeze (USA) 2
	Come Back Little Sheba (USA) 2		Private's Progress (UK) 2
	The Snows of Kilimanjaro (USA) 2		The Baby and the Battleship (UK) 2
	Genevieve (UK) 2		*The Searchers* (USA) 2
	Call Me Madam (USA) 2	1957**	Anastasia (USA) 5
	A Queen is Crowned (UK) 2		Doctor at Large (UK) 3
	Road to Bali (USA) 2		Yangtse Incident (UK) 3
1954	The Glenn Miller Story (USA) 5		Campbell's Kingdom (UK) 2
	Calamity Jane (USA) 4		Giant (USA) 3
	The Purple Plain (UK) 3		The Teahouse of the August Moon (USA) 2
	On The Waterfront (USA) 3		The Spanish Gardener (UK) 2
	Magnificent Obsession (USA) 2		The Story of Esther Costello (UK) 2
	The Caine Mutiny (USA) 3		Woman in a Dressing Gown (UK) 2
	Doctor in the House (UK) 3		Heaven Knows, Mr Allison (USA) 2
	The Robe (USA) 2		High Society (USA) 2
	Hobson's Choice (UK) 3		Tea and Sympathy (USA) 2
	Sabrina Fair (USA) 2	1958**	The Wind Cannot Read (UK) 3
	Rear Window (USA) 2		The Bridge on the River Kwai (UK) 3
	Trouble in Store (UK) 2		The Young Lions (USA) 2
	The Belles of St Trinians (UK) 3		Pal Joey (USA) 2
	Knock on Wood (USA) 2		Indiscreet (UK) 2
	From Here to Eternity (USA) 3		The Defiant Ones (USA) 2
1955	*The Dam Busters* (UK) 5		Carve Her Name With Pride (UK) 2
	Doctor at Sea (UK) 3		Ice Cold in Alex (UK) 2
	Marty (USA) 3		Peyton Place (USA) 2
	The Country Girl (USA) 3	1959** ***	Room at the Top (UK) 2
	East of Eden (USA) 2		The Inn of the Sixth Happiness (UK) 2
	A Man Called Peter (USA) 2		I'm All Right Jack (UK) 2
	All That Heaven Allows (USA) 2	1960** ***	Sink the Bismarck (UK) 2
	A Star is Born (USA) 2		The Millionairess (UK) 2
	Love Me or Leave Me (USA) 2		Inherit the Wind (USA) 3
	I Am a Camera (UK) 2		
	Young at Heart (USA) 2		

Notes: Films analysed in detail are given in italics.

* The 'score' figure given for each film refers to the number of mentions it received in the following annual award categories: *Picturegoer* 'Best Actor'; *Picturegoer* 'Best Actress'; *Kinematograph Weekly* 'Top Box Office Film'; *Kinematograph Weekly* 'Best Individual Performance'; *Kinematograph Weekly* 'Most Popular Star'; *Motion Picture Herald* 'Top Ten Films'.

** There are no *Motion Picture Herald* citations for the British Box Office in this year.

*** There are no *Picturegoer* awards for this year.

altered dramatically between 1945 and 1960. Billings's ebullient optimism, in his review of 1946—

> More than anything else the Box-Office balance sheet of 1946 shows that this has been the best year on record for the British film industry. Of the estimated yearly takings of £110,000,000, contributed by the 25,000,000 British filmgoers who regularly attend their 'local', a substantial sum is now 'stopping at home'. This is good news.[4]

—had by 1960 given way to a more circumspect tone:

> Let's face it, 1960 hasn't exactly been a vintage film year, but what it lacked in quality it gained in variety. Moreover it was a comparatively prosperous year and for these reasons: one, the lifting of the Entertainments Tax, which has made a tremendous difference to gross takings in West End and key provincial halls; two, the aforementioned variety of the pictures, particularly those made by British producers, who have again stolen a march on the Yanks; and three, the masses' growing discontent with television programmes. They not only want a change of fare, but an excuse to retire from the parlour.[5]

Over these fifteen years, the 'struggle' between the trade itself and the film critics responsible, through their reviews, for the discourse surrounding films, was conducted against a background of major social changes: postwar austerity and reconstruction gave way to the consumer boom and apparently increased affluence of the 1950s, of which one feature was the widening of leisure choices and the overall decline of cinema as the dominant cultural form. In this context it is legitimate to ask what 'the popular' connotes, and whether indeed it is possible to discover what was widely enjoyed at various moments.

The fan magazine *Picturegoer* carried out an annual poll of its readers and awarded its 'gold medal' to the most popular male and female actors in respect of their performance in a particular film; they also published the top ten names in each category yielded by their poll. From the 1930s until 1958, when the magazine ceased publication, the *Picturegoer* poll provides a consistent and useful summary of audience preferences, albeit confined to those cinema-goers who regularly subscribed to the magazine. On its own, this would be an inadequate guarantor of the contemporary success of individual actors in films; but it does offer a useful corrective to film distributors' annual assessments, which were more directly concerned with the profitability of films or the future market potential of stars.

The most frequently quoted distributors' assessment is that published in the *Motion Picture Almanac*: this was an American publication summarizing the activities of the US film industry at home and abroad, in which a simple list of the ten most popular films and stars at the British box office during the preceding year was given, apparently based on returns from distributors in Britain and presumably intended for the benefit of the US industry. The entry for the British box office occupies less than one of the one thousand pages in the publication. This is

4   *KW,* 19 December 1946, p. 46.

5   *KW,* 15 December 1960, p. 8.

nevertheless a useful—and relatively accessible—rough guide to the dominant trends in popular cinema; though what it offers is limited by its derivation from the experience of distributors routinely dealing with the US industry (if not owned by US interests) and by its address primarily to interests which were in direct, and often bitter, competition with the British film industry during the period.

The periodic evaluations conducted within industry trade papers such as *KW* and *Motion Picture Herald* were addressed to those involved in the business of selling films to audiences, and accordingly aimed to inform their readers about the degree of success achieved by various products. For the historian, the problem in dealing with these assessments lies in their inconsistency and variety and, most difficult of all, in the lack of information about how given judgements were formed. *Kinematograph Weekly*, the major British trade paper during the period, used over forty different categories in its assessments published in December each year: only four of these, however, appeared consistently. Several factors account for the lack of simple data about box-office receipts for particular films, and for the often eccentric proliferation of categories in *KW*'s annual awards.

During the latter part of the 1940s, cinema was undoubtedly the dominant form of popular culture in the UK, and seemed, to optimists at any rate, to be an expanding industry. Economic relations between Britain and the dominant US film industry in the austere postwar years were complicated by the British government's sporadic and ill-judged attempts to protect the home industry. Plotting the fiscal performance of individual products must have been an accountant's nightmare; and this, combined with the hope that the market would become more buoyant, might explain the lack of reliable data. But cinema audiences peaked in Britain in the late 1940s, with 1,600 million admissions per year, thereafter declining continuously through the 1950s, the most dramatic fall occurring between 1955 (1,182 million) and 1960 (501 million).[6] By 1965 they were down to 327 million; and the relentless fall continued, until by the late 1980s cinema admissions were a mere 5 per cent of what they had been in 1946.[7] Therefore, while the British economy as a whole appeared healthier during the consumer boom of the 1950s, the cinema industry had no respite. The major competitor in the field of entertainment was, of course, broadcast television; and references to this competition litter the cinema trade papers throughout the 1950s.

A correlation of films and stars cited in varied sources can offer a more trustworthy picture of 'popularity', at least in its quantitative dimension, than can dependence on any one source alone. A discussion of individual films selected according to such a correlation offers interesting historical insights to set alongside those available in studies whose *raisons d'être* and starting-points are more firmly located in questions about particular genres, directors, stars, or production strategies. The problem with studies of the latter sort has always been their tendency to overemphasize film texts whose actual exposure to the mass audience was relatively marginal, because of their intrinsic interest

6   James Curran and Vincent Porter (eds.), *British Cinema History* (London: Weidenfeld and Nicolson, 1983), p. 372.

7   Geoffrey Nowell-Smith, 'On history and the cinema', *Screen*, vol. 31, no. 2 (1990), pp. 160–71.

for critics and scholars. This overemphasis, and the concomitant marginalization of films which might have enjoyed greater success at the box office, becomes problematic to the degree that the canons by which critics and scholars have evaluated films are different from those by which it is legitimate to understand either the predilections or the 'reading activities' of the mass audience.

The vicissitudes of the various branches of the film industry are germane to a discussion of popularity because these relate to both the number and the types of films offered to audiences. As far as audiences themselves are concerned, we might speculate that although cinemas had substantially diminished in number by the mid-1960s while typical admission prices had risen appreciably, the overall range of leisure choices open to audience members had not changed as much as these facts might imply. Going to the cinema, from the 1960s onwards, was just one amongst a range of entertainment options. What this qualitative social change does suggest, however, is that the concept of popularity in relation to cinema has a different meaning in the period after the 1960s than it did in the 1940s. This must be taken into account in assessments of the social consequences of cinematic representations towards the end of the postwar period. Popular cinematic imagery was far less widely consumed in the 1960s than it was in the 1940s; and it should also be remembered that correlations of various assessments of popularity in any given year are conducted against a background of overall and absolute decline in the popularity of the institution of cinema. The demise of the fan magazine in the late 1950s is a reminder of this.

If the distinguishing feature of British society in the 1940s was a stoical collectivism, by the 1960s there was instead an impatient fragmentation. Is there any evidence of this in the content of films achieving large-scale box-office success? It is certainly true to say that characteristic themes treated in popular films underwent marked changes through the period, and that at any given moment all of the most popular films tended to share some common concerns. However, unless we are to subscribe to the idea that films in some way reflect the society in which they circulate, understanding the significance of such changes is a complex matter. Given that the meanings of a film are the product of active negotiation between reader and film text operating within a discursive field constructed via the activities of the industry and its critics, how did audience members 'read' the images they were offered?

Here we are immediately plunged into the realm of speculation. Although the answer to this question can never be known, its determinants may be considered; for example by means of detailed analysis of box-office successes yielded through a correlation of different sources, considering not only overall narrative themes, structures, and resolutions, but also details of representations of characters and the nuances of their relation to narrative development. So far, so good: but this only attends to the film itself. What of the audience? What forms of evidence are available here? It is possible to envisage an oral history enquiry which would attempt to reconstruct, through interviews and questionnaires, some traces of the audience. But aside from the logistical difficulties of such an undertaking, any conclusions would be subject to all the limitations inherent in its methods: hindsight, faulty memory, and unrepresentative samples of respondents, for example; though such conclusions would still offer fascinating correlative material along the lines of the Mass-Observation survey of cinema audiences in Bolton in 1938.[8] More satisfactory might be an examination of contemporary published material: if we cannot resurrect the audiences themselves, we do have access to discursive materials routinely circulating among them: in this form evidence does exist of the terms in which various films, characters, plots, and stars were discussed. We can discover which representations were acceptable, which were the subject of controversy. In short, if we cannot meet with the audience, we can reconstruct the discursive contexts of their cinema-going and their readings of films.

A cursory glance at the list of films popular at the British box office between 1945 and 1960 (see Table 3.1), compiled from a correlation of the sources outlined above, shows that overall the British market was dominated by the US (Hollywood) product[9]—which explains the anxieties of the British industry concerning what they perceived as major threats to their livelihood: US 'investment' in British films, and the perennial competition with the US industry for box-office revenue. In the late 1940s the share was more even, and the continuing success of Hollywood films with British audiences was masked by the fact that the smaller number of top box-office hits was dominated by British titles: hence the celebration, in many histories of cinema, of British film production at this time. During the 1950s, however, the US product was dominant, both in numbers of popular successes and within the handful of top-selling titles in each year. Towards the end of the 1950s and in the early 1960s, British films once again figure significantly both in overall market share and in the top hits listings—though given the contribution of US finance to these productions we should perhaps be wary of the claims about the 'revival' of the British cinema abounding in the press of the period: if the term is justified in cultural terms, it is certainly questionable in fiscal terms. By the mid-1960s, in any case, the situation was back to 'normal': a market dominated by imported material, with a none the less significant minority of popular box-office successes emerging from the home industry.

Kinematograph Weekly was the main forum for the distribution and exhibition branches of the British industry. Josh Billings's annual review was clearly intended as a kind of survey of work in progress addressed to distributors and exhibitors. The function of Billings's annual reviews, besides reinforcing the industry's sense of collectivity, was to attempt predictions of future performance in order to ensure profits, and hence survival. This attempt would have had implications for the range of titles available to audiences in succeeding years; for it is distributors and exhibitors who make the initial selections from which

8 Jeffrey Richards and Dorothy Sheridan (eds.), *Mass-Observation at the Movies* (London: Routledge & Kegan Paul, 1987).

9 The table lists 105 US and 101 British films. Only titles with a 'score' of two or more have been included here. The remainder, with one citation each, is heavily dominated by the US product—thus the picture overall shows the British industry dominated by US imports. In addition many of the British pictures were financed by US companies.

audience choice produces the box-office hit. Thus the politics of distribution, after those of production, constrain and order the very possibility of any particular film becoming a box-office hit. The large number—over forty in all—of different and changing categories employed during the period provides evidence of the industry's unease: attention to the details of these categories, to the day-to-day terminologies of product classification, allows the historian insight into the various attempts to stabilize it. It also allows consideration of the rather more elusive question of what a 'popular' film meant, in the terms of the trade, and how this meaning was subject to change as cinema audiences declined through the 1950s. These categories fall into three distinct groups: those directly concerning the all-important issue of monies received; those responding to the imperative to define the product as closely as possible; and those concerning the box-office drawing power of particular performers.

Of these, the latter group is the most stable: the importance of actors to the marketing of films and the subsequent assessment of their success was apparently uncontested. Three categories citing an actor's name in respect of a particular film appeared consistently throughout the period: 'Best Individual Performance', 'Most Popular and Consistent Star', and 'Most Promising Newcomer'. 'Best Individual Performance' is the category for which Billings appears to draw most heavily on conventional notions of quality: on the values of 'art' as opposed to the more quantitative values—those of 'commerce'—implied in his use of the term 'popularity', where he habitually referred to the numbers of tickets sold, the length of queues or the perceived demand for films featuring a particular performer.

During the 1945–60 period the number of citations for 'Best Performance' increased: perhaps the decline in overall audience figures made the assessment of an individual star's popularity increasingly uncertain, throwing Billings back on his experience in recognizing performance skills to estimate future popularity. In 1957 he commented on the changes he perceived: 'As for the giants of yesterday, Bob Hope, Gary Cooper, Clark Gable and Fred Astaire, they seem to be as dead as the dodo. The Tommy Steeles, the Frankie Vaughans and the Elvis Presleys have completely taken over their territory.'[10]

10 *KW*, 12 December 1957, p. 9.

In 1946 Billings cited only one actor in his category 'Best Individual Performer'—Celia Johnson for her performance in *Brief Encounter*. In 1951 he listed Michael Redgrave in *The Browning Version*, Alec Guinness in *The Mudlark*, Judy Holliday in *Born Yesterday*, and Bette Davis in *All About Eve*. By 1957 the number of 'Best Performances' had risen to ten. However, although Billings did occasionally refer to individual performances in his prose accompaniment to the annual review, this practice was on the whole unusual. Most of his text is concerned with an assessment of distributors' output and with the contours of the successful film. Again and again he stressed that individual performance, stars, technological innovations, and the like can never compensate for a poor script.

The wide-screen and colour can unquestionably make a good film even more attractive, but, like many a so-called star, these embellishments are no compensation for an indifferent script. There never has been and there never will be a substitute for a strong story.[11]

11 Ibid.

As far as individual actors are concerned, Billings was undoubtedly most at ease with the category 'Most Popular Stars'; though it is interesting to note the relatively poor correlation between his assessment of who these were and that of *Picturegoer*'s annual readership poll. *Picturegoer* cited ten male and ten female actors each year in its annual 'Best Actor' and 'Best Actress' awards, whereas Billings was more erratic, giving forty-three names in 1948 and only five in 1953 and 1959. In general the number was between ten and twenty-five. The correlation between these and the *Picturegoer* assessments was never more than 50 per cent, and frequently much less. In 1946, when Billings cited Celia Johnson for 'Best Individual Performance', he was actually far more enthusiastic about James Mason and Margaret Lockwood, who were among *KW*'s sixteen 'Most Popular and Consistent Stars'. In 1951 he cited seventeen names, only four of which also figured in *Picturegoer*'s list—Alec Guinness, Susan Hayward, Doris Day, and Glynis Johns; and in 1957 there were twenty-three, of which seven also appeared in the *Picturegoer* assessments. Despite his regular (Dirk Bogarde, Frank Sinatra, Richard Todd, Heather Sears, Yvonne Mitchell, Ingrid Bergman, and Deborah Kerr) attention to actors, however, by the late 1950s Billings clearly had reservations about the scope of their power at the box office: 'I've mentioned who I believe to be the most popular stars, but, with the exception of Kenneth More, who is unquestionably a big draw here, I know of no actor who can turn an ordinary film into a box office success mainly on the strength of his name'.[12]

12 Ibid.

KW's product classifications are far less stable than those concerning actors, revealing the increasingly desperate attempts to stem the inexorable decline in cinema admissions through the period. In general the picture is one of a disappearance of categories at the end of the 1940s, some rather odd experiments in the early 1950s, and an appearance of new categories towards the end of that decade. The generic categories are the largest group, and within these the musical is the most consistently used (1945–7, 1949–58). The western first appeared as a separate category in the postwar review in 1950 when *Winchester 73* was cited as 'Best Western'; and this category was used throughout the 1950s, except in 1954 when the rather curious 'Best Outdoor Film' described *The Far Country*. In the late 1940s the categories *documentary, interest*, and *artistic* were used: in 1948, for example, *XIV Olympiad—The Glory of Sport* was named 'Best Full Length Documentary', *This Modern Age* 'Best Interest Series', and *Hamlet* the 'Most Artistic Film'. However, none of these categories survived beyond 1950. In 1958, a new category, horror, made its first appearance (referring to the Hammer production *Dracula*), and was joined in 1959 by 'Best Series', which confirmed the box-office drawing power of the 'Carry On' films. *Carry on Sergeant*, the first of the series, had appeared in Billings's list of 'Others in the Money' in 1958, and *Carry on Nurse* was *KW*'s 'Biggest Box Office Attraction' in 1959. Yet in 1954 and 1955, when the first two 'Doctor' films, *Doctor in the House* and *Doctor at Sea* were among the box-office hits, there was no category designating films from a series. This category seems to be a hybrid between a generic classification and one which attends, like 'Best Straight X Certificate' (*Room at the Top* in 1959 and *Suddenly Last Summer* in 1960), 'Best Offbeat' (*The Shaggy Dog* in 1959), and 'Best Gimmick' (*House on Haunted Hill* in 1959) to features of the film understandable in terms not of narrative content so much as potential marketing strategies. The only categories which, in attempting to define both content and mode of address, can unarguably be called generic, and which were routinely used during the 1950s, were the musical and the western. It was not until the 1960s that greater precision was attempted in generic definitions employed: 'Best Thriller' (*The Birds* in 1963), 'Best Historical Drama' (*Zulu* in 1964), 'Best Costume Comedy' (*Tom Jones* in 1963), and so on; indicating—in their appeal to specialized audience preferences—the increasing fragmentation of the cinema audience which characterized that decade.

In the mid-1950s two short-lived categories attended specifically to new technologies in the production and exhibition of films; 'Best 3-D' (*House of Wax* in 1953 and *Hondo* in 1954) and 'Biggest CinemaScope Attraction' (*The Robe* and *Three Coins in the Fountain* in 1954, *There's No Business Like Show Business* and *The Seven Year Itch* in 1955, *The King and I* (this film was also cited as 'Best Musical') and *Smiley* in 1956, and *Island in the Sun* and *Anastasia* in 1957). CinemaScope and 3-D can best be understood as attempts to draw audiences into the cinema by promising them a form of entertainment unavailable on the domestic television screen. The presence of these categories in the mid-1950s also draws attention to the fact that many cinemas were not yet equipped to screen CinemaScope films; and that such films might thus have required extra encouragement. By making a special case in this way, Billings and *KW* perhaps hoped to encourage investment in this new technology.

Finally, within these product definitions, some attention was paid to the nationality of origin of films. Here the chauvinism of the British is strikingly evident, all films being classified as either 'British', 'American', or 'Continental'. The category 'Best British Film' was, as would be expected in the British market, the most consistent; but even so it did not appear every year, being most in evidence at the beginning of the period (1945–51, 1953, 1957). The category 'Best American Film' appeared, rather oddly, at just the time in the mid-1950s when the US product had achieved its maximum dominance of the British market (1954–6, 1960). The category 'Most Successful Continental Film' appeared in the early 1950s and was fairly consistently used thereafter (1952–8, 1960). In 1959 there was a 'Gimmick' category, and one for

'Straight X Certificate', but none for 'Continental'; and in 1960 non-English-language films were referred to simply as 'Foreign', though the implications of the *risqué* were retained—thus the 'Most Sensational Foreign Film' in 1960 was *The Green Mare's Nest* (Autant-Lara, France/Italy, 1960). Billings returned to the appellation 'Continental' during the 1960s.

Apart from its chauvinist lumping together of all non-English-language films, this is a particularly interesting category, since few 'Continental' films achieved the status of box-office hits, certainly earlier in the period; yet they did offer a new marketing possibility, and can perhaps best be understood in this way. They were invariably European films, mainly French and Italian, and so perhaps the use of this category also offers early evidence of the industry keeping half an eye on Europe as an economic entity. On the whole, however, it is true to say that in the routine parlance of the trade papers and film fan magazines of the period the term continental implied the sexually explicit; and as such offered a product, like 3-D or CinemaScope, unavailable on the television screen.

The uncertainties of the film business in the period between 1945 and 1960, and the concomitant innovations in marketing strategies of the late 1950s, are also in evidence in the third group of categories, those relating to the primary function of film as perceived by exhibitors and distributors—namely to generate profit at the box office. The categories which appeared consistently throughout the period were 'Biggest Box Office Attraction', with a separate listing of 'Runners-Up', and 'Best Output', which cited a distribution company. These were the two most important items of information for exhibitors: which films made the most money, and which distribution company routinely offered the best booking opportunities. There was considerable attention, most marked in the late 1940s, to specifically British operations; and during the 1950s attention was paid to novel marketing strategies with such categories as 'Best Double Bill', 'Best British Double Bill', 'Best Re-Issue Double Bill' (1951, 1953–60), or the colourfully named 'Super Special Long Run Propositions at Special Prices' (1958) and 'Hard Ticket Giants', 'Block Busting Exploitation Offerings' (1959–60), which, like 3-D and CinemaScope in the earlier 1950s, drew attention to films which could not be fairly accounted for in the overall national box-office picture. The 'Super Special Propositions' in 1958 were *The Ten Commandments, South Pacific*, and *Around The World in 80 Days*; and the same titles reappear as 'Hard Ticket Giants' in 1959, accompanied by *Gigi* and *The Nun's Story*. In 1960 the term was 'Block Busting Exploitation', and the film was *Hercules Unchained*.

Although most of these titles attracted considerable razzmatazz and long queues in urban centres, none appeared in the 'Biggest Box Office Attraction' listings: these categories, then, appear to embody a suggestion to exhibitors about new strategies for filling (or saving) their cinemas. By the end of the 1950s it had become inescapably clear that cinema was no longer the dominant form of mass entertainment, and that in order to survive at all outside the 'art house' it would have to reorganize itself radically. These raucous categories represent an attempt to do this; and the films themselves, with their lavish production values and grand-scale panoramas, recall the struggles in the USA between the MPPC cartel and the 'independents' in the early years of the century, as the cinema institution engaged in a formative contortion similar to that which was to characterize the late 1950s.

In this exploration of the changing meanings of the notion of 'the popular' as it referred to the relation between films and their audiences (a relation always mediated by the box office, the object of Billings's and KW's scrutiny), it is the category which measures successive films' drawing power at the box office which is of greatest interest. In the succession of 'Biggest Box Office Attractions' between 1945 and 1960, there is evidence of the gradual shift in audience preferences: for KW 'the popular' is simply that which the most people prefer and will pay to see. Any sociologically motivated interpretation of such preferences, though, must also take into account the overall and absolute decline in audiences during the period and the related politics of distribution.

The simultaneous popularity of different genres and stars, not to mention the vagaries of release dates, make it difficult to claim with certainty that any single film was the 'top hit' of its year. Nevertheless this correlative method is sound enough to offer groups of titles which, taken together, can be analysed to reveal common themes. Discovering thematic unities amongst groups of films whose only common feature, at first glance, is a temporal one, requires an analytic method which can be employed over a range of different genres. I selected (on the basis of their 'popularity' at the British box office) groups of six films from 1945–6, 1950–1, and 1955–6, and performed a careful textual analysis of each film. These analyses involved a dual enquiry into the status and narrative experience of characters; taking into account first their functional contribution to the unfolding of the narrative, and secondly the degree to which the character allowed (or invited) audience insight into the diegesis. This method entailed a schema whereby all characters in any film could be classified in one of four groups (central, major, minor, figures); and the schema allowed comparisons between films contemporary with each other, and between films separated by a temporal interval. Having analysed each film in isolation according to this method, I was then in a position to consider individual films and groups of films in terms of thematic and structural similarities and dissimilarities. In this approach in which film texts are privileged, dictating questions or observations about their social and/or political contexts, I hope to have avoided the pitfalls of a reflectionist analysis. The elaborate correlation of sources employed to generate sample films for analysis is fundamental to this mode of enquiry, since it is contemporary success at the box office, or contemporary audience choice, which determines the selection of film objects in the first place and therefore allows the following question: what changes are discernible in the content and narrative structure of films found to be 'popular' at different moments?

In the mid-1940s a common theme in the majority of the most successful films at the box office concerned the status and behaviour of women. Time and again, films offered a central female protagonist who transgressed the implied social order either wilfully, as Barbara (Margaret Lockwood) did in *The Wicked Lady*, or as a consequence of 'tragic' circumstances, such as those suffered by Diana (Anna Neagle) in *Piccadilly Incident* (1946). Frequently, the films focused on the psychic make-up of the character in an attempt to explain her troubles by reference to her past experience: Francesca (Ann Todd) in *The Seventh Veil* (1945) and Maddalena (Phyllis Calvert) in *Madonna of the Seven Moons* (1944) are examples of characters whose narrative path is constructed in this way. The case of Laura (Celia Johnson) in *Brief Encounter* is exemplary of this narrative method at its most uncompromising, since the entire film is structured in the form of her 'silent'—given in voice over to the audience alone—address to her husband, in which she details the agonies and delights of her extramarital liaison. The consequence of this narrative method is that problems which might, from a more distanced point of view, reasonably appear to be general social concerns—in this case the attempt at re-establishment of prewar conventions of family life following the disruptions of the war period—are suggested to be the discrete and private concerns of a lone (female) individual.

By the mid-1950s, by contrast, the thematics of popular films are concerned more with men than with women, with narrative structures tending to a generalization from the particular, as opposed to the 1940s personification of social—generally expressed as female—concerns. Here we have a mythologizing process at work: the narrative experience of central characters (by now usually male) is idealized, rather than being relegated to the realm of the private where, whether tragic or fortunate, characters' experience is not inevitably seen in symbiotic relation with that of the wider social group.

Thus the angst-laden performances of James Dean in *Rebel Without a Cause* (1955) and *East of Eden* (1954) are made to stand for the general problem of socializing the young in middle-class America and, in the case of the latter, for an even more generalized interrogation of American values. Both films implicitly pose the question 'what is the American way of life?' exploring it through a dramatic construction in which the central character is posed as embodying wider concerns. This is true of such apparently diverse films as *Rebel Without a Cause, East of Eden* and *The Searchers* (1956), as well as of the British pictures *The Dam Busters* (1954), *Reach for the Sky* (1956) and *Doctor at Sea*, in which the question relates to Britain and the British way of life. The point which concerns us here is that all these films enjoyed outstanding success at the British box office in the mid-1950s.

This major change in the thematics of 'the popular' over a ten-year period provokes further questions about the critical discourse surrounding these films. My textual analyses were followed by collecting critical responses to the sample films from a variety of sources, both British and American: trade journals, film journals, fan magazines, and national press and more general papers which sometimes reviewed, or referred to, new films.[13] In general, the less specialized the source the more likely it was that a radically oversimplified reading of a film would be presented. Nevertheless, this set of sources remains, for the historian, the best contemporary evidence of audience understandings of the films. Clearly the caveat underlying my remarks about changes in the thematics of the popular—that only generalized propositions based on a plurality of instances have any validity—is also operative in the case of these published responses to films.

What is immediately of interest here is that, rather than the striking change in the thematics of the popular noted in the films themselves, there appears to be a striking consistency: critics and reviewers seem to be virtually unanimous in the sociological and aesthetic models on which they implicitly draw in their summary judgements. Moreover these models, unlike the thematics of films, did not change appreciably between the mid-1940s and the mid-1950s. The majority of critics affirm, in their responses to films, the conventional status quo as typically confirmed in narrative resolutions, referring additionally to the canons of 'high' art as these were understood in postwar Britain[14] in their applause for a particular performance—Redgrave in *The Browning Version* and *The Dam Busters*, Johnson in *Brief Encounter*—or in their denigration of a particular film whose 'popular' tone reveals, to the critic, a lamentable absence of such an aesthetic. It is in practice often difficult to separate aesthetic references from those pertaining to social mores: this confusion between cultural and ethical values has, I suspect, substantive consequences for the maintenance of middle-class hegemony during the so-called 'classless' 1950s. *Tribune* noted approvingly the 'Beautifully sincere and natural playing of Celia Johnson' in *Brief Encounter*, endorsing her eventual repudiation of the 'affair' with Alec (Trevor Howard) by referring to the 'guilt, humiliation and [a] heroic integrity at the centre'. It is tempting to infer that Johnson's 'playing' could be considered 'natural' precisely *because* of her 'heroic integrity' revealed in her appropriately felt 'guilt and humiliation'. Margaret Lockwood's performance as the ebullient, unashamedly transgressive heroine in *The Wicked Lady* was, on the other hand, 'inept to the point of exasperation'; though for this evidently misogynist critic, James Mason in the same film 'aroused both admiration and sympathy'.[15] The implicit opposition between (high) drama and (low) melodrama which underlies reviews throughout the period surfaced clearly in the *News Chronicle* review of *The Dam Busters*: 'Drama . . . never once degenerates into melodrama, nor the humour into the irrelevant flippancy of comic relief'.[16]

13 Such as: *Picture Post, New Musical Express* (formerly *The Accordion Times*), and some women's magazines—*Woman, Woman's Illustrated, Woman and Beauty, Woman's Own*.

14 John Ellis 'Art, culture, quality: terms for a cinema in the forties and seventies', *Screen*, vol. 19, no. 3 (1978), pp. 9–50.

15 *Tribune*, 23 November 1945.

16 *News Chronicle*, 17 May 1955.

In addition, many reviews in the 1940s revealed an alignment between 'high art' values and French cinema, which had given way by the end of the 1950s to a repudiation of the sexual explicitness of French (by now 'Continental') films. *Brief Encounter* was equated by many with both 'art' cinema and, in what seemed a self-evident corollary, 'French' cinema:

> ... it would be difficult to find a more profound study of love outside the French cinema.

> ... this is a poet's film, harsh, cruel and lovely.[17]

17 *Britain Today*, February 1946; *Monthly Film Bulletin*, December 1945.

We should also note, however, the context of these critical judgements. Since much of the British trade and critical press during the 1950s was deeply concerned about the survival of the home industry, there is always an imperative in their writing to encourage—to search for indications, however insubstantial or tenuous, of future success, as well as to exhort audiences to attend. This tendency took a positively jingoistic turn as the decade progressed and the British industry crumbled before its critics' very eyes.

Running through the shifting alliances and discords which characterized the British film industry from 1945 onwards there is a thread of agreement: an anxiety shared by all, though expressed and understood in implacably different ways, about the growing cultural dominance of Britain by the USA. Stafford Cripps at the Board of Trade in 1945, for example, saw the problem in terms of imports and exports: 'I am anxious', he said, 'to leave the strong Rank combine effective for meeting and possibly dealing with American competition'.[18] Whereas Ralph Bond, a leading member of the film technicians' union ACT, offered a rather different perception of the dual imperatives of Rank's export drive in the USA and his investment in distribution and exhibition in Britain: 'It is a curious but evident fact that the more cinemas Mr Rank owns the more he is dependent on America to provide films to fill them'.[19]

18 Public Record Office, Board of Trade 64/2188 (November 1945): quoted in Margaret Dickinson and Sarah Street, *Cinema and State: The Film Industry and the British Government 1927–84* (London: British Film Institute, 1985), p. 170.

19 Ralph Bond, *Monopoly, the Future of British Films* (London: ACT, 1946): quoted in Dickinson and Street, *Cinema and State*, p. 172.

The antipathy towards America which lurks beneath these remarks, as well as in the more specific responses to films by critics and reviewers, also surfaces as a thematic element in many British productions during the 1950s, as well as in the implicit chauvinism of *KW*'s blithe division of the world into 'British', 'American', and 'Continental' in its annual review categories. A general sense that British cinema audiences were receiving a diet inappropriately dominated by Hollywood pervaded both critical writing and trade reviews, as well as informing the various governmental interventions in the regulation of the trade. British critics' alignment of the Hollywood film with the aesthetics of 'low'/mass/industrial culture and their attempts to find in the British film the values of 'high' culture can perhaps be understood as a solidly based suspicion of US infiltration of the UK market, couched in the terms of intellectual snobbery.

An examination of *Kinematograph Weekly* through the 1950s reveals, in addition to the perceived threat from American competition, an attention to the problem for the British industry of competition from broadcast television. Apart from routine news coverage of the various negotiations conducted between industry bodies and television companies, there are occasional feature articles which address the problem in general terms. An audience survey of 1956, for example, urged exhibitors to look to their laurels, and attempted to assert that television, while unarguably an alternative form of entertainment, was not necessarily a replacement for the cinema.[20] A few years earlier, in 1953, Josh Billings had gone even further. In the chatty prose accompanying his annual review, he referred to the extremely popular Rank Organisation documentary about the coronation, *A Queen is Crowned*:

20 *KW*, 13 December 1956, pp. 8–9.

> Every exhibitor who played the film, and most did, makes it his top. . . . Rank Organisation deserves full credit for its foresight and courage in tackling the subject . . . despite fears by many that the broadcasting and televising of the memorable ceremony would destroy the commercial potentialities of the celluloid impression. As it turned out the BBC recordings furnished the finest and most widely distributed trailer in the annals of show business. . . .[21]

21 *KW*, 17 December 1953, p. 10.

Despite Billings's optimism and the rather more circumspect findings of *KW*'s 1956 audience survey, however, there seems little doubt in retrospect about the deleterious effect the rise of broadcast television had on cinema audiences in Britain. The number of television licences issued rose from not quite 350,000 in 1950 to well over thirteen million in 1965.[22] In the same period, as we have seen, cinema lost over three-quarters of its audience. It was a spiralling decline: as admissions fell, cinemas closed and audiences dwindled. Although the drop in overall revenue was less steep than that in audience numbers because of the rise in admission prices, gross revenue nevertheless declined by about half between the mid-1950s and the mid-1960s.[23] In 1952 the Cinematograph Exhibitors Association attempted to institute a boycott against companies which sold films to television; but they were unable to prevent other trade associations from signing an agreement with the BBC in 1956 for the sale of films.

22 Curran and Porter, *British Cinema History*, p. 372.

23 Dickinson and Street, *Cinema and State*, p. 228.

It is interesting to note that the routine screening of films on broadcast television, which began in 1956–7 with, among others, a transmission of John Ford's *Stagecoach* (on 29 September 1956), coincided with the sharpest fall in cinema admissions (from 1,182 million in 1955 to 501 million in 1960). By 1958 the two television channels in Britain were between them broadcasting about 150 films a year—an average of three every week.

All these issues—the changes in the thematics of the popular between the mid-1940s and the mid-1950s; the consistent critical support for the conventional status quo (in sociological terms) and the routine dependence on the values of high art (in aesthetic terms); the increasing defensiveness on the part of the British industry and its critical support towards popular successes produced in Hollywood rather than

Elstree—are condensed in the case of the 1951 George Cukor film, *Born Yesterday*. This film, released on the cusp of the new decade (its UK release date was 6 June 1951), was one of the top box-office hits of 1950–1. For the purposes of the present discussion, this film may be regarded as paradigmatic not only in its narrative structure but also in the tone of the responses it elicited from British reviewers.

Billie Dawn (Judy Holliday) is 'reborn' during the course of *Born Yesterday*'s narrative—but the (re)birth signalled in the film's title lays claim to a wider significance. Like any heroine of the 1940s her transgressions must be remedied; like the central characters of 1950s films her recoupment is achieved by means of her initiation into the twin ideals of high culture and democratic politics. Thus, in the figure of Billie Dawn, American democracy is also born again: freed, like her, from the corrupt and avaricious embrace of self-serving senators and entrepreneurs. In narrative terms she is moved from her initial position as consort to the grossly corrupt, but also culturally innocent, junk dealer Harry Brock (Broderick Crawford) to a new position at the narrative's close as wife to the literate, honest writer Paul Verrall (William Holden). The transformation is visually signalled through her dress, particularly via the motif of the spectacles through which she learns to 'see' the world with greater clarity (or at least to see it as it is seen by her journalist mentor/lover). This was a narrative resolution heartily approved of by the film's reviewers on both sides of the Atlantic:

> Beneath the comedy, which is the picture's primary content, there is important meaning with respect to such matters as honesty, democratic principles, integrity and good citizenship.[24]

> Garson Kanin's comedy is a pleasing lesson in the virtues of democracy, enlivened by smart, sometimes witty, dialogue and by characterisation which, if broad and simple, is always lively.[25]

In *Born Yesterday* Billie Dawn emerges from the 1940s as her conception of 'independence' is remodelled, as it were, to conform to the model required of women in the 1950s. Her complete renovation is indicated to the audience in the last scene of the film when, having been stopped for speeding along Capitol Hill, Paul inadvertently shows their brand new marriage licence, instead of his driving licence, to the traffic cop. In a close-up we see her new name, Emma Verrall. Emma was the name her father had given her, Verrall the name Paul has given her. Thus the prodigal daughter is reclaimed for patriarchal democracy, and the audience is left with the edifying conclusion that the 'good' Paul and Emma are set on their matrimonial path, while the 'bad' Harry and his corrupt lawyer Jim Deverey (Howard St John) must face the consequences of their illegal usurping of the democratic processes of law-making. As in many films of the later 1950s, the two central male characters Paul Verrall and Harry Brock epitomize the dualism—in this case offered as a polarization—in contemporary political values. Harry Brock (blind, like a badger?) the junk dealer, like Cal in *East of Eden*, is motivated by individualistic materialism while the goals of the journalist

24 *Motion Picture Herald*, 25 November 1950.

25 *Monthly Film Bulletin*, vol. 18 (1951), p. 227.

Paul Verrall (sees all?), like those of Cal's twin brother Aron, have more to do with the spiritual, with ideal social values. It is between these two figures that Billie Dawn must choose, which means that she must define herself in terms of one or the other.

At various points in the film the significance of Billie's choice is signalled by the *mise-en-scène* in which the canons of Western art are visually locked into the propositions of Western democracy. We see an Egyptian obelisk in the distance between two pillars of the colonnade outside the National Gallery of Art, signifying the impressive longevity of history and culture (not to mention, for the feminist reader, their phallic dimensions); we see a small statue of Eros on a fountain, signifying the developing love between Billie and Paul; and, as Paul quotes for Billie a speech in which Napoleon claims that he would rather have been a humble peasant, we see Manet's *The Old Musician*, a painting about the choices that must be made by youth on the threshold of adult life, thus implicitly about the concept of free will. In this way the choice now available to Billie is signified, while at the same time the assertion is made that this choice is a consequence of her acculturation. This dimension of the film, however, seems to have been either missed or ignored by British reviewers, who insisted on the absence of high art values in American popular cinema:

> Americans are easily bewitched by the word 'democracy' and a number of recent Broadway successes . . . have lightly and ingeniously expounded its simpler virtues. . . .

> Compared with her, Eliza Dolittle was a blue stocking and a mistress of phonetics. . . .[26]

26 *Sight and Sound*, March 1951;
Manchester Guardian,
30 April 1951.

There is more to Billie, however, than a relatively simple *tabula rasa* being completed in a manner appropriate to the American myth. Judy Holliday was an accomplished comedian and, in this role, played up the *ingénue* aspects of Billie's character so that Paul's earnestness is constantly put into question by her apparently naive, but often astute, questions and responses:

PAUL: Has he ever thought of anyone but himself?
BILLIE: Who does?
PAUL: Millions of people do.
       The whole history of the world is the story of the struggle between the selfish and the unselfish. . . . Can you understand that?
BILLIE: You're crazy about me, aren't you?
       That's why you get so mad at Harry.
PAUL: Yes.

Thus the unanswered question about the nature of intelligence, an important theme of the film, is foregrounded in the interaction between Holliday's performance and her character's diegetic experience (the much celebrated card-playing sequence is an earlier instance of this); and additionally, to the alert reader at least, she offers a powerful critique of the very process the narrative requires her to embrace. It is here that we can see at its clearest the collision between the strong heroine of the 1940s and the submissive supporting role typically allotted to women in films of the 1950s. In a film contemporary with *Born Yesterday*, *All About Eve*, Margot Channing (Bette Davis) summarizes the point:

> One career all females have in common, whether we like it or not, is being a woman.
> Sooner or later we've got to work at it no matter how many other careers we've had or want.
> And in the last analysis nothing's any good unless you can look up just before dinner, or turn around in bed, there he is.
> Without that you're not a woman. You're something with a French provincial office, or a book full of clippings, but you're not a woman.

Compelling though Billie Dawn is as a character—she is certainly the central character in the film, as Margot Channing is in *All About Eve*—she is always given in relation to the two opposing men, Harry and Paul.

The interesting thing is that whereas in 1951 in *Born Yesterday* the audience is invited to empathize with Paul's conception of the almost sacred nature of American 'democracy' and the centrality of high culture to this ideal, later in the decade this position is revealed (in popular cinema, at least) to be a hopelessly impractical one. In *East of Eden* it is Cal's materialist pragmatism which wins the day. British reviewers, while continuing to subscribe to the dominant social discourses concerning morality, the family, citizenship, and so on, also betray an increasing unease about the aesthetics of popular culture:

> Steinbeck has provided an old-fashioned heavy sentimental drama, and Kazan has slickly tailored it in the modern, neurotic manner to suit a sick society.

> . . . a film dedicated to display, that mistakes mannerisms for style, artifice for art.

> Inflation is not only a headache with politicians and augurers of the stock markets: it hits one with a sickening thud from the screen. Before even the lights went down on *East of Eden*, I knew that it was inflated. One of those glossy melodramatic folders, all big names and hideously tinted photographs, had been handed to me, and at the top of it were the words: 'GREAT BOOKS, GREAT PLAYS, GREAT TALENT MAKE GREAT PICTURES (signed) Jack L. Warner.' Do They? What about GREAT GUFF? *East of Eden* is that.[27]

27 *Daily Worker*, 9 July 1955; *Sunday Times*, 10 July 1955; *New Statesman*, 16 July 1955.

But this thinly veiled distaste of the middle-class British aesthete for the melodramatic form itself, as well as for the unseemly American habit of loudly proclaiming one's virtues in the marketplace, conceals, it seems to me, a more deep-seated unease about what was clearly understood, by the middle of the 1950s, to be the threatening invasion of American cultural influence in Britain.

Part II Social Histories

Part II: Social Relations

4 Scenarios of Exposure in the Practice of Everyday Life: Women in the Cinema of Attractions

CONSTANCE BALIDES

A Windy Day on the Roof

(All illustrations in this article appear courtesy of the Paper Print Collection, Library of Congress)

In *What Happened on Twenty-Third Street, New York City* (Edison, 1901), a man and woman walk down a busy city street. As the woman passes over a grated vent in the sidewalk escaping air blows her skirt up around her knees. In *What Demoralized the Barber Shop* (Edison, 1901), two women (or men dressed as women) stand at the top of the stairs that lead to a basement barber shop and lift their skirts to reveal their legs and striped stockings. Pandemonium ensues as the men in the

1 The films discussed in this essay are held in the Paper Print Collection, Motion Picture, Broadcasting and Recorded Sound Division, Library of Congress, Washington, DC. See Kemp R. Niver, *Early Motion Pictures: The Paper Print Collection in the Library of Congress* (Washington, DC: Library of Congress, 1985) for descriptions of films in the collection. Thanks to the staff in the Motion Picture Division for their very helpful assistance, and especially Madeline Matz.

2 American Mutoscope and Biograph Company (AM and B), *Picture Catalogue*, 1st edn. (New York: AM and B, November 1902), p. 63. The tradition of 'living pictures' is discussed by John Hagan in 'Erotic tendencies in film, 1900–1906', in Roger Holman (comp.), *Cinema 1900–1906: An Analytical Study by the National Film Archive (London) and the International Federation of Film Archives*, vol. 1 (Brussels: Fédération Internationale des Archives du Film, 1982), pp. 231–8; and early erotic film displays are discussed by Judith Mayne in 'Uncovering the female body', in J. Fell, C. Musser, J. Mayne, and R. Koszarski, *Before Hollywood: Turn-of-the-Century American Film* (New York: Hudson Hills Press in association with the American Federation of Arts, 1987), pp. 63–7.

3 For a feminist debate on Méliès's fascination with the female form, see Lucy Fischer, 'The Lady vanishes: women, magic, and the movies', in John L. Fell (ed.), *Film Before Griffith* (Berkeley, CA: University of California Press, 1983), pp. 339–54; and Linda Williams, 'Film body: an implantation of perversions', *Cine-tracts*, vol. 3, no. 4 (1981), pp. 19–35.

4 In the films I have been able to view, black women are occasionally represented but in a racist way that assumes they are an inappropriate object of white male desire; as, for example, in *A Kiss in the Dark* (AM and B, 1904).

shop below attempt to get a better look. In the *Gay Shoe Clerk* (Edison, 1903), a female chaperone and customer enter a shoe shop. In an insert close-up of the female customer's foot and lower leg, the male clerk ties the laces of the woman's new shoe in an agitated manner as her skirt is raised to show a white petticoat and stockinged leg. Finally, in *A Windy Day on the Roof* (AM and B, 1904), a woman is hanging laundry on the roof of her tenement building while a man is painting the side of the building below. The wind blows the woman's clothing, which enables the painter to look up her skirt.[1]

In this catalogue of what appears to be a case of the Freudian fetish, a male fascination with women's ankles and raised skirts is less surprising than the situations in which these scenes of exposure occur. Walking on a city street, going shopping, and hanging laundry are everyday activities, and in these films women perform the various tasks of daily life. The everyday, however, becomes the narrative context for turning women characters into spectacles.

That women should be constructed as sexual spectacles, even in very early cinema, is not in itself surprising. A market in pornography existed during the Victorian era, and pornographic films, sometimes taking the form of tableaux vivants (or 'living pictures' with 'strong poses' as they are described in early film catalogues), drew on a tradition of nineteenth-century entertainments. Risqué spectacles, moreover, are an important part of the thematic repertoire of early cinema.[2]

Both pornographic and erotic films from this period justify the display of women by relying on the pretext of a theatrical performance or out of the ordinary situation. In *The Pouting Model* (AM and B, 1902), two female pages dressed in leotards open the curtains of a side show to reveal a tableau of a naked woman who is being painted by a clothed male artist, and in *Trapeze Disrobing Act* (Edison, 1901), a female acrobatic performer partially disrobes while swinging on a trapeze in a vaudeville theatre as male onlookers, country rubes, watch from a balcony. Méliès, whose films often play on the appearance and disappearance of characters, uses the situation of a magician's act to show a woman's clothing being removed in *Les Apparitions Fugitives* (Méliès, 1904).[3]

In contrast to these theatrical situations, in the films whose descriptions open this essay it is the public visibility of the female characters *per se*—sometimes enhanced by an accidental incident—that provides the sketchy narrative justification for display. In this paper I analyse such films from the USA before 1907 in which women— frequently white, working-class women[4]—are sexualized in scenarios of everyday life. Certainly this representation could be assessed in terms of its continuity with a long line of objectified images of women, and the fetishism of the female body in some of the films could be explained in terms of the compensatory mechanisms of the male psyche regarding castration. The approach I take in this paper, however, is more precisely historical and is motivated by the following question: how was this everyday visibility of women possible?

The elaboration of a reply—as film analysis and film history—involves both historicizing theoretical arguments about space in film, especially the issue of narrative space, and delineating a discursive field within which the films discussed would have made sense. In an attempt to avoid an analysis that looks at 'what the text says *truly* beneath what it *really* says' in favour of one that assesses 'the statement in the exact specificity of its occurrence', to quote Michel Foucault,[5] films are placed alongside historical discussions of two key issues, prostitution and sexual harassment. One (although, of course, not the only) way to analyse the intelligibility of these films—the social sense they make—is to discuss them in relation to other historical sites in which the visibility of women as sexual in the context of the everyday was being produced.

Recent film scholarship stresses that early or 'primitive' cinema (up to 1907) is a particular regime of representation and cinema practice and not a rudimentary precursor of a later classical Hollywood style (from 1917). This work is characterized by a precise historical attention to the early period, and films are analysed for their distinct visual strategies, formal organization, and type of spectatorial involvement, as well as for their specific exhibition contexts.[6] For Tom Gunning early cinema is an exhibitionist cinema organized around 'presenting a series of views', and it 'displays its visibility' in a way that directly solicits the attention of spectators.[7] Gunning historicizes these formal qualities by linking them to the investment in shocks and thrills in other contemporary popular entertainments such as magic theatre and amusement parks. These characteristics contrast with classical Hollywood cinema's concern for narrative coherence and its use of strategies that invite a more absorbed attention from the spectator. Indeed, Gunning and André Gaudreault highlight the difference of the early period by referring to it as the 'cinema of attractions'.[8]

Given the particular meanings that adhere to women's bodies in social life as well as representation, the attraction of women within the cinema of attractions will have political implications over and above those of a general—though certainly historical—conception of exhibitionism. Judith Mayne distinguishes between various kinds of display arguing that while the alterity of early cinema Gunning describes is apparent in some films, in others there is a traditional (classical) orchestration of the woman's body as object of the look of a male subject, a gendered duality in which the woman is 'capable of possessing a look only when that look solicits the attention of a male viewer'.[9]

The point to stress is that sexual difference is inscribed in film representation early on and that women become a certain kind of attraction in the cinema of attractions. This can be illustrated by three films that take exercising as their 'topic', *Getting Strong* (AM and B, 1904), *Physical Culture Lesson* (AM and B, 1906), and *Al Treloar in Muscle Exercises* (AM and B, 1905), as well as *What Happened on Twenty-Third Street, New York City* (all of which are single-shot narratives).[10] These films are the most explicit inheritors of what Linda

5 Michel Foucault, 'The discourse of history', in Sylvère Lotringer (ed.), *Foucault Live: (Interviews, 1966–1984)*, trans. John Johnston (New York: Semiotext(e), 1989), p. 21; and Michel Foucault, *The Archaeology of Knowledge and the Discourse on Language*, trans. A. M. Sheridan Smith (New York: Pantheon Books, 1972), p. 28.

6 There is a large body of work on early cinema, some of which is cited throughout this paper. For an extensive overview, see Charles Musser, *The Emergence of Cinema: The American Screen to 1907* (New York: Charles Scribner's Sons, 1990).

7 Tom Gunning, 'The cinema of attraction(s): early film, its spectator and the avant-garde', *Wide Angle*, vol. 8, nos. 3–4 (1986), p. 64. Also see Tom Gunning, 'An aesthetic of astonishment: early film and the (in)credulous spectator', *Art and Text*, no. 34 (1989), pp. 31–45.

8 The term 'cinema of attractions' was introduced by Gunning and André Gaudreault in a paper, 'Cinéma des premiers temps: un défi à l'histoire du cinéma?' given at Cerisy in 1985. In 'The cinema of attraction(s)', Gunning uses the term to describe films until 1906–7, dates that are revised to 1903–4 in his later article, 'An aesthetic of astonishment'.

9 Judith Mayne, *The Woman at the Keyhole: Feminism and Women's Cinema* (Bloomington, IN: Indiana University Press, 1990), p. 166.

10 For a discussion of the single-shot narrative, a dominant genre until 1903, see Tom Gunning, 'Non-continuity, continuity, discontinuity: a theory of genres in early films', in Thomas Elsaesser with Adam Barker (eds.), *Early Cinema: Space, Frame, Narrative*, pp. 86–94.

Williams identifies as the protocinematic in Eadweard Muybridge's studies of motion in the 1870s and 1880s in which the 'supposedly *scientific* study' of human movement is organized in terms of sexual difference. Williams argues that in these photographic studies, women are 'already fictionalized' and their bodies, through a particular use of *mise-en-scène*, are invested with a 'diegetic surplus of meaning'.[11]

11 Linda Williams, 'Film body: an implantation of perversions', pp. 33, 26, 24.

Getting Strong

In *Getting Strong*, two women in nightclothes enter a bedroom to find a third woman seated at a dressing table combing her hair. The two women instruct the third in the art of exercising, and they help her remove her dress and corset so that she, too, can exercise without the constraint of her street clothes. In *Physical Culture Lesson*, a man demonstrates exercises to a woman in a bedroom. Both characters remain clothed, although the woman does reveal her stockinged legs. Between exercises she goes to a dressing table to powder her nose. Physical proximity produces the necessary incentive for transforming the situation from one of instruction to one of romance, and the film ends with the couple kissing. If the art of exercising is given a 'surplus of meaning' by locating the activity in a suggestive location—the bedroom—in both films the display quotient adhering to the female body is increased by showing the women attending to their physical appearance. The *mise-en-scène* and use of props contribute to producing these situations as erotic.

12 Not all exercising films are risqué. There are more straightforward demonstrations in *Physical Culture Girl, No. 3* (AM and B, 1903) and *In a Boarding School Gym* (AM and B, 1904), despite the suggestive title.

13 The sight of his exposed body may well have produced an unintended pleasure for female spectators. Miriam Hansen discusses such an unexpected female response to *The Corbett-Fitzsimmons Fight* (Veriscope, 1897) in terms of the importance of the public nature of cinematic reception for an alternative public sphere. See Miriam Hansen, *Babel and Babylon: Spectatorship in American Silent Film* (Cambridge, MA: Harvard University Press, 1991).

By contrast in *Al Treloar in Muscle Exercises*, Treloar appears wearing exercising trunks and performs on an undecorated stage. While the display of his body is surprisingly revealing, it does not involve undressing as it does for the woman in *Getting Strong*, nor exposing a concealed part of the body as in *Physical Culture Lesson*.[12] A didactic quality of Treloar's performance is reinforced by the use of a stand with changing display cards (associated with vaudeville) indicating the type of exercise Treloar is demonstrating—and he periodically glances at these cards to ensure proper coordination with his movements. The authority of Treloar's social status as a physical culturist is reinforced by the *mise-en-scène*, which makes his display a demonstration of his skill.[13]

Getting Strong

What Happened on Twenty-Third Street, New York City most explicitly raises the issue of the sexual display of a female character in the context of everyday life. The comic gag that ends in revealing a woman's legs involves rudimentary stereotyping (a stout woman in plain street clothes walks near but not over the grate) and the use of *mise-en-scène* to highlight the display (the woman in the gag wears a frilly light-coloured dress, which both makes her stand out as she comes into view and provides a strong contrast with her dark stockings). The film is structured around the incident of display, in which, as Mayne points out, the woman's body is 'set in place in a chain of motions not her own' in a narrative of display and concealment.[14] Mayne further suggests that the everyday location has the effect of naturalizing this narrativization.

14 Mayne, *The Woman at the Keyhole*, p. 163.

Getting Strong

In addition to the woman's exposed legs, however, there are displays of another kind in *What Happened on Twenty-Third Street, New York*

City. The use of location shooting on a well-known street, the general view of everyday life in the modern metropolis—a busy city street with pedestrians and traffic—and an acknowledgement of the fact of filming through characters' looks to the camera are displays associated with actuality films.[15] Miriam Hansen argues that one of the consequences of the exhibitionism in the cinema of attractions is an address that is 'predicated on diversity, on distracting the viewer with a variety of competing spectacles, which has the effect of soliciting the viewer, as a member of an anticipated social audience . . .'.[16] *What Happened on Twenty-Third Street, New York City*, in holding a number of attractions in place, is an example of the textual inscription of such a diversity.

This is further illustrated in the different implications of characters' glances in the direction of the camera. Hansen argues that one effect of the woman's look is to produce a 'modicum of distance between the performer and her objectified image . . .'.[17] The woman's look is clearly tied to her sexual display, and for Hansen and Mayne this involves different implications. The looks of other characters cannot be solely understood in these terms. The glances of two men who walk in diagonally crossed paths after the display has occurred as well as that of a boy who enters from the foreground at the end of the film can be read as a more general comment on filming *per se* in keeping with the implications of such looks to the camera in actualities.

A relationship between the attractions of sexual display and actuality filming is also established in the advertising for the film. *What Happened on Twenty-Third Street, New York City* is included in the 'humorous' category in a 1902 film catalogue, *Edison Films*. It is described in a way that capitalizes on its association with an actuality film, which is taken to further enhance the display of the woman:

> In front of one of the large newspaper offices on that thoroughfare is a hot air shaft through which immense volumes of air is forced by means of a blower. Ladies in crossing these shafts often have their clothes slightly disarranged (it may be said much to their discomforture). As our picture was being made a young man escorting a young lady, to whom he was talking very earnestly, comes into view and walks slowly along until they stand directly over the air shaft. The young lady's skirts are suddenly raised to, you might say an almost unreasonable height, greatly to her horror and much to the amusement of the newsboys, bootblacks and passersby.[18]

The location is identified as a real one where ladies have been subjected to the vagaries of wind currents. There is a stress on the accidental, if fortuitous, situation in which the cameraman was able to catch this commonplace occurrence with the implication that the event was not staged (against what appears to be the textual evidence for such a claim). In a masculine nod to the male reader/exhibitor contained in the parenthetical remarks ('it may be said . . .' and 'you might say . . .'), there is also a speculation on the extent of exposure ('an almost unreasonable height'). Diversity in this case reinforces the assumption

15 These elements, for example, are present in the actuality film, *At the Foot of the Flatiron* (AM and B, 1903), which also makes use of the wind, but not for the purpose of sexual display.

16 Hansen, *Babel and Babylon*, p. 34.

17 Hansen, *Babel and Babylon*, p. 39.

Physical Culture Lesson

Physical Culture Lesson

Al Treloar in Muscle Exercises

18 *Edison Films*, no. 135 (September 1902), p. 86 in Charles Musser, Thomas E. Jeffrey, and Reese V. Jenkins, *Motion Picture Catalogs by American Producers and Distributors, 1894–1908: A Microfilm Edition* (Frederick, MD: University Publications of America, 1985).

Al Treloar in Muscle Exercises

of an appeal to a masculine audience. The display of the woman occurs in the everyday just as it might do in real life, foregrounding the sexual nature of women's public presence.

From the hindsight of the Marilyn Monroe sequence in *Seven Year Itch* (Wilder, 1955) that replays the scenario of vent, air, and exposure, the situation of the comic gag in *What Happened on Twenty-Third Street, New York City* might have the familiarity of the return of the repressed to a contemporary spectator. Such a whiggish response, however, loses a sense of the fabrication of the situation of display in the film. Indeed all manner of everyday situation is exploited in films of the period to the end of exposing a woman's body or some illicit sexual situation or both.

Workplace locations are used, especially ones requiring physical proximity between men and women, for example, between a female manicurist and a male client in the film, *In a Manicure Parlor* (AM and B, 1902) and between a female secretary and her male boss in *The Broker's Athletic Typewriter* (AM and B, 1905). Other work situations involve the display of female bodies, such as a corset shop in *The Way to Sell Corsets* (AM and B, 1904) and in *A Busy Day for the Corset Model* (AM and B, 1904);[19] a photographer's studio in *One Way of Taking a Girl's Picture* (AM and B, 1904), and *Animated Picture Studio* (AM and B, 1903), in which a dancing woman is filmed for a moving picture; and a department store in *Four Beautiful Pairs* (AM and B, 1904).

Exercising is not the only activity, moreover, to be mined for its risqué potential. Women are shown getting undressed in front of windows as men pass outside in *As Seen on the Curtain* (AM and B, 1904) and *Pull Down the Curtains, Susie* (AM and B, 1904); being fitted for a dress by seamstresses in *Her New Party Gown* (AM and B, 1903);[20] walking on the street in *What Demoralized the Barber Shop* and *Love in the Suburbs* (AM and B, 1903); shopping for shoes in the *Gay Shoe Clerk* or for an adjustable reclining chair in *The Adjustable Bed* (AM and B, 1905); and doing housework in *A Windy Day on the Roof*.

I am not arguing that the films constitute a 'genre', such as keyhole films, or that they can be grouped around a particular formal strategy, such as characters' looks to the camera. Most of the films are single-shot narrative comedies with physical gags and punitive endings in which prurient male voyeurs are chastised. Others are erotic displays that rely more on situation and *mise-en-scène*. Some incorporate erotic display with cinematic tricks such as 'stop motion substitution'.[21] While the flimsy justification for display, moreover, could be viewed as simply quaint and comic (or as a sign of desperation from a patriarchal unconscious), my focus in this paper is on the way the inappropriateness of these scenarios of exposure is articulated in spatial terms.

By making the space of the everyday the place of display of women's bodies or some unexpected sexual intimacy, the films produce everyday space as something other, something else besides a location for the practice of everyday life. In *What Happened on Twenty-Third Street, New York City*, this is heightened by the fact that display occurs on a city

19 The description of this film in Niver, *Early Motion Pictures*, p. 43 somewhat exaggerates the extent of undressing by the models.

20 The title of this film in the AM and B production records is *Having Her Gown Fitted*. See Niver, *Early Motion Pictures*, p. 135.

21 For a discussion of punitive endings, see Nöel Burch, *Life to Those Shadows*, trans. and ed. Ben Brewster (Berkeley, CA: University of California Press, 1990). Gunning discusses stop motion substitution and the substitution splice in Méliès's films in Tom Gunning ' "Primitive" cinema—a frame-up? or the trick's on us', *Cinema Journal*, vol. 28, no. 2 (1989), pp. 3–12.

street. In all these films, however, the everyday becomes a particular kind of space.

The formulation that space takes place in film is used by Stephen Heath to theorize the implications of narrative space in classical Hollywood cinema. For Heath narrative involves a process of centring in the orchestration of film space and in the spectator's relationship to it. Space becomes place through the continual inscription of the spectator in the diegetic world of the film, which is effected through the spectator's identification with the camera and with the looks of characters. This process is likened to perspectival vision as it developed in codes of representation in the fifteenth century, and it is understood in relation to Althusser's conception of the interpellative process of ideology.[22]

22 Stephen Heath, 'Narrative space', in *Questions of Cinema* (London: MacMillan, 1981), pp. 19–75.

While Heath's influential theorization of narrative space in classical cinema does not appear to have an immediate applicability to an analysis of early cinema, given its alternative regime of representation and cinematic address, the formulation, space takes place, aptly characterizes the construction of space in the films discussed in this paper. Heath's argument is also pertinent in its broad implication that there is a relationship between representation and subjectivity, and that spatial practices in film involve the spectator in a process that reproduces social relations in society more generally.

These political concerns regarding the analysis of space in film are refocused in this discussion of early cinema in the direction of the work of Michel Foucault. Although this paper is not dealing with the issue of spectatorship *per se*, a consequence of such a shift is the assumption of a different notion of the subject from that generally used in contemporary film theory. Foucault, who is less interested in subjectivity understood as a process involving an underlying mechanism, whether ideology or desire, focuses on institutional practices and discourses, which are 'productive' or constitutive of the terms according to which it is possible for individuals to be subjects in particular historical periods. If this conception of the subject loses a sense of the complexity of psychic processes (and the unconscious investments of spectators in the imaginary of cinema), it gains in an understanding of the historicity of the formations within which individuals become subjects.[23]

23 Foucault in *The Archaelogy of Knowledge and Discourse on Language* is critical of relying on a notion of 'psychological subjectivity' (p. 55) in historiography as well as of analysing phenomena in a meta-explanatory manner.

Space takes place in the films in this study in the sense that the location of everyday activities (space) becomes a locus of display (place). While this does not involve a textual inscription of the spectator's look through strategies of continuity editing, there is an invitation, even in single-shot films, for spectators to look in a certain way. In *What Demoralized the Barber Shop* and *A Windy Day on the Roof*, for example, male characters who are so concerned with looking up women's skirts are giving an indication of how the women's actions are to be understood.[24] If these situations orient looking, they also represent space in terms of implicit rules of operating and social relations.

24 Charles Musser discusses an 1897 Edison version of *What Demoralized the Barber Shop*, which appears to be quite similar to the later version, in Charles Musser, *Before the Nickelodeon: Edwin S. Porter and the Edison Manufacturing Company* (Berkeley, CA: University of California Press, 1991), pp. 113–14.

In Heath's argument space becomes meaningful as place when certain relations of looking are enacted. In his focus on the implications of *narrative* for classical film space, Heath also prioritizes a particular view of *space*, one in which vision is central. In order to further historicize the notion that space takes place in the films in this study, it will be useful, however, to displace this priority given to vision. Michel de Certeau in *The Practice of Everyday Life* develops an analysis of space that also uses the distinction between space and place.[25] If in Heath's formulation, space (in classical cinema) is meaningful in as much as it *becomes* place in the movement of narrative ('narrative clarity . . . hangs on the negation of space for place . . .'),[26] in de Certeau's analysis space *and* place are distinct regimes of location. In other words de Certeau delineates a space different from that of perspectival vision:

> Escaping the imaginary totalizations produced by the eye, the everyday has a certain strangeness . . . whose surface if only its upper limit, outlining itself against the visible. Within this ensemble, I shall try to locate the practices that are foreign to the 'geometrical' or 'geographical' space of visual, panoptic or theoretical constructions. These practices of space refer to a specific form of *operations* ('ways of operating'), to 'another spatiality' . . . .[27]

In de Certeau's schema space, on the one hand, is a 'practised place' capable of accommodating various uses and defined in relation to 'the operations that orient it, situate it, [and] temporalize it . . .'[28] These operations actualize a location by concretely bringing it into existence. Space is also associated with tactics, which insinuate themselves into authorized constructions of place and can undermine them. Place, on the other hand, involves a sense of the stable structuring of a location through a conception of 'proper' rules and a univocal ordering of elements. Place is bound up with perspective and a panoptic vision. It is also linked to voyeurism. De Certeau describes someone standing on the top of the World Trade Centre, a person whose body is 'no longer clasped by the streets':

> His elevation transfigures him into a voyeur. It puts him at a distance. . . . The exaltation of a scopic and gnostic drive: the fiction of knowledge is related to this lust to be a viewpoint and nothing more.
> Must one finally fall back into the dark space where crowds move back and forth . . . ?[29]

De Certeau invokes what would seem to be a long-standing masculine anxiety in which the threat of the city ('the dark space') is identified with the figure of woman, an association that is problematized by Patrice Petro in her work on Weimar cinema.[30] In this description de Certeau also identifies place with a masculine vision (the distanced view of the voyeur), linking perspective to a sexually implicated looking (the 'lust to be a viewpoint and nothing more').

In some discussions of de Certeau's work there is a problematic tendency to construct a binary opposition between place and space in which place is associated with a deterministic and monolithic conception of use and space is understood to mean—somewhat

25 Michel de Certeau, *The Practice of Everyday Life*, trans. Steven F. Rendall (Berkeley, CA: University of California Press, 1984). This paper borrows part of its title from de Certeau's book.

26 Heath, *Questions of Cinema*, p. 39.

27 De Certeau, *The Practice of Everyday Life*, p. 93.

28 Ibid., p. 117.

29 Ibid., p. 92.

30 De Certeau's formulation is reminiscent of ones used by Charles Baudelaire and Walter Benjamin to describe the threat of the city to the male *flâneur*. For a critical analysis, see Patrice Petro, *Joyless Streets: Women and Melodramatic Representation in Weimar Germany* (Princeton, NJ: Princeton University Press, 1989).

31 See John Fiske, 'Popular forces and the culture of everyday life', *Southern Review*, vol. 21, no. 3 (1988), pp. 288–306. Fiske seems to imply a necessarily resistant quality to uses of space.

32 Griselda Pollock, *Vision and Difference: Femininity, Feminism and Histories of Art* (London: Routledge, 1989), p. 65.

33 For Burch in *Life to Those Shadows*, a 'visual flatness' in early cinema includes horizontal placement of figures in the shot and a 'lateralizing' effect on actor's movements. Before the woman discovers the painter in *A Windy Day*, this kind of articulation of space has the effect of producing two areas of action.

axiomatically—differentiated uses and resistance.[31] This is not the import of my argument. I am interested in reading the films against the background of both Heath's and de Certeau's distinctions in order to foreground the competing definitions of space in the films.

My interest, more precisely, is in analysing these spaces in terms of a sexual division of activity. This is also a concern of Griselda Pollock, who, in her work on impressionist painters, contrasts 'pictorial space' in which 'objects are placed in a rational and abstract relationship' (which resonates with the perspectival view of de Certeau's 'place' and Heath's narrative space as place) with 'experiential space', discussed in the work of women artists.[32] Like de Certeau, Pollock points to a space other than that constituted in relation to vision, but she does so in a way that foregrounds the difference gender makes. The distinction I propose for the analysis of films in this study is one between a masculine place, defined in terms of voyeurism, and a feminine space, defined in relation to the performance of everyday activities, a space whose modus operandi is not primarily visual.

That space in early cinema representation admits of different kinds of analysis is illustrated in *A Windy Day on the Roof*. The film is a single-shot narrative organized around a gag. It shows two simultaneous activities, a painter looking up a woman's skirt while painting the side of the building and a woman hanging laundry on a clothes-line on the roof. In the use of a painted backdrop of a cityscape and the choice of the clothes on the line (knickers and a camisole), the film further sexualizes the woman in the city. A comic tension, however, is produced as the spectator's attention is divided between the two activities. While the pressure of expectation regarding the imminent gag—what will the woman do when she discovers the painter looking?—gives a priority to the painter's activity, the fact that there are no cuts, inserts, or shifts of camera position to focus the spectator's attention, as one might expect in a classical Hollywood film, gives some autonomy to the woman's activity; it is not simply subsumed within the terms of the joke.[33]

The film ends when the woman discovers the untoward glance of the painter and throws a bucket of water on his head, whereupon the painter exits from the bottom of the frame. This gag of discovery and retribution can be analysed in various ways: as a straightforward joke on the inappropriate prurience of the male voyeur; as a symbolic castration; and as a sophisticated formal joke that foregrounds the presence of the frame. It is also about a conflict over the legitimate use of space (looking or domestic labour) and who will have the authority to define this use (the painter or the housewife).

The gag, in other words, plays out the conflict over characters' different relationships to space. On the one hand, there is an association between the man and vision in which the woman is a spectacle for the male voyeur's look. Space becomes a meaningful location as it is articulated in relation to characters' lines of sight (will the woman see the painter looking up her skirt?). On the other hand, there is an association between the woman and the everyday, where space is meaningful in relation to the particular activity enacted within it. The painter, like de Certeau's voyeuristic observer looking in on someone else's world, establishes the pre-eminence of sight in defining space, and his status as a man authorizes him to do so. The woman asserts her authority over space through her actions.

A Windy Day on the Roof illustrates a further sense in which space can be understood to take place. In the painter's look at the woman, the practice of everyday life (space) is subordinated to relations of looking (place). This is interesting in relation to de Certeau's conception of strategy, a *modus operandi* of place in which 'a subject of will and power . . . can be isolated from an "environment" '.[34] The effect of the attempt to sexualize the woman in *A Windy Day on the Roof* involves an isolation of the character from her environment: the woman is abstracted from the space of ordinary activities. In this abstraction—which is the inappropriateness of the scenario—de Certeau's 'other spatiality' (the space of everyday operations) is made invisible. The film ends with the woman alone in the shot and an assertion of the visibility of this other space—the space of everyday life.

During the late nineteenth and early twentieth centuries, the public visibility of women, especially their increased presence in public spaces—workplaces, lodging and boarding houses, department stores, city streets, and urban amusements—received a great deal of contemporary commentary. There was a widespread concern, which was expressed in studies of middle-class reformers and in the popular press, over the dangers facing the single 'girl' alone, 'on the town' and 'adrift' in the city. This person's sexual behaviour was an underlying anxiety.

Consternation, however, is not the only response to this situation. Kathy Peiss details the emergence of a subculture of working women around the 'cheap amusements' of commercialized leisure from 1880 to 1920 in New York City. Within a working-class understanding of social codes and relationships, aspects of the increased visibility of women and especially the notion of 'putting on style', which included a concern for fashionable clothing and an assertive display in public places, was a strategy of self-definition.[35]

With the proviso that implications of practices cannot be assumed from their discursive constructions, I analyse one aspect of the production of the visibility of women in reformers' reports on prostitution—the 'Social Evil'—during the early twentieth century. These reports produce a version of 'place' in the sense of an authorized conception of location in which women become the object of a scrutinizing gaze, and they contribute—as do the films in this study—to a historical field of discourses regarding working women's visibility in public places. If in *A Windy Day on the Roof* the housewife is sexualized irrespective of the fact that she is in the space of everyday life, in these vice reports it is the sexual visibility of women in the everyday that is cause for scandal.

A Windy Day on the Roof

34 De Certeau, *The Practice of Everyday Life* (general introduction), p. xix.

A Windy Day on the Roof

35 Kathy Peiss, *Cheap Amusements: Working Women and Leisure in Turn-of-the-Century New York* (Philadelphia, PA: Temple University Press, 1986), especially pp. 56–87. Peiss further discusses the significance of cinema-going within the culture of working-class women as well as the positive aspects of films representing everyday heterosexual encounters in the workplace and on the street. On the implications of women's increased public presence for cinema, also see Hansen, *Babel and Babylon*; Ben Singer, 'Female power in the serial-queen melodrama: the etiology of an anomaly', *Camera Obscura*, no. 22 (1990), pp. 91–129; and Lauren Rabinovitz, 'Temptations of pleasure: nickelodeons, amusement parks, and the sights of female sexuality', *Camera Obscura*, no. 23 (1990), pp. 71–89.

Catherine Stansell, in her study of New York in the nineteenth century, argues that prostitution, already a feature of life in the city, is viewed as a social problem between 1830 and 1860 when it becomes more visible on public streets. An account from the period, quoted by Stansell, illustrates this point: 'It [prostitution] no longer confines itself to secrecy and darkness, but boldly strikes through our most thronged and elegant thoroughfares'.[36] *Commercialized Prostitution in New York City* (1913), written nearer to the period under investigation in this paper, charts the perception of the extent of prostitution's incursion into public places:

> There is another group of miscellaneous places . . . the natural channels through which the varied life of a great city passes. These are freely used by the prostitute. Attention is called to them simply to emphasize the fact that wherever groups of people meet for innocent pleasure or for business, there the prostitute lingers to ply her trade. Such places include subway and railway stations, hotel lobbies, entrances to department stores, ferry slips, and post office buildings.[37]

It is not simply the visibility of prostitution *per se*, but a particular *kind* of visibility that is most problematic. Prostitutes 'linger' with people going about the routines of their everyday life, and they 'freely' use places in which ordinary life in the city is conducted.

The anxiety over the easy access to vice facilitated by such a situation focuses on places where prostitutes and male 'runners' and 'lookouts' solicit clients as well as the devious methods of procuring new prostitutes. This involves:

> Procurers [who] frequent entrances to factories and department stores, or walk the streets at night striking up acquaintance with girls who are alone and looking for adventure. They select a girl waiting on a table in a restaurant, or at the cashier's desk, and gradually make her acquaintance. They attend steamboat excursions, are found at the sea shore and amusement parks, in moving picture shows, at the public dance halls. . . .[38]

The Social Evil (1910) identifies additional places of danger, such as soda-water fountains and candy stores, employment agencies, penny-in-the-slot arcades, and delicatessen stores.[39]

While reformers detail the existence of the business of prostitution in the spaces of everyday life, however, they also produce the visibility of prostitution, especially for the middle classes. Many reports include the findings of field investigators, which are frequently presented as case studies. One investigative procedure is described as follows:

> A census was taken in 27 different tenements where immoral conditions were found to exist during the month of February, 1912. . . . In the different apartments 56 women were found who, on the basis of dress, conversation, and general bearing, were classed as 'suspicious'. . . . At times [the male investigator noted] children were playing in front of doors behind which prostitutes plied their trade.[40]

36 Christine Stansell, *City of Women: Sex and Class in New York 1789–1860* (New York: Alfred A. Knopf, 1986), p. 173. Stansell quotes William W. Sanger's, *The History of Prostitution: Its Extent, Causes and Effects Throughout the World* (New York: The Medical Publishing Co., 1921), a major nineteenth-century report on the subject.

37 George J. Kneeland, *Commercialized Prostitution in New York City* (New York: The Century Co., 1913), p. 65.

38 Ibid., p. 86.

39 Committee of Fourteen, *The Social Evil in New York City: A Study of Law Enforcement by the Research Committee of the Committee of Fourteen* (New York: Andrew H. Kellogg Co., 1910), p. 65.

40 Kneeland, *Commercialized Prostitution*, pp. 26–7.

41 See, for example, Committee of
    Fourteen, *The Social Evil in New
    York City*, p. xxiv.

Part of the investigator's skill involves an ability to read codes of dress and behaviour of the women in the tenements. This paradigmatic example of a Foucauldian scenario of nineteenth-century discipline involving surveillance and individualization is inflected in relation to gender. A frequent complaint by reformers was that the invisibility of the act of sex in the prostitution exchange produced a problem for law enforcement and prosecution.[41] In the above report, the invisibility of the act (behind the closed doors in front of which children play) is displaced onto the visibility of 'suspicious' characteristics in certain women. Thus the investigator's job involves reading women's bodies for the implication of illicit sexuality.

While the presence of prostitution in everyday life is a problem *per se* in these reports, it is more precisely a problem of the indeterminacy of the boundary between spaces of the everyday and sexual spaces. This involves a slippage between respectable (ordinary) locations and immoral ones in which vice occurs and between types of women, respectable and morally loose. If Kneeland expresses some incredulity over the fact that prostitutes do ordinary things ('The prostitute herself frequents the hairdressing and manicure parlor . . .'), *The Social Evil* (1902) comments on the problem in a more straightforward manner: 'it would be a grievous error to suppose that all prostitutes, or even a very large proportion of them, are thus easily distinguished from the decent classes of society.'[42]

42 Kneeland, *Commercialized
    Prostitution*, p. 68. Committee of
    Fifteen, *The Social Evil: With
    Special Reference to Conditions
    Existing in the City of New York
    (A Report Prepared Under the
    Direction of the Committee
    of Fifteen)*(New York:
    G. P. Putnam's Sons, 1902), p. 80.
    The fluid boundary between
    respectable employment and
    prostitution for women and the
    proximity of prostitution to the
    daily life of working-class
    communities is discussed
    by Barbara Meil Hobson in
    *Uneasy Virtue: The Politics of
    Prostitution and the American
    Reform Tradition*(Chicago:
    University of Chicago Press,
    1990).

43 AM and B, *Picture Catalogue*
    (1902), p. 51.

The films in this study can be analysed in relation to these issues. While the choice of location, for example, a corset shop or a manicure parlour, carries 'advantages' already noted, the films also rehearse the issue of a lack of proper segregation between ordinary and sexual public spaces. *In a Manicure Parlor* plays out this dilemma at the level of the *mise-en-scène*. It shows two couples, a female manicurist and male client, on either side of a screen in a manicure parlour. While the couple on the right are occupied in conversation as the manicurist works on the customer's nails, the couple on the left kiss and hug. The split-screen effect in the film emphasizes the distinction between the two spaces that are represented. The man involved in the assignation reinforces its illicit nature by frequently looking around to ensure that he and the manicurist are not being detected. The 'well-behaved' pair[43] interrupt their conversation in order to hear what is going on, and at one point the manicurist chastises her customer when it seems that he is becoming susceptible to the bad influence on the other side of the screen (he is not keeping his hand in a bowl of water). This further illustrates the influence of immoral spaces on respectable ones, even if it produces the pleasure of seeing that it is illicit.

In *A Busy Day for the Corset Model*, there is a distinction between the diegetic space as it exists for the characters, which involves a respectable woman who is shopping for corsets and models at work, and that space as it is orchestrated for viewers of the film. The corset models are framed by the entryway to the room and stand on a raised platform in the centre of the shot; as they turn on the platform they hesitate to face

A Busy Day for the Corset Model

Four Beautiful Pairs

What Demoralized the Barber Shop

44 See E. J. Bellocq, *Storyville Portraits: Photographs from the New Orleans Red-Light District, Circa 1912* (New York: Museum of Modern Art, 1970), Plate 16. Shelley Stamp Lindsey discusses the representation of prostitution in film in 'Wages and sin: *Traffic in Souls* and the white slavery scare', unpublished paper delivered at the 11th Ohio University Film Conference, Athens, Ohio, November 1989.

45 Mary Gay Humphreys, 'Women bachelors in New York', *Scribner's Magazine*, vol. 20 (1896), p. 627. This is one of a series of articles by Humphreys on independent working women and bachelor girls in *Scribner's* during 1896. Thanks to Ben Singer's 'Female power in the serial-queen melodrama' for this reference.

forward in the direction of the camera. In *Four Beautiful Pairs* the ordinary space of the department store becomes a sexualized space through a visual joke involving the juxtaposition of the upper bodies of female shop assistants, who are standing behind a display counter, with the legs of mannequins wearing stockings in the display counter in front of the assistants. This gives the impression that the saleswomen are not wearing skirts. Finally, in *What Demoralized the Barber Shop*, it is unclear whether the women who are soliciting attention through their bold swaying are prostitutes on the street or women coming on to men in the barber shop. While the implication of the title (a demoralization) and the loud striped stockings (clothing that draws attention to itself) would appear to suggest that the women are prostitutes, the joke in the film is on the indeterminacy of the women's status, encouraged by the fact that their faces are not visible, as well as the men's incredulity that such a spectacle could be intruding into their public and homosocial space.[44]

Over and above the narrative heuristic involved in the choice of these locales, there is a wider social resonance to the dilemma of space enacted in the films, one in which the veneer of respectability is combined with the attraction of a prurient spectacle. In rehearsing the problem of the boundaries of space, the films point to the way the scandal of prostitution—its everyday visibility—could attach itself to women more generally. Indeed in discussions during the period, the public visibility of women could be reason enough for mistaking them as sexually available:

> The exodus of women, for one reason or another, to the cities in the last ten years parallels that of men. . . . Each year they come younger and younger. They have ameliorated the customs and diversified the streets; nor are they to be confused with any of the better-known types.[45]

In this commentary on women's increased presence on city streets from an article 'Women bachelors in New York' (1896) in *Scribner's Magazine* by Mary Gay Humphreys, single women in the city living on their own and working are differentiated from prostitutes, the 'better-known types'. The article is both a description of this new type of person, the bachelor girl, and a defence of her lifestyle. Humphreys walks a fine line between a number of possible criticisms of the single woman: she is not libertarian or feminist (that is, she is not a 'theorist'!); she is uninterested in homosocial or potentially lesbian forms of leisure that might be found in women's clubs; and, most particularly, although the bachelor girl has set up a household without the benefit of marriage, she is not promiscuous. Humphreys defends this new living arrangement:

> To be the mistress of a home, to extend hospitalities, briefly to be within the circumference of a social circle, instead of gliding with uneasy foot on the periphery, is the reasonable desire of every woman. When this is achieved [by the bachelor girl] many

46 Humphreys, 'Women bachelors in New York', p. 634.

temptations, so freely recognized that nobody disputes them, are eliminated.[46]

The worry over 'the many temptations' facing the bachelor girl is mitigated by the fact that despite her unmarried state, she has a domestic impulse, and these new households avoid marginalizing her in a place 'on the periphery'. To be sure, the defensive tone in Humphreys's article speaks to the pressure on single women not to be seen to be sexually active (the bachelor girl does not live alone because she is interested in sex). This situation was a double bind for women since they were at the same time subject to the threat of sexual innuendo and harassment on public streets and places of work.

> [The boss] sauntered up to our table, began to fling jokes at us all in a manner of insolent familiarity, and asked the names of the new faces. When he came to me he lingered a moment and uttered some joking remarks of insulting flattery, and in a moment he had grasped my bare arm and given it a rude pinch, walking hurriedly away. . . . I now found myself suddenly the cynosure of all eyes, the target of a thousand whispered comments, as I moved about the workroom. The physical agony of aching back and blistered feet was too great, though, for me to feel any mental distress over the fact—for the moment at least.[47]

47 Dorothy Richardson, The Long Day: The Story of a New York Working Girl, in William L. O'Neill (ed.), Women at Work (Chicago: Quadrangle Books, 1972), pp. 260–1. (Original publication date is 1905.)

In this fictionalized version of an incident of harassment in *The Long Day: The Story of a New York Working Girl* (1905) by Dorothy Richardson, the female narrator becomes a focus of the scrutinizing attention of her workmates, making her complicit in the sexual advance of the boss. The woman's physical reality, however, involves the 'agony of an aching back and blistered feet', the visceral residuum of her labour. The narrator's relationship to her work (in her experience of space, to use Pollock's formulation) asserts itself over her workmates' sexualizing gaze.

Discussions of sexual harassment in novels, serialized stories in magazines, and trade union journals during the period under investigation produced a network of advice for working-class and lower-middle-class women concerning how to negotiate life in the city. If the vice reports on prostitution and the films—in their orchestration of space through male voyeur's looks or prurient views for purported male spectators—rehearse a dynamic of place (in both de Certeau's and Heath's sense of place constituted in relation to vision), these discussions of sexual harassment foreground a conception of space, especially how women could negotiate being constructed as sexual within a masculine economy of place.

Of course, being put 'in place' is not the only way of understanding the social issue of prostitution or voyeurism in the films, especially as either might have been understood by women. Prostitution, as Stansell argues, cannot be reduced to the views of moral reformers, who tend to characterize prostitutes as victims or moral degenerates; it is better understood as a choice—albeit a circumscribed one—for women. Female subcultures were also an aspect of prostitution, whether in brothels or in an understanding of the codes of heterosexual dating, which for some working-class women involved casual prostitution or 'charity' in which sex was exchanged for favours rather than money.[48]

The focus on vice reports in this essay is a way of assessing one dominant construction of women as sexual in public places. In looking at the issue of sexual harassment, however, I draw on the work of feminist historians, who discuss women's experiences of prostitution, in order to underscore a notion of 'subculture'. The term is used in this context to imply ways of dealing with being located in a sexualized and 'voyeuristic' place (rather than the notion of a resistance to dominant interpellations). Various historical texts that rehearse the negotiation of power relations in contexts where women are inappropriately sexualized can be analysed to the end of reconstructing such a subculture.

In 1908 *Harper's Bazar* [*sic*], for example, invited its readers, especially the 'average girl' between 16 and 30 who has had 'the experience of coming to the city' over the past ten years to send in the story of her experience. Letters intended for the benefit of 'many thousands of girls who think of coming to the city within the next year or two' [*sic*], and who, 'adrift' are 'far more helpless and in peril than a man in the same straits' were published throughout the year.[49] While this exercise in readers' participation is concerned to impart certain moral standards, the letters both provide and give expression to a network of advice based on shared experience. One woman, after an offer of fifteen dollars a week from a doctor, describes the end of her job interview:

> As I was leaving his office, feeling that at last I was launched safely upon the road to a good living, he [the doctor] said, casually, 'I have an auto and as my wife doesn't care for that sort of thing, I shall expect you to accompany me frequently on pleasure trips'. . . . After that experience I was ill for two weeks. . . .[50]

Other writings point to the use of certain expressions coded for sexual innuendo. 'Sexual purity and the double standard' (1895) in *The Arena* notes:

> Already the introduction of the typewriter in the hands of lady operatives has started the low, familiar jesting that show the evil suspicions to which they are being subjected, as well as the temptations that surround them. In the city of Des Moines, where I live, there are many offices which employ stenographers where no self-respecting woman will long remain employed. I shall never forget the remark of a young friend of mine who has recently abandoned the profession of stenographer for that of nurse. In conversation with her about some trifling matter I made use of the expression, 'if you will be accommodating'.
> 'Oh!' said she, 'I do not want to hear you use that hateful expression.'

48 See Peiss, *Cheap Amusements*. Also see Ruth Rosen, *The Lost Sisterhood: Prostitution in America, 1900–1918* (Baltimore, MD: Johns Hopkins University Press, 1982) for a discussion of the subculture of prostitution.

49 'The girl who comes to the city: a symposium', *Harper's Bazar* [*sic*], vol. 42, no. 1 (1908), p. 54. For a historical overview, see Mary Bularzik, 'Sexual harassment at the workplace: historical notes', in James Green (ed.), *Workers' Struggles, Past and Present: A 'Radical America' Reader* (Philadelphia, PA: Temple University Press, 1983), pp. 117–35.

50 'The girl who comes to the city: a symposium', *Harper's Bazar*, vol. 43, no. 3 (1908), p. 278.

51 J. Bellangee, 'Sexual purity and the double standard', in *The Arena*, vol. 2, no. 43 (1895), pp. 372–3.

On seeking to know why she felt so, she informed me that she was almost invariably met with that remark when seeking employment, and had come to detest it.[51]

That a woman should be 'accommodating' was one way male employers expressed their sexual expectations of female employees, a phenomenon associated with increased job opportunities for women. There was also an assumption on the part of some employers that low wages for women were legitimate because they could be supplemented by women through part-time prostitution or participation in an economy of 'charity'. The comment of one employer, after being questioned about the offer of a low wage for a stenographer's job, is illustrative: 'He said he expected young women had friends who help them out'.[52]

52 'The girl who comes to the city: a symposium', *Harper's Bazar*, vol. 43, no. 3, p. 277. Low wages and vice were argued to be causally related, a situation that was deplored in reformist and trade union journals of the period. See *The World's Work* and *Life and Labor*.

Serialized stories in popular magazines and novels can also be read as 'guides' on how a woman should conduct herself in public, especially in the event of some compromising situation. In 1910, *The Ladies' Home Journal* ran a serialized story, the 'true experiences' of a 'girl's long struggle' in New York City, a melodramatic and fictionalized version of some of the incidents reported in vice investigations. In a penultimate scene, the narrator/heroine is almost subjected to 'ruin' in a hotel room by a male friend. After escaping, she hails a cab and directs the driver to take her to the railway station:

> Huddled in the hansom I suddenly remembered that my purse was in my travelling bag in the hotel. However, in a chamois-bag, which I always carried when travelling pinned inside my shirtwaist, was money enough to pay the cab-fare and buy a ticket to New York.[53]

53 The Girl Herself, 'My experience in New York: the true story of a girl's long struggle in the big city as told by the girl herself', *The Ladies Home Journal*, vol. 27, no. 7 (1910), p. 59.

In the context of this tale of potential ruin there is an obliquely stated piece of advice to women travelling alone: carry a bag with money pinned inside your clothing.

The responses to incidents of sexual harassment in these texts are varied, and include indignation, anger, and political activism. Women's friendship is also seen as a form of solace and empowerment. In *The Long Day*, quoted earlier, the heroine leaves her job on the advice of the foreman: 'It's no place for a girl that wants to do right'. She subsequently roams the streets in an almost unconscious state, but is rescued by an old friend: 'and with Minnie Plympton's strong arm about my aching body, I was jolted away somewhere into a drowsy happiness'. This meeting follows an earlier discussion of the importance of women's friendship in the factory, 'the highest type of friendship'.[54]

54 Richardson, *The Long Day*, pp. 262, 265, 198: both Richardson and Elizabeth Hasanovitz turn to trade unionismn as one solution. See Elizabeth Hasanovitz, *One of Them: Chapters From a Passionate Autobiography* (Boston, MA: Houghton Mifflin Company, 1918). In practice, women also confronted sexism in unions. See Mary Bularzik, *Sexual Harassment at the Workplace: Historical Notes* (Somerville, MA: New England Free Press, 1981).

It is useful to place a film such as *The Broker's Athletic Typewriter* alongside such texts. A key attraction of the film involves a transformation of the real boss to a dummy made to look like him, a cinematic trick (probably through stop-motion substitution) that enables the female secretary to throw the boss around the room following his unwanted sexual advance. From the point of view of a working woman's subculture in which the issue of sexual harassment was not hidden, the thematic material of such a film as well as the autonomy exhibited by the secretary (who responds positively to an earlier advance from a more suitable male worker) would have, one can speculate, included the pleasure of revenge. In *Four Beautiful Pairs* the female shop assistants form a community, commenting to each other and laughing at a naive male customer who mistakes appearance (of the mannequins' legs) for reality (the bodies of the assistants).

Thomas Elsaesser, in categorizing work on this period of cinema, describes one approach in which early cinema is understood as 'part of a "cultural" or ideological–theoretical history'. In his discussion of the importance of the specificity of regimes of space in early cinema, Elsaesser also notes that 'the impression of intelligibility of an action' in a film depends on 'whether the system that governs its representation is intelligible to the viewer'.[55] In this essay I use the notion of intelligibility in a broad sense. Certainly the scenarios of exposure in the films, especially in the comedies, are transparent in their project of displaying women's bodies. By avoiding the assumption of an inevitable (and ahistorical) voyeurism in the representation of women, the implausibility of the films can be foregrounded.

This implausibility makes more sense in the relationship between the films, vice reports, and stories about sexual harassment. These texts can be seen to form a series with consonances on certain issues—working women's presence in public places, the everyday and sexuality, and the problem of permeable boundaries between ordinary and sexual spaces. Analysing such a series, a discursive field, is a way of assessing the terms according to which phenomena are visible and knowable in any historical period. One could also analyse films that explicitly thematize prostitution and sexual harassment, situating film in its historical context. The concern of this paper is, instead, to make explicit some of the historical terms according to which the films are comprehensible. How a film is understood, moreover, will depend on how its representation of space resonates with other experiences of space by viewers, who are differentiated in various ways.

55 Elsaesser and Barker, *Early Cinema*, pp. 5, 12.

Getting Strong

Towards the end of *Getting Strong*, the film in which three women exercise in a bedroom, one woman jokingly hits another and gestures with her arm as if to show her strength; the group begins to laugh; and the film closes when all three look directly at the camera. The effect, much as Hansen argues in relation to *What Happened on Twenty-Third Street, New York City*, is to produce a distance between the characters and their sexual display. In the case of *Getting Strong*, this distance involves a humorous comment on the idea of 'getting strong' and the characters' pleasure in each other's company. It also foregrounds the performative space occupied by the actresses. As the spectacle of objectification breaks down, the female characters' actions produce another scenario of the everyday, one that digresses from the film's intent to expose women's bodies. Analysing these other spaces—in which women characters perform everyday activities and actresses perform their roles—is another way of understanding the attraction of women in the cinema of attractions.

5 The Proletarian Woman's Film of the 1930s: Contending with Censorship and Entertainment

MARY BETH HARALOVICH

In the 1930s, many Hollywood films positioned women's narrative choices within the fragile contours of a patriarchal capitalism in which the morality of womanhood struggled with economic pressures. Products of the studio system, with stars and production values, these films also called upon a popular recognition of the material conditions which inform women's gendered and class identities. They circulated meanings about: the social and economic restrictions of 'shop girl' wages (*Our Blushing Brides* (MGM, 1930); *Employees' Entrance* (Warner Bros, 1933)); the terms under which love between the classes is possible (Dorothy Arzner's *Working Girls* (Paramount, 1930); *A Free Soul* (MGM, 1931)); the economic conditions which foster prostitution (*Faithless* (MGM, 1933); *Marked Woman* (Warner Bros, 1937)); sexual harassment in the workplace (*Our Blushing Brides; Employees' Entrance; Big Business Girl* (MGM, 1931)); the social and economic oppression of working-class women (*Baby Face* (Warner Bros, 1933); *Black Fury* (Warner Bros, 1935)); and, strangely enough, the possibilities of social change through Marxist theory (*Red Salute* (Reliance, 1935)).

A Hollywood proletarian woman's film raises a number of questions about the possibilities for oppositional meanings in the entertainment film. I shall address some of these issues and propose a methodology which derives from the contradictory elements of the genre. Through analysis of two films which cross the 1930s, I shall explore how these films work through contemporary economic conditions in different ways. While *Our Blushing Brides* invites women to recognize and identify with the choices available to women in the film, *Marked Woman* identifies the women in the film as other, addressing the female audience in a position of superior knowledge. The degree to which film censorship is responsible for this shift in the address to women by the proletarian woman's film of the 1930s constitutes a central issue.

In its concern with the economic parameters of woman's social existence, the proletarian woman's film de-centres what Maria LaPlace has concisely summarized as the distinguishing features of the 'woman's film'. While the proletarian woman's film can address 'the traditional realms of women's experience: the familial, the domestic, the romantic', it is also likely to focus on how the economic realities of woman's daily existence modify her presence within these traditional places. In the 'arenas [of] love, emotion and relationships' the proletarian woman learns that economic power informs both romantic and sexual relationships. And, as LaPlace argues, 'A central issue . . . in any investigation of the woman's film is the problematic of female subjectivity, agency and desire in Hollywood cinema'. In the proletarian woman's film, this problematic is firmly tied to the social relations of power which derive from the intersection of gender and economics.[1]

Not all films about working women adopt a proletarian consciousness. For example, a film like *Night Nurse* (Warner Bros, 1931) is not a proletarian woman's film. While the female protagonist of *Night Nurse* is a working woman, the problems she confronts are not directly related to the economic conditions of her existence. Further, the film's exploitation of the sexuality of its women characters and stars is poorly motivated by character traits or narrative structure. *Night Nurse* contains many scenes of flagrant maternal drunkenness, violence to women, and display of female sexuality. But it does not provide space for the intersection of woman's gendered identity and economic identities. A film like *Night Nurse* functions in this study as a baseline against which the proletarian woman's film may be identified.

As Charles Eckert's consideration of *Marked Woman* as a Hollywood proletarian film has shown, any representation of the 'real relations' of social life can only emerge in this context through the conventions of Hollywood cinematic practice.[2] While the proletarian woman's film uses signifiers of 'working class-ness' (clothing, apartments, speech, gestures) to differentiate class identities and contextualize character traits, the genre also participates in what Eckert has called 'the almost incestuous hegemony that characterized Hollywood's relations with the vast reaches of the American economy by the mid-1930s', namely, the merchandising of lifestyle.[3] In pressbooks for the proletarian woman's film, exhibitors are urged to address women audiences within similar contradictions. Advertising copy seeks to draw women to the cinema by asking them to recognize the contemporary economic issues in films about women's lives, while merchandising tie-ins and publicity stories hawk the visual pleasure of stars and consumer products. And film industry censors raised concerns about linking the American economy to problems with woman's self-identity.

1 Maria LaPlace, 'Producing and consuming the woman's film: discursive struggle in *Now, Voyager*', in Christine Gledhill (ed.), *Home is Where the Heart Is* (London: British Film Institute, 1987), p. 139.

2 Charles Eckert, 'The anatomy of a proletarian film: Warner's *Marked Woman*', in Bill Nichols (ed.), *Movies and Methods, Vol. II* (Berkeley, CA: University of California Press, 1985), pp. 407–25.

3 Charles Eckert, 'The Carole Lombard in Macy's window', *Quarterly Review of Film Studies*, vol. 3, no. 1 (1978), p. 4.

Tony Bennett describes popular culture as a 'terrain on which dominant, subordinate and oppositional cultural values and ideologies meet and intermingle'. He goes on to argue that 'the very organisation of cultural forms' is shaped by 'these opposing tendencies [and their] contradictory orientations'. In Bennett's view, popular culture easily accommodates contradiction and diversity by providing space for the combination and articulation of multiple social identities. 'Oppositional cultural values create a space within and against [dominant culture] in which contradictory values can echo, reverberate and be heard.'[4]

These assumptions about opposing tendencies and diversity suggest a methodology which can open up analysis of the text/context relationship to explore the possibilities for expression of a proletarian consciousness in Hollywood commercial entertainment. Multiple meanings can collide and coexist within the same text because popular forms are produced by the intersection of oppositional forces. While Bennett does not detail these forces, Annette Kuhn, in a recent study of censorship and power, argues for historical analysis which proceeds from a similar assumption. For Kuhn, power relations (both in the text and in its contexts) are a fluid 'process of negotiation between contending powers, apparatuses and discourses'. Kuhn shows how this assumption effectively de-centres the power of censorship and of power itself, insisting that 'the forces involved in film censorship at any conjuncture are [not] in any way fixed or decisive'.[5]

Four contending forces which combine to produce the proletarian woman's film emerge from these methodological assumptions about the fluid combination of historical forces and the need to explore the opposing tendencies and the specific apparatuses which characterize the Hollywood cinematic institution: first, the address to women through the exploitation of events and/or situations derived from the contemporary social economy of the Depression; secondly, the narrative and stylistic needs of the film text and the work of the text in organizing meanings; thirdly, the conditions of studio production, especially the 'entertainment value' of star discourses and the related display of production values, merchandising, and consumerism; and fourthly, censorship, through the development of the Production Code during the 1930s. As these four areas work together to produce the proletarian woman's film, their intersection contributes to the production of contradictions and to the potential for resistances to patriarchal ideologies within popular entertainment.

Because this study concentrates on the 1930s, it might be expected that the formalization of the Production Code in 1934 would result in the elimination or the suppression of films which take up social relations of economics and gender. While the degree to which Production Code censorship might have found the proletarian woman's film to be a problem is an important issue, it is just as important to identify the aspects of Hollywood cinematic practice which might subvert censorship concerns. The exploitation of contemporary problems related to women's sexuality calls the ideologies of patriarchal capitalism into

4 Tony Bennett, 'The politics of the "popular" and popular culture', in Tony Bennett, Colin Mercer, and Janet Woollacott (eds.), *Popular Culture and Social Relations* (London: Open University Press, 1986), p. 19.

5 Annette Kuhn, *Cinema, Censorship and Sexuality, 1909–1925* (London: Routledge, 1988), pp. 131 and 134.

question. When the four contending forces are analysed as they operate through specific films, tensions between 'censorship' and 'entertainment values' emerge with some consistency as they work together to allow the production of oppositional values in the Hollywood film.

Recent studies of the possibilities for social consciousness within the entertainment film have shown dissatisfaction with the attempts of popular entertainment to circulate oppositional or contradictory meanings, largely because it is assumed that classical Hollywood narrative is a decisive factor in meaning production. John Hill and Nick Roddick have each written about popular films which seem to recognize the material existence of class relations; and both conclude that classical Hollywood narration subverts any progressive meanings that these films may contain. Roddick's survey of Warner Bros social consciousness films of the 1930s and Hill's analysis of British realist working-class films of the 1950s and 1960s use widely different methodologies to assess the politics of these popular films; yet both writers insist that the ideologies inherent in character, causality, and the happy ending serve to personalize social conflict and to offer solutions which deny the complexity of social life.[6] The very fact of narration, it is suggested, requires the subversion of any socially conscious subject matter. This assumption about the ideological power of classical Hollywood cinema also suggests that narrative structure can unify the heterogeneous subjectivities of audiences and that Hollywood films in the final instance reproduce a dominant ideology.

This was an assumption shared by film censorship, as it operated through the Production Code Administration. Lea Jacobs and Richard Maltby have each analysed a particularly contradictory period in film history, 1930 to 1934, when the Production Code was being negotiated and the ideological value of narrative was in process of being discussed and institutionalized. Both Jacobs and Maltby argue convincingly that the development of the Production Code shows that the institution of Hollywood film censorship identified, and attempted to protect, dominant ideologies. Both authors centre their studies on a difficult problem for ideology: the 'sex film' or 'kept woman'/'fallen woman' cycle, in which impoverished or working-class women exchange sexual favours for economic security and for what Jacobs describes as 'class rise'. This research shows that the Production Code Administration regarded narrative structure as a strategy for controlling the production of meaning and for reducing the potential for oppositional subjectivities in contemporary audiences. Both Jacobs and Maltby suggest that the disruptive potential of ideological contradiction around woman's sexuality was understood as a threat to dominant values and capitalist culture. As film censorship developed in the 1930s, the Production Code Administration attended to narration and film style in order to alleviate ideological problems.[7]

In Jacobs's analysis of the conventions of the 'fallen woman' cycle, it is argued that the film industry recognized that the narrative logic of 'class rise', with its visual display of women and material rewards,

6   John Hill, *Sex, Class and Realism: British Cinema 1956–1963* (London: British Film Institute, 1986); Nick Roddick, *A New Deal in Entertainment: Warner Brothers in the 1930s* (London: British Film Institute, 1983).

7   Lea Jacobs, 'Censorship and the fallen woman cycle', in Gledhill, *Home is Where the Heart Is*, pp. 100–12; Richard Maltby, '*Baby Face*, or how Joe Breen made Barbara Stanwyck atone for causing the Wall Street crash', *Screen*, vol. 27, no. 2 (1986), pp. 22–45 (reprinted in the present volume as chapter 11).

worked against the morality of womanhood which the Production Code tried to protect. In his analysis of *Baby Face*, Maltby enlarges the context of censorship to include 1920s and 1930s consumerism. In *Baby Face*, Lily and Trenholm give their fortune to the latter's bank, which is on the verge of financial collapse. The film ends with the couple, broke but happy, working in the factory town from which Lily originally escaped. Maltby sees this ending as a narrative 'punishment' for the kept woman, for her 'existence as a spectacle of desire . . . in an economic moment when the possibilities for consumption were sharply restricted'. In Maltby's analysis of the ideological effects of Production Code censorship, the display of consumerism through woman-centred spectacle is regarded as incompatible with capitalism in crisis during the Depression.[8]

8 Jacobs 'Censorship and the fallen woman cycle', pp. 102–4; Maltby, '*Baby Face*', pp. 44–5.

However, comparison of two proletarian woman's films which cross the chronology of the 1930s reveals how studio production 'entertainment values' intersect with the exploitation of the Depression in different ways. Rather than being incompatible with capitalist culture, the proletarian woman's film displays the contradictory values surrounding woman's sexuality, the visual pleasures of consumerism, and the social economy of the Depression which are well grounded in the opposing tendencies which constitute the film's industrial and social context of 1930s cinema. Also, with *Our Blushing Brides*—a pre-Code 'shop girl' film, and *Marked Woman*—a post-Code film about prostitution, potential 'moral difficulties' are understood differently in each instance by the Production Code Administration. This analysis will show, through the four factors which produce the proletarian woman's film, how popular entertainment films, both before *and* after the 1934 Production Code, are made up of complex and contradictory discourses about the social relations of class and gender; and that two significant contending forces in the production of meaning are studio 'entertainment values' and censorship.

The early 1930s 'shop girl' film is especially useful for exploring how popular films accommodate the contradictions of the first years of the Depression. This genre exploited the Depression by exploring the sexual politics of the department store. In drawing narrative conflict from sexual harassment in the workplace, the 'shop girl' film draws upon the economic determinants which tie together relations of class and gender. Yet, while showing how economic privation threatens woman's virtue, the 'shop girl' film also fosters consumerism through fashion shows. (Indeed, *Our Blushing Brides* would be thirty minutes shorter were it not for the fashion shows.) This display of merchandise and spectacle contributes to the film's articulation of class difference and the contemporary economic stresses on women.

Our Blushing Brides is the last in a trilogy of popular MGM films about contemporary young women, all of which starred Joan Crawford. These films span the coming of sound and of the Depression. In the first two, *Our Dancing Daughters* (1928) and *Our Modern Maidens* (1929), Crawford danced her way through performances as 'wild and reckless'

Our Blushing Brides

flappers. Released nine months after the Crash, however, *Our Blushing Brides* retained the lavish spectacle and high production values of the first two films of the trilogy, while accommodating the Depression economy through a redesign of the Crawford character from party girl to hard-working 'shop girl'. This allowed MGM's star to make the social transition without leaving behind the glamorous Cedric Gibbons Art Deco sets and modern costumes of the two previous films.[9] The film centres on the working life of women employed as sales assistants and models for a large department store. Low wages require three women to share the rent of a cramped apartment, and they harbour no illusions about any future change in their situation. The owner of the department store is a wealthy and handsome playboy accustomed to satisfying his desires with the women his store employs. In a variation of the 'fallen woman' (in which, as Lea Jacobs notes, the visual display of the woman is dependent upon her fall into materialism),[10] the 'shop girl' recognizes the economic nexus of sexual harassment and struggles to reject the temptation of material goods. The 'shop girl' film can afford this virtue, since the visual pleasure of the star's display is partially guaranteed through her role as a department store model. While the lead character has the strength to resist the owner's advances, her co-workers/room-mates are more desperate—or more cynical—and allow men to provide them with material comforts in exchange for their virtue. The women discuss how their desires are thwarted by the economic exigencies of waged labour: in this way, the film explores the economic boundaries of women's sexual identities. The 'shop girl' film explains—and justifies —the economic parameters of choice available to working women.

Our Blushing Brides uses three types of narrative space in visually situating the ideological environment in which the women's class and gender identities intersect. First, there is the primary location of narrative action, the department store, a setting which integrates three systems of exchange: work, consumerism, and sexuality. The film

9   Donald Albrecht, *Designing Dreams: Modern Architecture in the Movies* (New York: Harper & Row in collaboration with the Museum of Modern Art, 1986), pp. 90–1, 124; '*Our Dancing Daughters*', *Variety*, 10 October 1928, p. 22; '*Our Modern Maidens*', *Variety*, 1929.

10 Jacobs, 'Censorship and the fallen woman cycle', p. 102.

immediately establishes Crawford's dual identity—as the star but also as an ordinary working woman. The film begins with dozens of women lining up at the time clock to begin the working day. While Crawford strikes a model's pose, she also jockeys for a place in front of the locker-room mirror with the other workers. Once she is on the job, however, *Our Blushing Brides* neatly brings forward the extraordinary qualities of the star and of the studio's production values, an industrial strategy which also informs the representation of class difference in the film. Crawford's room-mates, both of whom eventually (but not without struggle) allow themselves to succumb to material temptation, work at boring counter service jobs (selling perfume and blankets).

As the star in the role of department store model, Crawford's work constitutes a multiple site of exchange and looking. Her character takes pleasure in participating in commodity spectacle while modelling fashions she cannot herself afford for women of a different class. The store owner, who surveys the first fashion show in the film with his valued customers, is invested with the power of ownership in all three systems of exchange: labour, consumerism, and sexuality. He owns the model's labour, the lingerie, and the gowns they are selling, and—through the eroticism of his gaze—the women's sexuality, which is both waged labour and part of the display of merchandise.

The second type of narrative space is the living space which makes class differences visible and situates the working women within an economy of widely disparate incomes. There are two types of living space in *Our Blushing Brides*: that of the workers and that of extreme wealth. The three women share a small one-bedroom apartment. Meanwhile, on his grand estate, the store owner lures women into a lavish studio apartment built into the branches of a large tree. (About the display of production values through the tree house, *Variety* commented: 'seldom does Hollywood's lech for bigness lead to such ridiculous extremes'.)[11] In a charity fashion show at the estate, a shot/reverse shot shows the store models, in simple and ordinary

11 'Blushing Brides', *Variety*, 6 August 1930, p. 21.

clothes, visually dazzled by the fabulous gowns and sumptuous living environment available to their class opposites.

The third type of narrative space in the 'shop girl' film, and the one which draws relations of class and gender firmly into the arena of narrative conflict, is the space of sexual harassment. It is here that the shop girl confronts her economic dependency on the owner. The semi-clad Crawford is visually caught in the models' dressing room at the store by the gaze and physical presence of the owner. As he intrudes into her space from the doorway, his desire integrates his economic ownership of the store and of her labour with his sexual power.

In this scene, a woman is wedged between the uninvited gaze of a man at the rear of the frame and the camera at the front. She covers herself in protection from his gaze, resisting her forced display, while participating in a visual display for the camera. This scene of sexual harassment in *Our Blushing Brides* is similar to one in *Night Nurse* in

Our Blushing Brides

which a male resident doctor easily colonizes the space of the nurses' dressing-room through gestures and glances. But unlike *Our Blushing Brides*, the aggressive male gaze in *Night Nurse* is not motivated by specific character traits or goals. Instead, it suggests a more 'naturalized' assumption about male prerogative and sexual exploitation.

Our Blushing Brides establishes a visual and narrative contrast between a virtuous but dowdy existence on $12.50 a week on the one hand, and commodity spectacle on the other. While her room-mates meet unhappy ends, the Crawford character resists both temptation and sexual harassment. She ends the film wearing the clothes she might have previously modelled, romping with her husband-to-be, the store owner, in his tree-house apartment. Unlike the 'fallen woman', the shop girl's virtue is rewarded by marital happiness and 'class rise'.

Although the Production Code Administration observed that *Our Blushing Brides* was about 'the well-known primrose path', it was also found to be inoffensive in the meanings it offered about sexual politics: the story 'has been very discreetly handled and contains moral values of the highest quality. Beside this it has an abundance of entertainment value. It conforms to the Code and contains nothing objectionable'. *Variety* acknowledged more explicitly that the fantastic narrative resolution of *Our Blushing Brides* met the needs of both ideology and entertainment: 'Miss Crawford in steadfast chastity emerges as the ultimate winner, with the typical fictional accomplishment of a rich husband, without loss of ideals'.[12]

Variety derided this proletarian woman's film as 'Another of Metro's endless cycle of sex, satin and salesgirl hooey designed to capitalize the day dreams of flaps and stenogs'. Yet it also predicted that this combination of entertainment and address to contemporary women would have a 'box office response [which] will indicate both managers and populace [are] satisfied'.[13] Because records from the very early 1930s are incomplete, in demonstrating further how these films ask contemporary women viewers to recognize their own experiences,

12 JBM Fisher, Resumé, 9 June 1930, *Our Blushing Brides* case file, Special Collections, Academy of Motion Picture Arts and Sciences, Beverly Hills; '*Blushing Brides*', *Variety*, 6 August 1930.

13 Ibid.

desires and 'day dreams' in the lives of their cinematic sisters, it is necessary to look at a later example of a 'shop girl' film.

The advertising campaign for *Employees' Entrance* (1933) exploits the Depression and the lives of department store workers by firmly establishing an address to contemporary women which recognizes sexual harassment in the workplace. Touted as the 'most pressing moral problem of our times', the sexual power of employers results from women's problems in finding work in an economy with scarce employment. The film's advertising campaign asks: 'Has the depression brought BARGAINS IN LOVE? Is there a panic in morals . . . when millions of heartsick girls will pay *any price* for a job!' A flyer apparently meant for distribution 'To New York working girls—and their bosses!' shows eight scenes from *Employees' Entrance* which establish the workplace as the site of women's sexual exploitation. Released in 1933, on the cusp of the Code, many of these scenes were excised from the film through censorship negotiations. Yet the address to the gendered and class identities of contemporary working women was clear: 'Department store girls—this is your picture—about your lives and your problems'.[14]

It is interesting to compare the address to women of *Employees' Entrance* with that of the later *Marked Woman* (1937). One poster typical of the campaign for this film reads: 'Women! You've read about those notorious "clip joints"! You've heard how men are robbed by their hostesses! You've passed such places many times without knowing it! Now you can see a side of life you've never known!' The poster copy goes on to promise an exposé of 'racket slaves' and an opportunity to 'Meet the Girls who got caught in the racket!'[15] In considering *Marked Woman*, a proletarian woman's film made after the inauguration of the 1934 Production Code, a central issue must be the degree to which film censorship, as opposed to the three other factors—narration, studio production, and the articulation of the relationship of economics to gender identities in contemporary life—marks the film. *Marked Woman*

14 Pressbook for *Employees' Entrance*, Warner Bros Archives, Special Collections, University of Southern California.

15 Pressbook for *Marked Woman*, Warner Bros Archives, Special Collections, University of Southern California.

is a realist exploitation of contemporary conditions which intersect gender and economics, based on the well-known and sensational 1936 trial of Lucky Luciano for gangsterism and prostitution. Like *Our Blushing Brides*, *Marked Woman* accommodates a star discourse with the concomitant demands of glamour and merchandising.

One effect of this combination of star, censorship, and articulation of women's choices through gangsterism and vice is a shift in address to women viewers. Rather than positioning women characters as sharing experiences with women, as the 'shop girl' films do, *Marked Woman* separates the women in the film from the women in the audience. The 'you' of the sexually harassed department store worker has become the 'she' of the hostess/prostitute. This shift in address results from the historical context of *Marked Woman*.

In taking up prostitution and Lucky Luciano, the film of necessity established causal relationships between the economic conditions which foster prostitution and the sexual and economic exploitation of gangsterism. At the same time, Production Code censorship required that this knowledge be somehow hidden or adequately repressed. Even the 'entertainment value' generated by star and merchandising constituted a problem. In her return to the screen after a year's absence during her public contract dispute with Warner Bros, Bette Davis had to be repositioned, as star and actress, in a tough role. The film's pressbook shows how the studio deftly handled the wide range of knowledges in circulation around this film, managing to its advantage, but not suppressing, the film's contemporary realist basis.

Charles Eckert discusses how the film represents gangsterism and vice as capitalist practices of ownership and exchange of labour. Accounts of prostitution in the press of 1936 also show that specific knowledge about the economic exploitation of prostitution and about the economic causes of prostitution was widely circulated. *The Nation*, for example, stated: 'It is clear that in the vast majority of cases women have embraced the world's oldest profession because they knew no other way to make a living . . .'. *Time* presented short case studies of the operation of prostitution syndicates. And *New Republic* published a list of people who lived off prostitutes' labour, and summarized a report by the Florence Crittenton League on the histories of 561 delinquent and wayward girls, concluding: 'despite all moral indignation, prostitution is a comparatively advantageous profession—for a few years. It is the best job these girls can get.'[16]

Despite this circulation of public knowledge about prostitution, censorship required that in the film itself any specific reference to prostitution or to the Luciano case be suppressed: '. . . it is imperative that you establish it quite clearly that the girls, Mary, Emmy Lou, *et al.*, are merely hostesses in a night club and not, by any stretch of the imagination, prostitutes'. Yet, as the review in the *New York Times* shows, it required no stretch of the imagination to know not only that *Marked Woman* was about prostitution and Lucky Luciano, but also that film censorship required that such knowledge be repressed:

16 Eckert, 'The anatomy of a proletarian film', pp. 422–3; 'Prostitution in New York City', *The Nation*, 22 April 1936, p. 369; 'Women: bawdy business', *Time*, 25 May 1936, p. 15; 'New York's vice ring', *New Republic*, 10 June 1936, pp. 124–6. I am grateful to Diane Waldman for sharing these sources with me.

In the interests of the Hays office and the Legion of Decency, the sphere of influence of Johnny Vanning, the picture's Luciano, has been transferred from the bagnio to the bistro, and it is the hostess in the smart clip-joint, rather than the members of the older [*sic*] profession, who engage our attention.

Thus, while the Production Code Administration might have succeeded in eliminating explicit references to prostitution and the New York vice case, the film's narrative nevertheless retained the knowledge about the economic and sexual exploitation of prostitution.[17]

A second contemporary discourse is that of the star system. Bette Davis was assigned to *Marked Woman* after her return from England, having failed in her attempt to wrest control of her career from Warner Bros by freeing herself from the studio's seven-year option contract. Maria LaPlace argues that discussions about this lawsuit in the popular press circulated a conception of Davis as possessing 'qualities of strength, independence and devotion to career'. As LaPlace has shown in her analysis of *Now, Voyager* (Warner Bros, 1942), expectations about Davis inform the way the film's advertising 'exploit[s] spectator knowledge of [Davis's] previous roles and personal life as major marketing tools'.[18] While a similar strategy is adopted for *Marked Woman*, in this case the star must negotiate some potentially bumpy ground. Davis's return to the screen is in a genre whose lead character is typically played by a tough male. In its presentation of Davis's role as a hostess who turns against her racketeer boss, the pressbook stresses the 'versatility' of the actress and the 'emotionality' of her performance style. In a role which can exhibit her award-winning 'diversified emotional acting', Davis must be 'alternately tender, hard and gay, and versatile actress that she is, she does them all admirably'.[19]

In a letter to Jack Warner following the New York premiere of *Marked Woman*, Charles Einfield (director of publicity and advertising in New York) reassured Warner about Davis's financial value to the studio. Einfield's comments also indicate that performance has the ability to smooth the gaps between realist portrayals and expectations of star glamour. Einfield reported:

> [Women at the Strand Theatre in New York] don't talk about how beautiful she is, but how realistic she is. You hear women say, 'There's a gal who doesn't need a lot of junk all over her face and who doesn't have to put on the glamour to hold us in our seats. . . . She isn't afraid to let people see her as the tawdry character she is supposed to represent'. . . . Bette Davis is a female Cagney and if we give her the right parts, we are going to have a star that will pay off the interest on the bonds every year.[20]

The advertising and publicity copy offered to exhibitors in the *Marked Woman* pressbook takes a position similar to Einfield's. The pressbook acknowledges both opposing tendencies which combine to produce *Marked Woman*: the film's exploitation of censorable material

17 Joseph Breen, letter to Jack Warner, 1 December 1936, *Marked Woman* case file, Special Collections, Academy of Motion Picture Arts and Sciences, Beverly Hills; Frank S. Nugent, '*Marked Woman*', *New York Times*, 12 April 1937, p. 16.

18 LaPlace, 'Producing and consuming the woman's film', pp. 148 and 150.

19 Pressbook for *Marked Woman*.

20 S. Charles Einfield, letter to Jack Warner, 12 April 1937; Rudy Behlmer (ed.), *Inside Warner Brothers (1935–1951)* (New York: Viking Penguin, 1985), p. 39.

(gangsterism, violence, and prostitution) and the entertainment value of its star discourse and merchandising.

The pressbook begins with statements which remind exhibitors that Warner Bros is offering two proven profitable commodities: Bette Davis and gangster films. These two elements, already 'pre-sold' to the public, are linked together: first, 'Bette's Back' on the screen; and, secondly, she is starring in one of the studio's popular gangster/social consciousness films:

> PRE-SOLD IN HEADLINES[:] The most acclaimed star of 1936, after an absence of nearly a year, returns to make a film that is ACCLAIMED BY CRITICS in the trade press and by Hollywood correspondents as worthy of standing beside 'Public Enemy', 'G-Men' and other Warner Bros films of special social significance.

The pressbook goes on to reassure exhibitors that studio-produced advertising can handle any potential problems with the film. In offering the exhibitor 'carefully prepared advertising copy and subtly written publicity stories', the pressbook implicitly admits that censorship did not hide the 'true' content of the film. It also cautions exhibitors not to design their own 'stunts' around the 'theme of the plot' or the title.[21]

Several devices for exploiting the film's realist basis implicitly require audiences to recognize the film's unspoken subject matter:

> Brutal realism of picture calls for a warning sign in lobby front for faint hearted. Copy for sign can be taken right out of ad copy—'WE WARN YOU! Don't Come Unless You Really Want to Know Life, Excitement, Adventure! And If You Want to Know The Truth About The Other Side Of Life—Run, Don't Walk, To This Theatre'.

For a radio phone-in programme, the pressbook suggests a problem-solving context in which 'a girl . . . tells the predicament of one of the girls in the picture. Listeners get ducats for the best solution to the girls' problem.' And, in another approach which acknowledges the film's 'true' topics, Warner Bros adopts a reformist stance about the studio's contribution to the public interest. The pressbook offers the following copy for a one-minute radio plug:

> Motivated by the conviction that truth is more powerful than any fiction, Warner Bros has taken up the cudgel against a racket which is preying on American Society and have made a daring exposé of the 'clip joint' menace. Fearlessly flinging this challenging gauntlet in the face of the American apathy, Warner Bros brings 'Marked Woman' to [a theatre near you].[22]

Publicity stories about the film's production enhance both aspects of *Marked Woman*: its 'hard-hitting realism' and the glamour and spectacle of its production values. Two stories appear to address Production Code Administration concerns about 'excessive brutality and gruesomeness' in the depiction of Mary's beating and of Vanning slapping Betty. In 'Bette's Mother Fooled By Hard Make-up on Star', Mrs Davis is

21 Pressbook for *Marked Woman*.

22 Pressbook for *Marked Woman*.

reported as not recognizing her daughter through the bandages 'expertly applied by [a] Hollywood surgeon' and the bruises provided by the make-up department. In a story subtitled 'Newcomer To Movies, Taking Heavy Clip, Thinks That's The Usual Thing', the slap which causes Betty to tumble down the stairs to her death is described as unintentionally realistic, the result of the awkward physical meeting of the two actors, Jane Bryant and Eduardo Cianelli.[23]

The way the pressbook foregrounds women's gowns reveals how star and merchandising provide a discourse which competes with those around gangsterism and prostitution. The women's costumes, used to demonstrate the economic and sexual exploitation of the women by the gangsters, also demonstrate studio production values and the star system as they are offered as fashions and spectacle to the female spectator. As LaPlace suggests in her analysis of *Now, Voyager*, the conjunction of star–character–actress–consumer–woman is the site of multiple and contradictory consumerist discourses. In *Marked Woman*, the 'Morn to Midnight Fashions as Worn by Bette Davis' in her private life—'arising', 'off for the day's work at the studio', 'for tea', and 'dressed for a gala evening'—exactly reverse the work schedule of the women in the film, who, like the women in the song 'Lullaby of Broadway', say goodnight early in the morning when the milkman's on his way.[24]

Finally, a story about how 'Film Backgrounds Help Indicate Human Traits' explains how the 'tastefully done' Club Intime was changed into the Club Intimate to assist in 'building the character of the villain of the piece'. Vanning's goals and desires also effected changes in the women's costumes; but unlike the club *mise-en-scène*, the gowns are elided as signifiers of 'clip joint' as they are routed through the spectacle of merchandising and the star discourse of the film. The story relates that Vanning 'also turns the hostesses into high-powered chiselers with new manners, morals and above all, clothes. So Orry-Kelly . . . was able to get in some choice bits of his own art, including an evening gown for Miss Davis which he declares is the most beautiful he has ever produced'.[25]

This analysis of the *Marked Woman* pressbook shows that Production Code censorship prohibitions do not work in isolation in repressing the economic conditions taken up in the film. Rather, censorship works in concert with other conditions of Hollywood film production, notably the star system and merchandising, to displace concerns about any morally difficult meanings circulating through the film. And, while discourses of star and merchandising may compete with knowledge about the economic determinants of sexual exploitation, they do not simply erase the intersection of economics and gender at the basis of *Marked Woman*: 'It's better than being a salesgirl'.

In his exploration of the potential for progressive meanings in popular culture, Tony Bennett asks historians to re-code the signifiers of the past in order to see how they might produce oppositional meanings and political effects.[26] In its representation of capitalist culture in the 1930s, the proletarian woman's film exploits the economic context of the

23 Joseph Breen, letter to Jack Warner, 22 December 1936, *Marked Woman* case file; Pressbook for *Marked Woman*.

24 LaPlace, 'Producing and consuming the woman's film', see especially pp. 145 and 150; Pressbook for *Marked Woman*.

25 Pressbook for *Marked Woman*.

26 Tony Bennett, 'Hegemony, ideology, pleasure: Blackpool', in Bennett *et al.*, *Popular Culture and Social Relations*, p. 152.

94 Social Histories

Depression as the basis for its narrative conflict. As women characters confront the moral choices available to them, they must also recognize how economics intersect with gender. This knowledge about sexual politics is expressed through the film industry imperatives of censorship, the star system, and the display of production values and merchandising. The gender identities which emerge in this fluid combination of narration, censorship, studio production, and appropriation of contemporary problems are necessarily mobile, shifting, and contradictory.

6　The *Married Love* Affair

ANNETTE KUHN

In the summer of 1923, a British film titled *Maisie's Marriage* (co-written by Marie Stopes and directed by Walter Summers) became the target of a number of attempts at censorship. Institutional practices of film censorship are always obliged to assume as their object individual films: texts—representations with specific boundaries. And yet in any actual instance of censorship there is usually more than this at stake. Certainly in the case of *Maisie's Marriage*, the content of the film does not alone provide sufficient explanation either for the excessive efforts at censorship directed at it, nor for the consequences of those efforts, many of which were unforeseeable and some indeed the very opposite of what had been intended.

Maisie's Marriage became an object of censorship by virtue of its implication, at a particular historical moment, within a certain set of discourses and power relations, which penetrate the text and yet also exceed it. These include discourses and practices of film censorship; but also involved in the constitution of *Maisie's Marriage* as censorable are the operations on the one hand of the film industry and on the other of contemporary debates around sexuality and birth control. Each of these—censorship, the film industry, discourses on sexuality— constructs the film differently, and each is caught up in a struggle over the conditions under which the film was to enter the public domain. Each, too, inscribes different interests and power relations, some of them operating in contradiction.

The routine procedures of censorship at the time the film was released were instrumental in determining the limits of what was and what was not 'suitable' material for commercial cinema screens. Although in this respect *Maisie's Marriage* could not be faulted either in content or in style, the film's connection with the name of Marie Stopes made it extremely troublesome, all the more so because there was very little in the film itself that could seriously be objected to: while the film was produced as an object of censorship through its engagement with contemporary debates around sexuality and birth control, these issues are not explicitly articulated within it. This made it a peculiarly elusive object of censorship. One of the difficulties *Maisie's Marriage* posed *vis-à-vis* film censorship was that it was already a product of other contemporary censorships, notably of the widespread taboo on discussing sexual matters and the virtual impossibility of obtaining information on birth control.

Nevertheless, although the film is open to a variety of readings, meanings in *Maisie's Marriage* became relatively fixed in the moment of censorship, through which it was precisely constructed as 'controversial'. Film censorship creates censorable films: and a censorable film, once it has entered the public domain, becomes a marketable property exactly because of the lure of prohibition conferred by acts of censorship. The *Maisie's Marriage* affair offers one instance of censorship operating not only prohibitively in the regulation of the public sphere of cinema, but also productively in the actual creation of such a sphere.

Maisie Burrows, the eldest of ten children, meets and falls in love with Dick Reading, a fireman. When Dick proposes marriage, Maisie refuses him because she does not want a life like that of her parents, who have too many children and not enough money. Turned out of home by her father after a family row, Maisie wanders the streets in desperation, eventually attempting suicide by jumping off a bridge. She is rescued, but immediately arrested and sent to jail for two months. On her release, Maisie is taken in as a maidservant by her rescuer's wife, Mrs Sterling. The Sterlings have three children and a happy marriage, and from Mrs Sterling Maisie learns that she can enjoy married love without the consequences she so fears. One evening, when Maisie is alone in the house with the Sterling children, her degenerate brother calls and extorts money. In the ensuing fracas, the house catches fire and Maisie is rescued by Dick. The couple, joyously reunited, marry.

This, in brief, is the story of *Maisie's Marriage*, made and released in 1923. Besides being a love story of a kind commonplace enough in the popular cinema of the day, *Maisie's Marriage* also deals, implicitly at least, with birth control and marital happiness, proposing a direct causal link between the two. Such matters were the subject of widespread debate and much controversy in the early 1920s: and 1923 in particular was in a number of respects a key moment of transition in the politics of birth control in Britain.

In the early 1920s, the birth control movement had entered a new phase, and was beginning to secure a broader base for its objectives than it had enjoyed hitherto. One of its new goals was to persuade government and local authorities to sponsor clinics dispensing advice and contraceptives: the first, private, birth control clinics in Britain had opened in 1921. Arguments in favour of birth control began to stress its benefits in terms of the health, welfare, and general happiness of mothers and children, a shift from the earlier, predominantly eugenic, emphasis on the quality of the population. The movement was now ready to make a bid for party political support for its aims, or at least for a voice in Parliament. Although no party actually adopted any policy on birth control, a number of MPs were publicly supportive of the cause. Outside Parliament, the movement was also gaining ground within the Labour Party: the idea of birth control as a public health issue was certainly more attractive to the Left than had been the more characteristically middle-class eugenic approach. It was during this period that a number of Labour-controlled local authorities came into conflict with the government over the question of publicly funded birth control clinics. At the beginning of 1923, public awareness of all these issues was heightened spectacularly by a handful of *causes célèbres*. A health visitor, Nurse E. S. Daniels, was suspended and later dismissed from her job for giving advice on birth control to some of her clients. The case aroused a great deal of interest and much support for Nurse Daniels herself. At about the same time, two left-wing birth control activists, Rose Witcop and Guy Aldred, were prosecuted for circulating Margaret Sanger's pamphlet, *Family Limitation*, and found guilty of selling an obscene publication. And finally in February, Marie Stopes, eugenicist, author, and well-known birth control campaigner, went to court with a much-publicized libel suit.[1]

If the appearance of a film like *Maisie's Marriage* at such a moment constituted a strategic intervention in a broader debate, any relationship between the latter and the former pivots as much on discourses surrounding the film as on the content of the film itself. These include, but are by no means confined to, contemporary preoccupations around sexuality, sexual pleasure, and contraception. *Maisie's Marriage* is at once produced by these discourses and productive of meanings of its own, meanings which—in a series of complex and at times contradictory operations—recirculate and transform their originating discourses. The film encounters other practices, too—relations of power through which in specific ways at a particular conjuncture it becomes a cultural product of a certain kind. Predominant among these are practices of what may broadly be termed the cinematic institution, and within these, more specifically, practices of film censorship. Significant in the passage of *Maisie's Marriage* through these practices is the film's association with the name of Marie Stopes. Stopes is credited as writer of the film's story, though the scenario was actually written by her credited co-writer, Walter Summers, with Marie Stopes maintaining the right of final approval of script and control over the content of intertitles.[2]

In 1923, the name of Marie Stopes was a byword: her book *Married Love* (subtitled 'a new contribution to the solution of sex difficulties') had been an enormous success from its first publication in March 1918. By the end of the year, in fact, it was already in its sixth reprint. In November 1918, in response to demand from readers of *Married Love*,

1 Jeffrey Weeks, *Sex, Politics and Society: The Regulation of Sexuality Since 1800* (London: Longman, 1981) chapter 10; Sheila Rowbotham, *Hidden from History* (London: Pluto Press, 1973) p. 150; Jane Lewis, 'The ideology and politics of birth control in Interwar England', *Women's Studies International Quarterly*, vol. 2, no. 1 (1979), pp. 33–48; Robert E. Dowse and John Peel, 'The politics of birth control', *Political Studies*, vol. 13, no. 2 (1965), pp. 179–97.

2 British Library, Stopes Collection (hereafter BL-SC) ADD 58507, memo of meeting with producers of film, 11 April 1923; for biographical information on Stopes, see Ruth Hall, *Marie Stopes: A Biography* (London: Andre Deutsch, 1977).

Stopes published another best-seller, *Wise Parenthood*, a short treatise on birth control—of which there had been only a brief discussion in *Married Love*—which included recommendations as to methods of contraception. These successes were followed in 1920 by *Radiant Motherhood*, in part advice manual for first-time parents, in part eugenic tract. Marie Stopes's constituency was at first limited largely to the book-buying public—to the middle classes, that is—though within a few years her ideas did begin to achieve much wider circulation.

Marie Stopes's growing fame was perhaps due as much to her notoriety—her books were looked on in some influential quarters as nothing less than scandalous, even obscene, and in certain countries they were even banned—as to the social needs evidently addressed by her work. Her writings certainly provoked huge public response, much of which revealed hitherto untapped depths of ignorance, fear, sexual frustration, and conjugal misery.[3] At the same time, since they could lay claim to a certain scientific respectability and were endorsed by various eminent medical practitioners, Stopes's ideas could not be dismissed entirely as the outpourings of a crank. The combination of scientificity with sexual subject matter, moral conservatism, and romantic appeal guaranteed extensive publicity and a degree of acceptability—as well as controversy—for her work.[4]

In 1923, Marie Stopes's public profile was raised several notches when the trial opened in February of a libel suit she had brought against a Catholic doctor, Halliday Sutherland, who had made some uncomplimentary remarks about contraception in general and Marie Stopes in particular in one of his books. During the nine-day trial, other issues were raised, notably the alleged obscenity of *Married Love*. The trial attracted a great deal of publicity, and was reported in all the popular newspapers. On an unclear jury decision, the judge finally ruled in favour of Sutherland, a verdict which produced further public furore, as well as a good deal of sympathy for the loser. The judgement was taken to appeal, and reversed on 20 July. (The verdict did eventually go against Stopes, however: in November 1924, the Lords ruled four to one in favour of Sutherland.)[5]

During the first half of 1923, then, Stopes and her books were much in the public eye. Controversy raged and sales boomed throughout the year: of *Married Love* alone the number of copies sold virtually doubled (from 241,000 to 406,000) between March and December.[6] In the period between the February verdict and the July appeal in the Sutherland case, Stopes made her first—and, as it turned out, her last—foray into cinema as a vehicle for her ideas. *Maisie's Marriage* was produced by Samuelson's, a British company with a reputation for quality productions. The film's original title was *Married Love*, but despite its celebration of marital harmony it was in no sense a cinematic version of the book: it made no pretence at being either a scientific treatise or a manual of advice, but was in fact a work of fiction—a 'fast-moving popular melodrama' not very different from the fare on offer at the time in commercial cinemas. Stopes was later to allege that the idea of calling

3 Ruth Hall (ed.), *Dear Dr Stopes: Sex in the 1920s* (Harmondsworth: Penguin, 1981).

4 Weeks, *Sex, Politics and Society*, p. 192; Lewis, 'The Ideology and Politics of Birth Control', pp. 35–8.

5 Muriel Box (ed.), *The Trial of Marie Stopes* (London: Femina Books, 1967); Hall, *Marie Stopes*, chapter 13.

6 Hall, *Marie Stopes*, p. 243; Marie Carmichael Stopes, *Married Love: A New Contribution to the Solution of Sex Difficulties*, 11th edn. (London: G. P. Putnam's Sons Ltd., 1923).

the film *Married Love* had not been hers: be that as it may, its producers were evidently well aware of the publicity value attaching to that particular title. The film was made in just two weeks—in an effort, perhaps, to seize the crest of the Sutherland trial publicity wave. It was trade-shown on 11 May, and scheduled for a June release.

Married Love was well received by at least one national newspaper,[7] and the film trade was not unsympathetic either—an attitude which was to be modified in light of subsequent events. It was, however, pointed out early on that the title might well generate expectations that the film could not fulfil. One trade reviewer nevertheless concluded that 'Whatever may be the suggestion of the title, the film itself is a straightforward human story of sentimental rather than sexual appeal', while another noted that 'in spite of its title, the story . . . will appeal to the popular imagination'.[8] But if some critics emphasized the appeal of the story as against the 'misleading' character of its title, there was already some unease in the trade about the latter. *Kinematograph Weekly*, a journal which saw itself as representing the more 'respectable' elements of the exhibition arm of the film industry, expressed serious misgivings about the choice of title, saying that this was exactly the sort of thing to bring the trade into disrepute.[9] Exploiting the name of a controversial book was far too crude a piece of gimmickry, it seems, to be tolerated in an industry still aspiring to shed the socially inferior image of a sideshow catering to the most vulgar.

However, before *Married Love* was to find its way into the cinemas of the land, it ran into more formidable obstacles. On the day of its trade show, the film was submitted to the British Board of Film Censors (BBFC), where it languished for more than a month before being released. The Board took exception to the film immediately, on the grounds that

> there are many scenes and sub-titles which render this film in our opinion unsuitable for exhibition before ordinary audiences; while the title, taken in conjunction with the name of the book and the authoress referred to, suggests propaganda on a subject unsuitable for discussion in a Cinema Theatre.[10]

Films based on 'notorious books' were to prove repeatedly troublesome to the Board in 1923, and there was a particular dislike of the use of titles of publications that dealt with topics which they regarded as exceeding the proper social function of cinema—namely to entertain.[11]

The BBFC had evidently seen through the producers' attempt to capitalize on the publicity value—and the 'forbidden' connotations—of the title *Married Love*. But if this title suggested that the film dealt with issues 'unsuitable' for the cinema, namely sex and birth control, was there anything in the film which might be regarded as objectionable from the standpoint of British film censors of the early 1920s? The BBFC's verdict, despite the implication that the film contained objectionable scenes and intertitles, must have been that there was really

7 *Daily Telegraph*, 14 May 1923.

8 *Bioscope*, 17 May 1923, p. 61; *Kinematograph Weekly*, 17 May 1923, p. 73.

9 Leader, *Kinematograph Weekly*, 17 May 1923, p. 59.

10 BL-SC ADD 58507, BBFC to Napoleon Films, 11 May 1923.

11 British Board of Film Censors, *Annual Report 1923*. Other book-based films which ran into censorship trouble at this time include *Three Weeks*, founded on a racy Elinor Glyn novel, and *La Garçonne*, based on a book by French writer Victor Margueritte which was banned in Britain: Public Record Office, Home Office Papers (hereafter PRO-HO) 45/20045; PRO-HO 45/11446.

very little, if anything, in its content that could specifically be objected to. And yet they were most reluctant to grant it a certificate.

In this atmosphere of uncertainty, the BBFC took the unusual step of asking the Home Office for guidance. On 18 May, a week after the film was submitted for censorship, officials from the Home Office called at the Board's premises in Wardour Street to view *Married Love*.[12] In the interim there had been a protest from Marie Stopes to the BBFC President, T. P. O'Connor (who was a Catholic—a fact which was to figure large in Stopes's assessment of events), and a discussion between O'Connor and the film's producers.[13] Presumably, no agreement had been reached, and O'Connor told the Home Office that he was inclined to refuse to pass the film. The Home Office representatives, however, took a slightly less negative view about the film's actual content ('there is nothing of an objectionable nature that could not be easily removed by the censor's pruning knife'), though they did agree that there were problems about the title. Their private opinion, nevertheless, was that 'a Birth control–Marie Stopes–propaganda film ought not to appear with a censor's certificate if this could be avoided'[14]—an acknowledgement that the trouble was not the actual film but its association with a 'notorious' public figure and a topic that was at once taboo and controversial.

In other circumstances, perhaps, *Married Love* might—with the collusion of the Home Office and the Board of Censors—have been at this point quietly suppressed. But it was not, for several reasons. Because neither the BBFC nor the Home Office possessed any legal powers of film censorship, they could do no more than advise the bodies which did hold such powers, namely the local cinema licensing authorities. Prominent among these was the London County Council, which since the BBFC's inauguration a decade earlier had assumed the role of pace-setter for censorship practices up and down the country. The Board of Censors was eager to maintain good relations with the LCC, which was also represented at the 18 May meeting. However, on the question of *Married Love*, the LCC disagreed with the BBFC, finding it unobjectionable. This difference of opinion provoked anxieties at the Home Office about possible discord between the BBFC and local cinema licensing authorities, or indeed between the various authorities themselves, as to the film's censorability. For if either of these things were to come about, the national uniformity of censorship practices, which the Home Office had been striving for a number of years to attain, would be immediately undermined.

At stake as well was a potential challenge to the BBFC's hitherto rather shaky authority and credibility. After ten years of indecision and struggle, it was hoped within the government that the Board's tenuous legal position was about to achieve at least conventional consolidation, and that local authorities would soon automatically look to it for advice on the censorship and certification of films. To this end, the Home Office was preparing a new set of recommended model conditions for cinema licences: these were to include, for the first time and after some legal

12 PRO-HO 45/11382, Home Office memo, 24 May 1923.

13 BL-SC ADD 58507, Napoleon Films to Marie Stopes (MCS), 14 May 1923; MCS to T. P. O'Connor, 15 May 1923.

14 PRO-HO 45/11382, Home Office memo, 24 May 1923.

15 PRO-HO 158/23, The censorship of cinematograph films, circular 373, 422/78, 6 July 1923; also PRO-HO 45/11191 and 45/22906.

tussles, a condition to the effect that no films without the BBFC's certificate were to be exhibited without the express consent of the licensing authority. When the Home Office was called in to give advice on *Married Love*, these new conditions were in the process of being drafted: they ultimately formed the basis of an advisory circular sent to local authorities on 6 July.[15] In this delicately balanced situation, any upset in relations between any of the parties involved—Home Office, Board of Censors, local authorities—brought on by the *Married Love* affair was to be avoided. 'I am afraid', said the government official who reported on the meeting, 'that the film is bound to cause controversy but it is a pity it has come at a time when we were hoping to secure greater

16 PRO-HO 45/11382, Home Office memo, 24 May 1923.

uniformity.'[16]

Married Love remained at the BBFC for several weeks while the Censors were trying to come to a decision about it. In response to a protest at the continued delay, the Board wrote to the producers saying the film had been viewed four times and that 'careful and prolonged

17 BL-SC ADD 58507, Brooke Wilkinson to Napoleon Films, 29 May 1923.

consideration' was still required.[17] But finally on 7 June a list of alterations was agreed between the two parties. After all the delay, the changes demanded by the BBFC were few and on the whole minor in nature, the most significant being that the film's title should be changed to *Maisie's Marriage* and that posters and other promotional material were not to say that it was based on Marie Stopes's book *Married Love*. Apart from this, objection was made to eight intertitles, only one of

18 BL-SC ADD 58507, Napoleon Films to MCS, 2 July 1923.

19 London County Council, Music Hall and Theatres Committee, 27 June 1923; BL-SC ADD 58507, Napoleon Films to MCS, 20 June 1923; LCC to Napoleon Films, 3 July 1923; LCC to various London cinemas, June and July 1923; LCC to MCS, 16 July 1923.

which was to be deleted: for the rest, amendments only were requested.[18] These changes having been agreed, the BBFC passed the film 'A' (for 'public' exhibition—recommending exhibition to adults-only audiences). Perhaps as a trade-off for the certificate, the London County Council lent the weight of its support to the BBFC's demands for changes, and checked a number of attempts within its area to show the film in uncensored form, or to advertise it 'misleadingly'.[19] The Board expressed the hope that other licensing authorities would be equally

20 PRO-HO 45/11382, Brooke Wilkinson to Home Office, 27 June 1923.

vigilant.[20]

This hope, however, was to prove vain. Within a fortnight of the agreement, it was brought to the BBFC's attention that the producers of *Maisie's Marriage* had not in fact made all the changes requested, that uncensored prints of the film were in circulation, and that in many places the name of Marie Stopes was being used in promoting the film in breach of the spirit of the understanding between the Board and the film's producers. Some exhibitors, it seems, were publicising the film as

21 PRO-HO 45/11382, handwritten Home Office minute, 28 June 1923; BL-SC ADD 58507, correspondence between BBFC and Napoleon Films, 22, 25, and 27 June 1923; *Daily Herald*, 28 June 1923.

22 BL-SC ADD 58507, Cinematograph Exhibitors' Association to MCS, 6 June 1923; *Kinematograph Weekly*, 7 June 1923, p. 61; 21 June 1923; p. 51.

'*Maisie's Marriage* a story of married love written by Dr Marie Stopes'. Worse still, there were reports that some local authorities had judged the film unobjectionable, and were allowing the uncut version to be exhibited in their areas.[21] 'Respectable' elements of the film trade, having already given their support to the BBFC in the matter of the film's censorship, expressed their disapproval of certain exhibitors flouting the Censors.[22]

These reports were not without foundation. Marie Stopes later conducted an informal survey of local authorities, discovering that a

23 *Morning Post*, 11 July 1923; BL-SC ADD 58507, correspondence between MCS and Chief Constables, July 1923; Frederick White to MCS, 9 August 1923.

24 PRO-HO 45/11382, minute by S. W. Harris, 27 June 1923.

25 PRO-HO 45/11382, circular 446, 368/3, 30 June 1923.

26 Hall, *Marie Stopes*, p. 245, footnote quoting a local newspaper advertisement for *Maisie's Marriage*, 21 July 1923; PRO-HO 45/11382, correspondence between Home Office and Sheffield Chief Constable, July and August 1923.

27 PRO-HO 45/11382, MCS to Home Office, 11 July 1923; Home Office to MCS, 12 July 1923; BL-SC ADD 58507, MCS to Home Office, 14 July 1923; Home Office to MCS, 17 July 1923.

28 Hall, *Marie Stopes*, p. 245.

29 All references to *Maisie's Marriage* herein are based on the print of the film in possession of the Samuelson family, which was loaned to the author by David Samuelson. This print has a censor's certificate which is placed *after* the title card.

30 BL-SC ADD 58507, Napoleon Films to MCS, 2 July 1923.

number of them had indeed permitted the exhibition of *Maisie's Marriage* in uncensored form. She was angry at not having been consulted about changes made to the film, whose distributor afterwards claimed that before it was put into circulation, all of the cuts had in fact been restored.[23] In the version of the film discussed here (see below) some, but certainly not all, of the changes demanded by the BBFC have been made. It seems likely that several different versions of the film were in circulation.

Whatever the case, the Home Office was convinced that a 'fraudulent and impudent evasion'[24] had indeed taken place, and was moved to take the unprecedented step of intervening directly at local level in the censorship of a film. On 30 June, a confidential administrative circular was issued to local licensing authorities in England and Wales, endorsing the BBFC's and the LCC's actions with regard to *Maisie's Marriage*, and expressing the hope that local authorities would 'only allow the revised form of the film to be exhibited under the conditions agreed to by the publishers'.[25] But even this remarkable excursion into state censorship failed to produce the desired result.[26] Furthermore, the film's producers managed to find out about the Home Office's 'confidential' circular, and within three weeks of its issue, Marie Stopes had threatened the Home Office with legal action and had a personal interview with the Home Secretary himself, who responded in somewhat conciliatory manner by assuring her there had never been any intention that her name should be forbidden from appearing on the film or in advertising for it. Nevertheless, while admitting that the BBFC's ruling had no status in law, the Home Office refused to climb down to the extent of withdrawing the 30 June circular.[27] Only a few days later, in a renewed wave of publicity, the judgement on appeal in the Stopes–Sutherland libel case was handed down. This coincidence of events finally assured the success of *Maisie's Marriage*.[28] Censorship had produced the very opposite effect to that which had been intended by the Censors.

Not ours to preach nor yet to point a moral—yet if, in the unfolding of our story, there is aught that comforts, helps or guides, then are our efforts doubly paid.

So begins *Maisie's Marriage*,[29] at once disclaiming and confirming its status as a film with a message. After this, the story begins:

The Burrows family live in Slumland but their prototypes dwell in all our cities—wherever our artificial civilisation has planted its weeds where the struggle for existence is hard and ruthless and the narrow dogma of our disciplined beliefs turn life and the joys of living into meaningless phrases.

The 'Slumland' setting is a concession to the Censor, who objected to the geographical specificity of the original Camberwell.[30] Maisie's family, the Burrowses, are characterized as representing a particular social group, whose misery is signalled in the scene of poverty, overcrowding, and familial discord which follows the opening intertitle: mother overworked and weary, children quarrelsome, babies snivelling, father drunk and violent. Next we are introduced to Maisie, the film's heroine and the eldest of the ten Burrows children, at work as a waitress: smart, pretty, polite, and smiling, yet capable of handling with firmness and determination customers' sexual advances. If the other Burrowses are specimens of the 'weeds' referred to in the introduction, this weed-choked garden has somehow produced a perfect rose in Maisie.

What is already implicit in the contrasting characterizations and locations of these first two scenes—that Maisie does not really belong with her family—is soon confirmed in the story that follows. The agency of the inevitable separation of Maisie from the Burrowses comes in the character of Dick Reading, a fireman stationed opposite Maisie's place of work, an only child who enjoys an affectionate relationship with his mother. The young pair are brought together by Dick's dog, and their encounter inspires in Maisie both intimations of erotic pleasure ('dim tremulous thoughts of waking womanhood') and fear of what yielding to such impulses will bring ('It's drudgery—drudgery—drudgery—then there'll be children we can't afford to clothe or keep'). Unwilling to face the prospect of becoming like her cowed and worn-out mother, Maisie refuses Dick's offer of marriage, despite the fact that she loves him. But Maisie's parting from her sweetheart also brings about her separation from her family: Maisie's brutish father, overhearing her telling Dick 'I'm afraid you'd be like my father in a few years', throws her out for her ingratitude:

> Now listen ter me, girl—if yer father's roof ain't good enough ter shelter yer—yer'd better pack yer fings and clear—and good riddance to yer.

Maisie, like many another romantic heroine, is now alone in a world which turns out to be full of pitfalls for an attractive and sexually innocent young woman. On her first night away from home, she falls into the questionable company of prostitutes, and narrowly avoids losing her virtue to a man whose wife's frigidity has forced him to seek solace elsewhere. Fortunately, he turns out to be a gentleman and Maisie escapes intact, only to be frightened out of her wits ('Forms that lurk in every shadow—Faces that leer at every turn') merely by finding herself where no decent girl ought to be—out alone on the streets. Desperate, she tries to commit suicide by jumping off a bridge, but in a suspenseful scene involving much cross-cutting, is saved from drowning by Paul Sterling, a successful and comfortably off writer whose wife immediately takes pity on Maisie and offers to take her home. But Maisie's troubles are far from over: her suicide attempt brings her to court, where she is sentenced to two months' imprisonment.

Through a series of lacks—of a proper family life, of a man, and (most crucial of all) of a particular type of knowledge—Maisie is exposed to a whole range of perils. It is not merely that, in common with many an *ingénue* heroine of silent cinema, Maisie's virtue is constantly at risk: so too are her liberty and even her life. But the conventions of the narrative genre to which this story belongs—the popular romance—as well as the imperatives of the vehicle of its telling—popular cinema—require a happy ending. For this to be possible, Maisie's lacks must be liquidated and Maisie herself brought from danger to safety.[31]

The first lack—of a family—is in some measure dealt with by the intervention of the Sterlings, who take Maisie into service as a maid when she is released from prison. The Sterling family is all that the Burrowses are not: small, financially secure, and happily ensconced in a delightful home with a huge garden. The Sterlings have three charming and adored children, whose antics awake in Maisie 'the longing that has dwelt unaltered through the ages in every woman's heart'. But it is clear that the Sterlings cannot provide Maisie with the 'proper' family she lacks. Aside from a not inconsiderable class difference, Maisie can never be a 'real' mother to the Sterling children; nor even, as it turns out, can she be an adequate mother-substitute: they already have a nanny, and when Maisie is eventually given sole charge of them, disaster strikes—the house catches fire. Maisie may long for happiness of the kind the Sterlings enjoy, but she can never attain it by becoming part of that family. Instead she must deal with the lack of a proper family by making her own, which in the world of the popular romance means only one thing—the liquidation of another of the narrative's lacks, Maisie's of a man. Maisie must marry.

And that, of course, is exactly how the story—'like all true fairy tales', in the words of the film's closing title—ends. But what of the problem that separated Maisie in the first place from both her man and her family of origin? What of her fear of the consequences of marriage? Here again the agency of the Sterlings—or more precisely that of Mrs Sterling—is crucial. For it is Mrs Sterling who explains that what Maisie most fears is not after all inevitable:

1. IT: 'I will tell you a story, dear, a parable. There were two men each owning a garden of roses, but the trees of the first grew wild and untended'.
2. MCU two-shot Maisie and Mrs Sterling talking. FADE.
3. MS a sickly-looking rose bush.
4. IT: 'But though the blossoms grew heavy on the branches, they were meagre and colourless'.
5. MCU several unhealthy looking roses. FADE.
6. As shot 2.
7. IT: 'But the other was wiser—armed with knowledge he pruned his tree carefully'.
8. As shot 2.
9. MCU hands pruning a rose.
10. IT: 'Each bud was cared for and nurtured, and though his roses were fewer—each bud had turned into a perfect flower'.

31 This approach to the analysis of narrative is based on the work of Vladimir Propp, *The Morphology of the Folk Tale* (Austin, TX: University of Texas Press, 1968).

11.	MS	some perfect roses. DISSOLVE.
12.	CU	one perfect rose. DISSOLVE into face of baby. FADE.
13.	MS	two-shot Maisie and Mrs Sterling talking. Maisie remains unreassured.
14.	IT:	'Before I married, I used to think of my lover— somewhere in the world—searching for me—passing all others by—never resting till we met—and I think this is true, dear'.

Maisie, the rose among the weeds, now has it within her power not only to produce perfect roses of her own, but also to secure lasting conjugal bliss with a true lover. All that remains is for the former sweethearts to be reunited in a dramatic scene in which Maisie is rescued from fire by Dick and his ever-faithful dog. Not only does Maisie get her man, she will, it is suggested, also enjoy both 'married love' and a planned family.

Maisie's Marriage may be read at a number of levels, though only one of these is strictly necessary to the production of a 'culturally competent' reading of the film. At this most readily available level, *Maisie's Marriage* may be regarded as an ordinary love story, with elements of drama, suspense, and action, and with characterizations and narrational strategies typical of the fiction cinema of the period. Among these are a 'woman-in-peril' theme (Maisie endures trials by water and by fire); drama and suspense created through action and cross-cutting (evident notably in the two scenes in which Maisie is rescued); tender love scenes (Dick's proposals of marriage); melodramatic conflict (family rows, Maisie in court standing trial for attempted suicide); sentimentality (Dick's dog, the Sterling children, their kittens); themes of female virtue and male rapacity (two scenes in which Maisie deals with sexual harassment at work, her excursion into London low life with the prostitutes); and a 'fairy-tale' ending (the wedding of Maisie and Dick in the final scene). All things considered, *Maisie's Marriage* is certainly readable as no more complex than a commonplace popular romance, in which lovers are parted through no fault of their own, and after a series of vicissitudes are reunited and marry.

In this type of story, the narrative pivots on the cause of the lovers' parting. In *Maisie's Marriage*, it is fear—fear not so much of sex itself as of what the heroine sees as its inevitable consequences—which separates the lovers. A satisfactory resolution of the narrative calls for a dissolution of Maisie's fears about sexual love and marriage, which is brought about in turn by her enlightenment on certain issues. It is at exactly the level of questions of sexuality, sexual pleasure, family limitation, and marital harmony that the film exceeds its purely narrative enunciation, embodying a discourse that, while taking the narrative as its starting-point, also transcends it. This excess lies partly in what may be termed the moral address of the film, and it is at this level that the 'message' of *Maisie's Marriage* is articulated.

By definition, narrative films with 'messages' adopt a position on, or speak on behalf of, issues which are in some sense external to the individual fiction in question, but are nevertheless dovetailed with it. The merits of such films are commonly judged according to the seamlessness with which fiction and 'message' are interwoven, since there is always a risk that the one may dominate the other. If the 'message' dominates, a film can be dismissed as 'mere' propaganda, while if the story is dominant, it easily becomes submerged, or—and this may simply be another way of saying the same thing—the film may open itself up to a range of different, and potentially conflicting, readings. Given the ascendancy of fictional narrative in cinema and the expectations this generates in audiences, the latter type of 'film with a message' can be rather unstable as a bearer of meaning. If *Maisie's Marriage* is considered in these terms—for fiction cinema had already achieved institutional dominance well before 1923—it is clear that the film belongs to the second category: that is, as a film with a message, if not as a romantic narrative, it may be regarded as in some degree 'open' and its moral message optional. It may nevertheless be useful to look at the film from the point of view of its enunciative qualities—as it articulates discourses through which different meanings are produced—if only because this raises the question of the precise conditions under which particular readings of a film become available.

This is pertinent to the question of the 'moral lessons' of *Maisie's Marriage*. For in order to read the film as being 'about' birth control, or 'about' sex or sexual pleasure, certain sorts of knowledge must guide its reading: for example, a prior awareness of the existence of Marie Stopes, of the general tenor of her ideas, and perhaps a more direct acquaintance with the content of such books as *Married Love* and *Wise Parenthood*. The events surrounding the various attempts at suppressing the film would certainly suggest that such knowledge was at issue. All parties involved in these events agreed that the film's capacity to disseminate ideas, to make money, or to make trouble, lay precisely in its association with the name of Marie Stopes and all that this implied, particularly in the summer of 1923. The conflict was never really about the film's content: it was about the conditions in which it was constructed as a film with a particular message.

What is the nature of this embattled message of *Maisie's Marriage*, then, and how does it engage those discourses which allow the film to be read as bearing a particular message? First of all, the message is not unitary: it incorporates a number of voices, some of which are more insistent than others. Among the most insistent must be the relationship the film sets up, notably in the scenes in the Burrows household, between large families, poverty, and unhappy home life. However, to make a connection between these things and the failure to limit fertility probably calls for a certain amount of knowledge about birth control, for the point is certainly not made explicitly in the film. Secondly and relatedly, it might be inferred from the ways in which Dick and his mother and more particularly the Sterlings are represented, that small families are happy and healthy families. Again, this does not on its own call forth the conclusion that they may be so by intention more than by chance, though this was hinted at in the one intertitle deleted at the BBFC's request. In explaining to Dick why she will not marry him, Maisie says: 'Your father died before he did the harm mine's done.'

It is in the sequence in which Mrs Sterling tells Maisie the parable of the rose growers, though, that the film approaches the birth control question more directly. The pruning metaphor, taken directly from *Wise Parenthood*,[32] encapsulates Marie Stopes's characteristic combination of eugenic and health/welfare arguments on behalf of birth control. To readers of the book among the film's audience, the reference would be obvious. But the sequence condenses into a few shots a rather specific set of pro-birth-control arguments (which would not have been universally endorsed even within the birth control movement itself). These images function purely metaphorically and their meaning is in no measure fixed by the intertitles. On its own, then, the 'parable' remains relatively 'open': though in the shot in which a close-up of a rose dissolves into a baby's face, it does provide the film's least oblique allusion to birth control. The metaphor of pruning is anchored to some extent, then; though significantly, not verbally. Contraception must remain unspoken in the text.

A 'moral' reading of *Maisie's Marriage* extracts is more than simply an endorsement of birth control, however, even if this might be its readiest message. The film is also 'about' sexual pleasure in marriage, which was in fact the central topic of *Married Love*. According to Stopes, the control of fertility was a necessary, but by no means sufficient, condition of marital happiness. She advanced the view—revolutionary in its time—that sex was a good thing (though only within marriage) and its enjoyment a positive value in itself, essential to conjugal harmony and family contentment. To this end, she exhorted husbands to be sensitive to their wives' sexual needs and desires, and both husbands and wives to perfect their love-making techniques.[33] Nothing of this, of course, is explicit in *Maisie's Marriage*, though to readers of *Married Love* references to Stopes's views on sex would be obvious enough at various points throughout the film.

The scene in which Maisie visits a nightclub ('A mystic underworld behind closed doors, where Bacchus and Aphrodite fox-trot to a negroid Pan') is one such moment. She is paired off with a man, manifestly drunk, who confides in her that the wife he loves is frigid ('Man's a man—flesh and blood—can't mate with an icicle!'). In the subjective sequence which follows, the man's affectionate advance to his wife is rebuffed, while she devotes her attention to a pet pekinese. In *Married Love*, Stopes suggests that if married couples were to cultivate an enjoyment of sex for its own sake, husbands would have neither the need nor the desire to resort to prostitutes,[34] an eventuality which would evidently take care of several social problems at a stroke. Similarly, a scene involving the Sterling children and their pregnant cat invokes Stopes's arguments in favour of openness with children on sexual matters:[35]

32 Marie Carmichael Stopes, *Wise Parenthood: The Treatise on Birth Control for Married People*, 10th edn. (London: G. P. Putnam's Sons Ltd., 1922), chapter 1.

33 Stopes, *Married Love*, chapter 5.

34 Ibid., chapter 3.

35 Marie Carmichael Stopes, *Radiant Motherhood: A Book for Those Who Are Creating the Future*, 4th edn. (London: G. P. Putnam's Sons Ltd., 1925), chapter 18.

Child: Why must we be special kind to Amelia, Mummy?

Mrs S: It's because Amelia is going to be a mother and have several little kitten-children just as I have you.

For Marie Stopes, sexual pleasure in marriage and a frank and open attitude to discussion of sexual matters went hand-in-hand with a happy and loving partnership between husband and wife. The flamboyantly sentimental manner in which this aspect of Stopes's teaching was at times expressed in her writings[36] also has its echoes in the film, where such expression fits well with the generic requirements of the romantic narrative. As Mrs Sterling says to Maisie,

> Before I was married, I used to think of my lover—somewhere in the world—searching for me—passing all others by—never resting till we met—and I think this is true, dear.

To a considerable extent, then, *Maisie's Marriage* is readable as a film with a message by virtue only of its implication within discourses on sexuality, sexual pleasure, and birth control. It acquires its moral address in its engagement with such discourses, especially as these latter are articulated in the writings of Marie Stopes. This does not, however, mean that a moral reading of the film was available only to readers of Stopes's books, simply that prior knowledge of this kind offers the readiest access to a certain reading of the film. Stopes's name was known to millions who had never read a word she had written: she was a highly controversial figure and her work touched on topics which had the seductive lure of the taboo. Moreover, at the time *Maisie's Marriage* appeared, her court appearances in the Sutherland libel suit had placed her in the forefront of public awareness. If many people did not know precisely what Marie Stopes's ideas were, they certainly knew what they were about: sex and birth control. Whether the name of Marie Stopes was attached to them or not, these were burning issues of the day. It is in this context that the moral address of *Maisie's Marriage* must be understood. To the extent that such an address speaks through the film text, it may be heard in part or in whole; soft and muted, or loud and clear. Indeed, it need not even be heard at all, for the film is perfectly intelligible without it. And yet it was the film's moral address that inspired the mobilization of all the machinery of censorship; and it is precisely through censorship that the film is constructed as troublesome, as conveying a 'controversial' message. In this sense, censorship did for the film what the film could not have done for itself.

But if *Maisie's Marriage* acquires certain meanings by virtue of discourses originating outside the film text itself, such meanings pervade the text at an unconscious as well as at a conscious level. These are centred upon the problem of *knowledge*. Maisie lacks knowledge of a particular kind, and it is Mrs Sterling who, with her happy family and loving husband, possesses and passes on the knowledge that Maisie lacks. In this respect, *Maisie's Marriage* departs somewhat from other 'films with a message' of the period, which tend to construct institutions

36 'The half-swooning sense of flux which overtakes the spirit in that eternal moment at the apex of rapture, sweeps into its flaming tides the whole essence of man and woman . . . .' (*Married Love*, p. 130). This is by no means untypical.

and practices such as science, medicine, social welfare, and the law as repositories and agencies of knowledge. Even where, in line with the demands of narrative cinema, such knowledge is spoken by a character in the fiction, that character invariably stands in for an institutional source. But if the Mrs Sterling character in *Maisie's Marriage* is a stand-in, what exactly is she representing? Women's traditional knowledge of matters emotional, sexual, and reproductive? Possibly, but the portrayal of the Sterlings—of Mrs Sterling in particular—suggests otherwise: that Mrs Sterling, independent-minded, happily married purveyor of useful knowledge and good advice, is none other than Marie Stopes herself.

This conclusion acquires added force from an examination of the class relations of knowledge proposed in the film. The working class is constructed as either lacking in knowledge, or incapable of articulating knowledge, or both. Yet since the narrative demands that the working-class heroine acquire it, the missing knowledge must be provided from some source. Sure enough, it is: and a middle-class woman, who also happens to be the employer of its recipient, is that source. Knowledge is imparted, then, not so much through gender solidarity—a woman passing on female lore to another woman—as through a relation that, for this one purpose only, crosses a social class divide. It is class difference, then, rather than gender solidarity which here provides the condition for the communication of narratively crucial knowledge. The 'truth' about sexual pleasure, about birth control, about married love, is not universally available in society, nor is it evenly distributed between the different classes. But it can nevertheless be communicated across class barriers by good works—acts of personal kindness, generosity, or patronage by the middle class towards the working class. If this sums up Marie Stopes's personal view of her mission to educate the working classes in matters sexual and reproductive, it represents only one of several positions in circulation at the time within the birth control movement on the question of the dissemination of knowledge.[37] In this sense, in its subtextual address, *Maisie's Marriage* adopts a somewhat partisan stance in its advocacy of birth control—a stance precisely privileging Marie Stopes (or 'Marie Stopes').[38]

At the same time, however, the subtextual organization of knowledge in *Maisie's Marriage* as originating in 'Marie Stopes' may enter into conflict with the narrative and cinematic imperatives of the genre to which the film belongs, and which produce its most insistent reading. If the popular romantic narrative requires that lovers be subjected to needless separation in order that they may ultimately be reunited, it also demands that the reader understand more than the unfortunate couple about exactly what it is that has separated them. The reader must be aware that the lovers' parting is unnecessary in order that the pleasure of its poignancy may be fully indulged, while the reader remains safe in the knowledge that matters can, and certainly will, be sorted out in the end. In the case of *Maisie's Marriage*, then, generic imperatives would suggest that spectators of the film ought to know what Maisie does not know. But, as has been noted, while in 1923 some audience members

37 Dowse and Peel, 'The Politics of Birth Control'.

38 Here Stopes—regarded as 'author', as a creative subjectivity behind the film to which her name is attached—is to be seen as distinct from 'Stopes'—a convenient label for a subtext, a structure which underlies the film but is not reducible to the input or conscious intent of a person or persons. See Peter Wollen, *Signs and Meaning in the Cinema* (London: Secker and Warburg, 1972), pp. 167–8.

might well have been in this position, many undoubtedly would not: for this would call for knowledge which was in many respects esoteric at this time.

To the extent that *Maisie's Marriage* addresses a knowing spectator, and to the extent that readers of *Married Love* and *Wise Parenthood* would be forearmed with the necessary knowledge, the film's address must surely be, in some degree at least, class-specific. Given the social composition of the book-buying public, the film divides its audience, more or less along lines of class, into groups with differing narrative viewpoints. Since the film was constituted as censorable almost entirely in regard to its status as a 'message' film, the problem from the BBFC's point of view was the section of the audience that did not know—namely, the working class.

It has already been argued that the excess of censorship activity inspired by *Maisie's Marriage* had a great deal to do with the film's association with the name of Marie Stopes. And it is clear that the various parties involved in the censorship process were well aware of this, too. They were obviously at some level conscious also of the film's instability as a carrier of knowledge of certain kinds. The BBFC's most significant demands—that the title *Married Love* not be used and that no suggestion be made in advertising the film that it was based on Marie Stopes's book—show this clearly enough, for they are aimed precisely at inhibiting the availability (especially, presumably, to that section of the audience that 'did not know'—the working class) of a 'moral' reading of the film. Hence the strongly expressed irritation of both Censors and Home Office officials, and the unprecedented resort by the latter to direct intervention at local level, when infringements of these prohibitions came to light.

But Marie Stopes's figuration in *Maisie's Marriage* operates at several levels, not all of them subject to the operations of censorship. First, and most obviously, Stopes figures as the film's author: in the opening title, she is co-credited (complete with academic qualifications) with its writing:

G. B. Samuelson presents
MAISIE'S MARRIAGE
A Story specially written for the Screen
by
DR MARIE STOPES DSc PhD
in collaboration with
CAPTAIN WALTER SUMMERS

At this level, censorship was powerless to intervene, much as those involved might have wished to do so: Marie Stopes, leading light of the Society of Authors, was in a position to see to it that she kept her writer's credit, on the screen at least.[39] As regards the film's advertising and promotion, these matters rested ultimately in the hands of the film trade, of exhibitors in particular, rather than either with Marie Stopes on the one hand or with the Film Censors on the other.

39 On Stopes's protest to the Home Office that attempts were being made to delete her name from the film, S. W. Harris expressed the private opinion that 'I never imagined this could be part of the undertaking (desirable as it might be!).' PRO-HO 45/11382, handwritten Home Office minute, 12 July 1923

Secondly, and more importantly, Marie Stopes—or perhaps rather her writings and other propagandizing activities—figures as the locus of that knowledge which makes possible a reading of *Maisie's Marriage* as a film with a certain message. It is at this reading, as has been suggested, that the operations of censorship were largely directed. But even these efforts at prohibition had unexpected, even contradictory, effects: far from limiting the availability of a 'moral' reading of the film, they actually proposed such a reading, certainly once the prohibition was made public. Finally, though, there is one more level at which Marie Stopes—or in this case 'Marie Stopes'—figures within the film: this is in its subtext, in which 'Stopes' is constituted as the enunciative source of narratively crucial knowledge. The subtextual level is beyond the reach of any institutional practices of censorship. As the BBFC's paltry demands for alterations indicate, there was little in the film's surface content that could be regarded, in terms of these practices, as 'prohibitive'. Apart from serving to justify the BBFC's delay in releasing the film, the very minor changes asked for are perhaps to be interpreted as symptomatic of an awareness—in part conscious, in part unconscious—that the real roots of the film's troublesomeness lay elsewhere..

Part III Institutional Histories

7 Copyright Protection in Theatre, Vaudeville, and Early Cinema

JEANNE ALLEN

Recent film theory and criticism have explored the relations between modes of visual representation and the socio-economic relations that pervade a culture in a particular era. John Berger and Jean-Louis Comolli have described those qualities of representational style which affirm and support economic practice and social relations. In *Ways of Seeing* Berger[1] argues that oil painting dominated visual representation in Europe between 1500 and 1900 because its illusionistic capacity to capture the texture, lustre, solidity, and tangibility of possessions was congruent with new attitudes towards property and exchange. Oil painting defines the real as 'what you can put your hands on'. Similarly, Comolli refers to the late nineteenth-century emergence of film as a manifestation of the 'ideology of the visible' which dominated that century:

> The second half of the nineteenth century lives in a sort of frenzy of the visible. . . . There is again the development of the mechanical manufacture of objects which determines by a faultless force of repetition their ever identical reproduction, thus standardizing the idea of the (artisanal) copy into that of the (industrial) series.[2]

The process by which certain modes of representation become dominant in society rests for Berger and Comolli on a sympathetic congruence between ideology and the technical qualities of artistic creation. But the actual social practice which affirms one form of artistic creation over another is described or implied by both as the operation of public preference, the audience's intuitive recognition that ideology is best served by this artistic practice.

1 John Berger, *Ways of Seeing* (Harmondsworth: Perguin, 1972).

2 J.-L. Comolli, 'Machines of the Visible', in T. de Lauretis and S. Heath (eds), *The Cinematic Apparatus* (London: Macmillan, 1980).

This discussion of the relations between theatre, vaudeville, and film in the USA at the turn of the century, an era of inter-media competition for the American audience, will discuss in concrete and specific terms the relation between cultural ideology and modes of artistic representation by analysing how one social institution, the legal system, served a critical role in translating the 'ideology of the visible' into the business practice of American mass entertainment industries.

Long before the current critical debate outlined the issues of art's material significance, economic and legal circumstances required that courts make determinations about art as material/intellectual property. The courts were asked to arbitrate the claims of competing mass culture industries, and whether those decisions were philosophically valid is perhaps less an issue than that those decisions contributed to the relative success of various kinds of mass entertainment.

What Comolli and others have referred to as the 'ideology of the visible' emerges as a governing principle in the legal decisions concerning the intellectual property of mass culture at the end of the nineteenth and the beginning of the twentieth centuries in the USA. As a means of defining the reality of property in an era of big business, the courts' decisions to protect the material form of an idea from being duplicated in a visually intelligible and appreciable way rested on the premise that property (reality) took primarily visible forms.

Properties which lent themselves most readily to a visible identification were best protected by law. And as a corollary, the commodity which could best be protected against theft provided the safest basis on which to invest the large sums of money required to market a product to mass audiences. What Comolli describes as the ideology of an age was translated into explicit legal decisions which provided a strategic weapon for an entertainment industry whose product was well adapted to the courts' prescriptions.

Distinctions between originals and copies or forgeries, or between an artwork as physical artefact and the performances directed by the artefact, confronted judges and courts with philosophical questions concerning the essence of artistic creation as intellectual property. Those questions were complicated by arising in an era of transition from manual to mechanical means of production so that the issue of the basic identity of the work of art, or the question of wherein artistic originality lay, was challenged by the proliferation of the means and forms of expression in a highly competitive marketplace. The law's conception of originality and copy in an age of increasing mechanical reproduction did not offer the same degree of protection to these mass entertainments: consequently, the law of copyright can be regarded as a significant additional element in accounting for the relative ability of these theatrical arts to compete with each other. The law's premise of distinguishing original and copy, idea and material artefact, publication and performance proved better suited to protect the motion picture and control competition in that industry than either theatre or vaudeville.

In outlining key legal decisions that affected three forms of dramatic art which competed for the American audience between 1890 and 1920, this discussion will indicate (1) the significance of the industrial context from which these theatrical entertainments emerged at the end of the nineteenth century, (2) the problems of ascertaining the essential identity of artistic property to be protected by law, and (3) the significance of legal decisions on this matter in charting or directing the shape and relative success of these forms of dramatic entertainment in the world of national business enterprise.

Nineteenth-century industrialization in the USA was characterized by the mechanization of the processes of production. The greater economies of scale made possible by mechanization accompanied the quest for national distribution. 'The American System' of standardized interchangeable parts, assembly-line construction, and division of labour which constituted factory organization between 1830 and 1880 increased the level of production and lowered the per unit cost at the same time that the initial investment in machinery required an extension of the consuming audience to make this investment profitable. The quest for a national market, pursued first by the railroads, fostered the style of 'cut-throat competition' which business historians such as Thomas Cochran and William Miller have argued resulted in the big business practices of the 'age of the robber barons'.[3] Arrangements such as combinations, pools, interlocking agreements, and monopolies were attempts to stabilize the market and diminish the waste encouraged by massive competition and its duplication of effort.

In this era of mechanization and invention, a cornerstone in strategies of market control was the ownership and protection of a discovery which enhanced the competitive position of a manufacturer. The laws which governed intellectual property as possession underwent a process of refinement and abridgement in the nineteenth century as economic production was transformed by mechanical processes (patent law) and by modes of marketing that emphasized the reputation of the producer (trade mark) and the publicity for the product (copyright).

Patent and copyright law protects intellectual property: ideas, discoveries, and inventions. Despite national laws forbidding the operation of business monopolies in the USA, these two 'natural' forms of monopoly were allowed as designated by Article 1, Section 8 of the US Constitution giving Congress the power 'To promote the progress of science and useful arts by securing for limited times (17 years for patent, 28 for copyright) to authors and inventors the exclusive right to their respective writings and discoveries'. The patentee enjoys 'the exclusive right to make, use and vend the invention or discovery' and the holder of copyright has the sole liberty of 'printing, reprinting, completing, copying, executing, finishing and vending' the work.

As a principal foundation of commercial success, patents in the second half of the nineteenth century increasingly became less the domain of a single inventor and entrepreneur who founded a manufacturing business and more a product of research departments—factories of invention—of

3   T. C. Cochran, *Basic History of American Business* (Princeton, NJ: van Nostrarid, 1959).

major electrical and chemical industries. Gradually patent law, designed to protect the inventor's rights to the commercial benefits of invention, became industry's loophole to acquire the fruits of monopoly by buying patent rights, hiring inventors, and developing branches of engineering research to maintain superiority in patent production and control. Corporate legal departments grew and became an essential wing of management able to influence and respond to governmental legal policy regulating the terms of competition.

Competition between the related American theatrical entertainments of theatre, vaudeville, and film between 1895 and the 1920s was resolved by the end of that era in favour of film. Reasons for the supremacy of film entertainment vary from its relatively inexpensive attendance fee, the inability of vaudeville to satisfy the public demand for novelty, film's facility for more fully satisfying the audience's desire for realistic spectacle, to film's propensity for incorporating the appealing elements of theatre and vaudeville into a single readily transportable retail commodity. Public taste, cost advantages, and inter-media borrowing and absorption have been the most common explanations offered to account for the demise of vaudeville and the eclipse of the legitimate theatre by film in the first two decades of the twentieth century.

While factors of business competition proved the determination of survival and hegemony in American mass culture, they do not explore the comprehensive impact of industrialization and resulting business practices which emerged from the era of rapid mechanization in the USA. Differences in the ability of theatre, vaudeville, and film to compete in the marketplace are not described in terms of their relative degree of adaptability to industrial practice. Nevertheless, as entertainment commodities, each of these theatrical arts is tied to an exchange system governed by the nature of a basic property which is merchandised. That property is intellectual, a discovery or invention which is then presented to the public in some material form. In order to succeed commercially the property of the entertainment industries must be protected from piracy, theft, unfair competition. During the nineteenth century laws of copyright which sought 'to promote science and the useful arts' by allowing the inventor to enjoy the financial fruits of invention were increasingly applied to forms of mass entertainment.

Patent and copyright laws with their explicit reference to ideas and inventions, a domain of property which includes the arts as well as science and engineering, became a fulcrum of industry for the growing businesses of the popular arts and entertainment of the nineteenth century. Art as original ideas and as undergoing, like the rest of the economy, a transition to machine production similarly became a battleground for the laws which sought to protect artistic creation as property.

The very scale of production practised in this era suggested the urgency of determining the status of a work of art as a commercial property and the conditions that obtain for the protection and exploitation of that property. In the competition for business success, mass culture industries sought and responded to legal decisions which determined what aspects of their property could be controlled and defended and hence what pursuits might reward the considerable financial investment that national distribution required. Did one form of mass entertainment offer greater control, greater opportunity for monopoly protection? Did the law, in responding to mechanization and the possibility of reproduction and pirating, grant the same benefits to each culture industry? In particular, the competition between three coexistent dramatic entertainments—vaudeville, theatre, and film—demonstrates in fairly gross terms the triumph of that mass culture industry which was most suitably adapted to the practices of turn-of-the-century business and the legal structures which governed it.

American vaudeville grew out of the concert room, music hall amusements of American taverns of the 1850s and 1860s. The forms of entertainment practised there were not categorically distinct from the forms of popular entertainment that evolved out of Europe in the previous three centuries. The minstrel show's singing and dancing, circus acts of acrobatics and magic, the comic sketch or joke were tied to a pre-industrial folk idiom with a long history. Two modifications marked American vaudeville in the second half of the nineteenth century: the attempt to clean up and refine its image of drinking, brawling, and prostitution in order to appeal to a middle-class family audience (expanding audience size vertically along class lines) and to extend its system of distribution and exhibition which paralleled the nationalization of American industry and manufacturing; and, perhaps more directly, the evolution of the theatrical road show and syndicates (expanding audience size horizontally along geographic lines).

Credit for this transformation has generally gone to Tony Pastor and the partners, B. F. Keith and Edward F. Albee. Keith, more than any other figure in vaudeville's business history, has gained the reputation for institutionalizing vaudeville and making it pre-eminent among all competing entertainment forms at the end of the nineteenth century.

The reference is somewhat ironic if one compares the nature of the industries over which these entrepreneurs presided. While their roles might have been comparable, the businesses they managed were separated in many key aspects by a century of industrialization which transformed the USA. The vaudeville act *per se*, the product merchandised, bore little resemblance to other products of manufacture which pervaded the American economy and living style in 1900. The wax figures for the dime museums of Sylvester Poli, before he entered the vaudeville business, required a greater involvement with the world of industrial manufacture than did vaudeville. One might argue that in vaudeville the working classes of industrial America, and later its middle classes, found an anachronism, a reactionary mode of entertainment that bore few, if any, traces of the industrialized world of the workplace. Like the Currier and Ives prints of the 1840s and 1850s, vaudeville's pre-industrial appearance maintained nostalgic ties with a rural America and a pre-industrial Europe whose descendants migrated to the cities where they accommodated themselves to the new order of factory organization. Only rarely did the world of the machine make its way to the vaudeville stage, as when Singer toured the road-show circuit with his 'performing sewing machine' or 'The Speed Mechanics' dismantled and reassembled a Ford onstage in eight minutes.

While the vaudeville act itself was a non-mechanized popular art, the format for assembling the acts into a unified performance bore a resemblance to machine structure, as the photoplay for film continuity would a decade or so later. The vaudeville act was a discrete interchangeable unit in a system of eight or nine acts. Resembling a specialized machine component, it was performed three times a day, six days a week for as many weeks as the circuit lasted. Indeed, by changing circuits and achieving popular success, some vaudeville performers could present a single act for as many as twenty years, again not unlike those actors and actresses who entered the touring circuit of legitimate theatre and played The Count of Monte Cristo or Rip Van Winkle for decades. The vaudeville performer presented entertainment of a pre-industrial nature but in an industrialized format.

The fact that a performer could potentially become so identified with a single act suggests that the ability to possess or own an original act as a means of one's livelihood would be essential to the performer and to the employer who would compete with other vaudeville businesses or other entertainment forms in seeking the audience's patronage. Yet there seems to be little indication that a vaudeville act as an original idea or intellectual property enjoyed extensive protection of law at any period in the history of vaudeville.

Copyright protection generally lagged behind the business exploitation of intellectual property in the nineteenth and early twentieth centuries. The first US copyright law of 1790 included maps and charts as well as books and was extended to engravings, etchings, and prints in 1802. In 1856 dramatic compositions and the right of publicly performing the same were protected by copyright. Paintings, drawings, chromo-lithographs, statues, models, designs, photographs and their negatives were not protected until 1870, considerably after all these forms had been merchandised in a competitive market. This gap between the time when artistic products were marketable commodities and when they were protected by copyright allowed those businessmen who built the largest scale of distribution to maximize the exploitation of the artist's work commercially with minimal if any remuneration to the artist. Only social value granting unique status to the original protected the commercial value of the artist's property.

Copyright law generally manifested a lag in responding to commercial exploitation arising from mechanical reproduction, but vaudeville or variety acts seem never to have qualified for strong protection in the first place. Vaudeville was not tied to print or publishing, to a centuries-long tradition of artistically respectable entertainment, or to a mode of notational representation which was capable of making subtle discriminations. Its domain was effervescent, non-literary, too close to personal style and modes of behaviour belonging to public domain rather than private property. Originality lay in execution and subtle variation. As a kind of folk art derived from traditions of public entertainment, vaudeville was not well adapted to legally supported conceptions of respectable art, private property, or originality tied to material form which validated other artistic entertainments. For instance in the case of *White-Smith Music Publishing Co.* v. *Apollo Co.* in 1908 the court decided that a perforated piano roll was not an infringing copy of the musical composition embodied in the roll, because the roll was not a written or printed record of the musical composition in intelligible notation. Similarly the twin requirements of visual appreciability and intelligibility that were applied here were later applied to the motion picture soundtrack which similarly was determined 'not visually appreciable as to its underlying elements'. Although sound recordings were protected after 1909, the US courts ruled that once a recording of a musical composition was sold it was not protected by copyright from being played and broadcast by radio transmission. Music became a staple of radio programming requiring only the initial investment in the recorded performance of the composition. *The dominance of the concept of intellectual property as being visually perceivable and its copies being visually intelligible gives visual representation dominant legal and economic sanction.*

The trade papers of the period not infrequently offer advertisements or statements by outraged performers who claim that someone has 'stolen' their act which they first performed on such-and-such a date. And the pattern of big-time vaudeville breaking an act that was copied or duplicated by numerous small-time vaudeville competitors in major urban areas argues for the limited ability of performer and entrepreneur to gain legal protection.[4] One might argue that the lack of union power or perhaps the lack of sustained dependence on individual performers or acts by owners of vaudeville houses and chains precluded a forceful lobby for legal protection. The transiency of the performers, the lack of vertical integration in the business which would involve the vested interest of owner in performer, may have shifted the problem of theft to labour, unorganized at least until the 'white rat' strike of 1901, which was broken by non-union performers and 'special offers' to union members from owners.

Vaudeville acts might seek copyright protection at both state and federal levels. At the state level common law copyright, derived from British copyright law which dated back to the Stationers Act, gave artistic creation protection until publication at which point it entered the public domain. The case of *Ferris* v. *Frohman* in 1909 determined that performance was not the equivalent of publication under US law although it was so considered in Great Britain. This gave vaudeville performance qualification for property protection at the state level but the laws varied from state to state, they were not spelled out in the state statute books, and in the absence of decided cases in most states, lawbook writers attempted to forecast judicial reaction to particular controversies.

4 For example, 'Keith's Big Small Timer Cleaning Up In Boston', *Variety*, 7 October 1911; 'Big Managers Desperately After Big Small Time', *Variety*, 12 July 1912.

Although state protection is referred to as common law copyright, copyright *per se* is actually a federal property right. Common law copyright did not allow complete ownership without fear of strangers making similar use of the act for their own profit. This could be acquired only through federal copyright which, contrary to the operation of common law, required the registration of a description of the act with the Office of Copyrights. Until the Copyright Law of 1909, when the law offered protection to dramatico-musical compositions (a sketch consisting of a series of recitations and songs but containing little action or dialogue for example) vaudeville acts would have to have qualified under the provisions for dramatic or musical copyright. In these cases a notational system which bore a direct relation to the performance was necessary. As late as 1914 the courts ruled that the voice, motions, and postures of an actor and mere stage business possess no literary quality and cannot be protected by dramatic copyright. While vaudeville was both musical and dramatic in broad terms, the array of qualities the courts looked to to define drama and to tie musical performance to published compositions proved considerable obstacles for vaudeville performers. While musical copyright did protect the composer from having others publish and perform a particular song, the variety act which used music, dancing, some dialogue, action of various kinds generally had to qualify for dramatic copyright. The problems of defining a drama were indeed complex: courts used nebulous criteria of 'sufficient' plot and dialogue, narrative structure, 'morally uplifting' content, audience emotions raised above those personal emotions evoked by the lyric song.

In a number of suits alleging infringement, several characteristics of non-legitimate theatre performance (burlesque, revue, variety) were excluded from copyright protection. *Martinetti* v. *Maguire* involved the alleged copyright to a theatrical spectacle entitled *The Black Crook*, frequently cited as the beginning of burlesque in the United States. Judge Deady denied Maguire copyright protection both because *The Black Crook* lacked originality and because it was a spectacle. The latter label was based on the revue's scant dialogue and dependence on action: 'a sort of verbal machinery tacked on to a succession of ballet and tableaux. . . . To call such a spectacle a "dramatic composition" is an abuse of language, and an insult to the genius of the English drama'.[5] The ability of vaudeville acts to qualify for protection under dramatic copyright seemed partially tied to the extensive use of language, although the case of pantomime and later silent film posed a quandary for judges who later admitted that a performance could be dramatic without dialogue.

That lyric song might be regarded as producing a personal emotional response rather than offering a dramatic form focuses the issue of identifying dramatic originality in terms of the audience's emotional response. In 1868, in *Daly* v. *Palmer*, the court decided that *After Dark* infringed the copyright of *Under the Gaslight* because the former is 'recognised by the spectator . . . as conveying substantially the same

5 E. S. Rogers, 'The Law of Dramatic copyright', *Michigan Law Review*, vol. 1 (1902), p. 112.

6 'Dramatic Copyright', *The Law Journal*, 14 May 1869, p. 267.

impressions to and exciting the same emotions in, the mind, in the same sequence or order as the original'.[6] In *Bloom and Hamlin* v. *Nixon*, also in 1903, the circuit court of Pennsylvania's eastern district was asked to determine if mimicry of the performance of a song constituted an infringement of copyright. While they determined that imitation of the singer could not be regarded as infringing, the court reiterated the discrimination between lyric music which 'sounds the note of personal emotion' and drama: there is nothing dramatic, the court claimed, about either the words or the music.

The determination of emotional response as the basis of duplication of an original idea bears relation to the court's consideration of moral content in a theatrical representation. Judge Deady claimed an exhibition of women 'lying about loose' or otherwise is not a dramatic composition and therefore not entitled to the protection of the copyright act. In 1903, in *Barnes* v. *Miner*, the New York circuit court decided that *X-Rays of Society* and the act which copied it in format but not in exact content had neither literary nor dramatic merit and did nothing to 'promote the progress of science or the useful arts'. Again the court tried to discriminate between the two versions on the basis of the emotions they aroused and determined that they were different because the responding audience in one case was female and in the other male. Quoting from *Martinetti* v. *Maguire*, Judge Ray claimed that a real dramatic composition, if grossly indecent and calculated to corrupt morals, would not be entitled to a copyright.

After the copyright act of 1909, which introduced the category of a 'dramatico-musical composition', the court had to decide, in *Green* v. *Luby*, whether or not there was enough action and dialogue in addition to a series of recitations and songs to constitute a dramatico-musical composition. The question of what arts could be regarded as dramatic was decided in at least one instance on the basis of whether or not a series of events or incidents serves to form a connective narrative. In *Fuller* v. *Bemis*, Marie Louis Fuller filed for copyright in the office of the Librarian of Congress a description of a 'Serpentine Dance'. The dance consisted of a combination of lights, shadows, stage settings, and draperies in a striking tableau. When the dance was reproduced without authority, Fuller brought suit for an infringement of copyright. Judge Lacombe held that the serpentine dance was not a dramatic composition.

> It is essential to such a composition that it should tell some story. . . . An examination of the description of the complainant's dance, as filed for copyright, shows that the end sought for and accomplished was solely the devising of a series of graceful movements, combined with an attractive arrangement of drapery, lights and shadows, telling no story, portraying no character, depicting no emotion. The *merely mechanical movements* by which effects are produced on the stage are not subjects of copyright where they convey no ideas whose arrangement makes up a dramatic composition.[7]

7 Rogers, 'The Law of Dramatic Copyright', p. 114.

With its lower admission prices, greater number of performances and wide-ranging format, vaudeville enjoyed a position of pre-eminence among forms of theatrical entertainment in the USA; by 1905 it had achieved a rough parity with legitimate theatre in terms of number of theatres. Legitimate theatre shared with vaudeville a similar degree of response to the changes of the industrial era. The performance itself bears a few marks of the changing mode of production in the economy, while the system of marketing follows patterns familiar elsewhere in industrial society. But the principles of originality, narrative form, duplication of a part of the whole, visual resemblance between original and copy or intelligibility between notation and performance, worked more in favour of theatrical art than of vaudeville. Tied more closely to print and publishing, theatre enjoyed more thoroughgoing protection of its property of written document and performance.

Although a playwright could not copyright the basic idea of a play (for example, a man and woman from families feuding with one another fall in love), he or she could have protection for a published script and rights of performance. A novel could be adapted for the theatre unless the novelist published and copyrighted a dramatic version, and remakes or updated versions of older plays were permissible. Playwrights could not gain copyright for scenic contrivances or segments of the play unless they were ruled as central to the play's identity. The particular gestures or mannerisms of actors or actresses could not be copyrighted. Imitation of celebrity performers, then, was not ruled out by law.

Theatre's status as a traditional dramatic art and its documentation in a publishable format resulted in it being provided more protection by law than was vaudeville. Variations of a play's central motif or imitations of acting performances, however, were well within reach of business practice. Theatre costs, including distribution and exhibition, were greater than film, which partially accounts for film's competitive superiority in the entertainment industry.

Introduced to the theatre-going public in the period shortly after 1897 in vaudeville houses all over the country, film was much more a product of industrialization. The machinery of its production was closely related to mechanical engineering and photographic reproduction (electrical and chemical industries) common in that era of the factory. As the result of mechanical operations discovered and patented in the nineteenth century, film was fully within the domain of industries for which patents were a central property if not commodity. Indeed, the rise of a patents pool in the years between 1908 and 1918 which sought to monopolize exhibition equipment and tie the use of film to that equipment set a precedent for industrial business practice which, while it was legally terminated under anti-trust rulings, has reappeared as the basic *modus operandi* of film industry organization.

In addition to the patents on the machinery of production and exhibition, film copyright, like that of other entertainment industries, offered business entrepreneurs protection of their property and restraint on competition that was intensified by piracy and theft. In the case of

Edison v. *Lubin* tried before the Circuit Court for the eastern district of Pennsylvania in 1903, the court ruled that the Edison film, *Christening and Launching Kaiser Wilhelm's Yacht 'Meteor'*, was subject to copyright by the Department of the Interior under the title of a photograph. The act of Congress of 1870 which had extended copyright protection to photographs, it was argued, could include a series of 4,500 pictures 300 feet long as a light-written reproduction. The question of whether each of the photographs must be copyrighted individually was resolved by accepting the argument that

> the instantaneous and continuous operation of the camera is such that the difference between successive pictures is not distinguishable by the eye, and is so slight that the casual observer will take a very considerable number of successive pictures of the series and say they are identical.

That the film's value consists in its protection as a whole or unit additionally supported its being considered as a single entity. It follows, however, that injury to copyright protection consists not in pirating one picture, but in appropriating it in its entirety (does this open the door to the piracy of particular segments?). One wonders if this line of reasoning would eliminate the protection of original dramatic incidents within the course of a film narrative which the dramatic climax of *Under the Gaslight* (1914)—the railroad scene in the fourth act—had enjoyed in 1868.[8]

Protected under the photograph provision of the copyright act of 1870, film seems ideally synchronized to the courts' rulings on the relation between original and copy, which depended on a direct relation between notational system and performance, which emerged from the legal conception of intellectual property as material artefact and on criteria of visual appreciability and intelligibility. Film's security was reaffirmed in 1905 in *American Mutoscope and Biograph Co.* v. *Edison Manufacturing Co.* which upheld the 1903 ruling despite the fact that 'in taking the negatives the camera was placed in different locations'. In 1908 the Berlin Convention for the Protection of Literary and Artistic Works recognized the status of cinematographic works as subject to international copyright.

Despite film's compatibility with the law's philosophical premises about originality and intellectual property that had evolved out of copyright cases concerning theatrical entertainments—there may be several dramatizations of the same story, each capable of being copyrighted like the separate copyrights for a painting, engraving, or photograph with the same subject-matter—the case of *Harper and Bros et al.* v. *Kalem Co.* over Kalem's film based upon *Ben Hur* introduced a curious rupture between film as material artefact and film as performance. The Circuit Court for the southern district of New York ruled in this case that the production of film as material artefact did *not* infringe Section 4952, Revised Statute US of 1901 which gives the author of a book, and his assigns, not only the sole right of printing,

8   'Dramatic Copyright', p. 267.

but also the sole right of dramatizing it, and in case of a dramatic composition the sole right of performing or representing it publicly. Invoking the case of *White-Smith* v. *Apollo*, which involved the discrimination between sheet music and perforated music rolls, the court maintained the distinction between infringing the copyright of a book and performing rights. They ruled that as a photograph Kalem's film did not infringe a copyrighted book or drama (the material artefact is not a *copy* because the pictures only represent the artist's idea of what the author has expressed in words, the narrative idea is not copyrighted but rather the concept as expressed by printed words). But when the film is put on an exhibiting machine, it was argued, it becomes a dramatization and infringes the exclusive right of the owner of the copyrighted book to dramatize it as well as the right to publicly produce it. One year after *White-Smith*, the courts upheld the primacy of the visual. The parallel between sheet music versus perforated piano rolls and theatrical dramatization versus film passing through a motion picture projector (both involving similar conceptions of mechanical reproduction) was not maintained. The principle of visual intelligibility caused the courts to recognize filmic representation as a *copy* of theatrical dramatization, although they had ruled a performance of a song produced by a perforated piano roll did not infringe the copyright on the sheet music of the song.

Despite this limitation on films based on plays, the two competitive weapons of patent law (protecting production and exhibition) and copyright law (protecting the film commodity) were paired in the film industry in the early part of the twentieth century as they were in so many other American businesses gaining national and even international dominance. Such pairing was not matched by either legitimate theatre or vaudeville. I am not arguing here that this was the sole factor that enabled film to gain hegemony over both of its theatrical competitors by the end of the 1920s. I do think that the coincidence of the Motion Picture Patents Company and the Berlin Convention in 1908 granting film international copyright recognition argues for an extended examination of the importance of the legal structure's support for certain entertainment commodities. Explanations of financial success based on popular preference or a drive towards realism ignore both the degree to which mass culture entertainment at the turn of the century participated in an economic transformation and the degree to which laws protecting private property supported the success of particular commodities and financial arrangements marketing them.

Although many of the copyright infringement suits reveal the competition *within* the businesses of vaudeville, theatre, and film, the fact that small-time vaudeville was used to launch film and that legitimate theatres were converted to film theatres indicates that difficulties in copyright protection added a further argument for conversion. The national distribution orientation of theatrical circuit owners (for example the United Booking Office) demonstrates the emphasis on developing a commodity best suited to that structure of marketing. If film minimized the cost of distribution and exhibition relative to theatre and offered greater protection from reproduction and theft than vaudeville, it was better suited to the scale of business of the twentieth century.

The Copyright Act of 1909 extended copyright protection to two additional classes of entertainment: dramatico-musical compositions and motion pictures other than photoplays. While the category of dramatico-musical composition would pertain to vaudeville performance to some extent, it is nowhere near the blanket category of non-photoplay motion pictures. A dramatico-musical composition may have less dialogue or less narrative than straight drama but it must have music and dramatic structure. It isn't a joke, a skit, an acrobatic or juggling act. But a non-photoplay motion picture can be anything recorded on celluloid.

We generally discuss the relationship between film and reality as an issue of representation, realism, or illusionism. But motion pictures, like oil painting in Europe between 1500 and 1900, manifest a claim to reality by virtue of their *materiality*. Unlike ideas or concepts, they are copyrightable intellectual property. Like the electrical and chemical industries, film gained a natural monopoly through protection of intellectual property that aided the competitive drive to dominate the entertainment industry.

The relation between the application of laws protecting industrial property and granting monopolies protected by government to the film industry and to other businesses demands further exploration. Did the legal precedents set by non-film businesses concerning trade marks and copyrights, advertising labels and prints which mushroomed in the era of film's business growth service this entertainment industry which bore some close relations to them? In his analysis of the protection of industrial property, H. A. Toulmin Jr points out in 1915

> As is becoming the modern custom amongst the large corporations, moving pictures of scenes about the plant or of the processes of its manufacture are being taken. These moving pictures can be copyrighted as well as motion picture photo-plays which are taken in and about the plant; they are now largely used for advertising commercial institutions.[9]

Stuart Ewen has also referred to those short films of the 1910s which featured a particular product as the protagonist in a filmic melodrama.[10] This manner of 'advertising' a product had found predecessors in the nineteenth-century American theatre, when David Belasco had once (in 1912) presented a set which reconstructed Child's Restaurant in unique and complete detail (for which promotional service Child's stocked the set with food consumed during the performance).

The growth of mass advertising in the era during which these theatrical arts competed for the American public provided a backdrop of business concern for the protection of brand names, advertising slogans and strategies, and in some cases, promotional entertainment itself. The

9 H. A. Toulmin Jr., 'Protection of Industrial Property', *Virginia Law Review*, vol. 3, no. 3 (1915), p. 177.

10 S. Ewen, *Captains of Consciousness* (New York: McGraw-Hill, 1977).

rulings that protected manufacturing similarly protected the intellectual property of entertainment industries and vice versa. The relation of entertainment industries to other businesses and mechanically produced commodities and their ability to succeed in the marketplace hardly seems incidental. By the 1920s the field of American mass entertainment demonstrated the hegemony of businesses adapted to and implicated in the structures of industrialization and the laws which governed and protected them.

8 'Spread like a Monster Blanket over the Country': CBS and Television, 1929–1933

WILLIAM BODDY

Exploring the Depression-era television activities of a US radio network may seem an unlikely historical project on two grounds: that a history of American television before its regulatory approval in 1941 or its commercial take-off point in 1947 is a tale of a non-event, at least as far as US consumers were concerned; and, moreover, that the various mechanical-scanning systems at issue in the early 1930s were technological dead ends whose limitations were already recognized by many in the field. Why explore technological blind alleys and commercial false starts? Furthermore, the subject's marginality seems compounded by a focus on the Columbia Broadcasting System, a young and much junior rival to the National Broadcasting Company in network radio, and a company which would play a relatively small role in the research and manufacturing sectors of the television industry. Conventional histories of US television view the substantial record of writing about the activity in television of the 1930s from the prospective of a reverse teleology from the technologies and institutional arrangements which marked the industry's full-blown commercial status. In such accounts, the history of television before 1940 is often reduced to a history of technology, starring the Radio Corporation of America's Vladimir Zworykin with walk-ons by Philo Farnsworth of Allan B. DuMont.

But such a teleological reading of TV's distant past neglects the richness of the record of the late 1920s and early 1930s, which saw not only technical experimentation (of both blind alleys and profitable future avenues), but also witnessed complex restructurings between

American motion picture, broadcasting and electrical manufacturing industries, and saw the beginnings of an aesthetic discourse on the television medium. In place of the technological teleology and the biological essentialism with which early television is often discussed (a progress of scientific conception, laboratory gestation, and commercial birth, growth, and maturity), I would like to briefly re-enter the thicket of early television activity in the USA to begin to unpack some of the larger determinations acting upon the medium. Television's commercial growth after World War II was so rapid, and television's debt to the programme forms and the commercial and regulatory structures of radio broadcasting so clear and pervasive, that one has the inescapable sense that the largest issues concerning the commercial application of television technology were in fact worked out before television's postwar era. Certainly television in the 1940s never underwent the period of improvisation and uncertainty that the radio industry did in the 1920s in the USA. Therefore, an examination of the manner in which one major actor in the early network radio industry—CBS—looked upon the prospect of television may underscore this larger, if often implicit, story of continuity and change.

Headed by the young cigar-company millionaire, William Paley, CBS saw television not from the prospective of a major electronics patent holder and manufacturer like RCA (owner of NBC), but from the perspective of a young broadcast network operator and entertainment company. CBS's record as an experimental television broadcaster from 1931–3 provides not only a rehearsal of many of TV's subsequent programme forms (comedy, musical programmes, sports, drama, and so on), but CBS's television activities at the time provide glimpses of how differently television was used by its tiny early audiences from the place television eventually found in the American home.

William Paley used the metaphor of the 'monster blanket' not to describe television in 1929 as he announced the swap of 50 per cent of CBS stock with Paramount Pictures, but rather to describe the chain of motion-picture theatres owned by Paramount. Paley envisioned a 'master combination' of the two companies and of the industries of radio and motion pictures brought about with the founding of the new medium of television. Paley's 'monster blanket', certainly an apt metaphor for the eventual structure of the network television industry decades later, was inspired not only by the geographical breadth of Paramount's theatres, but also by the major studios' vertical integration as producers, distributors, and exhibitors of feature films. Vertical integration provided the model for the subsequent network television industry and in particular for the deliberate moves by Paley after World War II to wrest talent, programme, and schedule control from broadcast sponsors in the new medium. Paley's tie-up with Paramount was mirrored by RCA's 1929 launch of its motion-picture subsidiary Radio-Keith-Orpheum. Such Depression-era links between the Hollywood studios and broadcast networks anticipate fifty years of uneasy manoeuvring between the two sectors in the US television industry, continuing through the present and prospective wave of studio and network acquisitions and consolidations.

Another possible inspiration for Paley's figurative monster blanket was CBS's successful 1930 takeover of a major talent agency, which by the mid-1930s would be responsible for half the bookings for major musical artists in the country. Inspired by the success of both the Music Corporation of America and NBC's own talent agency, CBS exploited this other model of business integration, where the functions of agent and employer were consolidated for network benefit, and which is also suggestive of several subsequent network practices in the television industry.

The precise role of television in Paramount's interest in CBS in 1929 is unclear. Zukor had approached the network's previous owner in 1927, and the unusual financial circumstances in Hollywood at the end of the 1920s brought about by the transition to sound (and the rivalry between RCA and American Telephone and Telegraph over sound-film patents and equipment sales) plus the expansion of theatre holdings by the studios complicate the picture. Paramount was silent on the background of the CBS deal except to note the appeal of network radio to boost motion-picture stars and theatre attendance. William Paley, however, was voluble on the stock swap, telling one group that the deal 'heralds an amalgamation of such far-reaching consequence as the linking up of a great radio network and the master organization in motion picture producing and exhibiting . . .'. The phrase 'we have made history' applied, Paley argued.[1] He elaborated:

> Spread like a monster blanket over the country is a great assemble of motion picture houses, exhibiting Paramount productions and those distributed by them. Over the same area a penetrating network of powerful radio stations has been engaging the attention of that same public and catering to its amusement needs in the home. There were great possibilities inherent if not actual that these two dominating forces in entertainment might find themselves in competition, if not in conflict. But now they have welded together in a master combination of direction, facilities, talent and resources and to the ultimate end that the public is to be better served and new peaks scaled in the arts of entertainment.
>
> It is more than an axiom that the public has to be amused, entertained. It is an economic necessity; what the motion picture has done for the worker wearied with a day of toil has been dealt with in pulpit and press and debated for years by statesmen and sages.[2]

After calling radio a 'lusty infant' in the speech, Paley corrected himself: 'Broadcasting is no infant; it is a giant. It makes people do things.' Suggesting that television's role was still unsettled, Paley remarked:

> One thing is certain, however. It is coming; whether it be in two years or five, it is sure to come. And with this amalgamation of interests we are prepared. Columbia can lean on Paramount for the new problems

1 William S. Paley, address, St Louis, January 1929 (Collection of the CBS Reference Library, New York). For a discussion of the CBS–Paramount swap, see Jonathan Buchsbaum, 'Zukor buys protection: the Paramount stock purchase of 1929', Cine-Tracts, vol. 2, nos. 3–4 (1979), pp. 49–62; and Michele Hilmes, Hollywood and Broadcasting: From Radio to Cable (Urbana, IL: University of Illinois Press, 1990), pp. 39–41, 50, 54.

2 Paley, address, St Louis, January 1929, p. 2.

3 Ibid., pp. 4–5.

entailing actual stage presentations in full costume to be broadcast, and Paramount knows it has an outlet in presenting its television features to the public.[3]

Paley argued that the eventual application of television was unclear: it might find a place in the home along the model of network radio, or a role in future motion-picture theatres, enhanced by supersized screens, full colour, and 3-D. 'The home can hardly be expected to be transformed into a modern theater having all the perfected devices and appurtenances available to the theater', he said in 1930.[4] Paley argued that television would not threaten the theatrical motion picture, and offered various rationales: that man was by nature a social creature ('he likes to rub elbows with his fellow men'); that science, like nature, always strikes a balance; and that 'moreover, someone will have to foot the bill for home television, and it is hard to conceive of an advertising sponsorship of the filmed efforts of Charlie Chaplin, Mary Pickford and Douglas Fairbanks'.[5]

4 William S. Paley, 'Radio and entertainment', in Martin Codel (ed.), Radio and Its Future (New York: Harpers, 1930), p. 66.

5 Ibid., pp. 63, 65, 67.

Richard W. Hubbell's *4,000 Years of Television* in 1942 described the euphoria surrounding the medium *circa* 1931:

> The word 'television' became DYNAMIC!!! It took on the attributes of a Lost Atlantis, a Fountain of Youth, a modern Midas Touch, the THING-TO-GET-IN-ON-THE-GROUND-FLOOR-OF! It would be lighting up every home, competing with the movies. It would KILL the movies! . . . it held out the allure of a Brunnehilde a-slumbering in the flaming crucible of science. A lot of people wanted to play Siegfried and rouse the maiden who slept.[6]

6 Richard W. Hubbell, 4,000 Years of Television' (New York: G. P. Putnam's Sons, 1942), p. 97.

CBS's prognosis for television in the years 1929–32 was mixed, but generally upbeat. Paley told the *New York Times* radio critic in 1932: 'I believe television will be in operation on a commercial basis by the end of 1932'.[7] In his announcement of the 1929 Paramount deal, Paley concluded:

7 Orrin E. Dunlap, The Outlook for Television, rev. edn. (New York: Harper and Brothers, 1932), p. 193.

> Our imagination can run wild, I know. I only want to point out, that whatever comes, be it television or any form of new entertainment which in any way has to do with screen presentation, stage presentation or radio presentation, that our amalgamation of interests finds us wholly prepared to take advantage of it. And that should be a comfortable feeling of satisfaction.[8]

8 Paley, address, St Louis, January 1929, p. 3.

With its significant interests in electronics manufacturing, CBS's senior network rival NBC/RCA also pursued television into the potential programme production centres of Hollywood. NBC/RCA maintained a typically imperial tone describing its ambitions in the new medium: as early as 1928, when applying for a commercial television licence, RCA told the Federal Radio Commission (FRC) that 'only an experienced and responsible organization, such as the Radio Corporation of America, can be depended upon to uphold high standards of service'.[9] A series of NBC memoranda outlines its approaches to early television and its relation to the film industry. NBC executive John

9 Quoted in Robert H. Stern, The FCC and Television: The Regulatory Process in an Environment of Rapid Technological Innovation (Ph.D. dissertation, Harvard University, 1950; New York: Arno Press, 1979), p. 56.

F. Royal wrote in 1931: 'The first television broadcast will, no doubt, be done by film. This will open up a very big question. Are we to make the film productions, or are they to be made for us? Can agencies have their own films made and submit them to us, the same as they do outside productions at present?'[10] Another NBC executive concluded in 1931: 'Obviously, the course to be followed is the creation of a film television department jointly directed by RKO and ourselves. The function of this department would be to create, obtain and supervise all film material to be used for television purposes.'[11] A memorandum from RCA's chief engineer in 1935 cited an earlier 'strong feeling' within the corporation that not only should NBC establish its own film production arm, but that it develop proprietary transcription standards to provide a 'handicap to the motion picture producers in entering the field'.[12] Another 1935 NBC memorandum sketched out the company's grand ambitions in television broadcasting:

> The ideal, of course, is that NBC should absolutely control its own network of stations. There may be, however, some opposition to this in these socialistic times. Obviously, a network of independent owners including perhaps many newspapers, is stronger, in a political sense, than a chain of stations owned by one organization. My own feeling is that a compromise can be reached through friendly interests, so that the National Broadcasting Company will be protected in its key cities and will be assured of cooperation in the other cities.[13]

The issues of industry structure in network television and the role of motion-picture studios in television programming have been perennial in the popular and trade literature since the 1920s.

In December 1930, the Federal Radio Commission approved CBS's application for an experimental television station. William Paley announced to the press: 'Through the Concerts Corporation and the Paramount–Publix Corporation, the Columbia network now has direct contact with famous concert performers, opera stars, and motion picture artists. I know they are all vitally interested in the progress of television.'[14] Like the 'monster blanket' of the vertically integrated motion-picture studio, the talent agency provided a model for network structure. Following the paths of the Music Corporation of America and NBC, CBS acquired and consolidated several concert bureaux and talent agencies in 1930, offering the benefits of what Paley described as 'combined, efficient and non-competitive management'.[15] Columbia Artists Bureau was making $2.3 million before commissions in 1935 booking live talent,[16] and the Columbia Concerts Corporation handled 50 per cent of the touring artists in the USA; *Fortune* wrote in 1935 of the Columbia Artists Bureau: 'unless you have a big name or are brought in by a commercial advertiser it is difficult to get a job with CBS through any agency except the Columbia Bureau'.[17]

In June 1931, CBS initiated experimental television broadcasts, seven hours a day, seven days a week from studios in the network's headquarters on Madison Avenue. The opening programme included

10 NBC memorandum from John F. Royal to G. F. McClelland, 29 August 1931 (Collection of the NBC Records Administration Library, New York).

11 NBC memorandum from H. B. Schaad to George Engles, 12 August 1931 (Collection of the NBC Records Administration Library, New York).

12 Letter from O. B. Hanson to W. R. G. Baker, 24 July 1935 (Collection of the NBC Records Administration Library, New York).

13 NBC memorandum from C. W. Horn to R. C. Paterson, 10 May 1935 (Collection of the NBC Records Administration Library, New York), p. 4.

14 William S. Paley, 'Columbia's television plans', press release, 16 December 1930 (Collection of the CBS Reference Library, New York), p. 1.

15 William S. Paley, 'Annual report', 16 January 1931, p. 4.

16 'Onward ever onward', Sponsor, 13 September 1965, p. 54.

17 'And all because they're so smart', Fortune, June 1935, pp. 154, 158.

talks by Mayor Jimmy Walker and Dr Walter Schaffer, chief engineer of Reichs-Rundfunk-Gesellschaft of Germany; a comic-monologue version of Little Red Riding Hood; two singing duets; a song by Kate Smith; a piano performance by George Gershwin; and an appearance by CBS's 'Miss Television', Natelie Towers.[18] Over the next eighteen months, CBS presented hundreds of vaudeville artists, singers, dancers, magicians, palm readers, sketch artists, animal acts, fashion shows, and make-up demonstrations. Notre Dame football games were presented via a miniature gridiron and a tiny metal football moved by invisible wires. Boxing sparring contests were staged on Tuesday nights in a small ring before the camera specially mounted on a movable pivot.[19] The *Television Ghost* began a regular series of television dramas described by CBS as 'Murder Stories as told by the ghost of the murdered. Closeup projection with weird effects'.[20]

The constraints of low sixty-line resolution, shallow depth of field, and a generally static camera demanded all the action be staged within an area of four square feet. Detailed instructions were offered for performers in a CBS memorandum, 'Hints for television broadcasters', written in 1931 by CBS's director of television operations, William Schudt:

> ACTION is a very important factor in visual broadcasting. It has been found that an active image comes through more clearly than any others. Act as much as possible in your program. Use your hands, head, and shoulders—also, where songs indicate, roll your eyes, and shake your finger at the televisor.
>
> While broadcasting you may move around in a TWO FOOT SQUARE SPACE without getting out of focus. Look into the light to either side of it. DO NOT LOOK up at the microphone.
>
> If you move out of the picture, the production man will give you a slight tap or push in the right direction. When such corrections are made, try not to look around in an amazed manner. Lookers-in will be quick to notice the unpremeditated move.[21]

The anniversary broadcast of the CBS station in 1932 inaugurated simultaneous audio transmission on the same channel and offered viewers the chance to witness an orchestra conductor directing a remote ensemble via television.

While CBS boasted of a New York television audience in 1932 consisting of ten thousand 'lookers-in', a CBS executive noted that 'The bulk of our television fan mail comes from enthusiasts scattered throughout a thousand-mile radius of New York . . .'.[22] The frequencies allocated by the FRC for experimental television broadcasting were in the short-wave portion of the spectrum, which meant that signals frequently travelled great distances. According to *Business Week* in 1931, television broadcasters admitted 'that interest in their efforts is confined almost entirely to the experimenter—the young man of mechanical bent whose principal interest is in how television works rather than in the quality of the images received'.[23] The *New York Times*

18 Columbia Broadcasting System, 'Television inaugural broadcast', transcript, 21 July 1931 (Collection of the CBS Reference Library, New York), pp. 2–9.

19 'Complete television log', *New York Sun*, 10 September 1932, p. 11; 'Grid games in miniature', *New York Sun*, 10 October 1931.

20 Joseph H. Udelson, *The Great Television Race: A History of the American Television Industry 1925–41* (University of Alabama: University of Alabama Press, 1982), p. 59.

21 William S. Schudt, Jr, 'Hints for television broadcasters', memorandum, 1931 (Collection of the CBS Reference Library, New York), p. 1.

22 William A. Schudt, Jr, 'Believes television for home is here', *New York Sun*, 18 June 1932.

23 'Television still has a long way to go', *Business Week*, 11 March 1931, p. 14.

shared some of CBS's television mail in 1932 from disparate points in North Carolina, Tennessee, Wisconsin, Vermont, Kansas, and Michigan. One viewer in Montreal told CBS:

> While experimenting with a television set last night we are quite sure that we intercepted some of your pictures from New York. We saw several pictures between 10.15 and 10.45 p.m. The first was a man and two others were women. They seemed to be different persons.[24]

24 Orrin E. Dunlap, 'Television's mail', *New York Times*, 7 August 1932.

Another viewer of CBS's experimental New York station, this one from Michigan, told the network:

> Last night I succeeded in bringing in the picture of a partially bald-headed man on my television machine. The image was quite clear, but I could not hold it long. There was some fading. The man moved his head quite often. The lips could be seen to move. I did not hear the sound. This is the only station I have succeeded in framing and I hope you can verify reception of this partially bald-headed person.[25]

25 Ibid.

Problems of recognizing television performers were not limited to distant lookers-in. CBS's director of television complained in 1931 that 'visitors at our studios who see our programs often make the mistake of comparing them with what they see on a movie screen'.[26] A reporter for the *Newark News* in 1931 was taken on a tour of CBS's studio, including a close-circuit screening of the next-door studio's transmission on a four-inch screen: the reporter concluded that 'the performers are in no danger of being recognized after a television broadcast'. She wrote that 'the whole effect is rather charming and the girls very pretty in a vague and fleeting way', but complained that 'the image is too illusory to be satisfying; you long to turn some dial to steady it and to bring it into sharper focus. Television is a promise but very little more.'[27] A sympathetic 1931 article in *Forbes* admitted that 'the sixty-line image leaves much detail to the imagination'.[28]

26 Schudt, 'Believes television for home is here'.

27 Charlotte Geer, 'Columbia's television', *Newark News*, 10 October 1931.

28 Thomas Calvert McClary, 'Television—its probabilities and possibilities', *Forbes*, 1 August 1931, p. 20.

Partisans of mechanical television appealed to faith in incremental and inevitable technical progress, and sought analogies to various other inventions at early stages—the automobile industry of 1904, the motion picture industry of 1908, the phonograph industry of 1910, and the radio industry of 1921. Others were unconvinced, such as the *New York Herald Tribune* which, in a 1931 article entitled 'Television needs an inventor', argued that

> present-day television is almost hopelessly imperfect and . . . little fundamental progress has been made since the first processes reached some success a few years ago.
>
> But if the history of other branches of invention is to be repeated by television what the world waits for now is an inventor with a new idea; something that will cut the knots of present difficulties not by the gradual loosening of detailed improvement, but by some totally new way of sending visual impulses over electric links.[29]

29 'Television needs an inventor', *New York Herald Tribune*, 1931.

After nearly two years and 2,500 hours of experimental programmes in television, CBS suspended the service on 23 February 1933. The network explained:

> We now feel that further operation with the present facilities offers little possibility of contribution to the art of television, and we have, accordingly, decided to suspend temporarily our program schedule . . . it is our intention to resume our experimental transmission as soon as we are sufficiently satisfied that advanced equipment of broader scope can be installed. Until then our activities will be confined to the laboratory and the maintenance of our close contacts with the other organizations in the field.[30]

There were several factors behind Columbia's abandonment of early television. It was increasingly clear that mechanical television had indeed reached the limits of its technology and that high-definition (400 lines or more) electronic television would require such wide bandwidths that the entire service would have to be moved into the relatively unexplored higher frequencies which would limit the service area of television broadcasters to line of sight transmission.

The financial contexts of broadcasting and the US economy were also changing. William Paley could tell his stockholders in January 1931:

> I dare say this is one of the few boards of Directors that can gather around a mahogany table these days to hear good news. I believe you all know in a general way that the broadcasting business has not suffered so severely as most others from the world-wide business slump, and I am happy to be able to tell you that the Columbia Broadcasting System has had at least a little more than its share of this good fortune.[31]

In 1929–30 CBS's gross sales were up 59 per cent, and its affiliates grew from thirty-eight to seventy-six stations. The prosperity continued through the early years of the Depression. Columbia's rapid growth allowed Paley to buy back the CBS stock which Paramount had purchased in 1929, since their agreement stipulated that Paramount buy back its stock if Columbia earned $2 million in profits within two years. That mark was reached by CBS in September 1931.[32]

While the repurchase left Paley with 40 per cent of the CBS stock and a check for $2 million from Paramount, it also brought a reorganization of the CBS board. Three representatives of the Wall Street investment bankers who had financed CBS's stock repurchase were added to the Columbia board, including Prescott Bush, George Bush's father.[33]

By 1933, however, network revenues were down, finally reaching 'the last industry to be overtaken by the depression', according to Paley.[34] The dim outlook for imminent regulatory approval of commercial television, the shortage of consumer or industrial capital to devote to the new medium, and the strategy of RCA at the time to move slowly in television, all contributed to a cooling of enthusiasm for television at CBS. Moreover, after the 1933 downturn, Columbia's radio

30 Quoted in Columbia Broadcasting System, 'Twentieth anniversary of CBS Television', press release, 10 July 1951 (Collection of the CBS Reference Library, New York), p. 5.

31 William S. Paley, 'Annual report', 16 January 1931, p. 1.

32 William S. Paley, *As It Happened* (New York: Doubleday, 1979), p. 84.

33 Frank C. Waldrop and Joseph Borkin, *Television—A Struggle for Power* (New York: William Morrow, 1938), p. 222.

34 William S. Paley, '1933 Annual report', 2 March 1934.

35 'And all because they're so smart', *Fortune*, June 1935, p. 81.

36 William S. Paley, 'Statement before an informal engineering hearing of the Federal Communications Commission', 16 June 1936 (Collection of the CBS Reference Library, New York), pp. 2, 4.

37 Laurence Bergreen, *Look Now, Pay Later: The Rise of Network Broadcasting* (New York: New American Library, 1980), p. 147.

38 William A. Nugent, 'Columbia Broadcasting's position: earnings growth shown during depression now slowing down', *Barrons*, 29 September 1941, p. 13.

39 Ibid; 'Thumbnail stock appraisal: six stocks with good peace prospects', *Magazine of Wall Street*, 26 December 1942, p. 289.

40 For discussion of CBS's plans for a Latin American radio network, see 'Plans Latin American network', *Printer's Ink*, 27 December 1940, p. 66; William S. Paley, 'Radio turns south', *Fortune*, April 1941, pp. 77–9; 'CBS Latin network', *Business Week*, 6 June 1942, p. 46; and E. Roderick Deihl, 'South of the border: the NBC and CBS radio networks and the Latin American venture, 1930–1942', *Communication Quarterly*, vol. 25. no. 4 (1977), pp. 2–12.

41 Peter C. Goldmark, *Maverick Inventor: My Turbulent Years at CBS* (New York: E. P. Dutton, 1973), p. 46.

revenues picked up again in 1934; by 1935 *Fortune* could write that 'to say that CBS has made money is to damn with faint praise'.[35] Between 1933 and 1937 television virtually disappeared in CBS's public announcements as the company became more concerned with enlarging its AM radio business and fighting back threatening regulatory reform. As the 1930s went on, CBS increasingly took on a sceptical, even hostile attitude towards new broadcast services like FM radio and television. William Paley's remarks before the Federal Communications Commission in 1936 were typical: 'Sudden, revolutionary twists and turns in our planning for the future must be avoided. Capital can adjust itself to orderly progress, it always does. But it retreats in the face of chaos.' Paley pointed to 'the need to go slow in adding to or revising the present commercial broadcast structure'.[36]

By the end of the 1930s CBS was a strong second to NBC in radio programme ratings and revenues; a Federal Communications Commission report in 1938 estimated the return on tangible investment at 80 per cent at NBC and 71 per cent at CBS.[37] The growing revenues of both CBS and NBC in the 1930s were built on rising radio-set penetration and the expansion of affiliate transmission facilities; network prime-time programming was generally produced or licensed by radio sponsors which controlled a specific 'time franchise' on a network schedule. By 1941, CBS was reaching 96 per cent of the nation's radio homes via 125 affiliates, having increased its number of affiliates 20 per cent between 1935 and 1939; and, as *Barrons* reported, 'no further expansion of revenues can be expected from the extension of facilities'.[38] At the same time, CBS in the early 1940s was in a very favourable financial position; in 1941 it had $7.5 million in cash in hand and an assets-to-liabilities ratio of over 2:1; in 1942 cash in hand totalled $12.5 million and the company's assets-to-liabilities ratio stood at 2.66:1.[39] Other investment opportunities were not far from hand for the cash-rich radio network.

By 1940 CBS was looking to new fields of investment for its enormous revenues from AM broadcasting: beyond television, these included the acquisition of Columbia Records Incorporated in 1939; plans for an eighteen-nation Latin American commercial network announced in 1940; and the company's acquisition of radio talent after World War II.[40] At the same time, with 90 per cent of its revenues generated by the sale of AM advertising time, CBS faced with some anxiety the prospect of technological upheaval in the form of FM radio and television in the 1940s. Its chief broadcast rival, NBC, was a subsidiary of the electronics giant RCA, and RCA's potential patent and manufacturing profits from commercial television were inextricably linked to NBC's plans for television. Despite CBS's five-person research staff under engineer Peter C. Goldmark begun in 1935, CBS's interest in television in the 1930s was primarily defensive, reacting to RCA's moves concerning the medium:[41] William Paley told a 1936 FCC hearing on possible allocations for FM radio and television: 'We should do nothing to weaken the structure of aural broadcasting in the present

42 Paley, 'Statement before an Informal Engineering Hearing of the Federal Communications Commission', 16 June 1936, pp. 2, 4.

43 'CBS moves in on television, plans transmitter on Chrysler Building', *Business Week*, 10 April 1937, pp. 20–1.

44 Columbia Broadcasting System, 'Gilbert Seldes is selected to direct CBS experimental television programs', press release, 20 August 1937 (Collection of the CBS Reference Library, New York).

45 William Boddy, 'Building the world's largest advertising medium: CBS and television, 1940–60', in Tino Balio (ed.), *Hollywood in the Age of Television* (London: Unwin Hyman, 1990), pp. 63–89.

band until experimentation in other bands has yielded us new certainties'.[42] In 1937 *Business Week* noted CBS's announcement of plans to build an experimental television transmitter at the top of the Chrysler Building in New York City, but added that no alliance of RCA rivals could challenge that company's patent position in television manufacturing.[43]

Despite CBS announcements in 1937 of the Chrysler Building transmitter, the creation of studios in Grand Central Station, and the appointment of the prominent critic Gilbert Seldes as its director of television, CBS leaders were cautious in their forecasts for commercial television.[44] An even more controversial period of CBS involvement in television was launched in 1941 when CBS unveiled the first of a long series of colour television schemes. That era was not to end until 1953 when the Federal Communications Commission, reversing an earlier decision, voted to kill the last of the CBS colour television proposals in favour of the RCA standards which prevail today in US television. But before that battle had ended, CBS had wrested programme supremacy from NBC to initiate a twenty-four year reign as the number one US network and had become the world's largest single advertising medium. But that is another story.[45]

9 Writing the History of the American Film Industry: Warner Bros and Sound

DOUGLAS GOMERY

1 Lewis Jacobs, *The Rise of the American Film* (New York: Harcourt Brace & Co., 1939), p. 297. The première took place on 6 August 1926: see *Variety*, 11 August 1926, pp. 4, 5, and 10.

2 Gerald Mast, *A Short History of the Movies* (Indianapolis: Bobbs-Merrill, 1971), p. 227.

3 Kenneth MacGowan, *Behind the Screen: The History and Techniques of the Motion Picture* (New York: Delacorte Press, 1965), p. 283; David Robinson, *The History of World Cinema* (New York: Stein & Day, 1973), p. 162; Peter Cowie (ed.), *A Concise History of the Cinema* (London: Zwemmer, 1972), p. 197; Laurence Kardish, *Reel Plastic Magic* (Boston: Little, Brown, 1972), p. 103; Kevin Brownlow, *The Parade's Gone By* (New York: Knopf, 1968), p. 657; Jean Mitry, *Histoire du cinéma: art et industrie*, ii (Paris: Editions universitaires, 1964), pp. 353–4; Georges Sadoul, *Histoire du cinéma mondial: des origines à nos jours* (Paris: Flammarion, 1949), p. 228.

4 A. R. Fulton, *Motion Pictures* (Norman, OK: University of Oklahoma Press), p. 155; Arthur Knight, *The Liveliest Art* (New

Numerous writers of the history of the American film industry have set forth the claim that Warner Bros' impending bankruptcy caused its innovation of sound. Lewis Jacobs, for example, writes: 'On August 26, 1926 [*sic*], Warner Brothers, in a desperate effort to ward off bankruptcy, premiered a novelty, the first motion picture with sound accompaniment, *Don Juan*'.[1] Textbook author Gerald Mast repeats the same assertion using slightly different language: 'Western Electric offered Vitaphone in 1926 to Warner Brothers, a family of struggling film producers whose company was near bankruptcy. The Warners had nothing to lose.'[2] Elsewhere Kenneth MacGowan, David Robinson, Laurence Kardish, Peter Cowie, Kevin Brownlow, Jean Mitry, and Georges Sadoul echo this conclusion.[3]

Other writers, coming after Jacobs's standard work, were not so bold. Some, like Arthur Knight, A. R. Fulton, and Henri Mercillon, ignore the issue of motivation.[4] Presto! Warner Bros adopted the new technology. Other accounts are a little more expansive, containing a sentence or two. Benjamin Hampton and Charles Higham (twice) credit Warner Bros' desire for more theatres, D. J. Wenden the overall industry structure, and Robert Sklar the industry's costly movie palaces.[5] Harry M. Geduld provides the longest account of the coming of sound in *The Birth of the Talkies*. Yet he avoids, and thereby complicates, this issue. For Geduld, Warner Bros first learned about sound because of an investment in radio. It then, for no apparent reason, adopted sound. Bankruptcy almost resulted when Warner Bros overcommitted itself in this one area.[6] Nowhere does Geduld explain why Warner Bros chose to gamble all its

York: Macmillan, 1957), p. 146; Henri Mercillon, *Cinéma et monopoles* (Paris: Centre d'études économiques, 1953), p. 18.

5 Robert Sklar, *Movie-Made America* (New York: Vintage Books, 1975), p. 152; D. J. Wenden, *The Birth of the Movies* (London: Macdonald & Jane's, 1975), p. 173; Charles Higham, *The Art of the American Film* (New York: Doubleday, 1974), p. 85; Charles Higham, *Warner Brothers* (New York: Scribner, 1975), p. 41; Benjamin B. Hampton, *History of the Movies* (New York: Covici, Friede, Inc., 1931), pp. 379 and 381.

6 Harry M. Geduld, *The Birth of the Talkies, from Edison to Jolson* (Bloomington, IN: Indiana University Press, 1975), pp. 107–8, 113.

TABLE **9.1. Warner Bros Pictures, Inc.: Net Profit and Loss**

Fiscal Year-Ending	Profit (Loss)
	$
31 March 1924	103,000
31 March 1925	1,102,000
27 March 1926	(1,338,000)
28 August 1926 (5 months)	(279,000)*
27 August 1927	30,000
31 August 1928	2,045,000
31 August 1929	14,514,000

Note: * A $669,000 loss at an annual rate.

Source: Warner Bros Pictures, Inc., *A Financial Review and Brief History: 1923–1945* (New York: privately printed, 1946), p. 28.

assets on an idea and system all its richer competitors had rejected, or how it financed all this new investment.

Warner Bros' published financial statements seem to support the Jacobs-inspired, traditional version. Using the data in Table 9.1, a narrative could be constructed in the following fashion. The company was losing large amounts of money, when on or about March 1926 it presumably decided to risk all on sound. Despite the mild success of *Don Juan*, the losses continued, albeit at a somewhat slower pace. But it was *The Jazz Singer* and its subsequent revenues in the beginning of 1928 which saved the company. Bankruptcy was averted; the turnabout was complete.

The 'bankruptcy hypothesis' is so well accepted that at least two scholars have employed it as a basis for their analysis of film and ideology. For example, Thomas Cripps writes:

> Warner Brothers, a studio of modest proportions and in straitened circumstances, saw 'talking film' as a gimmick that would attract revenue, while Al Jolson, a Broadway song-and-dance man, gambled on sound as a way to score a point on his rival, George Jessel. For the vehicle that would either carry Hollywood into the sound era or destroy both Jolson's career and the studio, they chose Samson Raphaelson's *The Jazz Singer* (1927).[7]

7 Thomas Cripps, 'The movie Jew as an image of assimilationism, 1903–1927', *Journal of Popular Film*, vol. 4, no. 3 (1975), pp. 190–207.

Even so sophisticated an analyst of film and ideology as Jean-Louis Comolli accepts the traditional explanation. He writes:

> It was necessary that Warner Brothers, a small company almost on the edge of bankruptcy, and which had nothing to lose, try its luck; the risk was, in August, 1926, the release and success of *Don Juan*, 'the first sound and singing film'.[8]

8 Jean-Louis Comolli, 'Technique et idéologie (5): caméra, perspective, profondeur de champ', *Cahiers du cinéma*, nos. 234–5 (1971–2), pp. 99–100.

Comolli goes on to conclude from this and other evidence that for the coming of sound technological change was not the moving force but rather the effect of the specific ideological functions served by the entrepreneurs of the American film industry. How much is Comolli's conclusion tied to this historical construct? Would it still hold if Warner Bros was *not* bankrupt?

Several factors can be isolated that are important for analysing any technological change. The innovating firm must, directed by its entrepreneurs, raise the necessary capital and devise a strategy to crack the market held by its competitors. Hence the innovator's situation *vis-à-vis* its competitors and the state of the business cycle must not be ignored. For Warner Bros' innovation of sound, every account of these factors has remained mere speculation, or has been sketched out only in the most superficial detail. Yet rich primary data do exist with which one can begin to answer these questions. During the 1930s Warner Bros and its principal licensor of sound equipment, Electrical Research Products, Inc. (ERPI), a wholly owned subsidiary of the American Telephone and Telegraph Company (AT&T), tangled in three major patent and contractual suits.[9] Secondly, in 1937 the United States Congress investigated AT&T's operations in non-telephone areas, including sound motion pictures. This probe produced several file drawers full of testimony, confidential memoranda, and almost all of ERPI's financial records.[10] Finally motion-picture trade publications, such as *Variety* and *Moving Picture World*, and general business publications like *Barrons* also charted the film industry's activities in the late 1920s. With these as yet unused sources, one can begin to revise the standard histories of the introduction of sound outlined above.

For Warner Bros one man secured the financial backing and provided much of the necessary business acumen. He was Waddill Catchings, the chief investment banker of Wall Street's Goldman, Sachs Company. A Mississippi-born graduate of the Harvard Law School, Catchings joined Goldman, Sachs in 1918. Not only an investment banker, he also authored treatises on economic problems. With William T. Foster he organized the Pollack Foundation for Economic Research in 1921, and co-authored two books during the 1920s on economic problems: *Business Without a Buyer* in 1926 and *The Road to Plenty* in 1928. Central to Catchings's economic theory was the necessity for the businessman–entrepreneur to take bold action. Only this behaviour, coupled with an adequate money supply, could ensure prosperity and eliminate severe depressions such as had occurred in 1920–1. Catchings demonstrated his faith in this principle in his investment work at Goldman, Sachs; during the boom of the 1920s he was the most optimistic of all the 'New Era' financiers.[11]

Warner Bros first came to Catchings's attention in December 1924. Henry A. Rudkin, senior partner of McClure, Jones and Reed, another New York investment house, advised Catchings that Warner Bros sought to expand and needed Wall Street help. McClure, Jones and Reed was too small to provide large-scale assistance. Was Goldman, Sachs interested? This seemed an extremely risky proposition even to Catchings. Up to this point, Wall Street had done little large-scale financing of motion-picture firms, with the exception of Famous

9 *General Talking Pictures Corporation et al. v. American Telephone and Telegraph Company et al.*, 18 F Supp. 650 (1937); *Electrical Research Products, Inc. v. Vitaphone Corporation*, 171 A 738 (1934); *Koplar (Scharaf et al., Interveners) v. Warner Bros Pictures, Inc. et al.*, 19 F Supp. 173 (1937).

10 US Federal Communications Commission, *Staff Report on Electrical Research Products, Inc.*, vols. i, ii and iii (pursuant to Public Resolution No. 8, 74th Congress, 1937).

11 Arthur M. Schlesinger, Jr, *The Crisis of the Old Order* (Boston: Houghton Mifflin, 1956), pp. 134–6; William T. Foster and Waddill Catchings, *The Road to Plenty* (New York: Houghton Mifflin, 1928), pp. 84–93; 'Warner Brothers pictures', *Fortune*, December 1937, p. 98; *Koplar*, 19 F Supp. 173, Record, pp. 279–83 (Waddill Catchings's direct testimony; the case concerns a stockholder's suit against the Warner brothers for manipulation of stock prices at the expense of other stockholders, and the testimony cited here was background to the crucial facts disputed in the case).

Players. On at least two prior occasions even the risk-loving Catchings had refused to issue securities for motion-picture corporations: he deemed none stable enough for Goldman, Sachs support. Moreover, Catchings had never even heard of Warner Bros. Nevertheless on Rudkin's recommendation he undertook the usual routine investigation as to the credit standing and expected economic future of Warner Bros.[12]

12 *Koplar*, 19 F Supp. 173, Record, pp. 283–5 (Catchings's direct testimony), pp. 1100–1 (Harry Warner's direct testimony).

Several aspects of the Warner Bros' operation impressed Catchings. One was its strict control of production budgets. Goldman, Sachs had never previously been sufficiently confident to finance motion-picture concerns because it had received no guarantee that their production departments could set limits for the cost of films. Warner Bros' rigid cost-accounting procedures, especially the day-to-day audits by production manager Jack Warner, set Warner Bros apart from the other firms he had considered. He also learned that Warner Bros used extremely economical methods in building their studio lot and acquiring props. Catchings agreed to finance Warner Bros, but *only* if it would allow him to dictate a master plan for long-term growth. Catchings had helped build up other companies. Both Woolworths and Sears-Roebuck had associated themselves with Goldman, Sachs as small, regional businesses and with its backing had grown into large, national corporations. Only with this long-term control could Catchings interest important banks in generating the necessary capital.[13]

13 Ibid., pp. 320–4 (Catchings's direct testimony), pp. 1106–7 (Harry Warner's direct testimony); *Electrical Research Products, Inc.* v. *Vitaphone Corporation*, 171 A 738 (1934), Affidavit of Waddill Catchings, pp. 1–2.

14 The four Warner brothers had a clean division of labour regarding their motion-picture firm at this time. Harry, the eldest, was chief operating and financial officer, Abe ran the distribution branch, Sam the technical and exhibition activities and Jack the production.

Both Catchings and Warner Bros' president, Harry Warner, knew that financing was the first and most important part of the company's operations that Goldman, Sachs, or any investment house, must change.[14] During its short existence Warner Bros had used two methods to obtain capital for film production. For a limited number of films Harry Warner would approach a rich individual and trade an interest in the profits of a film for a contribution to its backing. Warner Bros had to pay extremely high interest rates, sometimes as high as 100 per cent, for these loans. The more frequent method was the 'franchise system' under which Warner Bros divided the USA and Canada into twenty-eight zones and secured one franchise holder per zone, usually a major exhibitor. It would then obtain from each backer an advance towards a set number of films to be repaid with a percentage of the expected profits. The franchise holder in turn would then distribute the film within his exclusive territory. Warner Bros would pay extraordinary fees for these required advances. For the typical film, each of the twenty-eight backers would contribute several thousand dollars. For this, in most cases, Warner Bros returned double (and sometimes more) the original amount. Thus the effective interest rate was greater than 100 per cent. Catchings was sure he could procure cheaper rates. Moreover Warner Bros also lacked a distribution network to reap the significant advantages of economies of scale, a theatre circuit, and the publicity machinery to differentiate its films from those of other independent producers.[15]

15 *Koplar*, 19 F Supp. 173, Record, pp. 320–4 (Catchings's direct testimony); *Motion Picture News*, 4 April 1925, p. 1409; 7 February 1925, p. 557.

Negotiations between Catchings and Harry Warner commenced in January 1925. One month later, upon hearing that Warner Bros was trying to make a deal with Goldman, Sachs, the franchise holders rebelled. Normally unorganized, they appointed a committee to meet with Harry Warner. They were afraid that Warner Bros would try to terminate what had been an extraordinarily profitable relationship. At this point Harry Warner pursued an alternative. He knew that Vitagraph, a pioneer motion-picture producer with an international distribution network of fifty exchanges, was in severe financial difficulty. Its operations had generated extremely large losses for each of the past five years. Harry went directly to Vitagraph's president, Albert E. Smith, and offered to buy the corporation. Smith's most immediate problem was paying off $980,000 of current liabilities. Harry Warner offered to take over these debts, and purchase the shares of Smith, J. Stuart Blackton, and the estate of William T. Rock for $800,000. Warner Bros would then possess majority control.[16]

16 *Variety*, 4 February 1925, p. 23.

Harry Warner closed the deal in March 1925, and announced it to the surprised franchise holders in April 1925. Warner Bros now had twenty-six exchanges in the USA, four in Canada, ten in England, and ten in Continental Europe. It also acquired one studio in Brooklyn, New York, another in Hollywood, a large laboratory, a film library, real estate, and story rights. This takeover was the first move in Warner Bros' gamble to break the bind of the franchise holders and move up in importance in the industry. It was also the last financial manoeuvre done without the direct approval of Waddill Catchings. Its daring captured Catchings's imagination and he agreed to finance Warner Bros' future operations. In March 1925, Goldman, Sachs and McClure, Jones and Reed underwrote 170,000 new shares of Warner Bros stock to finance the Vitagraph deal. In May, Catchings joined the Warner Bros' board of directors and was named chairman of the board's finance committee.[17]

17 *Moving Picture World*, 2 May 1925, p. 25; *Motion Picture News*, 2 May 1925, p. 1925; 2 May 1929, p. 2020; *Koplar*, 19 F Supp. 173, Record, pp. 330, 1101–11.

Immediately Catchings set out to obtain the necessary permanent financing for production. After much effort he established a revolving credit line of $3,000,000 at 5 per cent interest. To secure such a sizeable loan Catchings went right to the top of the American banking fraternity. The leading commercial bank in the United States at the time was the National Bank of Commerce in New York; it had never granted a loan to *any* motion picture company. Catchings managed to persuade board chairman, James S. Alexander, at least to study the matter. The National Bank of Commerce completed an extremely thorough study and decided to make an exception with Warner Bros. Alexander added an extra 1 per cent call-charge to the normal 5 per cent demanded of its best customers. This charge would accrue even if the account were never used. Having persuaded the National Bank of Commerce, Catchings then approached the Colony Trust Company of Boston. Again he achieved success. With agreement from these two conservative giants, four other large banks easily fell into line. Pooling the loans, the revolving credit was established. Catchings had solved the short-term crisis for funding production.[18]

18 Ibid., pp. 353–63 (Catchings's direct testimony); John Sherman Porter (ed.): *Moody's Manual of Industrials* (1925), pp. 1899–1900.

He next turned his attention to acquiring funds for capital expansion. He and Harry decided Warner Bros needed more exchanges, first-run theatres, better promotion, and the remodelling of existing production facilities. In the autumn of 1925 Catchings orchestrated a $4,000,000 three-year, 6.5 per cent debenture. Warner Bros expanded in the required directions. It acquired ten medium-sized first-run theatres in cities including Seattle, Baltimore, Cleveland, and Pittsburgh. These theatres became the nucleus of its new chain with Sam Warner in charge. Warner Bros also leased first-run theatres in key locations, beginning with an eleven-year commitment to the Orpheum in Chicago's Loop.[19] The only available Broadway theatre was the Piccadilly; this Warner Bros purchased for $800,000, and immediately renamed the Warners'. Unfortunately it was the smallest major theatre in the Broadway area, seating only 1,500. Warner Bros began planning its biggest theatre: the 3,600 seat, $2,000,000 Warners' in Hollywood. Moreover it signed an agreement with Alexander Pantages to use his vaudeville artists as presentation acts in its new theatres. In the second area, Warners opened eight new distribution exchanges in the USA and Canada to provide a complement equal to Famous Players. It added twenty-one new exchanges in South America and the Far East. The return was immediate. Sales throughout the world helped offset some of its new investments. Warner Bros also added $250,000 in improvements to Vitagraph's Hollywood studio.[20]

Catchings and Harry Warner set their sights on the top. In July 1925, Warner Bros opened a $500,000 national advertising campaign in the major general-interest magazines and selected newspapers, including a special coordinated blitz through the Hearst Newspapers.[21] Catchings and Harry Warner wanted the Warner Bros name to become as well known as Famous Players, or First National. In July 1925, Catchings even bid $8.5 million to take over Universal. Carl Laemmle wanted $10 million. Catchings considered this a reasonable price. However, Laemmle and Robert Cochrane would not let Catchings's accountants examine Universal's books. Without this information to convince bankers, Catchings called off the deal. This was Catchings's first attempt at a merger, but not his last. Ultimate success would come with the takeover of First National itself in October 1928.[22]

As a final expansionist move towards acquiring more publicity, Warner Bros sought to buy a radio station. Sam Warner was fascinated with the new technological improvements in radio that seemed to appear almost daily. He and Warner Bros' chief electrician, Frank N. Murphy, coordinated the purchase of the necessary equipment to set up a station. KFWB opened in the spring of 1925. Warner Bros was the second motion-picture producer with a station, and the only one in Hollywood. KFWB openly copied the publicity methods of the then nationally popular radio master of ceremonies and theatre entrepreneur, Samuel Rothafel (Roxy). Harry Warner even advised the Motion Pictures Producers and Distributors Association to establish a station for the whole industry.[23]

It was as an outgrowth of these radio dealings that Sam Warner, through Western Electric salesman, Nathan Levinson, became interested

19 *Moving Picture World*, 5 September 1925, p. 74; *Variety*, 26 August 1925, p. 21; 23 September 1925, p. 36; 5 July 1925, p. 21; *Koplar*, 19 F Supp. 173, Record, pp. 390–400 (Catchings's direct testimony).

20 *Variety*, 12 August 1925, p. 23; 2 December 1925, p. 36; 16 December 1925, p. 7.

21 *Variety*, 10 June 1925, p. 30; *Moving Picture World*, 1 August 1925, p. 550; *Variety*, 23 September 1925, p. 36; *Moving Picture World*, 13 June 1925, p. 769; *Variety*, 1 April 1925, p. 27; 8 April 1925, p. 29.

22 *Variety*, 15 July 1925, p. 26; 28 October 1925, p. 27.

23 *Moving Picture World*, 21 February 1925, p. 769; 21 March 1925, p. 286; 11 April 1925, p. 592.

in Western Electric's newly developed sound (on disc) system. Together they convinced Harry to see a demonstration in the early part of May 1925. However they did not tell him the nature of the films because, as Harry later recalled:

> if [they] had said talking picture, I never would have gone, because [talking pictures] had been made up to that time several times, and each was a failure. I am positive if [they] said talking picture, I would not [have] gone.[24]

24 *General Talking Pictures*, 18 F Supp. 650, Record, p. 1108.

Nevertheless Harry went. In a small screening room he first saw a man speaking. Next a five-piece jazz orchestra appeared on the screen. Harry became interested. His companion, Sidney J. Weinberg, Catchings's assistant, was ecstatic. Spurred on by the banker's enthusiasm, Harry conceived an idea of how to use this new invention. He later remarked to Catchings: 'If it can talk, it can sing'. Warner Bros could record the greatest vaudeville and musical acts and present them in small to medium-sized theatres. This would provide for these theatres presentations equal to, or better than, those currently available, at a much lower cost. It was an entrepreneurial vision that would require the large amounts of financing only Catchings could provide.[25]

25 *Koplar*, 19 F Supp. 173, Record, pp. 366–8 (Catchings's direct testimony); p. 1101 (Harry Warner's direct testimony). For a similar, less detailed account, see Joseph P. Kennedy (ed.) *The Story of the Films as Told by the Leaders of the Industry* (Cambridge, MA: Harvard University Press, 1927), pp. 320–2.

In June 1925, Warner Bros signed a contract with Western Electric, and its representative, Walter J. Rich, to produce vaudeville shorts experimentally. Slowly the two parties cooperated on the problems of production, and jockeyed for the best market position *vis-à-vis* Famous Players, Loews, and First National. The *Don Juan* show was the product of the year-long production effort. Contractual complications arose on the financial side. Warner Bros signed two sets of agreements with Western Electric—one in April 1926, and a second in May 1927. Constant negotiations stalled any major thrust into the market. Slowly Harry carried out and perfected his strategy of 'vaudeville shorts'. Success would come in the first part of 1928 when these shorts, *The Jazz Singer* and the new part-talkies would begin to generate revenues commensurate with the $3 million investment Warner Bros had accumulated in three years, most of it during the first year.[26]

26 The innovation of Vitaphone by Warner Bros and the reaction of Fox and the rest of the film industry are described in the author's Ph.D. dissertation: 'The Coming of Sound to the American Cinema: A History of the Transformation of an Industry', University of Wisconsin–Madison, 1975, pp. 110–253.

Although the investment in sound in 1925 and 1926 was sizeable, it represented only one-fifth of Warner Bros' increase in assets. The other phases of its growth continued. Warner Bros even began to experience some return on these investments. Ernst Lubitsch's *Lady Windermere's Fan* established box-office records on its debut in January 1926 at the Warners' theatre in New York City: crowds had to be turned away. Lubitsch, guaranteed at least $150,000 per year, was Warner Bros' top director.[27] In February 1926, *The Sea Beast* with John Barrymore also proved to be exceptionally popular. In an attempt to duplicate the successful 'road-show' strategy of the 'Big Three', Warner Bros even worked out a deal with legitimate theatres to showcase the film at two dollars top admission. In April 1926, at its first sales convention (of three) Harry Warner announced twenty-six features for the 1926–7 season, sixteen fewer than the previous season. However these

27 *Moving Picture World*, 9 January 1926, p. 161; *Variety*, 14 April 1926, p. 23.

28 *Variety*, 24 February 1926, p. 24; *Moving Picture World*, 8 May 1926; 15 May 1926, pp. 212–13; *Variety*, 30 January 1926, p. 446; *Moving Picture World*, 8 May 1926, p. 116.

29 *Moving Picture World*, 1 May 1926, p. 44; 24 April 1926, p. 582; Warner Bros Pictures Inc., *A Financial Review and Brief History* (New York: privately printed, 1946), p. 30.

30 *Moving Picture World*, 16 January 1926, p. 220.

31 *Moving Picture World*, 1 May 1926, p. 2; 15 May 1926, p. 226; 18 September 1926, p. 173; 17 April 1926, p. 2; 20 March 1926, p. 4.

32 *Moving Picture World*, 1 May 1926, p. 2; 10 July 1926, p. 88; *Variety*, 30 June 1926, p. 49.

33 *Moving Picture World*, 5 March 1927, p. 18; *Electrical Research Products*, 171 A 738, Plea, Exhibit D, p. 335.

twenty-six 'Warner Winners' would cost more than the previous years' forty-two features. In addition he announced nine new 'road-show' specials, including John Barrymore in *Don Juan* and *Manon Lescaut*, and Syd Chaplin in *The Better 'Ole*.[28] Moreover Harry had just signed George Jessel to duplicate his popular role of *The Jazz Singer*. Waddill Catchings, in the closing address to this April convention, praised Warner Bros for its solid advance during the past year, and predicted a bright future with greater potential than any other firm in the industry.[29]

Warner Bros had extended itself in still other areas in the first half of 1926. It opened its second radio station, WBPI, in New York City. Headquartered at the Warners' theatre, and under the direction of Sam Warner, it generally employed vaudeville talent currently at the theatre.[30] On 4 May, Sam Warner launched a transcontinental tour of a 'radio station'. Controlled by KFWB, Frank Murphy and his crew could set up the portable station in twenty minutes at any theatre using a Warner Bros film. It would then broadcast the stage show, sponsor contests, and generally create publicity for Warner Bros' pictures and exchanges. The 'station' toured throughout the summer months. Sam also oversaw yet another new aspect of Warner Bros' operations. In April 1926, Warner Bros re-equipped Vitagraph's Brooklyn laboratory with modern apparatus; it had a capacity to process four million feet per week. Warners also expanded into foreign production by closing a deal to co-produce ten films with the Bruckman Film Company of Germany.[31]

With all this capital outlay, it was not unexpected that the yearly financial statement, issued in March 1926, stood in the red. The loss was large, $1,338,000, but the company had more than doubled its asset base. It now possessed an international distribution network, owned a growing chain of theatres, and was producing higher-priced films. Moreover it had the support of the nation's best banks in its climb towards the top of the industry.[32] By August 1927, revenues had grown sufficiently to cut its rate of loss in half. Foreign operations had become quite lucrative. Rentals in Great Britain improved substantially even in 1926, and would grow by more than $2 million for the fiscal year ending 31 August 1927. Yet Catchings and Harry Warner continued to invest, especially in higher-priced pictures. By August 1927, despite having tripled its asset base in two years, Warner Bros had turned the corner and even registered a small profit. The gigantic success of sound motion pictures, built on the solid base of earlier investments, would turn potential long-run gain into immediate rewards in 1928.[33]

Throughout this period Catchings continued to secure the necessary finance. As soon as the Vitaphone operations began to demand larger amounts of credit, Catchings was commensurate to the task. The initial Vitaphone contract called for a $500,000 investment; by February 1927, Warner Bros had accumulated over $3 million in assets. To obtain this capital, Catchings kept refinancing the revolving credit of $3 million. Catchings continued his persuasive cajoling; the bankers remained cooperative. In fact in August 1926, the Central Union Trust Company of New York agreed not even to notify Warner Bros' creditors of their pledged accounts receivable when it extended Warner Bros a new loan for $1 million. In September 1926, he secured yet another $1 million from S. W. Strauss and Co.; Harry Warner used this to improve the former Vitagraph studio in Hollywood. Catchings would continue this adroit financing until 1930. By then Warner Bros' asset base had grown from slightly more than $5 million in 1925 to $230 million, a 4,600 per cent increase in five years.[34]

34 *Koplar*, 19 F Supp. 173, Record, pp. 455–9, 473–5, 479, and 560–5 (Catchings's direct testimony); John Sherman Porter (ed.), *Moody's Manual of Industrials* (1927), pp. 385–6; *Variety*, 1 September 1926, p. 5; 24 November 1926, p. 10.

Several specific and general conclusions emerge from this short history. In terms of the question posed concerning the cause of Warner Bros' innovation of sound, the firm was never 'near bankruptcy'. In its early years it was a profitable operation, but one that could only become more profitable with a sizeable expansion in several important areas. To effect this growth, Waddill Catchings and Harry Warner secured funds for production, distribution, exhibition, and promotion. These investments created short-term losses. In fact it was simply a case of well-financed, well-planned short-run indebtedness. Moreover Catchings had the support of America's most important banks throughout this period of expansion. And sound was only one part, albeit a very risky one, of the investment surge. It succeeded only because the early expansion had created the necessary structural base.

Warner Bros' expansionary activities in the boom of the mid-1920s were part of a plan to move it up in the industry. At the time the industry's Big Three, Famous Players, Loews, and First National, dominated the industry. Fox, Film Booking Office (FBO), Universal, Pathé-Producers Distributing Corporation, and Warner Bros composed a second tier. Fox and Warner Bros would, and did, successfully challenge the 'Big Three'. In fact, Warner Bros was so successful it acquired First National in 1928. FBO and Pathé-PDC would become the basis of Radio-Keith-Orpheum. Universal was too conservative and fell in importance to join United Artists, a special case, and the only independent of the 1920s to emerge as an important firm, Columbia. The other independent producers of the 1920s either went out of business or became an almost insignificant part of the market.

On a larger scale this account of Warner Bros' expansion is only one example of a possible revisionist history of the American film industry. For the bankruptcy question, a priori one would begin to challenge the usual conclusion, as well as the terms in which that explanation is written. Other areas should be subjected to similar probes. But we must be careful. We must create our first principles and methods. We must examine the accepted notions of bias and cause, and begin to search out new sources of primary data.

10 The Disney–Fleischer Dilemma: Product Differentiation and Technological Innovation

MARK LANGER

An examination of competing three-dimensional animation technologies at the Disney and Fleischer studios during the 1930s reveals problems in previous historical accounts of their genesis and use. The first of these technologies was the Stereoptical Process, invented by Max Fleischer and John Burks of the Fleischer Studios, Inc. in 1933. The Stereoptical Process was a three-dimensional setback system arranged horizontally, with the camera in front of the cels and background. Cels containing the animated characters were photographed in front of a three-dimensional set mounted on a turntable. The turntable could be rotated in order to get the effect of a pan or tracking shot. The background set was constructed with a vanishing point at the centre of the turntable so that the further an object was from the lens, the more slowly it appeared to move. When photographed, it appeared as if the two-dimensional cartoon characters were moving within a three-dimensional environment.[1]

The Multiplane camera, developed by a Walt Disney Productions team headed by William Garity, was a vertical arrangement with the camera above the elements to be photographed. Unlike the earlier Stereoptical Process, the Multiplane camera used two-dimensional elements for each plane within the background. Artwork of different planes was held in individual light boxes, separated from other artwork by some distance. This made the various foreground and background planes spatially distinct. A greater illusion of depth was achieved by moving the camera down towards the background elements.[2]

1 Max Fleischer, US Patent 2,054,414, 15 September 1936; Seymour Kneitel and Izzy Sparber, *Standard Production Reference* (Miami: Fleischer Studios, Inc., 1940), p. 29.

2 C. W. Batchelder, *Multiplane Manual* (Burbank, Calif.: Walt Disney Studio, c. 1939), pp. 1–6.

3 'Invents movie 3rd dimension',
NY Morning Telegraph, 11 March
1934, n.p.; William Stull, 'Three
hundred men and Walt Disney.
That's the analysis of one
reporter', *American
Cinematographer*, vol. 19,
no. 2 (1938), pp. 50, 58;
C. W. Batchelder, 'Multiplane
camera lecture for ass't
directors', Walt Disney Archive,
Standard Production Reference,
13 January 1939, pp. 29–31.

4 This study will not attempt to
separate the individual
contributions of Max Fleischer or
John Burks to the development of
the Stereoptical Process, nor that
of Walt Disney, Ub Iwerks or
William Garity to the Multiplane
camera. A mention of a single
name may depict an exclusive
individual, or an entity
representing the technological
work of several people. Joe
Adamson, 'A talk with Dick
Huemer', in Danny Peary and
Gerald Peary (eds.), *The
American Animated Cartoon*
(New York: E. P. Dutton, 1980),
p. 33; Lotte Reiniger, 'The
adventures of Prince Achmed or
what may happen to someone
trying to make a full length
cartoon in 1926', *The Silent
Picture*, no. 6 (1970), pp. 2–4;
Peter Adamakos, 'Ub Iwerks',
Mindrot, no. 7 (1977), p. 24;
William Moritz, 'Resistance and
subversion in animated films of
the Nazi era: the case of Hans
Fischerkoesen', *Animation
Journal*, vol. 1, no. 1 (1992),
pp. 5–33.

5 Leslie Carbaga, *The Fleischer
Story* (New York: Nostalgia
Press, 1976), p. 71; G. Michael
Dobbs, 'Koko komments',
Animato, no. 18 (1989), p. 35;
Leonard Maltin, *Of Mice and
Magic* (New York: Plume, 1980),
pp. 109–10; Richard Schickel,
The Disney Version (New York:
Avon, 1968), pp. 164–5; Ralph
Stephenson, *The Animated Film*.
(New York: A. S. Barnes, 1973),
p. 37.

Neither technology was particularly efficient. Both were extremely expensive in their use of labour and materials. Light reflections from the surfaces of cels were a major problem with both processes, and the Multiplane camera had particular trouble with dust accumulation on the image surface. The employment of the Stereoptical Process was very time-consuming due to the remarkably long camera exposures required.[3] Why then were these technologies developed and used? Recounting a progression of three-dimensional animation processes from Carl Lederer's apparatus used in the 1910s, Lotte Reiniger and Carl Koch's device employed in the 1920s, through Ub Iwerks's development of a horizontal Multiplane camera before 1934, and Hans Fischerkoesen's appropriation of the Multiplane and Stereoptical technology in the 1940s is a task for other historians.[4] This study concentrates on the methodological problems posed by past considerations of the Disney and Fleischer processes.

Historical representations of the development of the Stereoptical Process and of the Multiplane camera explain the genesis of these new technologies in two major ways: either the technologies were introduced through the imagination of an inventive genius, or they were developed as a movement towards greater realism in animation. In other words, accounts of the development of the Stereoptical Process and Multiplane camera involve either a belief in the 'great man' theory of history, or a belief that animation history followed an evolutionary or teleological progression towards mimesis.

Historians representing these two groups overlap to a certain extent. Among the 'great man' proponents are such people as Leonard Maltin, Richard Schickel, Ralph Stephenson, Frank Thomas, Ollie Johnston, G. Michael Dobbs, and Leslie Carbaga.[5] Thomas and Johnston state:

**The Stereoptical Process,
US patent, 15 September 1936**

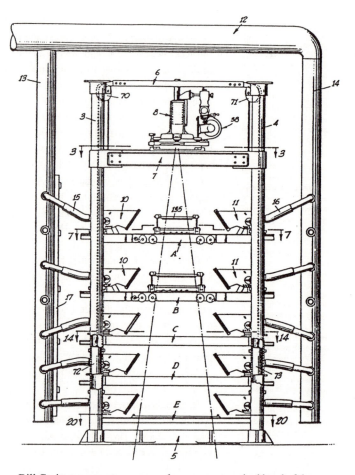

Bill Garity, an expert on camera lenses, was nominal head of the department, but Walt worked with each man on an individual basis. . . . They were called into sweatboxes and story meetings and often just sat around listening, getting the feel of what Walt was after. . . . Once they were asked to build an arrangement that could hold separate layers of artwork at varying distances from a still camera . . . it worked and Walt liked the result and suddenly was talking about building another one, larger and more complicated, that might be used for shooting animation. . . . And so the first multiplane camera was born.[6]

Similar thinking informs Leslie Carbaga's *The Fleischer Story*, in which the author dubs the Stereoptical device 'The most wondrous of Max's highly acclaimed innovations'. G. Michael Dobbs sees the Stereoptical Process as a physical simulacrum of Max Fleischer's thought: 'Max Fleischer . . .', avers Dobbs, '. . . was very literal-minded, and his method of adding three dimensions to cartoons reflects this belief. You want three dimensions, you use a three-dimensional model as your background!'[7] Historians who promote evolutionary or teleological arguments include Leonard Maltin (again), David R. Smith, and Richard Hollis and Brian Sibley. Hollis and Sibley maintain

6 Frank Thomas and Ollie Johnston, *Disney Animation: The Illusion of Life* (New York: Abbeville, 1981), pp. 262–4.

7 Carbaga, *The Fleischer Story*, p. 71; Dobbs, 'Koko komments', p. 35.

8 Leonard Maltin, *The Disney Films* (New York: Crown, 1973), pp. 12–13; David R. Smith, 'Beginnings of the Disney Multiplane camera', in Charles Solomon (ed.), *The Art of the Animated Image: An Anthology* (Los Angeles: The American Film Institute, 1987), p. 41; Richard Holliss and Brian Sibley, *The Disney Studio Story* (New York: Crown, 1988), p. 30.

. . . there was the perennial difficulty of conveying 'depth', something that hadn't mattered in the early comic cartoons but that was of vital importance in creating the realistic mood Walt wanted for *Snow White*. An illusion of depth was eventually achieved by . . . the huge but extremely versatile 'multiplane camera'. . . .[8]

In such considerations, the 'great man' theory and teleology coalesce. Great inventors provide the technology to aid in the inevitable march of progress. While one should not wish completely to deny concepts of individual endeavour or progress as historical factors, one must question the assumptions that underlie these concepts. The 'great man' theory views individual creativity as the motor of history. Is innovation an individual act, or does it have an institutional dynamic? Do personal or institutional interests best provide a motive for the creation of these new, expensive, and unwieldy technologies?

Secondly, teleological or evolutionary approaches join with the 'great man' theory in projecting history as a line of continuous development in one direction. These approaches reflect a belief in technological innovation as part of an ideology of progress. Something is invented by someone and technological, industrial, or social change follows. Raymond Williams has criticized this type of technological determinism for assuming that

9 Raymond Williams, *Television: Technology and Cultural Form* (New York: Schocken, 1975), p. 13.

> new technologies are discovered by an essentially internal process of research and development, which then sets the conditions for social change and progress. The effects of the technologies, whether direct or indirect, foreseen or unforeseen, are, as it were, the rest of history.[9]

Absent from such considerations is the possibility that research and development is a symptom, rather than an agent, of social change and progress. While Williams discusses the external dynamic of a system that incorporates technological innovation, this article examines the particular cultural subsets of the American animation industry, with focus on the actions of Walt Disney Productions and the Fleischer Studios, Inc. Broader parallels between this internal dynamic and the film industry at large or the social/economic system as it existed in the 1920 to 1942 period may be implied. However, the external dynamic will not be examined specifically in this study.

In historical representations of the Multiplane camera and Stereoptical Process, the consequence of invention is portrayed as primarily aesthetic rather than social or economic. Oddly enough (in light of the fact that animation does not use a three-dimensional, live performance as its starting-point), this aesthetic/historical system is strikingly comparable to that voiced by André Bazin, who stated that 'Cinema attains its fullness in the art of the real'. To Bazin, the basic need completely to represent reality was the driving force behind technological advancement. Thus, technological innovations such as sound, colour, and wide screen created a closer relationship between cinema and its surrounding world.[10] Similarly, animation historians view

10 André Bazin, *What Is Cinema?* Vol. 1 (Berkeley: University of California Press, 1971), p. 15; Robert C. Allen and Douglas Gomery, *Film History: Theory and Practice* (New York: Knopf, 1985), pp. 70–1.

the development of style and technology within American studio animation to 1942 as an unbroken march towards mimesis. Richard Schickel, for example, sees the Multiplane camera as a logical aesthetic extension of Disney's adoption of sound and colour: 'The multiplane camera thus becomes a symbolic act of completion for Disney. With it, he broke the last major barrier between his art and realism of the photographic kind.'[11]

It is the end point of this march that poses a challenge to the assumptions behind these historical methodologies. Both the Stereoptical and Multiplane technologies led to dead ends. Use of the Stereoptical Process was discontinued by 1941, and the Multiplane camera was employed with decreasing frequency through the 1940s. No significant amount of further technical refinement or development was made of either apparatus. Historical methodologies previously applied to three-dimensional animation technology all assume that history unfolds in a rational, continuous manner. The 'great man' theory accounts for the invention of these technologies as a logical extension of a visionary personality. The evolutionary or teleological approaches presume some sort of continuity, whether through the permanent institutionalization of these technologies, or through their organic relationship to some further development. The aesthetic assumptions see these technologies as a logical development towards mimesis. Mimesis was later abandoned in favour of increasingly 'flat' and stylized graphics used from 1942 throughout the US animation industry. As will later be demonstrated, this stylistic change, which is usually credited to such studios as Warner Bros or UPA, can be observed within the films of those very studios that were allegedly heading toward mimesis. These films include *Bone Trouble* (1940), *Fantasia* (1940), *The Reluctant Dragon* (1941), or *Dumbo* (1941) at Disney; and *Goonland* (1938) and *Mr Bug Goes To Town* (1941) at Fleischer.

Through an examination of both the institutional history and the style of films produced by the Disney and Fleischer studios during the 1930s and early 1940s, I wish to propose the need for alternative historical models of innovation and competition to those used by previous animation historians: models not so dependent on the presumption of a rational order governing the behaviour of individuals, institutions, technologies, or aesthetic movements. Such models take into account not only the strategies of institutional interaction between Fleischer Studios, Inc. and Walt Disney Productions, but also the coexistence of different styles within the discourse of each studio.

Janet Staiger, in *The Classical Hollywood Cinema*, notes that many of Hollywood's production practices resulted from a tension in its economic practices. Staiger defines this tension as a movement towards standardizing the product for efficient, economical mass production, and a simultaneous movement towards differentiating the product as the firms bid competitively for a consumer's disposable income.[12] Staiger points out that innovation was an economic necessity, even though it

11 Schickel, *The Disney Version*, p. 169. A categorical but ahistorical description of the Multiplane camera and Stereoptical Process can be found in Russell George, 'Some spatial characteristics of the Hollywood cartoon', *Screen*, vol. 31, no. 3 (1990), pp. 296–321.

12 Janet Staiger, 'The Hollywood mode of production: conditions of existence', in David Bordwell, Janet Staiger, and Kristin Thompson, *The Classical Hollywood Cinema: Film Style and Mode of Production to 1960* (New York: Columbia University Press, 1985), p. 88.

13 Staiger, 'Standardization and differentiation', in ibid., p. 97. Staiger's earlier thinking appears to be influenced by Paul A. Baran and Paul M. Sweezy's *Monopoly Capital: An Essay on the American Economic and Social Order* (New York: Modern Reader Paperbacks, 1968). Later, Staiger called for a less deterministic view of product differentiation through advertising: *Cinema Journal*, vol. 29, no. 3 (1990), pp. 6, 21–3.

14 Lester Telser, 'Advertising and competition', *Journal of Political Economy*, no. 70 (1964), pp. 537–62; Norman Schneider, 'Product differentiation, oligopoly and the stability of market shares', *Western Economic Journal*, no. 5 (1966), pp. 58–63. An historical overview of the debates surrounding product differentiation can be found in William Breit and Kenneth G. Elzinga, 'Product differentiation and institutionalism: new shadows on an old terrain', *Journal of Economics Issues*, vol. 8, no. 4 (1974), pp. 813–26.

15 Martin Shubik, 'Game theory and the study of social behaviour: an introductory exposition', in Martin Shubik (ed.), *Game Theory and Related Approaches to Social Behaviour* (New York: John Wiley and Sons, 1964), pp. 4–5.

16 Eric Rasmusen, *Games and Information: An Introduction to Game Theory* (Oxford: Blackwell, 1989), p. 21.

often involved higher production costs. Competition between different film companies led them to differentiate their products. Through product differentiation, one firm could emphasize how its goods differed in kind, and presumably in quality, from those of other companies. Elsewhere Staiger has explored this topic more thoroughly in relation to film advertising.[13] In the present study, product differentiation will be explored from the point of view of technological innovation and industrial competition. According to Staiger's model, innovation and product differentiation in the animation industry resulting from the development of the Stereoptical Process and the Multiplane camera would have enhanced long-term stability at the Disney and Fleischer organizations.

Staiger's view of institutional behaviour suggests a paradox. Although innovation and differentiation are meant to improve a company's long-term profits, their coincident costs do not appear upon reflection to be in the interests of an institution's financial health. Each innovation is presumably met by a response from the institution's competitor, resulting in a never-ending cycle of expensive product differentiation and a consequent erosion of profit. While Staiger earlier viewed product differentiation as an essentially rational decision that aids economic stability, empirical studies have shown that product differentiation is often associated with industrial instability in commercial sectors.[14] Indeed, within a few years of the development of the Stereoptical Process and the Multiplane camera, Fleischer Studios, Inc. was out of business and Walt Disney Productions was in severe financial trouble. Other determinants, such as labour strife and changes in the marketplace, were contributing factors to these troubles. However, competition and technological development were among the difficulties encountered by both organizations.

Central to Staiger's model is the concept of a conflict mechanism within the film industry. If one accepts this model of industrial organization as the impetus behind innovation and product differentiation, then one accepts a model suitable for analysis through game theory. Although it began as a form of strategic studies, game theory in the past few decades has been applied to the study of business, economics, social behaviour, and biology. Game theory has been defined by Martin Shubik as a method of studying decision-making in conflict situations.[15] In general, game theory concerns the actions of competing individuals or groups who are conscious that their efforts affect each other. Eric Rasmusen states: 'Game theory is not useful when decisions are made that ignore the reactions of others or treat them as impersonal market forces'.[16]

Evidence suggests that the Disney and Fleischer studios were keenly aware of each others' actions. While by the early 1930s Walt Disney Productions was considered to be the leader in terms of artistic innovation, Fleischer Studios, Inc., through cost control and the popularity of their 'Popeye' character, created animated films that were far more profitable to the Fleischers and their distributor Paramount than were Disney's when distributed by United Artists or RKO. Fleischer

Studios, Inc. was the leading animation studio on the east coast of the USA, dominating in prestige and profitability its local competitors Van Beuren and Terry. Max Fleischer resented Disney's having lured away many of his top employees with high salaries, and was conscious of Disney having utilized many Fleischer-developed processes, such as the Rotoscope. Walt Disney Productions took little notice of such west coast competitors as Celebrity Productions, Harman & Ising, or Leon Schlesinger. For example, while requesting screenings for the training of studio staff in 1935, Disney stated: 'I think it is all right to show Fleischer's stuff, but I would keep away from the local product'.[17] While many early animation companies were preoccupied with the development of new technology, by 1934 Walt Disney Productions and Fleischer Studios, Inc. were the only animation studios conducting research and development on a sustained basis. Both companies were highly competitive and non-cooperative.[18]

Game theory provides a means of accounting for the behaviour of competing institutions such as Walt Disney Productions and Fleischer Studios, Inc. Games are distinguished by their goals as either zero-sum games or non-zero-sum games. Poker and elections are examples of zero-sum games in that the winner takes all and the loser gets nothing. Any advantage that accrues to one player in a zero-sum game results in a corresponding loss by the other player. Non-zero-sum games correspond more to the conditions of mature oligopoly that existed in the film industry in the 1930s. They are not based on the premise that what one player wins, the other must lose. Non-zero-sum games leave open the possibilities that both players might gain advantage, that one might benefit while the other loses, or that both might lose. As a result, non-zero-sum games leave the possibility for both conflict and cooperation.

Non-zero-sum games divide into two categories—cooperative and non-cooperative games. A cooperative game is one in which the players make binding commitments with each other. In a non-cooperative game, they do not. As Eric Rasmusen has observed: 'Noncooperative game theory is economic in flavour, with solution concepts based on players maximizing their own utility functions subject to stated constraints'.[19] In terms of game theory, the competition between the Fleischer Studios, Inc. and Walt Disney Productions may be categorized as a non-zero-sum non-cooperative game, wherein each player sought to maximize his own position.

Much scholarship, such as Donald Crafton's and Kristin Thompson's work on the adoption of the cel method, Harvey Deneroff's writings on labour organization, or my own work on studio hierarchies, has emphasized the movement towards commercial standardization in the American animation industry.[20] The need to provide a standard product resulted in other forms of regulation. Most animated films were one reel in length. Standardization encouraged the production of animation series constructed around a central 'star' character, such as Felix the Cat, Ko-Ko the Clown, or Mickey Mouse. Even as the dictates of commerce standardized animation production, commerce also motivated a

17 Walt Disney, Memo, 18 September 1935, Walt Disney Archives.

18 While Ub Iwerks did some development of a horizontal three-dimensional process at Celebrity Productions, this effort did not proceed independently of the one at Walt Disney Productions beyond 1934. Max Fleischer, US Patent no. 1,242,674, 9 October 1917; 'Mickey Mouse as actor a dud at making money', *New York Herald-Tribune*, 12 March 1934; 'Disney's "Pigs" eat up profits', *New York Telegraph*, 18 November 1933; A. M. Botsford to Russell Holman, Memo, 1 March 1938, *Gulliver's Travels* Production File (private collection); Austin Keough, Max Fleischer, and Dave Fleischer, *Agreement*, 24 May 1941, pp. 11, 12; Richard Fleischer, interviews with the author, 8 November 1990 and 18 May 1991; Grim Natwick, interview with the author, 28 January 1990.

19 Rasmusen, *Games and Information*, p. 29.

20 Donald Crafton, 'The Henry Ford of animation: John Randolph Bray', and 'The animation "shops" ', in *Before Mickey: The Animated Film 1898–1928* (Cambridge, Mass.: MIT Press, 1982), pp. 137–216; Kristin Thompson, 'Implications of the cel animation technique', in Teresa de Lauretis and Stephen Heath (eds.), *The Cinematic Apparatus* (New York: St Martin's Press, 1980), pp. 106–20; Harvey Raphael Deneroff, 'Popeye the union man: a historical study of the Fleischer strike', unpublished dissertation, University of Southern California, 1985; Mark Langer, 'Institutional power and the Fleischer Studios: the *Standard Production Reference*', *Cinema Journal*, vol. 30, no. 2 (1991), pp. 3–21.

*Mickey Mouse and Bosko
(courtesy of the Walt Disney
Corporation and Warner Bros)*

21 Greg Ford, 'Warner Brothers
[*sic*]', *Film Comment*, vol. 11,
no. 1 (1975), p. 16.

22 Legal considerations played a
part in product differentiation, as
evinced by the lawsuit brought
against Van Beuren by Walt
Disney for copying the Mickey
Mouse character. 'Van Buren [*sic*]
scoffs at Disney suit', *Motion
Picture Daily*, 15 April 1931.

23 Rasmusen, *Games and
Information*, p. 29.

countervailing tendency towards product differentiation. For example,
the Warner Bros Negro boy character Bosko has been seen as imitative
of Disney's Mickey Mouse in terms of his physical proportions, simple
black on white 'inkblot' design, squeaky voice, and musical routines.[21]
But Bosko was also clearly differentiated from Mickey Mouse by the
use of long trousers and the lack of tail and mouse ears. Imitation of the
successful product of one company was counterbalanced by the need to
distinguish the product of one company from that of another firm.[22]
Product differentiation was common in the American animation
industry during the 1920s and 1930s, but was accomplished primarily
through graphic style or character design. Product differentiation by
means of technology was far more expensive. During the period,
innovation of animation technology was motivated chiefly by
competition between the two major animation companies—Fleischer
Studios, Inc. and Walt Disney Productions.

The Disney–Fleischer competition suggests the non-zero-sum,
non-cooperative model called the Prisoner's Dilemma. The Prisoner's
Dilemma is found in many different situations, such as oligopoly
pricing, auction bidding, salesman effort, political bargaining, arms
races, or other forms of conflict in which all participants are adversely
affected.[23] The Prisoner's Dilemma model supposes that the two players
are criminals who have been apprehended and jailed after the
commission of a crime. Each of the prisoners is informed by the police
that if he denounces the other one, he will go free, while the other
prisoner will go to jail for three years. If both prisoners remain silent,
each will receive a one-year sentence. If both prisoners denounce each
other, each will get two years in prison.

The best collective strategy would be for both prisoners to remain
silent. This way, each prisoner would serve only one year in prison.
However, since the two prisoners cannot communicate, neither can trust
the other. In the absence of trust, if the game is played *only once*, the
best policy is to betray one's partner. This will result in an equal chance
of either a two-year sentence or escaping punishment altogether,
depending on whether the other prisoner is silent or also opts for
betrayal. If the same players play a *series* of rounds, the best strategy

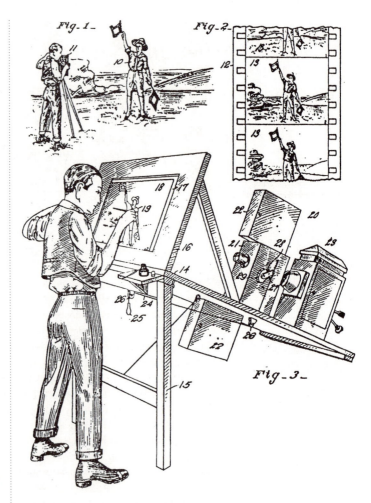

Fig. 1.

Fig. 2.

Fig. 3.

changes. Since each player can assess the results of the strategy, each prisoner can infer what the other prisoner did by evaluating the outcome of each round. This allows tacit cooperation to take place. If each prisoner continues always to betray the other, their combined sentences will be longer than that with any other strategy. The best way to maximize gains would be for the two prisoners to cooperate tacitly, and remain silent. Empirical studies of the Prisoner's Dilemma have shown that players rarely act in their own long-term interests. Instead, they irrationally attempt to beat their competitor in each round.[24]

Competition between two non-cooperative companies can be likened to the Prisoner's Dilemma. Each of the companies strives to find some advantage over its competitor, even though rational long-term economic interests argue against this approach. One potential advantage arises through the product differentiation that results from technological development. As earlier observed, differentiation of product began in the earliest years of animation, but technological differentiation became a central feature of the competition between Fleischer Studios, Inc. and

24 Malcolm W. Browne, 'Biologists tally generosity's rewards', *The New York Times*, 14 April 1992, pp. C1, C8; James E. Dougherty and Robert L. Pfaltzgraff Jr., *Contending Theories of International Relations* (New York: J. B. Lippincott, 1971), pp. 353–7; Alvin Scodel, J. Sayer Minas, and Milton Lipetz, 'Some descriptive aspects of two person non-zero-sum games', *Journal of Conflict Resolution*, vol. 3, no. 2 (June 1959), p. 115, cited in ibid.

Walt Disney Productions. Max and Dave Fleischer's first animated cartoon was manufactured in 1915. Although their films used the then common convention of depicting both the artist and the animated character in the same world, they were differentiated from contemporary animated films through the use of the Rotoscope. The Rotoscope allowed an animator to copy live-action movement by means of the rear projection of live-action film frame by frame onto a piece of translucent glass set into a drawing-board. The improved smoothness of movement obtained by this process was a central part of the marketing publicity surrounding the Fleischer brothers' 'Out of the Inkwell' cartoons. As *The New York Times* noted in 1920, the Fleischer protagonist, Ko-Ko the Clown, had

> a number of distinguishing characteristics. His motions, for one thing, are smooth and graceful. . . . He does not jerk himself from one position to another, nor does he move an arm or leg while the remainder of his body remains as unnaturally still as if it were fixed in ink lines on paper.

In 1925, Max Fleischer invented the Rotograph as a further advance in technological product differentiation. The Rotograph was a rear-projection system which allowed superior image quality and ease of construction of scenes combining live action and animated characters.[25]

Disney's entry into national distribution of product also depended on product differentiation. Disney's first series protagonist in the 'Alice Comedies' was a live-action girl played by Virginia Davis. In the 'Alice Comedies' this character was matted into a cartoon world. Such practice differed from that of competing animation series which featured animated protagonists. Although the Fleischer 'Out of the Inkwell' cartoons mixed live action and animation, their protagonists were drawn figures (albeit rotoscoped in the case of Ko-Ko the Clown) in a live-action world. Disney's distributor, Margaret J. Winkler, had been Max Fleischer's distributor. When Fleischer and Winkler parted company upon Max Fleischer's venture into distributing his own product, Winkler arranged to distribute the Disney product. She announced the 'Alice Comedies' in trade papers as 'Kid comedies with cartoons coordinated into the action. A distinct novelty'. Contemporary trade reviews made much of the distinctiveness and novelty of a live-action girl in a cartoon world. By emphasizing his live character Alice, rather than an animated rotoscoped character like Ko-Ko, Disney consciously used some conventions of classical Hollywood cinema as a means to differentiate his product from the products of others.[26]

A chronology of technological innovations at the Disney and Fleischer studios demonstrates a competitive pattern of innovation and product differentiation. From 1924 to 1926, Max and Dave Fleischer released their animated sound 'Song Car-Tunes' using the DeForest Phonofilm process. In 1928, Disney utilized the Powers Cinephone process to synchronize *Steamboat Willie*. Fleischer Studios, Inc. returned to sound production with *Noah's Lark* in 1929. Disney then

25 'Fleischer advances technical art', *Moving Picture World*, 7 June 1919; 'The inkwell man', *The New York Times*, 22 February 1920, p. 9; 'Offers new series of "Out of Inkwell" ', unidentified clipping, c. 1921, Margaret J. Winkler Papers, Film Study Centre, The Museum of Modern Art, NY; Milton Wright, 'Inventors who have achieved commercial success', *Scientific American*, vol. 136, no. 4 (1927), p. 249; Max Fleischer, US Patent no. 1,819,883, August 1931.

26 Certificate of Incorporation of the Red Seal Pictures Corporation, 7 September 1923, New York City County Clerk's Office; M. J. Winkler advertisement, *The Film Daily*, 11 May 1924; 'Alice's Wild West Show', *The Film Daily*, 16 March 1924; 'Alice's Wild West Show' and 'Alice's Day at Sea', *Motion Picture World*, 10 May 1924; Walt Disney, 'Letter to Margaret Winkler', in David R. Smith, 'Up to date in Kansas City', *Funnyworld*, no. 19 (1978), p. 33; George Winkler, interviews with the author, 25 May 1991 and 26 May 1991; Ron Magliozzi, 'Notes for a history of Winkler pictures', unpublished MS, 1991.

signed a contract with Technicolor, giving him exclusive rights for animation to the three-colour Technicolor process. This was used in Disney's *Flowers and Trees* (1932). The Fleischer Studios, unable to gain access to three-colour technology, made do with the bichromatic Cinecolor and two-colour Technicolor processes. In order positively to differentiate his colour films from those of Disney, Max Fleischer introduced the three-dimensional Stereoptical Process in his first colour film, *Poor Cinderella*, in 1934. After three-colour Technicolor became available to Fleischer Studios, Inc., the company moved to longer animated films with *Popeye the Sailor Meets Sindbad the Sailor* (1936). Walt Disney Productions countered with the development of the Multiplane camera, beginning in 1935 and culminating with its use in *The Old Mill* (1937). Several months later, the Disney studio released the feature *Snow White and the Seven Dwarfs* (1938). By co-opting the dominant feature-length format of classical Hollywood cinema, Disney differentiated his product, as he had similarly done with the earlier 'Alice Comedies'. His competitors could follow, or be left with what would be perceived as a less innovative, inferior, product. This is when the house of cards began to collapse. Following on the success of *Snow White and the Seven Dwarfs*, Max and Dave Fleischer drove themselves into insolvency by combining all of their technologies in the feature-length *Gulliver's Travels* (1939) and *Mr Bug Goes to Town* (1941). Disney narrowly escaped doing the same by applying his expensive technologies to the money-losing *Pinocchio* (1940), *Fantasia*, and *Bambi* (1942).[27]

The result of this institutional pattern of product differentiation closely follows the outcome predicted by the Prisoner's Dilemma. The Prisoner's Dilemma model does allow a competitor to win a particular round, as Disney did with the production of *Snow White and the Seven Dwarfs*. But such victories are minor anomalies in comparison with the long-term outcome of a competitive, non-cooperative strategy. With the exception of the anomalous success of *Snow White and the Seven Dwarfs*, technological differentiation of product did not provide benefit to either company. Walt Disney Productions remained viable in the 1930s and early 1940s largely because of income obtained from a stock offer and from ancillary business interests, such as product licensing, books, music, and revenue from comic strip and art sales, rather than because of income resulting directly or indirectly from the development of the Multiplane camera.[28]

Much less of the Fleischer Studios' income came from ancillary interests. Although some attempt had been made to market products based on Fleischer animated characters, the merchandising rights for the company's popular series of 'Popeye the Sailor' cartoons were held by King Features Syndicate. Cost controls imposed upon Fleischer Studios, Inc. that limited the company's use of new technology helped maintain that company's profitability. For example, Paramount contracts with the Fleischers specified that 'Popeye the Sailor' cartoons be black and white as late as 1942. This was seven years after Disney had completely

27 The $2,595,379 cost of *Pinocchio* was estimated to be in excess of one million dollars over projected income in the year of its release, while *Dumbo*, which made less use of the expensive Multiplane camera, cost only $600,000 and generated profit. Much of the studio's income was dependent on short subjects, which did not make extensive use of Multiplane, and income from ancillary sources, such as comic strips, licensing fees, etc. Walt Disney Productions lost $1,259,798 in 1940, $789,297 in 1941, and $191,069 in 1942. *Annual Report Fiscal Year Ended September 28, 1940* (Burbank: Walt Disney Productions, 1940), p. 3; *Annual Report Fiscal Year Ended September 27, 1941* (Burbank: Walt Disney Productions, 1941), p. 2; *Annual Report Fiscal Year ended October 3, 1942* (Burbank: Walt Disney Productions, 1942), pp. 2, 10; 'Disney loss cut', *Variety*, vol. 145, no. 7 (1942), p. 20; 'Walt Disney: great teacher', *Fortune*, vol. 26, no. 12 (1942), p. 154.

28 'The big bad wolf', *Fortune*, vol. 10, no. 5 (1934), p. 94; *Annual Report Fiscal Year Ended September 28, 1940*, p. 5.

converted to Technicolor production. Paramount's constraints kept production costs of 'Popeye' down to $16,500 per film, and effectively limited the use of the Stereoptical Process in these films. Fleischer one-reel colour films were to cost no more than $30,000, with only their two-reel specials and the first 'Superman' cartoon exceeding this figure. Budgets were considerably less than the $40,000 to $50,000 typically spent on a one-reel film by Walt Disney Productions. When these financial controls were relaxed for the Fleischer feature-length response to *Snow White and the Seven Dwarfs*, the Fleischers fell into the trap of the Prisoner's Dilemma. *Gulliver's Travels* went over budget, and Fleischer Studios, Inc. entered a crisis from which it never emerged.[29]

Other factors contributed to the fiscal woes of the Fleischer Studios, Inc. and Walt Disney Productions. After suffering a financial blow from a lengthy 1937 strike, the Fleischers were confronted with the expense of moving their company from New York to a new facility in the non-union labour environment of Miami, Florida during 1938. Walt Disney spent much of the profit of *Snow White* on his new studio in Burbank. Shortly after this, Disney also had to cope with a bitter strike in 1941. Profits of both companies were adversely affected by the loss of Continental European and Asian markets during World War II, as well as by currency restrictions in the UK. Some attempt was made to adjust to these conditions by an expansion of activity in Central and South America. Despite these factors, the Prisoner's Dilemma suggests that technological innovation was a decisive determinant in the sinking fortunes of the Disney and Fleischer studios. The continuation of technological innovation by these two animation companies contrasted with the practice of the dominant feature-length, live-action film industry. In the era of mature oligopoly, the feature film industry sharply reduced its degree of reliance on technological innovation for purposes of product differentiation following a period of expensive innovation in competing sound, colour, three-dimensional, and wide-screen technologies from 1926 to 1935. With the standardization of sound and colour technologies, and with the abandonment of wide-screen and 3-D, the feature film industry entered into a period of financial stability marked by relatively little technological innovation until after World War II. In comparison with the experience of the Fleischer and Disney companies, the stability of this dominant sector was relatively unaffected by the loss of markets during wartime.

Nevertheless, the importance of technological differentiation to the financial well-being of the institution was an article of faith held by Walt Disney and Max Fleischer. Both men clearly believed in an ideology of progress, wherein technological development played a key role. In a 1941 article in *American Cinematographer*, Disney stated: '. . . the public will pay for quality. . . . Our business has grown with and by technical achievements. Should this technical progress ever come to a full stop, prepare the funeral oration for our medium.'[30] Shortly after the collapse of Fleischer Studios, Inc., Max Fleischer recalled his career as a series of successful technical innovations, culminating with his

29 The Stereoptical Process was most generally used in the two-reel 'Specials' and in films of the more expensive 'Color Classics' series, such as *Little Dutch Mill* (1934) or *Hawaiian Birds* (1936). Isolated examples of the Stereoptical Process can be found in lower-budget black and white Fleischer cartoons. Examples include the 'Betty Boop' film *Housecleaning Blues* (1937) or the 'Popeye' cartoons *King of the Mardi Gras* (1935) and *Little Swee'Pea* (1936). More generally, depth effects were provided by exaggerated perspective drawing, as seen in the 'Talkartoon' *Sky scraping* (1930) or the 'Peopeye' *A Dream Walking* (1934). In an attempt to control the cost of production for the Fleischer features, three-dimensional effects were limited to an opening sequence of a ship in *Gulliver's Travels* and a descending camera track through the model of a city in *Mr Bug Goes to Town*. Most depth effects in the features were achieved through a return to exaggerated perspective drawing. After the returns from *Gulliver's Travels*, the Fleischer Studios, Inc. owed Paramount $100,000 in payment of loans. Following the disastrous release of *Mr Bug Goes to Town*, Paramount was owed $473,000. King Features Syndicate, Inc. and Fleischer Studios, Inc., *Agreement*, 17 February 1937, pp. 15, 19; Botsford to Holman, Keough, Fleischer and Fleischer, *Agreement*, pp. 2, 3, 11, 12; 'The big bad wolf', pp. 91, 94; 'Instead of getting $80,000, Disney says he'll lose 56G on US tax short', *Variety*, vol. 145, no. 10 (1942), p. 19; Richard Murray, *Deposition*, *Dave Fleischer v. AAP Inc.*, *et al.*, US District Court Southern District of New York, 6 December 1957.

30 Walt Disney, 'Growing pains', *American Cinematographer*, vol. 22, no. 3 (1941), p. 106.

31 Max Fleischer to Jimmy (Shamus) Culhane, *c.* December 1945, Collection of Shamus Culhane, p. 2.

introduction of 'the very first attempt to incorporate a third dimensional effect in cartoons . . . by the "Setback" method of photography.'[31]

Was the Multiplane camera a competitive response to the Fleischer system? Preliminary research strongly suggests that early Multiplane camera development did imitate the Stereoptical Process. Although few documents on Multiplane development exist, Disney employee Ken Anderson recalled that in 1935 he created a three-dimensional model of a door for an early horizontal version of the Disney 3-D process. When photographed with foreground cel images, the result showed Snow White interacting with the three-dimensional set. A search at the Disney Archives has failed to document why this earlier system was abandoned, although the need to avoid patent infringement seems a likely reason. It should be remembered that both Ub Iwerks's three-dimensional apparatus and a later Walt Disney Productions model of the Multiplane camera developed for the last shot of *Fantasia* used the same horizontal format as the earlier Fleischer process. The Disney Horizontal Multiplane camera also had the potential for the use of three-dimensional materials or mock-ups.[32]

32 Use of this horizontal version of the Multiplane camera was limited to the last shot of the 'Night on a Bald Mountain/Ave Maria' sequence of *Fantasia*. Ken Anderson, interview by David Smith, 5 September 1975, Walt Disney Archives; Thomas and Johnston, *Disney Animation*, p. 264.

At the time of their introduction, these innovations were perceived as technologically differentiating one studio's product from those of others. 'News stories' planted by Paramount pointed out that Max Fleischer's 'camera wizardry' brought about an advance over the earlier two-dimensional animation system. *Popeye the Sailor Meets Sindbad the Sailor* was publicized as the 'first two-reel, full-color, three-dimensional film'. *The Old Mill* received an Academy Award for best animated short subject, and the Disney studio was awarded another Oscar for 'technical achievement' in the development of the Multiplane camera. As had been the case with the Stereoptical Process, the Multiplane camera was extensively publicized as an important technological innovation.[33]

33 'Popeye slams foes into third dimension through Fleischer's camera wizardry', and 'Popeye knocks Bluto into third dimension', in *Popeye the Sailor Meets Sindbad the Sailor Pressbook* (New York: Paramount, 1936), pp. 13, 15; Schickel, *The Disney Version*, pp. 164–5; 'Three-ply Mickey coming: Disney announces new process for tri-dimensional films', *The New York Journal-American*, 28 May 1937; Frank S. Nugent, 'This Disney Whirl', *The New York Times*, 29 January 1939, p. 5.

The publicity and awards given to these technologies might seem to support the evolutionary or teleological argument that their development was an advance on the road to mimesis. Yet, as mentioned above, the Multiplane camera and the Stereoptical Process were used infrequently after a few years, which suggests that they were more of a dead end than the road of progress. The economic consequences of using such expensive technologies simply did not justify their continued use.

Did economics stand in the way of aesthetic evolution? Historical contentions that the Stereoptical Process was developed for reasons of mimesis are arguable.[34] Max Fleischer maintained that he was opposed to mimesis in animation during the time in which he developed the Stereoptical Process.

34 See Russell George, 'Some spatial characteristics of the Hollywood cartoon' for considerations of the differences between live action and cartoon realism.

During the span from 1914 to 1936, I made efforts to retain the 'cartoony' effect. . . . Let us assume we desire to create the last word in a true to life portrait. We examine the subject very carefully and religiously follow every shape, form and expression. We faithfully reproduce every light, shade and highlight. Upon completion of this grand effort, we compare our result with a photograph. . . . What have we now? Nothing at all. We have simply gone the long way around to create something which the camera can produce in seconds. In my opinion, the industry must pull back. Pull away from tendencies toward realism. It must stay in its own back yard of 'The Cartoonist's Cartoon'. The cartoon must be a portrayal of the expression of the true cartoonist, in simple, unhampered cartoon style. The true cartoon is a great art in its own right. It does not require the assistance or support of 'Artiness'. In fact, it is actually hampered by it.[35]

35 Fleischer to Culhane, *c.* December 1945; Richard Fleischer, interview with author, 6 October 1990.

Examination of the use of the Stereoptical Process in Fleischer films does tend to corroborate Max Fleischer's remarks. In no film is the Stereoptical Process consistently used as a background element. While there may be economic reasons for this, the effect on the screen is a rupture of the films' visual continuity. Through an alternation of three-dimensional and two-dimensional backgrounds, attention is drawn to the Stereoptical Process as a technological gimmick. Rather than reinforcing the realist codes of classical Hollywood cinema, the Fleischer use of the three-dimensional setback system appears to have been employed chiefly as a form of spectacle that contrasted with the traditional appearance of cel animation used in the rest of the film. Leonard Maltin and Russell George suggest that audiences of the time would not be aware that three-dimensional sets had been used. It is difficult, if not impossible, to reconstruct the perceptions of an audience more than fifty years ago. Examination of contemporary promotional literature released by the Fleischer Studios, Inc. and its distributor, Paramount, indicates that every attempt was made to draw the audience's attention to the use of this new technology. The opening credits of many Fleischer films included a title line heralding the use of the Stereoptical Process.[36]

36 Maltin, *Of Mice and Magic*, p. 114; George, 'Some spatial characteristics', p. 315; *Popeye the Sailor Meets Sindbad the Sailor Pressbook*, pp. 13, 15.

The employment of the Stereoptical Process in animated cartoons was consistent with the use of other Fleischer processes with a mimetic potential, such as the Rotoscope. In both *Gulliver's Travels* and *Mr Bug Goes to Town*, the human world and the worlds of Lilliput or the insects are defined by their degree of determination by photographic images. Both Gulliver and the 'Human Ones' are rotoscoped. Most of the Lilliputians and the insects are not. The juxtaposition of the two styles emphasizes the artificiality or 'cartooniness's of the film. A similar juxtaposition informs the visual discourse involving the Stereoptical Process.

The Multiplane camera was first developed for use in Disney's 'Silly Symphonies' series, of which William Garity—head of the studio team that developed Multiplane—once stated: 'It is the present intent to maintain this series in the realm of the unreal'.[37] The Multiplane camera maintained a uniform use of flat surfaces with some space separating each level of artwork. Lacking 'real' three-dimensional surfaces (such as angles or curves) that would contrast with the flat plane of

37 William Garity, 'The production of animated cartoons', *The Journal of the Society of Motion Picture Engineers*, vol. 20, no. 4 (1933), p. 309.

conventional animation cels, the Multiplane camera's two-dimensional surfaces may not seem to offer as great a potential for visual discontinuity with conventional cel animation as did the three-dimensional backgrounds employed by the Stereoptical Process. Nevertheless, the most often cited examples of Multiplane use—the long tracking shots in *The Old Mill*, or the camera descent to Pinocchio's doorway as he prepares to leave for school—emphasize the camera's potential for spatial realism.

These three-dimensional effects were not the only reason for the development of the Multiplane camera. According to William Garity, a major reason for the camera's development was that 'almost any scene can be broken down in such a way that lighting, colour and optical control is achieved over any part or all of the scene. This control would not be at all practical if the technique was confined to a single plane.'[38] Special effects were a primary consideration in the design of the apparatus. The Multiplane camera was used for sequences that were often anything but mimetic, or stylistically continuous with the rest of the picture. Disney layout artist Kendall O'Connor recalls that sections of the cartoony 'Dance of the Hours' sequence in *Fantasia* and the surreal 'Pink Elephants' fantasy sequence in *Dumbo* were shot with the Multiplane camera. This was done to take advantage of the superior control that the Multiplane camera gave in achieving a higher degree of artificial stylization. For example, the device's detailed control of light on each plane permitted the use of a better flat black background for the stylized shenanigans of the 'Pink Elephants' sequence.[39] The episodic quality of *Fantasia* emphasized the ruptures and contrasts among disparate styles—such as the abstraction of 'Toccata and Fugue in D. Minor', the 'cartoony' burlesque of 'Dance of the Hours', and the realistic drama of natural evolution in 'The Rite of Spring'. As Disney films became more discontinuous in terms of narrative and graphic style during the 1940s, those Multiplane camera sequences that emphasized three-dimensionality increasingly tended to create discontinuity when juxtaposed with more 'cartoony' elements, or with live action, as seen in *Saludos Amigos* (1943), *The Three Caballeros* (1945), or *Song of the South* (1946).[40]

Conventional wisdom has it that American animation was rescued from the aesthetic dead end of realism by Warner Bros and UPA animators. Steve Schneider claims that the stylized backgrounds and movement in Chuck Jones's *The Dover Boys* (1942) heralded a new beginning in American animation as 'the first cartoon since the rise of Disney in which the demands of realism were almost entirely banished. . . . Later in the 1940s, some of the founders of the UPA studio cited the film as an inspiration for their innovations.'[41] Ralph Stephenson identified this new trend in post-World War II animation as 'moving away from realism. . . . UPA started this'.[42]

Such considerations look for continuity within the output of a studio. For example, while Schneider hails the change in Jones's style in 1942,

38 William Garity, *The Disney Multiplane Crane*, n.d., Walt Disney Archives, *c.* 1938, p. 3.

39 A. Kendall O'Connor, interview with the author, 24 May 1991.

40 For a closer analysis of the separate discourses in *Dumbo*, see Mark Langer, 'Regionalism in Disney animation: Pink Elephants and Dumbo', *Film History*, vol. 4, no. 4 (1990), pp. 305–21.

41 Steve Schneider, *That All Folks! The Art of Warner Bros Animation* (New York: Henry Holt, 1990), p. 73.

42 Ralph Stephenson, *The Animated Film*, pp. 48–9. Similar evaluations are found in George, 'Some spatial characteristics', p. 306; Maltin, *The Disney Films*, p. 274.

elsewhere in his book he observes somewhat contradictorily that Jones's 'Sniffles' cartoons 'stayed heavily under the Disney influence . . . [with] . . . slower and atmospheric pacing . . . realistic backgrounds, and a striving for "cuteness" throughout'. Jones continued to make 'Sniffles' cartoons in this style through 1946.[43]

43 Schneider, *That's All Folks!*, p. 60.

Similar problems arise in the categorization of Disney and late Fleischer films as 'realistic'. Histories portray the Disney and Fleischer studios as latecomers to the tendency towards abstraction and stylization pioneered elsewhere. Animation historians confirm the existence of unified styles within the products of these companies, uninfluenced by the production of other animation studios until the artistic mantle passed to Warner Bros and UPA in the 1942 to 1949 period. Earlier Disney and Fleischer abstractions, or stylizations, such as the apparent breaking and splicing of the film image in Fleischer's *Goonland*, the distorted images in the hall of mirrors in Disney's *Bone Trouble*, the story presented as still sketches in the 'Baby Weems' sequence in *The Reluctant Dragon*, the self-reflexive antics and lyrics in the 'Pink Elephants' sequence of *Dumbo*, or the simple outlines, flat background, and electronic, percussive score of the 'Jitterbug' sequence in *Mr Bug Goes to Town*, all appear to exist outside of history. The Stereoptical Process and the Multiplane camera do not obliterate these tendencies—they coexist with them, clash with them, complement them, and even support them.

No single historical methodology can account for all aspects of any item from the past. This study is not intended as a theory of history, even in the restricted context of animation technology. My observations merely suggest how previous treatments of the subject fail to account fully for the development and use of three-dimensional processes. Evolutionary or teleological theories do not account for the discontinuities in the use of the Stereoptical Process and the Multiplane camera, nor does the 'great man' theory account for the institutional structure of the American animation industry. Aesthetic changes do not necessarily occur in a coherent, linear manner. All of these methodologies assume a kind of rational, continuous unfolding of technological history. As this study demonstrates, innovation takes place in a context far more complex and fragmented than that envisaged in previous considerations of the Stereoptical Process and Multiplane camera.

11 *Baby Face,* or how Joe Breen made Barbara Stanwyck atone for Causing the Wall Street Crash

RICHARD MALTBY

In order to ensure the appearance of legitimacy for its actions, censorship is obliged to imagine an audience for the text it is censoring, and assess that audience's cumulative response to its various discourses. In this activity of imagining audiences, if not in the motivation for it, the behaviour of censorship resembles that of criticism. It is, indeed, at this point of correspondence that the examination of censorship procedures may prove useful to that critical activity which calls itself theory. Obviously, the institution of censorship is not independent of other social forces: the censorship procedures established by the Motion Picture Producers and Distributors of America, Inc. (MPPDA) during the 1920s and 1930s integrated 'self-regulation' within the larger institution of cinema production, distribution, and exhibition. Under the supervision of the Studio Relations Committee (SRC), the application of the Production Code preceded the profilmic event, and was in part justified to the producers in terms of the financial savings incurred by not shooting unusable material. Primary documentation regarding the procedures of censorship might be expected to reveal, with greater accuracy than, say, the reminiscences of directors, how the institution of cinema intended and expected its products to be received.

Such a documented guide to expected meaning may be of particular use in considering potentially subversive readings of Hollywood texts. The production of a subversive reading can be described as a process by which the critic constitutes himself or herself as the subject of a text in some way other than that which the text proposes. Necessarily, the subversive reading must claim knowledge of a preferred reading. It is evident from the extent of critical disagreement over, for example, the preferred reading of *Blonde Venus* (Paramount, 1932) or *She Done Him Wrong* (Paramount, 1933), that particular periods and representations present problems of ambiguity in establishing what constitutes a preferred reading.

In an account of *Dance, Girl, Dance* (RKO, 1940) as a critique of patriarchy, Claire Johnston privileges 'Dorothy Arzner' as an agency of extracinematic intention identifiable from within the realm of the cinematic.[1] In her analysis of *Blonde Venus*, E. Ann Kaplan goes a stage further in distinguishing between the intentions of 'Dietrich' in her performance and those of 'von Sternberg' in his direction of that performance: '[Dietrich's] understanding of the extracinematic discourse she is being placed in permits a certain distance from what is being done to her, providing a gap through which the female spectator can glimpse her construction in patriarchy'.[2] As the subject of creative play among the discourses of the text, the critic may feel able to move at will between the realms of the cinematic and the extracinematic, and the privileging of specific elements of the extracinematic may be further justified in the name of polemic. However, if the critic-as-subject is restrained only by the subjectivity of the critic, the limits of permissible reading become difficult to establish. As the above examples indicate, constructing a purely cinematic criticism which only engages 'what results from the cinematic apparatus'[3] is extraordinarily difficult and also necessarily ahistorical. Such criticism can discuss ideology only if it presupposes that the ideology it discusses is stable and unchanging.

Like censorship itself, history intrudes upon the playful critic as a machine for the repression of subversive meaning, providing among other things tools for the examination of intent. As such, it operates antithetically to structuralist and psychoanalytic approaches. It may, however, be employed dialectically in the hope of generating a synthesis which educates the text both from itself and from its historical specificity. There would seem to be at least potential fruitfulness in combining an analytical framework with an historical contextualization, which, while not determining a single reading, suggests limits to the range of meanings available at the moment of production.

In what has become the standard textbook for US film history courses, Robert Sklar argues that

> In the first half decade of the Great Depression, Hollywood's movie-makers perpetrated one of the most remarkable challenges to traditional values in the history of mass commercial entertainment. The movies called into question sexual propriety, social decorum and the institutions of law and order.[4]

Sklar implies an element of intent on the part of 'Hollywood's movie-makers' and also that the censorship procedures adopted by the industry in February 1930 were inadequate to prevent producers resorting to the more explicit depiction of sex and violence as a means

1 'Towards the end of the film Arzner brings about her tour de force, cracking open the entire fabric of the film and exposing the workings of the ideology in the construction of the stereotype of woman.' Claire Johnston, 'Woman's cinema as counter cinema', in Patricia Ehrens (ed.), *Sexual Stratagems: The World of Women in Film* (New York: Horizon Press, 1979), p. 141.

2 E. Ann Kaplan, *Women and Film: Both Sides of the Camera* (London and New York: Methuen, 1983), p. 52.

3 Ibid., p. 20.

4 Robert Sklar, *Movie-Made America* (New York: Random House, 1975), p. 175.

of holding on to a declining audience. Taking their cue primarily from Raymond Moley's paean of praise to business self-regulation, *The Hays Office*, most accounts of the period suggest that 'The years 1930–1933 passed without a notable improvement in the quality of pictures and without the elimination of those objectionable themes and treatments which had brought about the creation and adoption of the Code'.[5]

Revisionist historians have interpreted the 'official' account of the limited effectiveness of censorship as opening up the possibility of Hollywood's producing 'subversive' films.

> Suppose for the sake of argument that scarcely any Hollywood films of the 1930s were actively hostile to capitalism in a direct political sense. One could nevertheless make a case for saying that Hollywood was in certain ways strongly subversive of the dominant sexual ideology. How else can one explain the outrage of groups such as the League [*sic*] of Decency and Hollywood's attempts to censor itself through the adoption of the Motion Picture Production Code.[6]

The case for Hollywood's subversion of dominant sexual ideology is made in Molly Haskell's *From Reverence to Rape*, where she suggests that 'It was really in the early 30s that the revolutionary 20s spirit, at least the questioning of marriage and conventional morality, took hold'.[7]

Sklar refers to 'the golden age of turbulence' between 1930 and 1934 as 'an aberration, a surprise even to Hollywood itself'.[8] The aberration may, however, lie more in the interpretation than in the event. If the movies of the early 1930s were declaring their proclaimed sexual and other radicalism, they would constitute an aberration both in terms of the general trend in popular culture during the early Depression years, and the movies' ideological behaviour during the rest of their history. While such behaviour is possible, it is sufficiently unlikely to require substantial critical proof.

The textual evidence for Hollywood's 'challenge to traditional values' is conventionally provided by readings of a small group of films, invariably including *I Am a Fugitive from a Chain Gang* (1932), three gangster movies, Mae West, the Marx Brothers, and seldom totalling more than twenty movies, or less than 1 per cent of Hollywood's feature film output during the period 1930–4. It is too small and too familiar a sample on which to base so substantial a conclusion as that the film-makers of Hollywood were fomenting social or moral disorder, particularly when the list does not correspond very closely with those films with which the censors themselves—both inside and outside the Hays Office—were most concerned.

However, it is clear enough that many movies of the period contain symptoms of a cultural crisis within patriarchal capitalism: in crime films, the recurring motif of the death of the father, and the inadequacy of a figure who seeks to speak in the name of the father; the frequent depiction of a 'distaste for the nuclear family' which Kaplan identifies in *Blonde Venus*.[9] It is equally clear, though much less remarked upon, that a significant number of the films of the early 1930s, including many of

5 Raymond Moley, *The Hays Office* (New York: Bobbs-Merrill, 1946), p. 75.

6 Edward Buscombe, 'Bread and circuses: economics and the cinema', in Patricia Mellencamp and Philip Rosen (eds.), *Cinema Histories, Cinema Practices* (Los Angeles, CA: American Film Institute, 1984), p. 8.

7 Molly Haskell: *From Reverence to Rape: The Treatment of Women in the Movies* (New York: Holt Reinhart and Winston, 1974), p. 45.

8 Sklar, *Movie-Made America*, p. 176.

9 Kaplan, *Women and Film*, p. 56.

those discussed within conventional histories, were themselves accounts of the events of the previous decade, and, in common with much other cultural production of the period, reflected on how the events of that decade had led to the Crash.[10] It is in this broader context of capitalism's representation of itself at a particular moment of crisis that patriarchy's distinctive representation of Woman and female sexuality during this period can best be placed.

The decade after the World War I was witness to the extensive development of a mass consumer culture in the USA, marked most strongly by the growth of advertising. Elements of this culture found themselves in strenuous conflict with the cultural and social patterns of Victorian patriarchal sensibility, a conflict indicated by the widespread image of generational antagonism that pervaded much of the period's popular culture. Much of the conflict was oriented around a revision of prevailing codes of sexuality: as advertising promoted the act of consumption as therapeutic process, it encouraged, in its imagery, a revaluation of the cultural place of the erotic. Movies participated in this process in two distinct realms: narrative and spectacle. In narrative terms, as Lary May has documented, movies told stories in which an exuberant American female sexuality was revealed to be monogamous and innocent.[11] The DeMille films of the early 1920s were comedies of remarriage, in which a sexuality discovered outside the conventions of Victorian patriarchy was relocated within a revised version of the institution. Acts of consumption were crucial to this process; by providing novelty through a change of appearances, they offered the means to preserve monogamy. The culture of consumption promoted fashion as a mechanism of change that in itself not only increased the obligation to consume but provided a substitute for other, more politically active, forms of change. The prewar energies of middle-class feminism proved particularly vulnerable to such recuperative diversion.

> The emphasis on self-realization through emotional fulfillment, the devaluation of public life in favor of a leisure world of intense private experience, the need to construct a pleasing 'self' by purchasing consumer goods—these therapeutic imperatives helped to domesticate the drive toward female emancipation. With great fanfare, advertisers offered women the freedom to smoke Lucky Strikes or buy 'natural' corsets. They promised fake liberation through consumption, and many women accepted this new version of male hegemony.[12]

By offering themselves to their audiences as idols of consumption both within the movies themselves and through the secondary industries of publicity, stars took a significant role in advertising the therapeutic pleasures of the intense life.

> All the adventure, all the romance, all the excitement you lack in your daily life are in—Pictures. They take you completely out of yourself into a wonderful new world. . . . Our of the cage of everyday existence! If only for an afternoon or an evening—escape![13]

10 e.g. *I Am A Fugitive from a Chain Gang, Public Enemy*.

11 Lary May, *Screening Out the Past: The Birth of Mass Culture and the Motion Picture Industry* (New York: Oxford University Press, 1980), p. 211.

12 T. J. Jackson Lears, 'From salvation to self-realization: advertising and the therapeutic roots of the consumer culture, 1880–1930', in Richard Wrightman Fox and T. J. Jackson Lears (eds.), *The Culture of Consumption: Critical Essays in American History, 1880–1980* (New York: Pantheon Books, 1983), p. 27.

13 Advertisement in the *Saturday Evening Post* quoted in Robert S. Lynd and Helen Merrell Lynd, *Middletown: A Study in Modern American Culture* (Harcourt, Brace and World: 1929), p. 265.

The generalized advertising of US consumer goods was one of the ways in which Will Hays, President of the MPPDA, insisted that 'The Movies Are Helping America'.

> In pictures orderly and effective home-keeping equipment for sweeping, scrubbing, washing, stirring, mixing, sewing, made their appearance, and gradually it became plain that these things freed woman from enervating toil. From the picture to the fact was an inevitable procedure. Gradually these things liberated woman to express herself in terms more befitting her dignity.[14]

The culture of consumption described the newly dignified woman as 'manager' of her home, but in the movies she celebrated her liberation from domestic drudgery through an anxious concern with appearance, in preparation for erotic activity. Both the advertising industry and the movies 'engaged in a therapeutic renovation of sensuality . . . locating eroticism in settings characterized by affluence, respectability, and, above all, health'.[15]

Their promotion of consumer culture constructed and revealed the contradiction of its representation of woman as object but not subject of desire. Female sexuality was recuperated in narrative terms within the constraints of monogamy, but it pervaded the culture as spectacle—a spectacle publicly directed at women, and overtly representing a new realization of the female self. In DeMille's bath scenes and advertisements for toiletries sensuality was cleansed of 'Victorian associations with poverty, disease, and dirt'.[16] A recurring image showed women observing themselves in mirrors: 'I saw my body. I saw my legs, my torso, my long, long arms. . . . I had never looked at my body as a piece of statuary. . . . I had this marvelous feeling. I can still feel the chills all over my body'.[17] Stuart Ewen's analysis of cosmetic advertisements focuses more explicitly on autoerotic perception.

> Though the victorious heroines . . . always got their man, they did so out of a commodity defined *self-fetishization* which made that man and themselves almost irrelevant to the quality of their victory. Their romantic triumphs were ultimately commercially defined versions of the auto-erotic ones of Alban Berg's prostitute, *Lulu*, who declares that 'When I looked at myself in the mirror I wished I were a man—a man married to me.'[18]

As in pornography, the autoeroticism of the gaze in the mirror ratifies the voyeurism of the male gaze. However, the cinematic representation also established an irreconcilable contradiction between the indiscriminate availability of woman as an object of scopophilic desire and the narrative insistence on the constriction of her permitted sexuality within monogamy. This contradiction, and its apparent resolution around voyeuristic/narcissistic identification within contemporary psychoanalytic theory, is historically more specific than theorists of patriarchy sometimes imply. It depends on the appearance of permissive, autoerotic images of female sexuality, and while these

14 Will H. Hays, 'The movies are helping America', *Good Housekeeping*, January 1933, pp. 45, 130.

15 Lears, 'From salvation to self-realization', p. 28.

16 Ibid.

17 Actress Betty Blythe, in Kevin Brownlow, *The Parade's Gone By*, p. 436, quoted in May, *Screening Out the Past*, p. 230.

18 Stuart Ewen, *Captains of Consciousness: Advertising and the Social Roots of the Consumer Culture* (New York: McGraw-Hill, 1976) p. 48.

were a staple of visual pornography, such images only began to proliferate in the culture through advertising and the movies in the 1920s. It was precisely the spread of such images that the reform groups were criticising.

The film industry had been a substantial beneficiary of Progressive reform and Prohibition, but reformers maintained a wary concern over the possible deleterious effects—both physical and moral—of movies on their audiences. Throughout the 1920s the MPPDA managed to contain this concern through an elaborate public relations exercise which co-opted potentially troublesome organizations, such as the General Federation of Women's Clubs and the International Federation of Catholic Alumnae, into its 'Open Door' programmes to promote 'better movies', and isolated the demand for governmental supervision of the industry as extremist. A number of events at the end of the decade rendered Hays's coalition of 'responsible groups' increasingly unstable. In late 1929 the leading Episcopalian newspaper, *The Churchman*, began a campaign against the MPPDA culminating in allegations that it had 'retained' officials of the Federal Council of Churches of Christ in America in exchange for favourable opinions on movies. These disclosures initiated widespread criticism of the industry throughout the Protestant religious press from 1930 onwards, and the resultant publicity focused the attention of educationalists, parent–teacher groups and other organizations on the issue. A loose alliance between these interests and independent exhibitors hostile to the MPPDA as an instrument of monopoly developed to support legislation linking control of movie content to federal regulation of monopoly practices such as block booking, which exhibitors and reformers argued prohibited community supervision of movie standards.

This argument was taking place amidst a general reaction among white Protestants to the apparent permissiveness of the postwar decade—a reaction evident before 1929, but greatly exacerbated by the Crash. Throughout the culture there were attempts to explain and account for the failure of the system couched in terms seeking to preserve the economic base.[19] Victorian patriarchy strove to reassert itself by identifying the alleged permissiveness of the Jazz Age as the scapegoat for the collapse of the economy.[20]

The demands for movie reform should thus be seen as part of a broader reaffirmation of traditional patriarchal values at a moment of cultural crisis. This reaffirmation, itself a displaced expression of anxiety for the economic system among the middle class, focused primarily on a concern that the family unit was in danger of disintegrating.[21] Motherhood, which had 'virtually disappeared from films as the main aspiration for a woman',[22] underwent a strenuous revival. Periodicals aimed at middle-class women ran articles extolling the fulfilment to be derived from domesticity, recantations from ex-feminists, and proposals that women who did not need to work should return to the home.[23] The overt concern of movie reform groups

19 e.g. Harold J. Laski, Can business be civilized?' *Harper's*, January 1930.

20 e.g. Harold de Wolf Fuller, 'The Myth of Modern Youth', *North American Review*, June 1929; G. Murray, 'The Crisis in Morals', *Harper's*, January 1930; Mary Roberts Rinehart, 'The Chaotic Decade', *Ladies Home Journal*, May 1930.

21 e.g. Floyd H. Allport, 'Must we scrap the family?' *Harper's*, July 1930.

22 May, *Screening Out the Past*, p. 212.

23 e.g., Elizabeth Cook, 'The Kitchen-Sink Complex', *Ladies' Home Journal*, September 1931; Worth Tuttle, 'Autobiography of an Ex-Feminist', *Atlantic Monthly*, December 1933; Rita S. Halle, 'Do You Need Your Job?' *Good Housekeeping*, September 1932.

with the deleterious effect of movies on children aligned them with the larger trend, while the underlying anxieties of white Protestants regarding their declining control of the culture was reflected in the overt anti-urbanism and implicit anti-Semitism of the campaign.

One consequence of this public concern was an increase in the activity of the state and municipal censor boards, and in the unpredictability of that activity. The industry required a mechanism to safeguard its products from such uncertainties—particularly given the costs of re-editing early sound films. The officials administering the Production Code acknowledged the industry's obligation to defend 'the accepted standards of the American family',[24] and 'the sanctity of marriage which . . . is the very foundation of society',[25] but much of the early work of the Studio Relations Committee involved monitoring and codifying the activities of the state boards in order to advise the studios about probable deletions. In the first years of its operation the accuracy of its predictions was vital to the establishment of its credibility with the studio heads of production.

The behaviour of the state boards varied between states and over time. Cuts made in movies between 1930 and 1934 show a pattern of increasingly rigorous control; one manifestation of this pattern being the frequency with which officials of the board wrote to Hays or Colonel Jason Joy, the first Director of the SRC, complaining about current standards. One inference from such complaints is that movies were becoming ever more 'daring' in their presentation of sexuality and crime. Such a claim is extremely difficult to measure in any absolute terms, but the impression of a continuous 'decline' of moral standards during the early 1930s is a simplified view of a complex situation in which the general cultural climate was moving towards an increased moral conservatism.

The debate among the institutions of censorship over what the SRC described as 'social problem' pictures was centred around the efficacy of narrative recuperation in contradicting scopophilic pleasure, expressed in terms of the extent to which a film's morality was to be assessed on the basis of 'the effect of the whole',[26] or on the details of its depiction. Until March 1933, Code officials continued to argue the producers' case that 'pictures that leave a certain final moral lesson' should be permitted a dramatic licence to include 'details that give the audience the opportunity to contrast good and evil'. The censors were not inclined to accept the argument.[27] Dealing with an already completed product, they were primarily concerned with the elimination of detail: outright rejection of entire films was rare, and invariably began a process of negotiation to discover what deletions would make the film acceptable. While the SRC sought to persuade the censors that the Code provided an adequate alternative to their statutes, most of its negotiations with the studios had to do with ensuring that it could defend a narrative through the interpretation of a Code principle such as 'Sympathy with a person who sins is not the same as sympathy with the sin or crime of which he is guilty'.[28]

24 Lamar Trotti, memo, 23 July 1931, Production Code Administration (PCA) *Back Street* Case File, at the Library of the Academy of Motion Picture Arts and Sciences, Los Angeles, California.

25 Joseph Breen to Dr James Wingate, then Director of the New York State censor board, 5 May 1933, RKO Production File, *Ann Vickers*, RKO Archives, Los Angeles.

26 Joy to Wingate, 5 February 1931, PCA *Little Caesar* Case File.

27 e.g. Wingate to Joy, 11 February 1931, PCA *Little Caesar* Case File.

28 'The Reasons Supporting Preamble of the Code', reproduced in Moley, *The Hays Office*, pp. 245–6.

29 Gerard B. Donnelly, SJ, 'An open letter to Dr Wingate', *America*, 29 October 1932, pp. 85–6.

30 'Children and the movies', editorial reporting an address on the Payne Fund Studies by William H. Short, Director of the Motion Picture Research Council, to the Spring 1933 meeting of the Society of Motion Picture Engineers, *America*, 6 May 1933, p. 100.

31 Wingate to Hays, 5 June 1931, PCA *The Big Brain* Case File.

32 Joy to Breen, 15 December 1931, PCA *Possessed* Case File.

33 Joy to William Orr, MGM New York, 14 June 1932 (unsent) PCA *Red-Headed Woman* Case File.

The reform lobby ignored such sophistry by insisting that the manner of presentation led audiences to identify with the sinners and hence sympathize with the sin. 'We feel justified in the complaint that our most competent stars are guilty of endowing unchastity with glamour.'[29] Their concern was primarily with detail, because it was the details of behaviour in the movies that children, in particular, remembered and imitated.

> They pay little attention to film morals or retribution, and the idea that a moral at the end cancels out in the child's mind unwholesome material that he has seen earlier in the picture is utterly mistaken.[30]

A second issue between the MPPDA and the censor boards was the industry's predilection for the crude but reliable market mechanism of rushing imitations of profitable pictures into production, generating seasonal cycles. When such cycles provoked controversy, the takings of individual movies were undoubtedly increased, but they provided the reform lobby with evidence of the industry's lack of social responsibility. On occasion, Hays invoked the powers of the MPPDA Board of Directors to control production: most notably, in September 1931 when the Board resolved to cease production of gangster pictures.[31] The solution of one problem, however, provoked another:

> With crime practically denied them, with box-office figures down, with high-pressure methods being employed back home to spur the studios to get in a little more cash, it was almost inevitable that sex, as the nearest thing at hand and pretty generally sure-fire, would be seized upon. It was.[32]

By the end of February 1932, Colonel Joy was complaining to Hays that a cycle of 'kept woman' films, inaugurated in mid-1931 with *Possessed* (MGM, 1931) and *Back Street* (Universal, 1932), was becoming a major problem. He clearly saw this cycle as comparable to the gangster films.

> In the gangster picture the gangster was not a hero. . . . And yet, because he was the central figure, because he achieved power, money and a certain notoriety, our critics complained that an inevitable attractiveness resulted. . . . They said we killed him off, but that we made him glamorous before we shot him. This is what you are apt to be charged with in this case. While the red-headed woman is a common little creature from over the tracks who steals other women's husbands and who uses her sex attractiveness to do it, she is the central figure and it will be contended that a certain glamor surrounds her. . . . I have a real fear not only of what the censors may do to the picture, but what the public itself will say.[33]

The controversy over the 'kept woman' cycle grew with the release of MGM's *Red-Headed Woman* in June 1932. Written by Anita Loos, it was a comedy in which Jean Harlow progressed up the social and material ladder by a series of affairs: 'Essentially it is an exposition of the theory that the wages of sin are wealth, luxury and social position,

34 Martin Quigley, *Decency in Motion Pictures* (New York: Macmillan, 1937) p. 38.

the only desiderata being physical charm and the willingness to accept the proffered prices.'[34]

What distinguished *Red-Headed Woman* from previous examples of the cycle was that the film made comedy out of what had previously been exclusively the material for melodrama and moreover provided a comic rather than a melodramatic conclusion: the film ends with Harlow living in luxury in Paris.

The ammunition it gave to the reform lobby was only part of the problem. In July 1932 Joy wrote despairingly to New York, 'probably right now half of the other companies are trying to figure out ways of topping this particular picture'.[35] Paramount's response, orchestrated by its new head of production, Emmanuel Cohen, included the purchase of William Faulkner's *Sanctuary* and the signing of a contract with Mae West. Both actions caused Hays and his officials considerable anxiety because, as Hays told Adolph Zukor, Paramount's behaviour 'disturbs the other companies and the whole inter-company relationship'.[36] Hays's fear was that the other studios would feel themselves obliged to imitate and outdo each other in competing for the sensational element of the urban trade, and in the process destroy the remains of his and the Association's credibility with the 'Open Door' coalition whose support he needed to resist the reform lobby. Protesting the news that Paramount were planning to film West's stage play *Diamond Lil*, Harry Warner implied that his company would, indeed, resort to such tactics.[37] Within three weeks, his head of production had produced an outline for *Baby Face*.

35 Joy to Carl Milliken, 7 July 1932, PCA *Red-Headed Woman* Case File.

36 Hays to Adolph Zukor, 16 November 1932, PCA *She Done Him Wrong* Case File.

37 H. M. Warner to Hays, 19 October 1932, PCA *She Done Him Wrong* Case File.

38 *Baby Face*, Short Story, no author shown (screen credits identify the author as Mark Canfield, one of Darryl Zanuck's pseudonyms), 9 November 1932, 8pp., at the Warner Library of the Wisconsin Center for Film and Theater Research, Madison, Wisconsin.

Darryl Zanuck's short story[38] is clearly borrowed from the Harlow film: it refers to the 'psychology of the "red-headed woman"' and similarly tells a story of social climbing through sexual adventure—one which is, however, unrelieved by comedy. It represents an escalation in explicitness from the comparable plots of the working-girl/Cinderella stories of the previous decade (*Love 'Em and Leave 'Em* (Famous Players–Lasky, 1926); *It* (Famous Players–Lasky, 1927)), by transforming the flirtatiousness of the Clara Bow/Louise Brooks flapper into an overt exploitation of female sexuality. Baby Face's predatory allure comes through her capacity to convince men of her innocence as she seduces them, but the mercenary nature of her motivation is explicit: 'all men wanted was her body, so she had given it to the highest bidder'. It also shifts the plot's locale from the site of consumption, a department store, to the site of contemporary financial crisis, a bank.

Escaping from the Depression landscape of a Pennsylvania steel town, Baby Face goes to 'the City', where, by way of a series of affairs with her immediate bosses, she progresses up the hierarchy of the Mercantile Trust Company, eventually transferring her affections from one of its managers to his fiancée's father, a director of the bank. When the younger man discovers this liaison, he shoots the director and then commits suicide. After a decent interval in Paris she takes up with the playboy President of the bank, having convinced him of her innocence.

In due course she marries him, and he lavishes furs, jewels, and securities on her. The bank suffers a collapse for which he is held responsible. He asks her to return his gifts to pay his bail, but she refuses. Just before she sails for Europe, she realizes that she really loves him. She returns to discover he has killed himself.

Haskell suggests that in most of her films, Harlow 'was no friend to her own sex',[39] but her misogyny was usually relieved by its comic context. Baby Face 'hates women',[40] and in her attitude to men evidences signs of a return to the original Theda Bara Vampire of *A Fool There Was* (Fox, 1915). Bara herself described the character as 'the vengeance of my sex upon its exploiters'[41] while Sumiko Higashi identifies a salient characteristic of Bara's which Baby Face shares:

Although the Vampire represented the full unleashing of the male's sexual instinct, she herself was always in control. She had not enough feeling to lose herself and was coldly calculating instead. It might even be construed that as a supernatural version of the whore, she was frigid.[42]

Baby Face enacts this role for most of the story, but at the end she succumbs to the conventional fate of the later, less powerful figure of the vamp, losing her power by falling victim to the very weakness she has previously exploited—romantic love; which, as a result of her previous behaviour, is available to her only in its tragic form of loss. The story describes a moral landscape of mutual exploitation, but does so within a narrative firmly constructed around the premise that such behaviour is itself immoral and not to be emulated.

Studio writers Gene Markey and Kathryn Scola produced a story outline on 21 November 1932. It begins with Lily Powers (Baby Face) the explicit victim of patriarchy. Her father exploits her to the point of trading her sexual services to a local politician in exchange for protection for his beer flat. Lily's refusal of the politician's advances is indirectly responsible for her father's death when his still explodes. The writers also introduced a supplementary character, Kragg, the town cobbler, as an alternative father-figure. Their outline[43] describes him as 'a gnarled, twisted, old German, a cripple—with a bitter resentment of the world . . . he reads Nietzsche, and he is steeped in the philosophy of nature—contempt for the weak. . . . Old Kragg is a sort of Mephistopheles. Through this girl he can get his revenge on society.'

In a 'brief but poignant scene' after the funeral of her father, he explains to her 'that she has been the victim of men—whereas she should make men her victims. That, just as a man can make use of men to rise in the world—even more easily can she, using her own weapon—sex!'

The introduction of Kragg has two, contradictory, effects. It provides a philosophical justification, referred to at several points in the script, for Lily's behaviour towards men. In one of her encounters with Stevens, the younger bank manager, the outline suggests

39 Haskell, *From Reverence to Rape*, p. 114.

40 *Baby Face*, Short Story, p. 1.

41 Quoted by Sumiko Higashi, *Virgins, Vamps and Flappers: The American Silent Movie Heroine* (St Albans, Vt.: Eden Press Women's Publications, 1978), p. 61.

42 Ibid., pp. 59–60.

43 *Baby Face*, Story Outline, 21 November 1932, at the Warner Library, Wisconsin Center for Film and Theater Research.

we establish her tremendous sex attraction for him. (We go as far in this scene as the censors will allow). . . . She resents—and rightfully—his coming to her for only one purpose, after he has spent the evening with his fiancee and his fashionable friends. Moreover, she resents the fiancee—because, with her Nietzschean ideal, she wants to be the one woman. . . . (At this point the audience will sympathize with Lily—because it is made plain that Stevens' only feeling toward her is wanting to sleep with her).

By both Kragg's description and the outline's representation of the male-dominated world, Lily's behaviour is rendered explicable and even at times sympathetic. On the other hand, Kragg's misanthropy is emphasized, while the plot denies everyone, particularly Lily, happiness. The outline depicts a world in which morality is unreliable, suggesting that Lily's 'Nietzschean' assertion of the self is encouraged by such unreliability; but also revealing that these conditions produce only turmoil and personal misery. In most respects, Lily's story mirrors the rise and fall of the gangster: her 'illegal' progress is iconographically charted by the acquisition of clothes and furnishings; her abrupt fall is marked by a moment of self-recognition, although in this case it occurs at the death of the object of her love rather than her own. A connection is made to the economic sphere through the image of Lily's literal progress up 'the gigantic forty-storey skyscraper of the Old Manhattan Trust Company'.[44] Lily's distraction of Trenholm, the bank's director, is identified as being the cause of the bank's failure, which occurs immediately after their marriage. This sequence of events imposes a causality on the narrative, implying a quite different ideological charge to that conventionally identified in gangster movies: less a left-handed version of the American success story with a moralizing ending appended for the benefit of the censors than a demonstration of the social failure provoked by the excesses of the previous decade.

Over the next four weeks Markey and Scola wrote a script which broadly followed the story outline. In Lily's rejection of her father, immediately prior to his death, she makes clear the perversity of the nuclear family she has been raised in. Declaring that her mother was right to leave him and is 'better off dead—than livin' with a thing like you!', Lily

> turns on him fiercely—all the pent-up bitterness of the years loosened in a sudden flood of rage.
> *Lily*: Yes, I'm a tramp! An' who's to blame?
> (looking at him with terrible loathing)
> My father! A swell start you gave me! Ever since I was fourteen—what's it been? Men!
> (screaming at him)
> Dirty, rotten men! An' you're lower than any of 'em!
> (her voice breaks hysterically)
> I'll hate you as long as I live![45]

44 Ibid., p. 9.

45 *Baby Face*, Final Script, 17 December 1932, at the Warner Library, Wisconsin Center for Film and Theater Research, pp. 20–1.

Later, the presentation of an idyllic view of family life becomes the occasion for a restatement of Kragg's philosophy. Alone on Christmas afternoon, Lily sees the family in the apartment next to hers gathered around their Christmas tree, father and children playing together. In her apartment she discovers a present from Kragg: Nietzsche's *Thoughts out of Season*. A passage is marked:

> 'Face life as you find it—defiantly and unafraid. Waste no energy yearning for the moon. Crush out all sentiment.' . . . She looks up and stares into the fire. . . . Her eyes are somber—bitter. When she came in this Christmas afternoon she was feeling sorry for herself. But now—from her friend, Kragg—this gospel of Nietzsche has brought her back to her hard point of view. Survival of the fittest![46]

46 Ibid., p. 82.

Kragg's function is to supply strength and purpose at precisely those moments when Lily's exclusion from family is announced. He offers an alternative patriarchy not simply in his plot location as substitute father, but explicitly in terms of his critique of the existing social structure as false consciousness.

With Trenholm, the bank president and the only man to see through her 'act' as the innocent victim of male sexual aggression, Lily reverts to conventional sexual mores in refusing to sleep with him until they marry: I'm just a little disappointed. . . . I was hoping you *wouldn't* be just like everybody else. . . . Silly of me, wasn't it?'[47] In these scenes it remains unclear as to how manipulative—of Trenholm and the audience—is Lily's attempt to revise the movie as a romance. When she refuses to return the money, her action is shown as uncertain, as if she is trying to convince herself:

47 Ibid., pp. 117–18.

> I have to think about myself! I've gone through a lot to get these things! My life's been miserable and hard! I'm not like other women—all the gentleness and kindness in me has been killed! All I've got are *these* things!
> (she hugs the case close to her breast)
> Without them I'd be nothing—I'd have to go back to what I was!
> (then with bitter fury)
> *No. I won't give them up![48]*

48 Ibid., pp. 131–2.

All her subsequent actions demonstrate her inability to enact her philosophy; her inability, in fact, to reject her prescribed role as Woman. The script leaves the process of her self-revelation ambiguous, only confirming it in her final discovery of Trenholm, still alive at Lily's return, in order that he may hear her declaration of love. Lily is finally redeemed/recuperated at the moment that she is also made to suffer through the recognition of her loss: she is accepted into the structures of patriarchy at the same time that she is punished for her earlier transgression of them. Kragg and Nietzsche have conveniently disappeared from the film's final reassertion of patriarchal romance. Lily, who began the movie in humourless imitation of Harlow's red-headed woman, ends it in imitation of Garbo's Susan Lennox.

The script of *Baby Face* shows 'the work that narrative and thematic organization performs to accommodate and recuperate developments like the independent woman stereotype'.[49] In doing so, it kept to the letter of the Production Code, as it was then being interpreted. The script was submitted to the Studio Relations Committee in the second week of December 1932.

> . . . it presents a problem, and a rather serious one from the censorship standpoint. With regard to the Code there is nothing we can find in it which is in violation, despite the fact that the theme is sordid and of a troublesome nature. However, we will do our best to clean it up as much as possible, and the fact that Barbara Stanwyck is destined for the leading role will probably mitigate some of the dangers in view of her sincere and restrained acting.[50]

After some internal discussion at the SRC, Dr James Wingate wrote to Zanuck on 3 January 1933. Remarking that it was hard to judge 'a story of this type' from the script alone, he expressed a naive confidence in Zanuck's supplying 'such moral values as may seem necessary to counterbalance the story, which without them might seem to stress to too great a degree the element of sex'. He reinforced the point by reminding Zanuck that *Red-Headed Woman* had been banned in several Canadian provinces and severely cut by the US state boards. He suggested Warners emphasize the moral lesson by so revising the ending

> as to indicate that in losing Trenholm she not only loses the one person whom she now loves, but that her money also will be lost. That is, if Lily is shown at the end to be no better off than she was when she left the steel town, you may lessen the chances of drastic censorship action, by thus strengthening the moral value of the story.

The draconian morality which insisted that female sexuality could not be shown to be profitable affected not only the scale of Lily's final punishment, but also her earlier conduct:

> . . . you ought to avoid making the facts of each relationship too explicit. This can be done by never really showing through dialogue or action that the man in each case is really paying for the apartment and supplying Lily with money and clothes in return for her affection.[51]

Wingate's letter made further detailed suggestions for deletions or changes in dialogue or action, premised, as SRC recommendations then were, by the comment that such material would be eliminated by state censor boards. Infractions of the Code were largely limited to specifically prohibited profanities, and the tone of this letter was typical in being advisory rather than demanding.

Production was completed in February 1933, and Wingate discussed it with Zanuck on 28 February. Wingate was particularly concerned about removing elements from the opening scene which implied that Lily's father was selling his daughter to the politician 'for immoral

49 Christine Gledhill, 'Developments in Feminist Film Criticism', in Mary Ann Doane, Patricia Mellencamp, and Linda Williams (eds.), *Re-Vision: Essays in Feminist Film Criticism* (Los Angeles, CA: American Film Institute, 1984), p. 40.

50 Wingate to Hays, 20 December 1932, PCA *Baby Face* Case File.

51 Wingate to Zanuck, 3 January 1933, PCA *Baby Face* Case File.

purposes'. Zanuck appeared, for once, to be cooperative, and Wingate emerged from their conference enthusiastic enough to write to Hays that Zanuck appreciated the problem created by sex pictures, and would not make them were it not for pressure from the sales department who had ordered 20 per cent of their product to be 'women's pictures, which inevitably means sex pictures'.[52]

52 Wingate to Hays, 28 February 1933, PCA *Baby Face* Case File.

The early months of 1933 comprised the low point of the industry's fortunes in the Depression. In late January Paramount and RKO were placed in receivership; Sidney Kent, President of Fox, was engaged in a legal battle with several of his board of directors to avoid the same fate. The crisis was primarily one of liquidity, with the companies failing to generate sufficient box-office revenues to sustain payments on the debts they had incurred in expanding in the late 1920s. In the atmosphere of uncertainty that preceded Roosevelt's inauguration, there was widespread fear that the entire industry was virtually bankrupt, and the immediate crisis deepened with the declaration of a bank holiday on 5 March. Box-office receipts were reported to have fallen by 45 per cent,[53] and weekly attendance was estimated to be as low as 28 million, a figure which supplied only 20 per cent of the income needed to defray weekly production costs.[54]

53 *Time*, 20 March 1933, p. 41.

54 C. F. Morgan, 'Climax of the Movie Tragedy Approaches', *Magazine of Wall Street*, 15 April 1933, p. 670.

The possibility of imminent economic collapse was not, however, the only problem the industry faced in early March. The exact nature of Roosevelt's proposals for government control of industry were not as yet clear, but bills hostile to the monopoly power of the major companies were to be presented to Congress, including a proposal by Representative Sirovich of New York for a wide-ranging Congressional investigation of the industry. State and municipal legislatures throughout the country were proposing a variety of local taxes on the movies as a readily available source of income. Hollywood's image of extravagance made it an acutely vulnerable financial target under such circumstances, and the reform lobby's growing ability to gain press coverage substantially increased that vulnerability. The first synopses of the Payne Fund Studies had been serialized in the September, October, and November 1932 issues of *McCall's*, and the claim that they would provide irrefutable scientific evidence of the detrimental effect of movies on children added considerably to the demands for governmental control.

The behaviour of the new Congress, and the extent to which it might regard such proposals sympathetically, was highly uncertain. There was a not unfounded fear that new members might believe that 'riding the movies is a profitable and tenable political position',[55] given the combination of moral disapproval occasioned by reports of the industry's financial dealings[56] and the untimely success of Mae West's first film, *She Done Him Wrong*. The election of Roosevelt meant that Hays, who had supervised Warren Harding's Presidential campaign in 1920, had lost his personal contacts with the administration; since the election there had been widespread rumours that he would be replaced

55 Lupton A. Wilkinson to Hays, 29 October 1932, Will H. Hays Archive, Department of Special Collections, Indiana State Library, Indianapolis.

56 *Upton Sinclair Presents William Fox* was published in early 1933, and free copies were distributed to every member of the new Congress.

by a Democrat. To add to the sense of alarm, there were reports that representatives of the various censor boards were planning a conference designed to produce a uniform policy on censorship.[57] Equally serious was the discontented presence in Hollywood of Martin Quigley, owner of *Motion Picture Herald*, instigator of the Production Code and a key figure in Hays's vital alliance with Catholic organizations.

57 Richmond, Virginia, *Times-Dispatch*, 7 February 1933.

> Q. is very much discouraged about the whole Code business. He feels that our folks here . . . continue to ignore it. . . . He feels that the staff which succeeded Col. Joy is not a good one. . . . I never saw him so down in the mouth about anything.[58]

58 Breen to Hays, 2 March 1933, Hays Archive.

Quigley's disaffection might have resulted in Catholic withdrawal from cooperation with the MPPDA, and that in turn might have led to a legislative victory for the Protestant-dominated reform groups.

An emergency meeting of the MPPDA Board of Directors was held on the evening of 5 March, primarily to consider measures to deal with the bank holiday. Hays, however, made it clear that more than economic action was required to deal with the crisis. A more rigid enforcement of the Code, he argued, was absolutely necessary if the industry was to maintain any public sympathy, and stand any chance of resisting the pressure for federal intervention not merely over its content policies, but also over its financial operations. He persuaded the Board of Directors to sign a Reaffirmation of Objectives that stated

> Not only is a continuous supply of motion picture entertainment doubly essential in these times of confusion and distress, but the tendency toward confused thinking and slackening of standards everywhere re-emphasizes the importance of the progressively effective process of self-discipline by which the moral and artistic standards of motion picture production have been steadily raised during the past eleven years. . . . It is inevitable that during a period such as we now face, disintegrating influences should threaten the standards of production, standards of quality, standards of business practice, built up and maintained by cooperation. . . . We realize the fact that whether American industry will be rebuilt after the depression on a higher or lower plane depends entirely upon the maintenance or destruction of the higher business standards developed through years of cooperative effort.[59]

59 Reaffirmation of the Members of the MPPDA, signed 7 March 1933, quoted in Moley, *The Hays Office*, pp. 250–1.

The Reaffirmation became the implement with which Hays began to reorganize the Code administration. It was not made public at the time, because it would have amounted to a public acknowledgement that the industry had violated the Code, but Hays immediately wrote to Wingate instructing him to tighten up the application of the Code not only on new scripts but also on pictures in production and those about to be finished.[60] Joe Breen, who had previously been supervising the application of the Advertising Code, was drafted in to assist Wingate where necessary. At the same time, company heads wrote to their heads of production in Hollywood, informing them of the new policy.

60 Hays to Wingate, 10 March 1933, 1933 Production Code File, Motion Picture Association of America Archive, New York.

During March Hays constructed a five-point programme for the 'organized solution on a co-operative scale of many of the problems of re-adjustment', covering ways in which the MPPDA member companies could pool facilities and hence reduce costs at the same time that they strengthened their operational hold on the industry. The Association's Annual Meeting on 27 March ratified the programme, although one of its elements, a temporary 25–50 per cent salary cut throughout the industry to meet the immediate cash crisis, had provoked strike threats by the Hollywood craft unions. The crisis had been somewhat alleviated by the partial restoration of confidence by the end of the month, and on 6 April Hays and the entire MPPDA Board entrained for California to put the production branch straight on the need for stringent economies and a more vigorous application of the Code. In addressing the producers on 20 April, Hays was insistent:

> The failure to maintain the clear promises the industry has made to the public for the protection of American family standards in motion picture theatres will jeopardize any permanent investment in the motion picture industry. . . . The result most disastrous of the violations is the legislative retaliation . . . peaking in this Sirovich investigation, the way they get sore because of what is in the pictures, in the advertising, and they take it out on us in this tax and other confiscatory measures. . . . To meet this emergency, and as a prime matter of economy and cost reduction, we have found it necessary to reaffirm our resolutions and strictly enforce them.[61]

61 1933 Production Code File, MPAA Archive.

62 *Motion Picture Herald*, 29 April 1933, p. 9.

If the producers ignored his 'clean up' campaign, Hays threatened, 'their superiors in New York would find a group who would obey orders'.[62] If the studios continued to evade the SRC, he would take the issue first to the company heads in New York, and then to the bankers and stockholders, and finally to the public. He insisted that the release of one censorable picture

> could force the entire Industry to submit to Federal censorship, which would mean—to use his own words—that 'the Industry would be placed in a straight jacket so far as censorship is concerned—and only be able to produce "Jack and the Bean Stalks" and fairy tales.' . . . they are going to be more rigid with the enforcement of the Code. This attitude is already evidenced in the letters we are now receiving from them on scripts. Prior to this time, we were told 'it is recommended, etc.', but recently letters definitely state, 'it is inadmissible, etc.' or something equally definite.[63]

63 Harry Zehner, memo to producers and writers, 26 May 1933, in Universal Studios Censorship file, USC Special Collections Box 778.

64 Cf. John Callan O'Laughlin to Hays, 10 April 1933. Hays Archive.

Although little of this action was made public, the firmness of Hays's stance was communicated to Congressmen through the MPPDA's highly efficient lobby operation in Washington, and undoubtedly played a significant part in defeating the Sirovich resolution on 12 May.[64]

The first two victims of the new policy were *The Story of Temple Drake* (Paramount, 1933) and *Baby Face* (Warner, 1933), both of which completed production in late February. Negotiations between Wingate and Zanuck during March had led to some further deletions in the Warners film, and a 'more wholesome and a brighter finish'[65] was added, in which the lovers were reconciled. However, an alarm bell had obviously been sounded by Wingate's mentioning that the cobbler preaches to Stanwyck 'the philosophy of Nietzsche to the effect that she should use the power that she has over men to rise in the world'.[66] By the end of March the revised film had arrived in New York, where it was unofficially rejected by the New York Censor Board. On 1 April, Hays received an assurance from Harry Warner that, in accordance with the Reaffirmation, no attempt would be made to release the film until further consultations over it had taken place.[67]

Modifications to *Baby Face* needed to go beyond simply the deletion of material or the substitution of 'protection shots', which most studios were by 1933 in the habit of taking on potentially dubious sequences. To bring it within the 'spirit of the Code', new scenes supplying 'the voice of morality' were required, and their provision was complicated by the fact that Stanwyck was unavailable for retakes. The solution, encapsulated in a letter Wingate sent Jack Warner on 11 May, was actually worked out by Joe Breen, who already occupied an important role in the censorship procedure.

> . . . the greatest lack of the picture now . . . is the fact that
> nowhere . . . is the heroine denounced for her brazen method of
> using men to promote herself financially. . . . This may seem to
> create the impression that her mode of living and course of action
> are condoned . . . we would suggest an attempt to use the cobbler in
> a few added scenes as the spokesman of morality.[68]

Breen was able to do what Wingate apparently could not: provide a practical solution to the studio's problem, and protect its investment. Wingate's universal unpopularity with the studio heads largely derived from his merely proposing deletions rather than suggesting improvements. The SRC, in the person of Hays and Wingate, insisted that the cobbler as Nietzschean philosopher of the immoral way be removed from the film. The SRC, in the person of Breen, put him back in with new dialogue. His initial advice:

> . . . A woman—young, beautiful—like you—can get anything she
> wants in the world! Because you have power over men!. . . . But you
> must *use* men, not let them use *you*! You must be a *master*, not a
> *slave*! Look! Here! Nietzsche says 'All life, no matter how we
> idealize it, is nothing more or less than exploitation!' That's what I'm
> telling you! Exploit yourself! Go to some big city where you can find
> opportunities. . . . Be strong—Defiant! *Use men—to get the things
> you want*![69]

became:

> . . . A woman—young, beautiful—like you, can get anything she
> wants in the world! But there is the right and wrong way—remember

65 Zanuck to Wingate, 29 March 1933, PCA *Baby Face* Case File.

66 Wingate to Hays, 2 March 1933, PCA *Baby Face* Case File.

67 Hays to Harry Warner, 14 April 1933, PCA *Baby Face* Case File.

68 Wingate to J. L. Warner, 11 May 1933, *Baby Face* Case File. Although the letter was signed by Wingate, it was undoubtedly written by Breen. All studio correspondence from the SRC was signed by its Director, but it was normal practice for letters to be written by officers.

69 *Baby Face*, Final Script, pp. 26–7.

70 Dialogue transcribed from print of *Baby Face* at the Warner Library, Wisconsin Center for Film and Theater Research. See also H. J. McCord to Wingate, 19 May 1933, PCA *Baby Face* Case File.

71 Wingate to J. L. Warner, 11 May 1933, PCA *Baby Face* Case File.

the price of the wrong way is too great. Go to some big city where you will find opportunities. But don't let people mislead you, you must be a master, not a slave. Keep clean, be strong—defiant! And you will be a success.[70]

Breen suggested that the book Kragg sends Lily should be *Self Help*, 'because the title lends itself to broad interpretation'.[71] While this suggestion was not taken up, his idea of substituting the quotation with a letter was. It read:

Dear Lily; from your letters I can tell that my advice was for nothing. You have chosen the wrong way. You are still a coward. Life will defeat you unless you fight back and regain your self-respect. I send you this book hoping that you will allow it to guide you right.[72]

72 Transcribed from print at Warner Library, Wisconsin Center for Film and Theater Research. See also H. J. McCord to Wingate, 13 May 1933, PCA *Baby Face* Case File.

All this remodelling was completed in a week, and on 20 May Wingate wrote to Hays:

As the picture appears now there is no evidence of any Nietzsche philosophy. On the other hand, as you will note, all the advice of the cobbler has been on the side of morality. . . . The affair with the office boy is cut in such a manner that he has no affair with her. All the men with whom she has affairs come to destruction. One loses his job, one is shot, another shoots himself, etc. The end of the picture has been changed so that it now closes with a picture of the board of directors showing that all of Lily's money had been repaid to the bank and that they haven't a cent and that Trenholm, the former president of the bank is working as a laborer in the steel mills.[73]

73 Wingate to Hays, 20 May 1933, PCA *Baby Face* Case File.

On 8 June, Breen wrote to Hays that the film now conformed to the Production Code, and suggested that Hays take the opportunity to congratulate the studio on 'the splendid spirit of helpfulness which the Warners have displayed in this matter and the promptness with which they set about to clean up a very bad picture and succeeded very well'.
Nevertheless, Breen reminded Hays the film's theme was still questionable and 'suggests a kind, or type, of picture which ought not to be encouraged'.[74] His endorsement did not, in any case, save the picture from minor cuts of dialogue and action by state censor boards, nor from a complete ban by five of the eight Canadian states.

74 Breen to Hays, 8 June 1933, PCA *Baby Face* Case File.

There is nothing particularly exceptional about what happened to *Baby Face*. *Temple Drake* and other 'kept woman' pictures in production at the time were subjected to comparable treatment, and a year later the same fate befell a number of other films caught between two dispensations of the Code, including Mae West's *It Ain't No Sin* (1934). The example of *Baby Face* does, however, serve to illustrate the extent of Code activity at an earlier period, where it is commonly supposed that little censorship activity took place. It also provides a case study of the balance between elements in the Code's moral accountancy. The narrative always presented a patriarchal moral, in which Lily's aberrant expression of her sexuality resulted in her punishment. The crime of which the narrative found her guilty was patricide, but the form of her punishment was changed from what had previously been the melodramatic fate of characters in comparable positions—deprivation, denial, and exclusion from society—to a more inclusive and perverse form of patriarchal revenge, by which she was returned to the world from which she had attempted to escape.

In this transformation, the character of Kragg retained the same narrative function as donor, but his ideological role shifted from that of alternative patriarch to true patriarch, to whose moral world Lily is returned at the film's conclusion. Where the script version offered only a pessimistic critique of the social consequences of the culture of consumption, the film's ending provided a reassertion of traditional Protestant values, in which Lily and Trenholm were announced to be '*working* out their happiness together'.[75] The realignment of Kragg's role to a point where, at the end of the movie, he becomes ideologically indistinguishable from the Director of the Bank who decrees Trenholm's return to the steel town, locates the film in an ideological context which Nick Roddick describes as 'a fundamentally just society which offered the individual, even under the most extreme circumstances, the chance to re-establish himself (rarely, if ever, herself)'.

The fact that the final version of the film was located in that context, however, has less to do with 'the studio's ideological commitment . . . to the nascent policies of the New Deal', as Roddick argues, than to external pressures on the studio and the industry to revise their product into a closer conformity with the expected norms of a culture in recession.[76] What makes *Baby Face* so appropriate an example of the processes of ideological repression is the way in which the cinematic inverts the causality of the extracinematic: the Crash, represented by the failure of the bank, is caused—which is to say, explained—by Lily's effect on men. The film exposes the contradictions inherent in patriarchy's bifurcated representation of woman, by which she is narratively punished for her existence as a spectacle of desire: it is accidental (in that it resulted from Stanwyck's unavailability for retakes), but it is entirely appropriate to the movie's optical politics that the revised ending cannot show Lily in the prison of working-class domesticity to which it has returned her.

Father Gerard Donnelly, SJ, editor of the Catholic periodical *America* and an influential figure in the organization of the Legion of Decency, rejected the theories of more extreme critics of the movies which historians have subsequently adopted when he commented that 'it would be absurd to claim that producers are deliberately trying to destroy the traditional teachings of the pulpit'.[77]

The movies of the early Depression represented the crisis of the period, but they did so within the parameters of their own systems of convention, which were themselves products of the industry's complex interaction with the culture and economy of which it was a dynamic part. Those conventions revealed the crisis in patriarchal ideology which

75 Dialogue transcribed from print of *Baby Face* at the Warner Library, Wisconsin Center for Film and Theater Research, my italics.

76 Nick Roddick, *A New Deal in Entertainment: Warner Brothers in the 1930s* (London: British Film Institute, 1983), p. 126.

77 Gerard B. Donnelly, SJ, 'An Open Letter to Dr Wingate', pp. 85–6.

accompanied the crisis in the institutions of capitalism. The extent to which patriarchy's contradictions were exposed was indicated by a Hays Office comment on Mae West:

> The very man who will guffaw at Mae West's performance as a reminder of the ribald days of his past will resent her effect upon the young, when his daughter imitates the Mae West wiggle before her boyfriends and mouths 'Come up and see me sometime'.[70]

78 Internal MPPDA memorandum, Ray Norr to Hays, 18 October 1933, 1933 Production Code File, MPAA Archive.

In an economic moment when the possibilities for consumption were sharply restricted, the contradictions contained within this image of woman became more apparent than they had been during its formulation over the previous decade. The image of fetishized sexuality as consumerist pleasure became more threatening for a culture in recession, and the potential subversiveness of the image brought forth louder calls for its repression. In that sense it may be argued that the campaign to repress the image of female sexuality was concerned with its threatened exposure of the contradictions within patriarchal capitalism, but the contradiction arose not around the representation of independent woman—a figure who was continuously contained, recuperated, and repressed within narrative—but around the representation of woman as an object of consumption/desire. The Depression interrupted the smooth development of a culture of consumption, and caused a temporary reconsideration of the iconography it had promulgated. The demand for the imposition of censorship was a rebellion against images of consumption, and it gained public credibility because those images had become too detached from the available reality. A recurrent criticism of both Hollywood and the previous decade was that they were guilty of the sin of excess. In the widespread criticism of Hollywood's 'excessive' salaries, the idols of consumption were represented as objects of idolatry to be condemned and punished. The 'kept woman' cycle was a vehicle for this condemnation, in two senses: it provided a target for it, and it also, with increasing vehemence, enacted it in the punishments it meted out to its heroines. To read *Baby Face* as an account of the conflicts of the previous decade is consistent with its existence as a text and an historical object. Judging whether audiences perceived it in these terms is rather more difficult because relatively few people were given the opportunity to see the film. Its reputation within the industry ensured a limited release, and, in common with the majority of films which provoked controversy during this period, it was prohibited from reissue in February 1935.

Part IV Textual Histories

12 A Scene at the 'Movies': The Development of Narrative Perspective in Early Cinema

BEN BREWSTER

She stole noiselessly down the broad staircase . . . and noiselessly approached the door of the big room where she had left her father. . . . Nobody saw her, nobody heard her, and she had a moment to gaze unobserved at the scene before her. It was like a scene at the 'movies', with all those books, and the piano, and the comfortable chairs, and the big portrait hanging over the fireplace, and the pretty lady behind the steaming tea-kettle, and the dog and the boys. . . . Only it was real! There were real bindings on the books, real reading in them, there was real tea in the teapot. The people were real, and their feelings for each other were real, too. She, standing on the outside, was the only unreal thing in this home scene. She looked at her father. Suddenly the room faded, disappeared, and a close-up of his face dawned on the screen before her, as it were. Why, her father was gazing at the lady behind the tea-kettle, as if—as if!—Laurel had seen too many close-ups of faces not to recognise that look! She drew in her breath sharply. It flashed over Laurel that perhaps this man wasn't really her father after all! She stirred, moved a foot: Mrs Morrison glanced over her shoulder. 'Oh! come here Laurel,' she exclaimed at the sight of her, and stretched out her arm, and kept it stretched out until Laurel had stepped within its circle.[1]

In this passage from a popular novel first published in 1923, the cinema is functioning as a metaphor for a kind of experience, or rather as the vehicle for a kind of fantasy. It is invoked for the segregation of the audience and the screen, the division between a place 'down here'

1 Olive Higgins Prouty, *Stella Dallas* (Boston: Houghton Mifflin, 1923). (New York: Paperback Library, 1967), pp. 38–9. This essay is reprinted as it appeared in *Screen*, vol. 23, no. 2 (1982), pp. 4–15, except for the addition of a note correcting a misdescription of *The Voice of the Child* and filmographic updating.

outside, from which one can watch unobserved, and a place 'up there' inside where what one sees is fictional, obviously, and yet seemingly more real than what is down here: Laurel Dallas outside the door is the 'only unreal thing in this home scene'. The segregation involves a reversal of the opposition between reality and illusion, and the projection of the spectator into the scene. And the novel goes on to move Laurel (despite her pangs of conscience: 'How could she—oh how could she have become a part of the picture on the screen, while her mother was still in the audience, out there, in the dark, looking on')[2] decisively into the world of Helen Morrison, shifting its point of identification to Laurel's mother Stella Dallas, who abolishes herself as visible to her daughter so as to be able to contemplate her in that world. Near the end, Stella out in the dark streets sees Laurel looking towards her from the lighted window of the Morrisons' house, but 'Laurel didn't know it. Laurel had no idea that her mother's eyes were in the depth of the mirror she had gazed into, at her own reflection'.[3] (The scene is faithfully reproduced in the 1925 film version of the novel. The 1937 version, far more uneasy about the fantasy, locates the cinema itself as one of its sources.)

What was the cinema so that by 1923 it could provide such a metaphor? Fifteen years earlier, such a cinema did not exist. It is a specifically English usage that makes the same term the name for the movie house and for the whole institution of the production, distribution, and exhibition of films (*Stella Dallas*, being American, uses 'movies'). But it is appropriate to the institution we know, so appropriate that we read it back into the whole history of the invention and utilization of moving pictures. But the movie house as the apparent centre of moving-picture-related activity only emerges in the decade after 1905; only then is there a hierarchization of the experience of moving pictures into the cinematic (primary) and the non-cinematic (peripheral). Before this decade there is no such division—apparatuses for the reproduction of an illusion of movement are integrated into a whole series of other practices—of science, education, religion, and entertainment. There are a few specialized film-show houses, but films are shown in vaudeville, music hall, or *caf'conc'* programmes, in fairground booths, in peep-shows, in church halls, accompanying popular lectures, and so on. Even as entertainment, they constitute one among a variety of attractions.

After 1905, however, marked most spectacularly by the nickelodeon boom in the USA, specialized houses devoted exclusively or principally to the viewing of films appear and are integrated more and more into a national and international network, containing its own hierarchy of first-, second- and *n*th-run houses, seat prices, publicity channels, fan magazines, press criticism, and so on, which is the cinema we know, the 'movies' Laurel can refer to so casually. Of course, all sorts of other uses of moving pictures continue—blue movies, educational films, films for religious use, scientific films, commercial films; but they are not seen in movie houses (except for a few rare occasions when they obtain the accolade of being real cinema, as with the transfer of some training films

2 Ibid., p. 53.

3 Ibid., p. 251.

Above, a sequence from Stella Dallas, 1925

for the armed forces into the cinema during World War II), so they are not cinema, just a kind of poor relation. Correspondingly, activities inside the movie house are hierarchized under the film—stage interludes, singsongs, Brenograph displays, in the auditorium; coffee, dinner, even steam baths in the building. And the film is hierarchized—main film, newsreel, travelogue, later A and B feature, and high and low genres. In one sense this cinema is just as heterogeneous as the precinematic uses of film were, but the heterogeneity is now held in a more or less peripheral location under the very specialized use of film described by Laurel in the universal form of 'a scene at the "movies" '. And the audiences, too, with all their differences of class, income, education, culture, and nationality, consume a single product in a social and geographical hierarchy measured by the interval between release date and their viewing.

But what about the combination of exclusion and projection that characterize that 'scene'? The movies are a form of visual entertainment—pleasure is obtained from what is seen up on the screen. However, for the curious reversal of reality and unreality noted by Laurel, more is required—the articulation of the look from spectator to screen with the looks from character to object and character on the screen. This is the field of what are known as point-of-view structures.

Films had been using point-of-view (POV) structures of the type analysed by Edward Branigan[4] for a long time before *Stella Dallas* was published. In the POV structure we see somebody see, then we see what they see from somewhere approaching their viewpoint (less commonly it is the other way round); vision is marked in the first of these shots, and often in the second, too. The simplest form of this is a type of insert. The scene with insert(s) is probably the earliest form of cutting within the scene; in it, some detail of the scene presented in long shot is shown in a 'magnified view'—not necessarily what would now be called a close-up, but a less inclusive camera set-up than the main scene. In *Falsely Accused* (1905) we are given magnified views of banknotes, a key being pressed into wax, and so on;[5] in *Mary Jane's Mishap* (1903) we have closer shots of the heroine's face. These are taken from the same angle as the main shots, but with a less inclusive view. They do not represent any fictional character's view, they are there for the audience. Even in *The Gay Shoe Clerk* (1903), where what we see in the magnified view (the heroine lifting her skirts for the shoe clerk to see her underwear) is undoubtedly the object of a look, it is still taken from the side, not from the clerk's own viewpoint.

In the true POV pattern, however, the second shot purports to be (and, more rarely, actually is) photographed from the place where the looking character is fictionally located. In *Grandma's Reading Glass* (1900) we see a boy with a magnifying glass looking through it at a newspaper, a watch, a bird in a cage, his grandmother's eye, a kitten, and these shots alternate with magnified views in a black circular mask (representing the glass and the look) of the print of the newspaper, the watch mechanism, the bird, the eye, the kitten's head. In *As Seen*

Above, a sequence from
The Gay Shoe Clerk, *1903*

4 Edward Branigan, 'Formal permutations of the point-of-view shot', *Screen*, vol. 16, no. 3 (1975), pp. 54–64.

5 For an example, see the still in Barry Salt, 'Film from 1900–1906', *Sight and Sound*, vol. 47, no. 3 (summer 1978), p. 151.

through the Telescope (1900) a peeping Tom with a telescope spies on a young man tying a girl cyclist's shoelace, but the view, much the same as that in *The Gay Shoe Clerk*, is now in a circular mask and represents the peeping Tom's point of view.[6]

POV here is, as I say, a special case of the magnified insert. But it would be wrong to see it as a development from the simple insert, leading on to more sophisticated uses of POV in later films. On the contrary, if anything, the development is the other way round. In *Grandma's Reading Glass*, the POV structure is the pleasure point of the film, its attraction—to make the break in continuity implicit in a cut within one represented space, the cut has to be made into the end of the film, not its means; in *As Seen through the Telescope* (and many other films such as *Ce que l'on voit de mon sixième* (1900–1) and *A Search for Evidence* (1903)), the structure is serving a simple pornographic narrative, the voyeuristic pleasure in the extra vision still explicitly thematized; in *The Gay Shoe Clerk* the pornographic insert is no longer a strict POV shot; in *Falsely Accused*, conveying straightforward narrative information has become the function of the insert, which function survives as the main role for the insert (and the cut within the same interior space) until the early 1910s (the other role, more especially in comedies, is the complicit closer shot of a character winking or grinning at the audience, as in *Mary Jane's Mishap* and many others).

This pattern, from pure spectacle via pornography to simple narrative, is a common one for the introduction of filmic devices, and the association of POV with the first two stages in the introduction of the insert suggests that POV begins as a primitive rather than as a sophisticated use of cutting. Even when a narrative hinges on what a character sees, this will often be conveyed without POV structures, even if a falsification of the diegetic space is implied: in *The Voice of the Child* (1911) a character is shown looking down at a picture and there follows a magnified insert of him holding the picture up in front of him to the camera so the audience can see what, in the fiction, he is supposed to be seeing.[7] By this time, of course, spatially more adventurous directors than Griffith were using POV structures where their narratives gave them the opportunity in much the way that later became standard —for example in *A Friendly Marriage* (1911), where the wife sees her husband and the vicar's daughter apparently lovers. But this 'reintroduction' of POV seems independent of and secondary to another sense of point of view in film narratives much more significant for the experience of segregation and projection described by Laurel Dallas. This is the sense in which changes of viewpoint not necessarily involving true POV make possible hierarchies of relative knowledge for characters and spectators.

A number of early films exploit the change in what can be seen produced by shifting the camera through 180 degrees. In *Women's Rights* (1899), the first shot shows two ladies gossiping by a fence, the second, from the 'other side' of the fence (in fact the filmmakers, with what seems now a misplaced confidence in the Kuleshov effect, use the

6   For a still, see ibid., p. 150.

Above, a grin to the audience in Mary Jane's Mishap, *1903. Below, a sequence including a magnified insert from* The Voice of the Child, *1912*

7   I now realize this is a partial misdescription, and there is no falsification of the space involved. In the main scene, the office typist gives the clerk, her boyfriend, a picture. He looks at the picture and gestures to the effect 'It's you'. In the cut-in, we see first the back of the picture as he is looking at the front. Inscribed on it are the words 'To my sweetheart'. He then turns it round to read the message on the back, and now we see the picture of the typist on the front. Thus, the shot never purports to be a POV shot. It is also worth mentioning that these are secondary characters whose motivations are of no concern to the narrative: the point of the shot is to establish the inscribed photograph, which the false friend will later slip into the coat pocket of the boss of these two characters, the hero of the story, so that it will be found by his wife and interpreted as a sign of infidelity.

same camera set-up and simply move the characters round to the other side of the fence), shows two young men creep up, pull the ends of their skirts through the fence and nail them to it, and the third, back on the 'original side', shows the ladies struggling to escape. This really hardly differs in its narrative effect from the gardener's turned back in *L'Arroseur arrosé* (1895), which of course consists of a single shot.

The Other Side of the Hedge (1905) uses a two-shot pattern round a hedge not unlike the three-shot one in *Women's Rights*, but to greater effect. In shot one, a courting couple sitting in front of a hedge are kept apart by a chaperone. The chaperone settles down for a nap between them. The couple then disappear behind the hedge, but the spectators, and the chaperone when she wakes momentarily and looks anxiously for her charges, can see their hats sticking up over the hedge a decent distance apart. Shot two is the 180 degree shot from the other side of the hedge: the hats, the spectator now sees, are attached to sticks and the couple are kissing in between them. The gap between the image given in one shot, and the truth given in the second, a truth denied the censorious chaperone, creates an irony out of the change in viewpoint. (It is interesting that two out of three contemporary accounts of this film—in *Biograph Bulletin*, no. 38 (1904), and *The Optical Lantern and Kinematograph Journal* (1905), as opposed to the manufacturers' 1906 'Hepwix' Catalogue entry—cannot describe it properly, because they cannot separate a description of the shots from a version of the story being told, when the point of the film is the eventually resolved discrepancy between them; this failure suggests an important threshold in the development of film narration.) On the other hand, neither shot is a true POV shot. In the first, although we see no more of the other side of the hedge than the chaperone, we see more than she does in that we see her. In the second, we are put into complicity with the couple who are assumed to know what we have seen, that the chaperone has been duped.

This kind of simple irony of differing viewpoints held together by narrative positioning can of course be linked to true POV. In *A Friendly Marriage*, the wife sees the husband and vicar's daughter, apparently lovers, whereas we already know that the husband loves the wife and is secretly earning a living, with secretarial help from the vicar's daughter; but the irony is resolved for the characters in the next shot, when the wife accuses him and he explains. More is at stake here than a mere wifely misunderstanding (as sexuality enters this platonic marriage, money and initiative in it shift from the wife to the husband), but the discrepancy between characters' and spectator's knowledge is only incidental to the narrative structure as a whole.

Narratives entirely constructed around these discrepancies are in fact to be found in the films Griffith made for Biograph between 1909 and 1912, despite the consistent refusal of POV structures in these films, and their reluctance to cut within the same space, especially in interiors. *The Drive for a Life* (1909) has one non-POV insert of an action and one insert of a letter, *Gold is not All* (1910) one insert of a letter; otherwise they consist of one-shot scenes and ordinary or alternating sequences. Yet both depend on hierarchies of relative knowledge and deception.

In *The Drive for a Life*, a man abandons his mistress in order to marry a respectable girl. (The *Biograph Bulletin*, no. 233 (1909), insists the former relationship is completely innocent and the 'mistress' French and a widow into the bargain, but the titles leave the precise relationships so vague as to make mistress the most obvious reading; moreover, it provides a better motivation for her subsequent actions and more powerful identification with her.) After he has said goodbye, the ex-mistress goes out on an errand, riding in a horse cab. Meanwhile, the man is showing off his motor car to his new fiancée. The two routes intersect, and the ex-mistress in her cab sees the couple in the car; but they do not see her. Driven into a jealous rage by this sight, she puts poison in some sweets (insert of this) and sends them with a forged covering note by special messenger to the fiancée. The man arrives at her house to reclaim his love-letters, discovers what she has done, and races in his car to arrive in the nick of time to prevent the fiancée eating the poisoned sweets.

The switchback that ends the film, between shots of the speeding car and the obstacles to its arrival on the one hand, and shots of the delivery, unwrapping, and preparation for eating of the sweets on the other, is the device for which Griffith is most famous (although he probably did not invent it), so it is worth emphasizing that it too depends for its suspense on the discrepancy of knowledge between the spectator and the fiancée receiving, opening, and preparing to eat the sweets supposedly sent by her lover. But more interesting for my purposes is the scene where the ex-mistress oversees the man with his new fiancée. It is filmed in one shot from the back of an unseen car travelling in front of the chauffeur-driven car in the back seat of which the man and his fiancée are seated. After a while, the cab enters left from a side road and drives along behind the couple's car. Finally the couple's car leaves frame right, and the mistress orders the cab to turn back the way it had come. The murderous jealousy which constitutes the narrative is set up in this one complex shot, through the spectator's sharing in the greater knowledge of the ex-mistress and recognition of the vulnerable ignorance of the couple.

Gold is not All adds a third layer to these two. It tells the parallel stories of two couples, a poor couple and a rich couple. They court and marry more or less simultaneously and both couples have children. The only direct link between them, apart from living in the same neighbourhood, is that the poor girl does the rich couple's laundry. The narrative alternates between the two stories, and we learn, not surprisingly, that one couple is poor but happy, the other rich but unhappy. But the symmetry between the two couples is deceptive: in fact the spaces they occupy are segregated into an inside, occupied by the rich couple, and an outside, occupied by the poor couple. This is marked not only by the fact that, whereas the rich couple's life takes place largely in interiors (sets), the poor couple are never seen inside their humble cottage; but also, and more significantly, by the fact that the rich couple live on an estate bounded by a wall. The key scene in the film, while both couples are courting, is filmed looking along this wall, with the street outside on the left and the park inside on the right. Both couples appear, initially each couple absorbed in itself. Then the poor couple see the rich couple over the wall and gaze at them in envy. The rich couple, oblivious, leave right, the poor couple shake their heads in sad resignation and leave left. This asymmetry of awareness is repeated throughout the film. Even in their own space, the poor cast many a backward glance towards the rich estate. The rich couple, on the other hand, are oblivious of the poor, until they intrude directly on them, when they (the rich) behave with embarrassed and uncomprehending

condescension (in the first scene the poor girl picks up the handkerchief the rich girl has dropped and hands it to her; during the climactic party at the rich house, the poor girl arrives with the laundry at the wrong door and has to be hurriedly redirected). But the narrative (and the titles) provide a third perspective: the rich are ignorant of the poor; the poor see the rich and envy them; the spectator knows rich and poor and knows the poor do not realize how unhappy the rich really are. Inside and outside on the screen duplicate inside and outside in the movie house.

This is the structure of Laurel's 'scene at the "movies"'. Point of view, in the sense of narrative perspective, the measurement of the relative perceptions and knowledge of the characters by the

Asymmetry of awareness:
the courting scene in
Gold is not All, 1910

development of the narrative, is here achieved without point-of-view shots. This is done by finding narrative actions and settings where the look and its object can be staged in one shot, or by dividing the narrative space into contrasting sections linked by much more generalized or even metaphorical looks (when the poor heroine of *Gold is not All* looks back over her shoulder 'at' the rich estate as she stands by the door of her cottage, it is not what she *physically* sees that concerns the narrative or the spectator). Notoriously, Griffith did not develop or ever really acclimatize himself to the 'just-off-the-eyeline-shot/reverse-shot' system which became the 'classical' method of scene editing by the end of the war. *True Heart Susie* (1919), which is an extension of the pyramid of knowledge of *Gold is not All* to feature length (Susie knows more than William, but the spectator knows that and what she knows, and also what neither knows) still prefers long shots and 'concertina' cut-ins to close-ups from the same angle. Early examples of that system I have seen—*The Loafer* (1912), *His Last Fight* (1913), *The Bank Burglar's Fate* (1914)—all use it in the context of fights, whereas the 'point-of-view' structure of the Griffith films is essentially passive (although it can give rise to subsequent aggression—the poisoned sweets). Although I cannot trace the process in detail, it seems clear that when the 'classical' system came to incorporate less aggressive contexts, it absorbed the Griffithian point-of-view structure, and combined together technical and narrative point of view.

One final characteristic of the establishment of this cinema: what might be called the extra twist of fictionality it brought with it. Many American films made before 1910 involve a plot where a worker hero (usually a foreman rather than a simple workman) is in conflict, usually over his girlfriend or wife, sometimes herself a worker, with another higher-ranking blackguardly employee—a supervisor (for example, *The Mill Girl* (1907), *The Paymaster* (1906)). The foreman displaces the supervisor in the mill girl's affections, or rescues her from his unwelcome attentions, and is then the victim of some conspiracy on the supervisor's part, which is finally uncovered, the happy couple are united, and the villain punished—or the girl is unjustly suspected of infidelity with a (less blackguardly) supervisor, leading to friction between the men, finally resolved by the opportunity for selfless heroism presented by an accident at work (*The Tunnel Workers* (1906)). The sets in these films are typically sketchy functional ones, providing a space for the action and painted décor indicating the milieu; but exteriors and a few interiors are filmed in 'real' surroundings—*The Paymaster* in a real (though disused) New England mill, *The Tunnel Workers*, spectacularly, at the top of the shafts of the works for the Pennsylvania Tunnel from New York City to Long Island. Thus the films can be said to have a naive realism—made for the nickelodeon market when the latter was already becoming reasonably unified but was still confined to a lower-middle- and working-class clientele, they reflect that milieu in the most direct possible way, confining themselves largely to it and filming directly in its real surroundings.

Fantasy perspectives: luxurious sets (top) and picture-book poverty (below) in Gold is not All

The films of the early 1910s I have been principally discussing have changed this. Their heroes and heroines are from the respectable, even rich, middle class and the locations and especially the sets are chosen, designed, and furnished to convey luxury and fashion. Even more strikingly, the poor have become a picture-book poor, living a carefree life in little cottages with roses round the porch. A shift in the centre of the fiction from the presentation of scenes to the presentation of differing character perspectives on scenes, and a displacement of point of view from a mechanism for articulating diegetic space to one for articulating characters' knowledge, go with a move from the direct photography of real environments to the presentation of a world much more penetrated by fantasy. The American cinema, not yet in Hollywood (although *Gold is not All* was filmed in Pasadena), is becoming a dream factory. The remark is not made either in a spirit of civically responsible condemnation, or one of surrealist celebration—the examples hardly suit either response: the story of *The Mill Girl* is no more socially responsible than that of *Gold is not All*, and by 1925 the latter seemed embarrassingly naive to Linda Arvidson, who played the poor girl in it[8]—but in order to re-emphasise the cinematicity of the 'scene at the "movies" ' that, by 1923, could be reappropriated by popular literature.

8 See Mrs D. W. Griffith (Linda Arvidson), *When the Movies Were Young* (New York: E. P. Dutton & Co., 1925), p. 147.

Filmography

For each film, this filmography gives the following information (when known): the original title, plus, for some foreign-produced films, a British release title in parentheses; the country of production; the company that produced it; the name of the director (d.); of the photographer (ph.); of the scriptwriter or author (sc.); and of the leading players (l.p.), with names of characters in parentheses; the release date in the country of production; and the length of the film for 35 mm prints according to contemporary catalogues or the trade press (one reel is approximately 1,000 feet). All films were viewed in prints held by the National Film and Television Archive, London.

L'Arroseur arrosé ('Watering the Gardener'), France, Lumière, ph. Louis Lumière, l.p. François Clerc (gardener), Duval (boy), 1895, 55 ft.

As Seen through the Telescope, UK, GAS Films, d. George Albert Smith, September 1900, 75 ft.

The Bank Burglar's Fate ('Detective Burton's Triumph'), USA, Reliance, d. John G. Adolfi, sc. C. D. Brown, l.p. Eugene Palette (yeggman), Sam De Grasse (Detective Burton), Billie West (telephone girl), 8 August 1914, 2 reels.

Ce que l'on voit de mon sixième ('Scenes from My Balcony'), France, Pathé Frères, 1900–1, 130 ft.

The Drive for a Life, USA, American Mutoscope and Biograph Co., d. D. W. Griffith, ph. G. W. Bitzer/Arthur Marvin, l.p. Arthur Johnson (hero), Marion Leonard (his mistress), Florence Lawrence (his fiancée), Dorothy West, Gertrude Robinson, Linda Arvidson (her sisters), Anita Hendrie (her mother), Robert Harron (messenger boy), 22 April 1909, 940 ft.

Falsely Accused, UK, Hepworth Film Manufacturing Co., d. Lewin Fitzhamon, May 1905, 850 ft.

A Friendly Marriage, USA, Vitagraph Co. of America, l.p. Earle Williams (Lord Towne), Lillian Walker (Lillian Cotton, later Lady Towne), Robert Gaillord (her father), Edith Clinton (her mother), Anne Schaefer (her aunt), Van Dyke Brooke (Towne's lawyer), Julia Swayne Gordon (Lady Somers), Hazel Neason (vicar's daughter), 5 September 1911, 1,000 ft.

The Gay Shoe Clerk, USA, Edison Manufacturing Co., ph. Edwin S. Porter, August 1903, 75 ft.

Gold is not All, USA, Biograph Co., d. D. W. Griffith, ph. G. W. Bitzer, l.p. Linda Arvidson (poor girl), Kate Bruce (her mother), Mack Sennett (poor boy), Marion Leonard (rich girl), Dell Henderson (rich boy), Gladys Egan (their daughter), Kathlyn Williams (his mistress), W. Chrystie Miller (grandfather), 28 March 1910, 988 ft.

Grandma's Reading Glass, UK, GAS Films, d. George Albert Smith, September 1900, 100 ft.

His Last Fight, USA, Vitagraph Co. of America, d. Ralph Ince, l.p. Ralph Ince (Tim, the prize-fighter), Anita Stewart (the bride), Gladdin James (the groom), 18 November 1913, 1,000 ft.

The Loafer, USA, Essanay Film Manufacturing Co., 20 January 1912, 1,000 ft.

Mary Jane's Mishap; or, Don't Fool with the Paraffin, UK, GAS Films, d. George Albert Smith, February 1903, 250 ft.

The Mill Girl—A Story of Factory Life, USA, Vitagraph Co. of America, l.p. Florence Turner (mill girl), Hector Dion (foreman), 28 September 1907, 700 ft.

The Other Side of the Hedge, UK, Hepworth Film Manufacturing Co., d. Lewin Fitzhamon, January 1905, 100 ft (stills originate in a Library of Congress paper print).

The Paymaster, USA, American Mutoscope and Biograph Co., d. Mr Harrington, ph. G. W. Bitzer, l.p. Gene Gauntier, Jim Slevin, Gordon Burby, 28 June 1906, 685 ft (stills originate in a Library of Congress paper print).

A Search for Evidence, USA, American Mutoscope and Biograph Co., ph. G. W. Bitzer, l.p. Kathryn Osterman, August 1903, 217 ft.

Stella Dallas, USA, Sam Goldwyn Inc., d. Henry King, ph. Arthur Edeson, sc. Frances Marion, l.p. Ronald Colman (Stephen Dallas), Belle Bennett (Stella Dallas), Alice Joyce (Helen Morrison), Jean Hersholt (Ed Munn), Lois Moran (Laurel Dallas), Douglas Fairbanks, Jr. (Richard Grosvenor III), 16 November 1925, 10,157 ft.

Stella Dallas, USA, Howard Productions, d. King Vidor, sc. Harry Wagstaff Gribble/Gertrude Purcell, l.p. John Boles (Stephen Dallas), Barbara Stanwyck (Stella Dallas), Anne Shirley (Laurel Dallas), Alan Hale (Ed Munn), 5 August 1937, 9,360 ft.

True Heart Susie, USA, D. W. Griffith, d. D. W. Griffith, ph. G. W. Bitzer, sc. Marion Fremont, l.p. Lillian Gish (Susie), Robert Harron (William), Clarine Seymour (Bettina), 1 June 1919, 6,213 ft.

The Tunnel Workers, USA, American Mutoscope and Biograph Co., ph. Frank Dobson, l.p. Jim Slevin, Kate Toncray, Guy Hedlund, 15 November 1906, 813 ft.

The Voice of the Child, USA, Biograph Co., d. D. W. Griffith, sc. George Hennessy, ph. Billy Bitzer, l.p. Blanche Sweet (wife), Edwin August (husband), Joseph Graybill (false friend), Edward Dillon (clerk), 28 December 1911, 998 ft.

Women's Rights (formerly catalogued by the NFTVA under the descriptive title 'Ladies' Skirts Nailed to a Fence'), UK, Riley Bros., October 1899, 75 ft.

13 Narrative/Diegesis: Thresholds, Limits

NOËL BURCH

This essay is undeniably vitiated by what is still a fundamentally empiricist stance. However, at the stage I have reached in my thinking about film, I feel the need to come to grips, albeit naively, with an issue which to many will smack of a specious essentialism, but which I regard as absolutely unavoidable.

I must confess, however, that I find myself hard pressed to define this issue in rigorous terms. For a start, I might say that what I see at stake is *the status of the experience of the mainstream narrative cine-film*. The problem is, perhaps, to situate the historical, social, aesthetic space which we call mainstream narrative film—the production/consumption cycle of the Cinema Institution—in terms of what is essential to that space, of what determines its unity, its specificity within the larger sphere of cultural production.

I have been inclined in recent years, borrowing a term from the earliest film semiotics (Souriau, Metz)[1] to refer to the general experience (within the mass audience of developed Western nations) of the classical film in terms of *diegetic production* at the level of transmission, *diegetic effect* at the level of reception, and *diegetic process* to encompass the two dieheses. Except as an abbreviation for diegetic process, this seems to me a word that has lost much of its usefulness, because it is either too vague to accommodate dialectical rigour or too mechanical: diegesis-as-thing. Now, one of my contentions is that this process can be triggered off in a filmic context independently of the presence of any narrative structure, and that one may consequently see it, rather than narrative, as the true seat of cinema's 'power of fascination'.

The issue also has a diachronic dimension, which is perhaps of more than speculative interest: are there, I might phrase it, any grounds for

1 In its simplest definition, the word *diegesis* 'designates the film's represented instance—that is to say, the sum of a film's denotation: the narration itself, but also the fictional space and time dimensions implied in and by the narrative, and consequently the character, the landscapes, the events and other narrative elements insofar as they are considered in their denoted aspect' (Christian Metz, *Film Language* Oxford University Press (New York: 1974)). See also Etienne Souriau, 'La structure de l'univers filmique et le vocabulaire de la filmologie', *Revue internationale de filmologie*, nos. 7–8, pp. 231–40.

hypothesizing an essential, constitutive difference between the spectatorial experience of the mainstream 'silent' (mute) film and the mainstream talkie, or between that of the classical narrative film in general and that of the audience in the Salon Indien, purportedly starting up from their seats as that 'train entering station' apparently bore down upon them? And is there any such difference between the experience of US television (taken as a limit instance among the televisions of the capitalist world) and that of the mainstream film viewed in a cinema? However, the theoretical (synchronic) axis of the issue remains central to my mind. Only when it has been satisfactorily posed can the historical issue be studied with the proper relevancy: is narrative itself really central to the very characteristic experience which we associate with classical narrative film?

This formulation is paradoxical by design. I believe that the apprehension of the mainstream or institutional continent of cinema as exactly coextensive with that of narrative is misleading: it hides the fact that however closely they have been associated historically, there are two distinct levels in the experience of the classical film. As certain limit instances show, the diegetic effect can be fully achieved in the total absence of narrative in any of its accepted forms (and I include, of course, the documentary narrative). Historically, narrative was no doubt the armature upon which the illusion of presence was effectively constructed, but in later years, and especially with the introduction of live sound, the autonomy of this presence became so great that it could survive in wholly non-narrative contexts.

I also wish to examine the possible distinction between the fully diegetic film and the imperfectly or weakly diegetic film. Again, in my opinion, such gradations depend not upon the absence or presence—or the relative degree of development—of narrative structures, but hinge, more fundamentally, on such factors as movement (both profilmic and camera), live sound, the readability of the picture track, and even, to an extent, upon the use of shot/counter-shot and the other strategies of camera ubiquity.

Finally, I will touch upon the evolution of modern commercial television, exemplified by that of the USA—and a certain popular cinema that is an outgrowth of it—which involves a deliberate 'de-tensification' of the diegetic process in favour of a form of 'induced disengagement', a fascinated non-involvement which is several removes in passivity away from 'the spell of motion pictures' . . . and which constitutes a new and potent weapon in the media arsenal of capitalism, pointing towards even more disquieting developments to come.

There is no reason to doubt the reports that some spectators started up from their seats when first they saw Lumière's train rushing at them where they sat, comfortably ensconced at their tables in the Salon Indien. However, I question fundamentally the notion, so often and so glibly bandied about, that this was the first manifestation of the cinematic illusion. As Christian Metz reminds us,[2] belief in the

2 Christian Metz, *Psychoanalysis and Cinema: The Imaginary Signifer* (London: Macmillan, 1982).

cinematic image as an analogue of real phenomena, if it ever was an hallucination (such as might be induced by drugs or psychosis, for example), has long ceased to be one; it is, indeed, a *willing* suspension of disbelief, an emotional involvement which may certainly attain great depths of anguish or compassion, but which is always grounded in the awareness that the subject is 'only watching a film'. It is in this respect, Metz further suggests, that the filmic experience resembles that of the fantasy rather than the dream.

The first spectators of *L'Entrée d'un train en gare* (1895), reacting with their whole bodies, to what they perceived as an external manifestation, were indeed in a brief hallucinatory state, their unfamiliarity with the messages they were receiving having induced a state of mild sensorial confusion.

Even such a sophisticated viewer as Maxim Gorky, though understanding no doubt how the Cinématographe worked, and prepared in any event for what he was going to see, seems to have experienced similar hallucinations: 'Carriages coming . . . straight at you . . . into the darkness in which you sit . . . a train appears on the screen. It speeds straight at you—watch out! . . . You imagine the spray will reach you and you want to shield yourself.' But even if these are not simply facile hyperbole-feigned hallucinations whose true experience are implicitly attributed to others—Gorky takes significant care to distinguish between these hallucinatory effects of moving photographs and the illusion of full presence which he equated with *reality*: '. . . no rumble of the wheels is heard', the train was 'but a train of shadows', you could not hear 'the gurgle of the water as it gushes from the hose'.[3]

Gorky's well-known text, with its call for sound, colour, and the presence afforded by the close-up (*Le Déjeuner de bébé* (1895) is the only film which he warms to in a personal sense) constitutes a precocious denunciation of primitive cinema's 'lack' as it was to be perceived by the middle classes, and especially the intelligentsia. He was also setting forth, over three decades before its accomplishment, the parameters of that ultimate goal of what gradually became the hegemonic tendency in motion pictures: the achievement of the full diegetic effect.

This achievement, which I situate at the dawn of synchronized sound, constitutes a major threshold. In the USA and Europe, classical cinema had in one sense reached full growth, with all its basic *visual* strategies (including the most enveloping version of the shot/counter-shot) since at least 1917.[4] Yet is it not verifiable in many ways that lip-synch sound immediately became an essential constituent of a fuller diegetic process than the silent cinema had known? This, I suggest, is the chief reason why involvement in silent film narrative requires a certain apprenticeship today: it is the relative weakness of its diegetic effect which perturbs the uninitiated viewer, rather than any difficulty in assimilating the standard narrative codes of the 1920s. I take this as a preliminary indication of the relative autonomy of the narrative and diegetic principles.

3 Maxim Gorky, 'A review of the Lumière programme at the Nizhni-Novgorod Fair, as printed in . . . July 4, 1896 . . .', in Jay Leyda (ed.), *Kino* (London: Allen and Unwin, 1960).

4 The earliest film I know which seems to display a complete mastery of the institutional *découpage* is Maurice Tourneur's *A Girl's Folly* (1917) in which the principle of camera ubiquity (in the film-studio sequences) is displayed with a skill still absent from such milestones as Barker/Ince's *The Italian* or DeMille's *The Cheat* (both 1915). Whatever the case, it is during these crucial years that the decisive threshold is crossed.

Conversely, it is undeniable that the reproduction, within this new substance of expression (film), of structures analogous to those of classical narrative *in general*, contributed historically to the gradual enrichment of the diegetic process—shot/counter-shot, for example, developed as an essentially narrative procedure—between 1906 and 1929. I none the less maintain that even before the advent of synchronous sound, relative autonomy is demonstrable. In fact, I believe that if there is any useful answer to the perennial question of cinema's specificity, it seems reasonable to suggest that within the broad spectrum of the classical narrative in general, it is the singular strength of its diegetic production that situates cinema apart, that has made it a uniquely powerful tool, not merely of social control but of social and even revolutionary mobilization as well.

The term *diegesis* was revived and appropriated by Etienne Souriau to account for a phenomenon which most scholars have associated peculiarly with cinema—and this in itself points to a privileged status among the other signifying practices. However, there is no doubt whatsoever that a literary narrative, for example, involves a diegetic process, most specifically by the adjunction to the description of the narrative action proper (which also partakes of diegetic production, of course) of descriptions of places, people, clothing, sounds, smells, and so on. Moreover, one can easily imagine (and in fact find, among the productions of the *nouveau roman*) non-narrative fictional writing, consisting solely of description and excluding the minimal components of narrative—*virtualité, passage à l'acte, achèvement*, according to the post-Proppian definition given by Claude Brémond[5]—which would none the less conjure up that imaginary world which we so easily evoke in connection with the diegetic effect. However, the almost inevitable unreadability—in the Barthesian sense—of non-narrative fiction, in contrast with the eminent readability of, say, those impressionistic documentaries or sequences of nature scenes with musical sound tracks used to fill gaps in television programming, does suggest that the diegetic effect in literature is more closely intertwined with the narrative process, no doubt because of the symbolic, discontinuous nature of the typographic sign—as opposed to the iconic, continuous nature of the cinematic sign. Hence, perhaps, in literature the more rapid breakdown of diegetic process upon the 'withdrawal' of narrative.

Literature also makes clear that the diegetic effect can be manifested with varying degrees of intensity: do not those sparse narratives imagined by Borges often seem closer to Propp's bare *résumés* of Russian folk-tales than to, say, a Balzac *conte*, precisely because they are more weakly diegetic than a text like *La Fille aux yeux d'or*?

Before proceeding further, I must deal with a question of terminology: is the diegetic effect equivalent to the 'illusion of reality' so generally ascribed to film (and leaving aside the historical aspect of this problem, as outlined above)? Though experientially, the phenomenon may be the same, from a theoretical point of view, a distinction between these two concepts appears crucial. For what we are

5 Claude Bremond, *Logique du récit* (Paris: Editions du Seuil, 1973), pp. 131 ff.

talking about is, of course, no illusion at all in any rigorous sense; whatever-it-is does not resemble reality, as any of us actually experience it, in any convincing way (a comparison with 3-D films is edifying in this respect). The historical maximization of the diegetic effect has in fact resulted from the accumulation of only a limited number of pertinent indices of phenomenal reality. The colour threshold itself was diegetically trivial in comparison with that of lip-synch sound. And the apparent non-pertinence here of the lack of any indices other than audiovisual (the sporadic careers of Smellorama, Sensurround are tangible signs of this), as well as the continuing audience preference for the imaginary three dimensionality of institutional screen space over the truly illusionistic three-dimensionality of stereo films, incline one to believe that the term 'illusion of reality' is a substitute, of nineteenth-century origin, for what is in fact a rationally selective system of symbolic exchange.

This is not to say, however, that the peculiar impact of the cinematic diegesis does not derive, as has often been stressed, from the fact that it involves almost exclusively iconic signification—and the replacement of the printed title by the spoken voice was a decisive step in the establishment of an iconic hegemony. After 1930, nearly all the narrative signifiers (with the important exception of music, and an occasional passage of offscreen commentary) are diegetic as well, whereas in literature, for example, there is usually a great deal of extradiegetic voice-over. But of course the diegetic effect in literature is always mediated in a way in which it is not in cinema, where the narrative and diegetic processes tend to fuse,[6] causing, of course, the frequent heuristic confusion between them.

The 'illusion of fusion' is also to some extent a construct, with a history of its own. The development of such narrative figures as the syntagma of simultaneity, successiveness, and proximity is coextensive with the emergence of strong spectatorial identification with the motion picture camera, that linchpin of the full-blown diegetic effect in film.

Is it meaningful to assign a single 'threshold of emergence' to the diegetic process which we today associate with moving photographic pictures and lip-synch sound? No doubt such a threshold was crossed when people around the world began seeing projected photographic images, familiar enough via the magic lantern, actually 'come to life' before their eyes, as Gorky had at Aumont's café: 'You anticipate nothing new in this all too familiar scene, for you have seen pictures of Paris streets more than once. But suddenly a strange flicker passes through the screen and the pictures stir to life.'

And surely the coming of the talkies was a decisive threshold as well. I am tempted to see 1895 and 1927 as the confines of a period of gestation, which saw the emergence of such acquisitions as colour and spoken titles, but above all of the system of narrative editing, and which climaxed as this latter merged with lip-synch sound to overdetermine the full diegetic effect.

6 Barthes speaks of the apparent fusion between connotational and denotational levels of signification in the still photograph. In the talking cinema the (con)fusion between these two levels is far more complete, not only because of the syntagmatic extension (in time) of the denotational level but also because of the complete material integration of the specifying textual level of signification which, with the photograph, is always writing, i.e. non-analogical. (The system of the silent cinema is much closer to the advertising poster than to that of the talkies.)

Can we, however, exclude from this historical space the experience of the viewers of the sophisticated magic lantern shows of late nineteenth-century Britain, which involved prefigurations of camera ubiquity, realistically tinted photography, voice, music, and sound effects?[7] Or, for that matter, the spectators of Daguerre's dioramas or Robertson's *phantasmagories*? And what of the stereoscope? What of photography itself?

It seems clear enough today that the introduction of the analogical replication of movement adds a decisive element to photographic signification. True, the enlargement to screen size through projection enhanced the analogical power of the photograph, and sequencing introduced a concatenation of the iconic signifiers impossible in the single photograph. But it is precisely the seamless concatenation of film frames which makes this plane of signification as continuous as iconic signification itself, naturalizing it in a way that even the dissolving views could not. Similarly, thirty odd years later, a technology born of the vacuum tube made it possible to naturalize the noun, integrating it into the iconic continuum in a way which neither the lantern-lecturer nor the cine-lecturer could achieve.

In his essay 'A scene at the "movies" ',[8] Ben Brewster stresses the centrality to the novelistic text of strategies of point of view and demonstrates how Griffith was at pains to introduce them early in his Biograph career, as he undertook to sophisticate the narrative mode of the early American film. In the exemplary *Gold is not All* (1910), audience identification with the poor-but-happy couple is effortlessly achieved through a *mise-en-scène* which produces the rich-but-wretched family as scene, viewed from the place of the poor couple, perpetually shown peering in at the rich from the outside, a situation of comfortable, 'ringside omniscience', paralleling that of the cine-spectator. And indeed, it is from the films of Griffith and his contemporaries that we may date the origin of a carefully hierarchized narrative system which makes it possible, lacking any but the grossest equivalents of the nuances of person enjoyed by the classical novel, to privilege the viewpoint of the character(s) with whom spectators are 'programmed' to identify (even if, as in *Gold is not All*, it is these characters' opposite numbers, insistently produced as *other*, who appear most often on the screen: our gaze has become the external gaze of the 'happy poor', *even in their absence*). It is this strategy of narrative viewpoint, often asserted without the recourse to 'subjective camera'—still a rare stance in 1910, even in the work of Griffith—which would henceforth perenially serve to naturalize such assertions as 'the poor are happier than the rich'.

Undeniably, identification with *the gaze that tells* is essential to the power of classical bourgeois narrative, both on the screen and in the novel. I would argue, however, that the specific experience defined by the cinema institution involves, as Jean-Louis Baudry and later Christian Metz have argued, a primal identification with *the gaze that sees*, the gaze that *is there*, with the point of view of the camera. In the current

7 Cecil Hepworth notes in his memoirs (*Came the Dawn: Memories of a Film Pioneer* (London: Phoenix House, 1951)) that when Burt Acres first showed him animated photographs projected on a screen, his familiarity with the lantern was such that he was not, at the time, particularly impressed. The implications of what he had witnessed did not become clear until some months later.

8 *Screen*, vol. 23, no. 2 (1982), pp. 4–15; reprinted in this volume as Chapter 12.

debate around these issues, I would argue resolutely in Baudry's and Metz's favour because my own examination of the genealogy of 'film language' supports their thesis.

Each of the successive identifiable acquisitions of this 'language' —more aptly: this mode of visual representation—may be analysed in terms of its role in the overdetermination of this quasi-primal identification. This relatively long process of gestation (1895–1925) comprised the re-creation on the screen of the perspectival box of the Renaissance, the mastery of the moving camera, and the refinement of all the other strategies of that camera ubiquity whose signified is summed up in the shot/counter-shot: *the absence/presence of the spectator at the very centre of the diegetic process.* All of these factors clearly converge upon a single, supreme effect, embarking the spectator on that motionless journey which is the essence of the institutional cinematic experience. Through this constant identification with the camera's viewpoint, the experience of the classical film interpellates us solely as incorporeal individuals.

One of the critical thresholds crossed in the course of this historical movement was the ban, by certain American companies around 1910,[9] against actors looking at the camera. In the land of Griffith, Barker, and DeMille, it was recognized much earlier than in France, for example, that the glance at the camera addressed itself explicitly to the spectator as corporeal individual, produced him/her as seated in a darkened theatre looking at dancing shadows on a screen. The music-hall entertainer's glance, the melodrama villain's, addressed the audience collectively—in contexts, moreover which were more presentational than representational (the bourgeois stage had long since eliminated the aside). The cine-actor's eye, on the contrary, when it encounters the cine-lens, drills straight at the individual, wherever he/she may be sitting. Now, in order to increase the cine-spectator's sense of being there, it was necessary to eliminate the camera from the (apparent) consciousness of the actors: they had ostensibly to ignore it. For the spectator to receive as directed at him/her a gaze at the camera had become tantamount to the hidden voyeur's shock when his/her gaze is unmasked and *returned*. As a condition of being able to 'take off', to enter that 'other scene' of the film, to feel him/herself freely evolving within it, the spectator had to feel him/herself *unobserved*. The ban on looking at the camera was, in particular, a fundamental condition for the integration of the close-up into the editing scheme—the closer the shot, the greater the shock of the glance at the lens—and for the full achievement of personal narrative identification.

Camera identification finds its firmest anchorage in that key figure, the shot/counter-shot, whereby the spectator becomes the invisible mediator between two gazes, two discourses which envelop him/her, positioned thus as the ideal, invisible voyeur. It is a measure of the extent to which the French cinema, still clinging to the presentationalism of the popular theatre, lagged behind the American as regards the assimilation of the institutional mode, that French actors were still

9 Cf. Kalton C. Lahue (ed.), *Motion Picture Pioneer: The Selig Polyscope Company* (New York: Barnes & Co, 1973), p. 63.

making asides at the camera as late as 1915 (cf. Feuillade's masterpiece, *les Vampires*).

It is becoming evident that the English 'gentlemen primitives' (of Brighton and elsewhere) displayed an uncanny sensitivity to these issues, due no doubt to the upper-middle-class origins that were unique among turn-of-the-century cineastes, and to their experience with the lantern. Williamson's famous film, *The Big Swallow* (1901)—correctly regarded as a 'lantern film'—seems almost to be an acting out of this entire effacement/identification process. An upper-class fop threatens the operator with his waving cane as he approaches the camera, nearer and nearer . . . finally swallowing both (in a puerile cut-away trick shot). Then as the huge face retreats, chewing, it smiles at . . . the audience. What is remarkable here, is that the gaze addressed at the operator is directed so far off-camera that today's spectator does not spontaneously perceive it as a glance at anyone behind the camera at all. Williamson already seemed to sense that a gaze at an offscreen character in the vicinity of the camera (basis for the shot/reverse-shot) must not be into the lens. Only when camera and operator had been removed from the primary diegesis could the actor look at the (second) camera, could he look at the audience with all the candour of the music-hall stars in primitive stand-up comedy films.

Gradually the rule became universal: a gaze towards the camera must never encounter the centre of the lens, a thin metal rim became the immutable frontier between an oblivious gaze just missing that of the invisible spectator and a gaze of direct address into his/her eyes: a character could look past—even through—the spectator at other characters, a landscape, and so on, but a look into the lens was permitted only in rare cases of extra-narrative or farcical Laurel and Hardy-type addresses to the audience. The spectator was allowed to experience an actor's or actress's gaze *almost but not quite* as if she/he were its recipient. The audience's invulnerability/involvement hinged henceforth upon a few scant seconds of eye-line angle.

Yet curiously enough, forty years after the Selig Polyscope Company had included in a list of dos and don'ts for actors an explicit ban on looking at the camera, there was produced, in Hollywood itself, a film which deliberately violated that time-honoured taboo. The 1940s and early 1950s were Hollywood's experimental years and this experiment, at least, has remained absolutely unique in Hollywood history for the very good reason that it was a commercial failure.

And yet Robert Montgomery's gimmick for *The Lady in the Lake* (1947) was in fact a very reasonable one: he would simply transfer directly to the screen the first-person narrative technique that had long been successful precisely in this genre of fiction, the hard-boiled detective novel. However, the establishment of a literal equivalence between the narratively subjective camera (the institutional camera is *always* diegetically subjective) and the novelistic first person, reintroduced effects that were profoundly disruptive of the diegetic process. On the one hand, the long takes and elaborate, not to say pedantic, camera movements tended towards a denaturalization, a mechanization of the flux of signification: the long invisible camera suddenly interposed itself again between audience and diegetic world. Above all, however, the fact of these characters constantly looking straight into the lens simply gave the whole game away! The secret of the maximization of the diegetic process is the spectator's invulnerability. Attempting to squeeze narrative identification into the same point in the mental space of the filmic experience as that already occupied, as it were, by the subject of primal identification, was to pit the pot of clay against the pot of iron, as the French proverb goes. The character of Philip Marlowe finds himself relegated to somewhere behind the spectator who suddenly finds him/herself thrust into the line of fire (and the choice of a rather distant tone for the detective almost seems to have been determined by the inevitable outcome of that unequal contest between the two modes of identification). In other words: how is it possible for 'me' to occupy 'my place' if 'I' am no longer invisible, if all those people keep looking 'at me'?

As recalled previously, the first-person tense of camera identification involves a split, isomorphic but not identical with the split in spectatorial consciousness between the 'I know full well' and the 'but all the same' by which Octave Mannoni, in a seminal text[10] has compared the conditions of the theatrical illusion with the mechanism of disavowal as it is encountered in analytic practice. There is the tacit, unconscious 'I' of camera identification, the 'I' that experiences the diegetic process as unmediated fantasy experience. And then there is the 'I' of character identification, non-specific to cinema and only incidentally ensured, within the institutional framework, by point-of-view shots. The point-of-view shot, if we do not simply mean one member of the shot/counter-shot, which more properly belongs to the subjectivity of 'primal', diegetic identification, is essentially contingent upon action, upon narrative incident. A film can easily contain no scenes in which the central character looks out of a window at something to which the editor cuts or any similar situation. And yet it is perfectly possible for that film to be in the first person by the constant presence of the central figure on the screen, by the use of close-ups suggesting his/her thoughts, or through the use of voice-over. In a sense, this is simply the equivalent of a well-known literary conceit, the disguised first person, achieved by comparable means. In fact the fundamental opposition between character identification and camera identification is that the former operates at the level of the (novelistic) signified of the classical film text, while the latter operates on the side of the signifier.

The Lady in the Lake, then, seeking to collapse the one into the other, could only succeed in expelling the subject from the film in a certain sense, and seriously compromising the full development of the diegetic process. A lesson learned pragmatically some forty years before was now at last demonstrated—theory in a practical state—for all to see.

Several such limit instances were produced in the immediate postwar Hollywood. Not surprisingly, all were carried out in conjunction with

10 Octave Mannoni, *Clefs pour l'imaginaire ou l'autre scène* (Paris: Editions du Seuil, 1969), pp. 9–33.

the telling of heavily coded crime stories. But whereas Montgomery's abolition of the impunity of the spectatorial subject may be said to introduce a major diegetic disruption, Hitchcock's quasi-abolition of editing in *Rope* (1948), Russell Rouse's abolition of dialogue in *The Thief* (1952) both demonstrate that neither of these major vehicles of narrative meaning are essential to the production of the (maximized) diegetic effect.

For although Hitchcock derives some truly surreal effects from the viscous flow of real time, his film is in fact simply a rigorous demonstration of Eisenstein's thesis[11] that one can recreate classical montage within the confines of the single take through strategies of framing, blocking, and camera movement alone. Hitchcock's constantly roving camera, always centred, always seeking the 'true' centre of the narrative (for example by remaining focused on the maid clearing the chest that conceals the cadaver rather than concerning itself with banal after-dinner talk) ensures camera ubiquity/identification as surely as the most traditional editing scheme.

However mediocre artistically, *The Thief* is even more interesting from a heuristic point of view. It shows that the suppression not only of dialogue but of the act of speech itself does not necessarily produce a throwback to the diegetic level of the (titleless) films of the late silent era.[12] As this film clearly demonstrates, the presence of synch sound effects is quite enough to raise the diegetic level to contemporary fullness (we keep expecting these characters to talk, they obviously have that capacity, we are just never there to hear it happen, but the synch sound effects are the guarantee of that potentially manifest presence).

We also encounter here a spectacular demonstration of the essentially narrative role, within the institution and especially since the mid-1930s, of the music which accompanies the diegesis. Incidental music in the sound film remains an extradiegetic narrative signifier, just as it was in the 'silent' film. In *The Thief* it can be said to replace dialogue which normally it would complement or reduplicate. But, like the textless picture narrative itself, it can only speak in clichés, it can exclude ambiguity only at the cost of having recourse to a broad, heavily coded symbolism. This film lays bare the role of dialogue in the constitution of singularity in the classical film. For the uncaptioned photoplay, not unexpectedly, can communicate only the most highly coded narrative, peopled by gross stereotypes. In the USA of 1952, this was almost bound to be an archetypal Cold War fiction—an unmarried scientist who betrays his country for some twisted, unknowable motive, is soon forced to go underground when something goes wrong and finally, after a protracted, graphic bout with his conscience, finally decides to turn himself in.

If the diegetic effect can be said to be weakened here at all, it is through the transference of the brunt of the narrative burden from dialogue (and even from language in general: written texts are also eliminated as much as possible) to music. But this weakening exists

11 Vladimir Nizhny, *Lessons with Eisenstein*, trans. and ed. Ivor Montagu and Jay Leyda (New York: Hill and Wang, 1962), pp. 94–139.

12 The undoubted rationale behind the elimination (or near elimination) of titles from such films as *The Wind* (1928), *Der Letzte Mann* (1924), or *Ménilmontant* (1924) was indeed the heightening of diegetic homogeneity and hence of character and narrative presence.

only as a cumulative effect, brought about by the continued sense of frustration produced by the gimmick: any single sequence, taken by itself, appears at full diegetic strength, the way almost no sequence in *The Lady and the Lake* can do.

Is a lapse such as that instanced in *The Lady in the Lake* of greater or lesser impact upon the integrity of the diegetic process than, say, Dreyer's sophisticated return to frontality and his quasi-elimination of shot/counter-shot in *Gertrud* (1964)?

Wary, henceforth, of the pitfalls of quantification, I hesitate to answer such questions. One thing is sure, however: for an audience culturally able to cope with the idiosyncrasies of *Gertrud*, the meanings produced by its 'diegetic deficiency' (if such it can be termed) are bound to be very different from those conveyed by the wrong-headed gimmick of *The Lady in the Lake*. To an unsophisticated mass audience, however, the two inadequacies might easily appear equivalent, both films still being *readable*, but not comfortably so.

Indeed, there are a relatively large number of films which, while adhering to many essential norms of the institutional system, introduce concerted, positive strategies which tend to weaken the diegetic process in one way or another. Jean-Pierre Lefebvre, in *le Vieux pays où Rimbaud est mort*, had his characters address the camera directly as a distancing strategy. The films of Ozu, as I have sought to demonstrate elsewhere,[13] involve temporary suspensions of diegetic presence (relative, that is, to a specific context: there are no non-diegetic images in Ozu). These suspensions are in the form of 'pillow shots', which punctuate all of his films after 1932. They are characterized by the temporary removal from the screen of the human figure,[14] of synch sound (after 1935), and of movement, and these last two, as we have seen, are directly associated with the two fundamental thresholds in the history of diegetic process in film. Nor, it should be noted, are we dealing with a procedure such as the freeze-frame which permanently suspends the diegesis at the end of many a classical film, and which constitutes a facilitation of the painful withdrawal from the thrall of the diegetic process. The pillow shots very definitely stand for a narrative duration, but one which they measure from outside the narrative properly so-called, and from the outer fringes of the diegetic space–time which may be said to contain it.

Chris Marker's eccentric film, *la Jetée* (1964), making a knowing return to the magic lantern lecture, undertakes to extend a comparable weakening to the entire film (the full diegetic effect being alluded to only once: a shot of the young woman opening her eyes). However, the outer limits of diegetic production have seldom been systematically tested. They have, of course, been crossed, at least since Viking Eggeling, many, many times. But it struck me some years ago that there was perhaps only one body of 'experimental' film-making which may be seen as applying itself specifically to the task of testing the limits of diegesis. I am referring to the work of Michael Snow.

13 Noël Burch, *To the Distant Observer* (London: Scolar Press, 1979), pp. 160–72.

14 Characters are the structural centre of the diegetic world, the link between narrative and diegesis.

The film which first called my attention to this aspect of Snow's work was *La Région Centrale* (1970–1). Here, it seemed evident, was a film which had achieved at last a self-reflexive utopia: the diegetic continuum was reduced wholly to the state of immanent referent—it was what we saw and heard, as opposed to the multiple layers of fiction and documentary films, whose diegetic space–time extends far beyond the shot. It became exactly coextensive, not with narrative—narrative cannot be random in the sense that these complex pans were—but with the process of filmic production itself. Of course, this process was *represented*—at one remove for the picture, at two for the sound (those bleeps 'controlling' the camera at the end of its universally articulated crane were fictional, after-the-fact creations). But both were primary within the diegetic sphere, both were forcefully *present*, through the interaction of the two tracks: however fictitious, this synchronism provided an irrefutable guarantee of 'liveness'. Thus, besides establishing what may be one inner threshold of diegetic production, the film indicated, by the very strength of its diegetic effect in the absence of any animate beings or of any 'natural' sound, that the minimal generation of diegetic process depends neither on narrative, nor synch sound originating in the image, nor even on profilmic movement, but can be generated by the image alone (the sound here is a digital translation of one dimension of the image). This is the case so long as the image is readable (at a certain speed, the blurring of the image suspends the diegetic process) and so long as camera identification is ensured through movement. It is interesting to note that in this context, the appearance on the screen of the camera shadow impinges not at all upon the diegetic process: in fact, I would hazard that it actually reinforces the 'I-but-not-I' and the 'there-but-not-there' aspects of the identificational process: 'I am the camera, but its shadow is not mine'. Subsequently, as I looked back over Snow's previous films, it became apparent that all of them, in one way or another, dealt explicitly with these issues.

The most comprehensive in this respect is Snow's best-known work, *Wavelength* (1968–9). During the forty-odd minutes which it takes for the camera-I to cross that Manhattan loft, the diegetic effect, the sense of camera identification indeed, is repeatedly lost and found again owing to various radical departures from and returns to the norms of conventional cinematography (as regards exposure, colour temperature, negative–positive relations, and so on). At the same time, the threshold between the domain of diegetic process and other possible modes of writing/reading is continually manifested in the contrast between inside and outside: even when the image has been almost entirely washed out by over-exposure or tinted a deep shade of pink, such depredations are perceived as taking place inside (due in particular to the room's emptiness of people and of profilmic movement), while outside, in the street, life goes on. It is remarkable that this decisive difference persists in spite of the fact that the departures from cinematographic norms affect that part of the frame as much as the rest. Here we have a further indication that movement constitutes one of the minimal conditions for diegetic production.

Wavelength also engages with the issue of the relations between narrative and diegetic process. Do the increasingly narrative moments of human activity strung out across the film—from the bringing in by movers of a 'casing shelved' to the discovery of a dead body by a young woman—determine actual intensifications of the diegetic effect? In my view, what we experience here is the *centring* of the diegesis which is typically brought about by narrative (and by constitution of character). As soon as this loft appears on the screen, with the roofs of trucks passing by outside those windows, generating what appears, at least, to be synch sound, institutionally determined expectations are such that it can only be perceived as waiting for something to happen, for some*one* to come in (such is the anthropocentric bias of the classical film). But the diegetic process as such is already fully engaged. Subsequently, someone does come in, the diegesis appears centred, in preparation for the appearance of recognizable narrative structures. Clearly, we are dealing with a perfectly coded succession, considerably more protracted than is usual, but that is all. Of course, as the film proceeds and as such expectations are not met, these normal images, when they reappear now and again, may have lost some of their credibility. Comparisons are difficult, since an acoustic sine wave soon begins to blot out the live sound—but perhaps this disruptive wail merely manifests our inevitable loss of faith through repeated depredations. None the less, when the woman finds the dead body—at the climax of the film's elementary narrative—full diegetic strength returns behind the sine wave, in much the same way that it seems to have hitherto been maintained through thick and thin 'out there', beyond the windows.

Consequently, it would seem, first, that even in the absence of narrative, even in the absence of images of humans or animals, the diegetic presence can be maintained through this or that essential component (here it is movement—however slow, it is enough to overdetermine camera identification—and synch sound that connote liveness for any audience). At the same time, it would also appear that analogical, profilmic movement and narrative tend to preserve the diegetic process absolutely intact even when the 'representational integrity' of the picture and/or soundtrack are under attack.

In fact, the film whose non-verbal title (←→) is rendered as *Back and Forth* (1977), shows how much obliteration the picture track can take before the diegetic process is so much as impinged upon. It is not until the camera, swinging back and forth across that occasionally peopled classroom, attains speed so high that the picture is no longer recognizably representational at all, and until the sound of the swinging camera boom has become a mechanical screech that blots out all ambient sound, that we can speak of a momentary suspension of diegetic process.

Another limit instance in the relations between narrative and diegetic process is revealed in *A Casing Shelved* (1977), a single-slide and tape

15 Annette Michelson, 'Towards Snow, part I', *Artforum*, June 1971, pp. 30–7.

piece designed to be presented and attended to in conditions so similar to those of the motion picture that it can, as Annette Michelson has pointed out, be legitimately assimilated to Snow's work as a film-maker.[15] A single still image is projected on a screen for nearly an hour. It shows a set of home-made shelves lined with dozens of objects belonging to the artist. The work's narrative is carried solely by Snow's own voice on tape, telling the story behind each of those objects in turn. It is hard not to be reminded of the primitive lecturer deciphering an image which was no doubt often incomprehensible to the gaze of the neophyte movie-goer. But the tenuousness of the visual guarantees, and in particular the absence of movement—even that of the dust particles that would betray the movement of a film—as well as the lack of spatio-temporal indices in the spoken commentary, make it very difficult to speak of a diegetic process or effect in connection with this piece, none the less saturated with narrativity.

Yet, however much these works by Snow may test certain outer limits of diegesis and narrative, another film makes it possible to isolate in exemplary fashion these two dimensions of cinematic representation, and perhaps better to understand as well the specificity of the diegetic effect and of primal identification with the camera. The Scottish physician–poet–film-maker Margaret Tait's beautiful film, *Place of Work* (1976), can be said to constitute an experiment in the maximization of the diegetic effect in the almost total absence of narrativity. The film is simply an exploration/meditation dealing with a house which, as the author announces briefly at the outset, she and her family are about to leave after many years spent living and working there. But although a ditch-digger may be glimpsed out on the road beyond the hedge, people are largely absent from the screen, as pans and fixed shots of the house and its garden follow one another in impressionistic order. The sound of the film, though not actually recorded synch, it appears, was edited and mixed to produce a perfect illusion of the live. The result, then, of these camera movements and of this sound, is a perfectly full sense of *being there*: the stage is set, once again, for 'people' (characters) to make their entrance.

Interestingly enough, however, the single moment of narrative emergence—an abortive emergence, at that—involves not humans but animals. During a series of garden views, a shot of a cat is followed by one of a bird. Nothing actually transpires, except for this imaginary transmission of a gaze: Tait's camera (and scissors) move on to other views. And yet any attentive audience, within the appropriate cultural and historical confines, will grasp, as soon as the bird appears, that this shot-change is potentially the first articulation in a tripartite narrative sequence: cat/sees bird/chases (kills? eats?) bird.

It is also interesting to note that the only centred appearance of a human being in the film (the ditch-digger is part of the scenery) not only fails to introduce narrative at all, but actually challenges the very identificational system upon which the maximized diegetic effect rests. At one point, as the camera explores the ground floor, it focuses on the open front door. A postman steps into view, withdraws again quickly when he sees the camera pointed at him. Tait's voice calls to him, telling him to come ahead, that it's all right, and he reappears to exchange a few words with the woman behind the camera. Here, I feel, is a momentary impingement upon the conditions of diegetic production as they have been established in this film. For at the point when Tait's voice calls out, we suddenly find that our position at the camera keyhole has been occupied. It seems there was someone there before us, or rather, someone is suddenly peering over our shoulder, urging us out of the way, as it were.

In these two moments, then, the film suggests, first, the boundary between the narrative and diegetic processes, and, secondly, between an illusionistic diegesis and one which acknowledges its process of production.

It has often been argued, in rebuttal of my attempts to define an Institutional Mode of Representation, essentially unchanged I claim, since its emergence in the late 1920s, and to theorize the visual and audial strategies which converged around that period to produce the full diegetic effect, that 'television has changed all that'. Before my massive exposure to US television style, I had seen no conclusive evidence of any fundamental differences between cinema and television in this respect. Today, having observed the way in which Americans relate to a television which runs twenty-four hours a day and whose chief function may be said to be the trivialization of everything, having observed the converging strategies of disengagement which have been built into the new medium as they have been into North American society as a whole, I have to admit that I was wrong.

It is strange to see the many ways in which US network television constitutes a return to the days of the nickelodeon: a continuous showing cut up into brief segments of from one to ten minutes, with an audience that drifts in and out, the incredible mixture of genres, the confusions between reality and fiction to which audiences are subjected—and seem so readily prone. Even *découpage* seems to be slipping back to 1910 in the proliferating evening sitcoms, with a prevalence of three-walled frontality and the medium long-shot. The use of offscreen laughter in these same shows seems clearly to be a way of situating the audience in a noisy theatre; but vicariously so, 'theatre' here being tantamount to *unreal*, not to be taken seriously. And this indeed is what so universally characterizes US television today: none of it matters, not the news any more than the soaps, not the election campaigns any more than the adverts (which often have built-in elements of self-derision that seem to say 'even these', presumably the true *raison d'être* of commercial television, 'are not to be taken seriously'). There has even been one astounding return to an undercutting lecture in the true spirit of the late nickelodeon period: the adventures of the stunt-driving *Dukes of Hazzard* are punctuated by an ironic, chortling, home-spun narration which unerringly de-dramatizes every situation.

For years we have assumed that the alienation effect was necessarily enlightening, liberating, that anything which undercut the empathetic power of the diegetic process was progressive. To be reminded that the scenes unfolding on stage or screen were artifice, to experience any mode of distancing was to be enabled to reflect upon a text and its production of meaning, and so forth. It is beginning to appear to me that US television, more advanced in this respect than any other, save perhaps that of Japan, mobilizes a number of strategies whose cumulative effect is to induce a certain disengagement, a certain feeling that what we see—no matter what it is—does not really count. Distancing, in short, has been co-opted. The contrast is striking with the type of engagement elicited by the classical cinema of the 1930s, 1940s, and 1950s and indeed by most Hollywood films today.

It would take many pages to outline the countless distancing effects to be found on US television, from the omnipresent star filter, as at home on the talk show or the newscast as it is in the variety show; to the very format of those obscurantist magazines—*That's Incredible, Real People*, and so on—which joyfully mingle file tapes (dutifully labelled as such), re-enactments (by the real-life protagonists of some 'strange event'), *cinéma-vérité* type interviews, studio presentations, as well as 'documents' varying considerably in status from the obvious fake (of telekinesis, for example) to the incontrovertible actuality. These distancing shifts in the status of representation, which at first glance ought to make a Godard green with envy, are in fact part of a brilliant strategy of disengagement, designed to place everything on the same plane of triviality, which is the general undertaking of US television.

However, the primary strategy of undercutting the diegetic process on US network television is the constant interruption through commercials, a kind of profilmic pendant of the plethora of accepted live interruptions peculiar, in my view, to the North American household's relation to their television set. And there is good reason to believe that the sluggish pace and pedantic repetitiveness of the daytime soaps is designed to mesh with the rhythm of housework.

By contradistinction, one is tempted to feel that the uninterrupted duration of diegetic production over a period of an hour or two might well be an essential element in that maximization of the diegetic effect which we associate with the classical film. Here too, the period from 1906 to 1914 is crucial, not only in laying the grounds for institutional editing, but also in the shift in programme format from a series of six-to-ten-minute shorts with songs or lantern slides between each, to one centred around a film well over an hour long.

The cool, disjunctive format of US network television may be seen as a veritable turning back of the clock, which is anything but innocent. 'Cinema' returns to a quasi pre-discursive state, abandoning the absorbing presence of the full diegetic process—which after all did elicit some kind of emotional, intellectual and perhaps even ideological involvement on the part of the spectator—in favour of a sort of bland detachment (clinically observed to be close to a state of narcosis or

16 Cf. Jerry Mander, *Four Arguments for the Elimination of Television* (New York: Morrow Quill, 1978), pp. 192–215.

hypnosis)[16] in which the repression in El Salvador is no more nor less involving than *The Price is Right*, and in which even the most outspoken (fictional) denunciation of, say, migrant workers' camps in Florida, will be taken with the same bemused incredulity as the exploits of *That's Incredible*. Faced with these developments, the left ideologue can no longer regard the classical film with its maximized diegetic effect simply as 'bad object'. I, for one, would henceforth argue that: (*a*) the dissolution of the diegetic effect must be carefully controlled in any audiovisual signifying practice with radical pretensions; and (*b*) the strong diegetic effect (in particular through recourse to the codes of 'liveness') must in some way or another remain a part of any such practice.

14 Heard over the Phone: *The Lonely Villa* and the de Lorde Tradition of the Terrors of Technology

TOM GUNNING

1 *The Lonely Villa* (Griffith, 1908); reprinted in Eileen Bowser (ed.), *The Biograph Bulletins, 1908–1912* (New York: Farrar, Strauss and Giroux, 1973), p. 97.

2 Avital Ronell, *The Telephone Book: Technology, Schizophrenia, Electric Speech* (Lincoln, Nebr.: University of Nebraska Press, 1989), pp. 4, 20.

3 André de Lorde and Charles Foley, *Au téléphone*; an English translation, *At the Telephone*, appears in Thomas Edwards (ed.), *One Act Plays for Stage and Study* (New York: Samuel French, 1925, second series).

There is something spooklike in the title of this Biograph subject, but we hasten to say that the incidents are of a decidedly material nature. . . .
    Publicity bulletin for *The Lonely Villa*[1]

Maintaining and joining, the telephone line holds together what it separates. . . . Being on the telephone will come to mean, therefore, that contact is never constant nor is the break clean.
    Avital Ronell, *The Telephone Book*[2]

. . . it's a most astonishing thing, but if I were to telephone twenty times a day, I should never get the hang of the blessed thing; it seems weird and uncanny.
    André Marex in André de Lorde's play, *Au téléphone*[3]

Near the opening of *Civilization and its Discontents* Sigmund Freud examines the contention that it is civilization itself, and specifically modern civilization, that might be responsible for man's discontent. Taking a sceptical view of the claim that man was happier in simpler times, Freud asks:

> . . . is there then no positive gain in pleasure, no unequivocal increase in my feeling of happiness, if I can, as often as I please, hear the voice of a child of mine who is living hundreds of miles away or if I can learn in the shortest possible time after a friend has reached his destination that he has come through the long and difficult journey unharmed?

4   Sigmund Freud, 'Civilization and its discontents', in James Strachey (ed. and trans.), *The Standard Edition of the Complete Psychological Works of Sigmund Freud*, xxi (London: Hogarth Press, 1961), p. 88. Ronell uses this quote in *The Telephone Book*, pp. 86–94. I signal here the inspiration and uncanny amusement Ronell's book provided for me, in spite of a wide divergence in method, and thank Mary Ann Doane for alerting me to it.

5   Stephen Kern, *The Culture of Time and Space (1880–1918)* (Cambridge, Mass.: Harvard University Press, 1983).

6   Ibid., 259–86.

7   Freud, 'Civilization and its discontents', p. 91.

8   Benjamin's arcades project has been brilliantly presented and discussed in Susan Buck-Morss, *The Dialectics of Seeing: Walter Benjamin and the Arcades Project* (Cambridge, Mass.: MIT Press, 1989). Wolfgang Schivelbusch's translated works on the history of technology are *The Railway Journey: Trains and Travel in the Nineteenth Century* (New York: Urizen Books, 1979— now available from University of California Press) and *Disenchanted Night: The Industrialization of Light in the Nineteenth Century* (Berkeley: University of California Press, 1988).

9   On the concept of the dream world of mass culture, see Buck-Morss, *The Dialectics of Seeing*, particularly pp. 253–86.

However, after listing some other clear benefits modern technology has bestowed on mankind, Freud gives the floor to 'the voice of pessimistic criticism' and adds:

> If there had been no railway to conquer distances, my child would never have left his native town and I should need no telephone to hear his voice; if travelling across the ocean by ship had not been introduced, my friend would not have embarked on his sea-voyage and I should not need a cable to relieve my anxiety about him.[4]

If the years around the turn of the century inaugurate (as Stephen Kern has indicated)[5] a new culture of time and space, we should not be surprised that Freud was particularly aware of the ambivalence of this new chronotope. On the one hand, distance (and the duration needed to cover it) is abolished. On the other hand, this technological conquering of space and time can be illusory. Families and friends are dispersed by the new technology as much as they are brought together, and the apparent compression of time can, in fact, cause a precipitate collapse of the processes of reflection. Kern theorizes, for instance, that instantaneous communication through cable and telephone artificially speeded up the July crisis that led to World War I, as technological haste propelled ultimatums and responses into a scenario of unstoppable confrontation.[6] When Freud compared the telephone's ability to overcome distance to the magical powers of a fairy tale[7] he was well aware of the dire consequences such magical gifts often entail.

Now at the close of another century, with new technological topologies confronting us, I believe we look back at the first experiences of technology with an uncanny sense of *déjà vu*. Not only do we confront the same ambivalence of optimism and anxiety, but the scenarios constructed around these primal ambiguities seem even more clearly legible. In the recent historicizing of film study, placing film within a history of the reception of technology has emerged as a primary challenge. Deriving inspiration particularly from Walter Benjamin's curtailed arcades project (and from such heirs to the Benjamin tradition as Wolfgang Schivelbusch),[8] the new exploration of the history of technology is more than technical. If Benjamin's method is fully understood, technology can reveal the dream world of society as much as its pragmatic rationalization.[9]

Although Freud does not really emphasize the dichotomy, I think that the opposition he sets up between technologies is revealing, particularly for early cinema. On the one hand he invokes those powerful devices of transportation and separation, the steamship and the railway. On the other hand, and apparently healing the breach, stand the machineries of communication and binding, the telephone and telegraph. As Schivelbusch has shown, the railway was the nineteenth century's mythic image of the new technology, embodying an excessive power that inspired terror as well as awe. Schivelbusch reveals that the railway's beneficial overcoming of space and time was balanced by the spectre of the railway accident, a figure as terrifying in fantasy as it was overwhelming in reality. The catastrophic effect of a train wreck on victims not injured physically led to the first medical diagnosis of traumatic neurosis and the acknowledgement that psychic events could have physical effects, paving the way for the theory of hysteria as formulated by Freud and Breuer at the end of the century.[10]

Lynne Kirby in her work on the image of the railway has proposed hysteria as a model for the spectator's experience of early cinema.[11] Thinking along the same lines, I have tried to theorize the particular effect of the non-narrativized cinema of attractions as an aesthetic of astonishment, exploiting a turn of the century taste for entertainment which confronted its spectator with a series of shocks.[12] The enduring film genre of early actualities of locomotives seemingly bearing down on camera and spectator exemplifies the audience address of a cinema which favoured direct visual stimulus over narrative development. But what about the role of technology in the period of narrativization which prepared the way for the classical paradigm? A film like D. W. Griffith's *The Lonedale Operator* (1911) shows how the new technology's ability to 'annihilate space and time' could support and interrelate with new narrative devices such as suspenseful parallel editing. The pattern of alternation brilliantly analysed in this film by Raymond Bellour[13] not only establishes gender positions (from Blanche Sweet, the threatened telegraph operator, to Frank Grandin, her engineer boyfriend) but also articulates the mode of technology each commands: the railway and telegraphy. The technology seems to follow Freud's typology. The railway separates the young lovers at the beginning while Blanche's morse code call for help reunites them. However the telegraph only *communicates* her plight to her lover and it is the speeding locomotive that brings them back together.

As Noël Burch and others (including myself) have pointed out, as cinema moved towards classical storytelling it had to overcome the self-contained and self-sufficient aspect of autonomous attractions addressed directly to a spectator.[14] Narrative development demanded the creation of a larger fictional whole assembled from a succession of shots. The individual shot was subordinated to an extended action in the new multi-shot narratives, with the direct address to the spectator sublated into a vectorized narrative expectation which carried the spectator from shot to shot. This was largely accomplished through a genre whose fictional action clearly required a succession of shots: the chase films so popular from 1903 to 1908. These films traced a clear line of diegetic action, creating a fully legible course for the spectator to negotiate as action moved from locale to locale and from shot to shot.

But with the appearance of parallel editing and the narrative devices of alternation it supplies, such simple tracing of physical action no longer suffices. Appearing as it does during the period of film's intense narratization, in which character psychology begins to motivate narrative action and the spatial and temporal relations between actions are no longer restricted to the clear linearity of the chase format, parallel editing typifies, without exhausting, the systematic nature that cinematic

10 Schivelbusch, *The Railway Journey*, pp. 131–45.

11 Lynne Kirby, 'Male hysteria and early cinema', *Camera Obscura*, no. 17 (1988), pp. 113–31.

12 Tom Gunning, 'An aesthetic of astonishment: early film and the (in)credulous spectator', *Art & Text*, no. 34 (1989), pp. 31–45.

13 Raymond Bellour, 'Alterner/raconter', in R. Bellour (ed.), *Le cinéma Américain* (Paris: Flammarion, 1980), pp. 69–88.

14 See Noël Burch, 'Passion, poursuite: la linéarisation', in *Communications*, no. 38 (1983), pp. 30–50; and Tom Gunning, 'Non-continuity, continuity, discontinuity: a theory of genres in early films', *Iris*, vol. 2, no. 1 (1984), pp. 101–12.

narration begins to display around 1908. It is the workings of this narrative system and its hardly accidental interrelation to technology that I wish to explore here. In the films I will discuss in this article the newly emerging forms of filmic narration display a relation (simultaneously thematic and structural) to the way technology structures modern life.

In the increasingly narrativized cinema of the transitional period (roughly 1907–13) the discontinuous shocks of early cinema become increasingly absorbed into a complex narrative process. This systemic approach to narrative creates a number of new tasks for the spectator, as he/she negotiates a series of spatio-temporal relations between events and interprets characters' motives. Placed in an active (yet also narrowly circumscribed) role before what (following Walter Benjamin) we could describe as a conveyor belt of narrative information, the newly formed cinematic spectator bears a striking similarity to the modern participant in technological processes. Integral to a process not in his/her control, the spectator must make the connections demanded or risk narrative incoherence.

Temporal simultaneity demands a more abstract sense of the interrelation of space and time and in many instances early film-makers incorporated recent technology into the plots of their films to naturalize film's power to move through space and time. The telephone supplies a particularly powerful example. In a key article Eileen Bowser demonstrates that portraying the unique spatial and temporal relations of a telephone conversation (different spaces but simultaneous time) called for ingenious solutions by early film-makers, which were eventually coded and became common practice.[15] True to the cinema of attractions' preference for the single shot, split-screens or split-sets predominate initially, with James Williamson's *Are You There?* (1901) using a none too stable curtain to separate the supposedly distant telephone lovers who are filmed within a single shot. Biograph's *The Story the Biograph Told* (1904) uses an actual superimposition of the two parties in a phone conversation (a solution I have not seen elsewhere), while Edwin Porter's *College Chums* (1907) creates an ingenious shot in which both participants appear in matted-in frames over a graphic image of a city, as animated letters pass between them conveying their conversation. Such split-screen devices remain an alternative method of conveying phone conversations into the classical period, with Lois Weber's three-way split-screen in *Suspense* (1913) providing the most elaborate example from the pre-feature era.

But after 1908 the most frequent device for portraying a phone conversation was parallel editing, cutting from one end of the telephone line to the other. While the earliest instances of extended parallel editing only occasionally portray telephone conversations, the fit between the spatio-temporal form of the event and that of its portrayal has a particularly satisfying effect which one suspects rendered the innovative technique particularly legible to film audiences. Griffith's first extended use of parallel editing appeared in *The Fatal Hour* shot in August 1908.

15 Eileen Bowser, 'Le coup de téléphone dans les primitifs du cinéma', in Pierre Guibert (ed.), *Les premiers ans du cinéma français* (Perpignan: Institut Jean Vigo, 1985), pp. 218–24. Most of this text has been incorporated into Bowser's *History of American Cinema*, vol. II, *The Emergence of Cinema* (New York: Scribners, 1990).

In this suspenseful tale of white slavery, a murderous clock device supplied the technological mediation, precisely counting off the minutes and marking the time between shots. In February 1909 Griffith shot his first film containing a suspensefully intercut phone conversation, *The Medicine Bottle*, followed in April and May of that year by his most famous telephone film, *The Lonely Villa*, a film which has become the *locus classicus* of parallel editing.

It is the genealogy of this film that I want to explore. With its last minute rescue; invasion of the bourgeois home; strict alternation between gender positions (the hysterical women inside the house, the threatening/rescuing males breaking in or rushing to the rescue); and, most important for my purposes, the technological link via the telephone that propels the climax into action, *The Lonely Villa* has become recognized as an archetype of film melodrama. But if the film is often cited as an *ur*-form of later rescue melodramas, we need to realize that it actually retells an older story which had already undergone a number of transformations. Retracing these various versions, we uncover a grim fable of technology whose fascination for early film-makers reveals some of the darker aspects of the dream world of instant communication and the annihilation of space and time.

A variety of film scholars have recently pointed to Pathé's *The Physician of the Castle* (1908) as the direct inspiration for Griffith's film.[16] The film, released in the USA in 1908 under the title *A Narrow Escape*,[17] has practically the same plot as *The Lonely Villa*. A doctor leaves his house to treat a patient after receiving a false message sent by burglars seeking to rob his house in his absence. When he arrives at the home of the patient he receives a desperate telephone call from his wife who tells him of the burglars' invasion. The physician jumps into his car for a wild race home, picking up two gendarmes on the way. He arrives home just in the nick of time to arrest the burglars about to seize his wife. Anyone familiar with Griffith's film recognizes an almost exact duplication. There are only minor plot changes (for example, the husband in Griffith's film is not a doctor; he calls home due to car trouble, only to discover the burglary in progress; and a gypsy wagon is dragooned into the race to the rescue in place of the disabled auto).

On the level of filmic discourse, however, the differences between the two films are significant. The Pathé film has twenty-six shots while *The Lonely Villa* has fifty-two. The most significant section of hyper-editing comes with the phone call. *The Physician of the Castle* devotes only four shots to this conversation (a long shot as the physician lifts the receiver; a parallel cut to a medium close-up (framed at the bust) of his wife on the phone telling of the burglary; a similar medium close-up of the physician as he hears the news; and a return to long shot as the physician hangs up the phone). Griffith, in contrast, develops the conversation over eighteen shots, including the husband briefly rushing out to check on his car and shots of the burglars' progress. In fact the suspensefully intercut telephone conversation far surpasses the actual race to the rescue to which Griffith devotes only seven shots.

16 The late Jay Leyda directed my attention to this and Barry Salt has published the most complete discussion of the film, in 'The Physician of the Castle', *Sight and Sound*, vol. 54, no. 4 (1985–6).

17 Cooper C. Graham, while a member of Leyda's seminar on Griffith Biograph Films at NYU, located the notice of the US release of this film. A synopsis can be found in *Moving Picture World*, vol. 2, no. 13 (1908), p. 270.

The Lonely Villa

The Lonely Villa

The Physician of the Castle

The Physician of the Castle

However, in researching the connection between these two films, I suddenly uncovered a number of other films from this transitional period with similar plots, which traced a path back to a 1901 play that served as the source for them all. Unfortunately, filmic analysis has to end here, since these earlier films exist only as catalogue descriptions which do not, alas, indicate the visual means of the portrayals of the telephone calls so central to their plot. But the differences in story-line command attention. The most detailed plot description comes from a film made by Edwin Porter for the Edison Company in August 1908 (between the Pathé and Biograph films) entitled *Heard over the Phone*. In contrast to the earlier demonstrations of patriarchial power restored with the aid of technology, Porter's film told a grim tale of defeat. In *Heard over the Phone* the disruption of the well-to-do suburban household comes from a hostler who is fired by the man of the house for mistreating the family's horses. As the father departs for New York City on business, the hostler vows revenge. I will quote from the film's original publicity bulletin for its description of the film's telephonic climax:

> BEFORE THE STORM: Mother and Child in sitting room—Mother reading to Child—Has presentiment of danger—Hears footsteps—Rushes to 'phone.
> AT HUSBAND'S OFFICE: Husband called up—Is startled—Thinks Wife unduly alarmed—Tries to allay her fears—Advises calmness.
> A TERRIBLE ORDEAL: Sudden interruption (Wife drops 'phone)—a masked face at the window—Husband hears a crash of broken glass—The Hostler's entrance—Wife screams—The attack—Child's pleading.
> AS IN A VISION: Husband wrought to a pitch of madness—In dreadful agony—Powerless to move—Hears every word—Witnesses as in a vision every scene enacted.
> MOTHER LOVE: Husband hears Wife's frantic appeal for mercy—His child's prayers—The curses and denunciation of the enraged Hostler.
> SUSPENSE: SILENCE—Hears Child's cry as Hostler secures her—The mother going to the rescue—The desperate struggle—The mother's cry as she regains her child—Frenzy of enraged and baffled Demon—A pistol shot—The mother's dying words as she crawls to the 'phone—The child's heart-rending sobs—Then silence.[18]

As anyone knows who has worked with early publicity bulletins, it is impossible to determine the visual treatment of this sequence. The text seems to indicate alternation between the two scenes. However the phrase 'As in a vision' may indicate some form of vision superimposition modelled on the vision scene as managed in nineteenth-century theatre. As *College Chums* and *Cupid's Pranks* (1908) show, Porter was adept at split-screen images. But, even without the actual film text, the narrative description of Porter's film is striking in its contrast to both the Pathé and Biograph films. The brutal violence, the father's incapacity to do anything but listen, and the specifically

18 *Film Index*, 5 September 1908, p. 14. I am indebted to Charles Musser for first alerting me to the existence of this film.

technological agony of the final silence carried over the telephone line provide a nightmare revision of Griffith's rescue melodrama.

Soon after Charles Musser directed my attention to this Edison film, my colleague, André Gaudreault, responded to my search for an original French catalogue description of *The Physician of the Castle* and sent me what appeared to be the description I needed. However, on closer inspection I realized that this text from the 1907 Pathé catalogue described an earlier version of *Physician of the Castle*, entitled *Terrible angoisse*, which shared Porter's grim ending. The description reads as follows:

> A successful lawyer at his country house for the summer is suddenly called to court. During his absence burglars break into his villa and the terrified young wife barely has time to rush to the telephone to call her husband. While she is telling him about the criminals, they seize her by the throat and strangle her, as well as her little boy. Hearing nothing more at the other end of the line, the devastated lawyer realizes what has happened and, mad with grief, rushes home. He throws himself on the corpses of his dear companion and his child.[19]

The rather shocking motifs of these two films (the destruction of a bourgeois family, technologically 'witnessed' by the *paterfamilias* who is incapable of intervening; his technological torment by sounds of unimaginable violence; and finally his devastation by deafening silence, as this aural medium mutely speaks of death) constitute the actual *ur*-form of *The Lonely Villa*, a nightmare of masculine impotence which the later film undoes and denies. These horrifying effects of a specifically modern agony, this demonstration of the suffering made possible through the illusory 'annihilation of space and time', are, in fact, the carefully managed effects of one of the first masters of suspense, playwright André de Lorde. De Lorde co-authored (with Charles Foley, whose short story provided the basic plot) the 1901 one-act play on which all these films were based, *Au téléphone*.[20] Although this play premièred at the Théâtre Libre with the founder of this innovative theatre of naturalism, André Antoine, in the lead, de Lorde was best known as the house author of the Grand Guignol, the Paris theatre of horror, and, after its première, *Au téléphone* soon became a well-known part of this theatre's repertoire.

The Grand Guignol had opened in Paris in 1897, featuring the grim naturalistic *rosse* plays that had shocked audiences at the Théâtre Libre a few years before, interspersed with satirical and *risqué* comedies. Working with manager Max Maury, de Lorde soon focused this formula on a particularly modern experience of agonizing suspense and horrifying climaxes. While certainly related to the nineteenth-century tradition of melodrama, The Grand Guignol differentiated itself by chronicling the triumphs of vice and the misfortunes, rather than the rewards, of virtue. Equally importantly, the theatre prided itself on its realism both in stage effects and in subject-matter. De Lorde particularly sought out a modern topology of horror, introducing the operating table

19 *Films et cinématographes Pathé* (Paris: Pathé Co., 1907), pp. 195–6 (my translation).

20 To my knowledge Kemp Niver was the first scholar to note *Au téléphone* as the source for *The Lonely Villa* in Bebe Bergsten (ed.), *D. W. Griffith, His Biograph Films in Perspective* (Los Angeles: John D. Roche, 1974), p. 91.

Au téléphone

(*Le laboratoire des hallucinations*) and the scientific laboratory (*L'horrible expérience*), the new treatment of mental illness at Salpêtrière (*Une leçon à la Salpêtrière*), the terrors of the speeding automobile (*40 HP*), and the dangers of colonialism (*La dernière torture*) to the stage. De Lorde's plays were brief, building, like Poe's tales, to a single emotional effect, one which de Lorde frequently described as 'the fear of being afraid'.[21]

Au téléphone embodies the psychological tension and the peculiarly modern effect of horror that de Lorde pursued. Its plot combines the action of *The Lonely Villa* with the ending of Porter's *Heard over the Phone* in a play consisting of two scenes in two locations. The first scene presents the vacation home of André Marex as he prepares to return to Paris on business and worries about train schedules and getting to the station on time. While the isolated location of their lonely villa has made train connections complex, Marex has had, at great expense, a telephone installed to aid his business. Using the phone to arrange a stopover at a friend's house that evening, he then departs, cautioning his wife and servant to be vigilant in his absence. After his departure, the male servant is drawn out of the house by a false message, leaving wife and child alone with an elderly female servant. Anxious, the wife calls her husband at the friend's home to which he had telephoned earlier. The phone call bridges the scene change, the second scene opening in the friend's apartment as the telephone rings. Marex at first tries to dispel his wife's anxiety, but suddenly she chokes with fear and Marex hears his home being broken into. He listens helplessly to the sounds of violent struggle, the screams of his child, and then complete silence. Marex cries out, 'they have murdered them', and the curtain falls.

In the play, the scene of distant violent death is conveyed only by the sounds heard over the telephone, mediated by Marex at the telephone. This technique supplied a tour de force for the actor playing Marex, through whose reactions 'the whole scene at the other end of the wire is brought vividly before the auditors', to quote a review from *The New York Dramatic Mirror*.[22] Marex moves from reassuring his anxious wife with rational discourse to uttering incoherent cries, until finally 'he drops the receiver unmanned, terror struck and maddened by the thought of his impotency'.[23]

Immobile, de Lorde's hero undergoes an agonizing paralysis, dramatically effective since the spectators are in the same fixed and helpless relation to unfolding events as Marex.[24] But if this technological torture serves mainly as a brilliant device in de Lorde's theatre of shudders, it also stands as a devastating fable of technology. Rather than allowing Marex to overcome space and time, the telephone torments him with distance and impotence. Electronic sound on the telephone can pass to and fro instantly, but the flesh and blood husband and father remains fixed and humiliated.

De Lorde frequently inverted the expected triumph of virtue in his horror plays. *La dernière torture*, for instance, deals with a group of French diplomats beseiged by Chinese rebels during the Boxer Uprising.

21 The Grand Guignol is chronicled in Mel Gordon, *The Grand Guignol: Theater of Fear and Terror* (New York: Amok Press, 1988), which includes de Lorde's essay 'Fear in literature'; and François Rivière and Gabrielle Wittkop, *Grand Guignol* (Paris: Henri Veyrier, 1979).

Le Grand Guignol

22 *Dramatic Mirror*, 11 October 1902, p. 16.

23 Ibid.

24 The obvious link between Hitchcock, Grand Guignol, and de Lorde in particular needs further investigation. The most effective scene in *Rear Window*, in which Stewart helplessly watches from across the courtyard as Grace Kelly is being beaten, clearly owes a great deal to *Au téléphone*.

The play ends as the French consul shoots his teenage daughter in order to prevent a 'fate worse than death' if she fell into the hands of the rebels. As soon as this act of murder is completed, the distraught father discovers that colonial troops have broken the seige. Seen today, this one-act play might well appear as a dark parody of Griffith's last-minute rescues.

Following the somewhat simplistic thesis which sees cinematic techniques as an answer to the narrative demands of nineteenth-century theatre,[25] it might seem that parallel editing provides the perfect technical solution to the dramatic situation of *Au téléphone*. However, cinema's ability to switch between locations instantly would in fact undercut de Lorde's effect of paralysis. And Griffith (and his Pathé predecessor) seem to understand this, matching parallel editing's mastery of space and time with the narrative transformation of the father's triumphant return in the company of the law to rescue his female family members. But if Griffith's film represents a secondary revision of de Lorde's nightmare, it also contains a moment that seems to hark back to the impotence of the *ur*-plot, a modified return of the repressed. Interestingly, this moment has no parallel in the simpler Pathé film. The shadow that de Lorde's *ur*-text casts over *The Lonely Villa* allows us to read this seemingly optimistic melodrama in another light.

This moment of extreme frustration comes when the burglars cut the telephone wire, thus creating a technological interruption which produces the greatest panic in the film, with both wife and husband making melodramatic gestures of despair (the husband in particular, staring out towards the camera, clenching his fists and bringing them to his head). The cut line brings to an end the eighteen-shot sequence which has alternated between ends of the phone line. Beyond the narrative omnipresence created by this parallel editing, this sequence also visualized a relation between husband and wife that goes beyond simple communication. Through a series of matching gestures the pair seem to be directly influencing each other physically, setting up an uncanny pattern of cause and effect.

As Rick Altman has shown in his penetrating structural analysis of *The Lonely Villa*, three times during the phone call Griffith cuts from the husband initiating a motion to the wife mirroring his gesture: first, both point towards the left presumably explaining their situations; secondly, as the husband tells the wife to get his revolver from his desk and fire it, he mimes pulling the trigger and the wife tries to shoot the gun; and finally the husband and wife both respond to the cut phone line by jiggling the phone switch. As Altman points out, each of these refers to a blockage in the plot (the broken down auto which the husband points towards; the unloaded revolver which does not fire; the cut phone line).[26] But, more explicitly, they all refer to technological breakdowns, with the cut telephone line producing the most panic. These cuts on gestures create an almost supernatural sense of the husband's ability to manipulate his wife: like a puppet master he makes the manipulative gesture which she completes as a performative gesture. The panic of the

25 The *locus classicus* of this argument is Nicholas A. Vardac, *From Stage to Screen: Theatrical Method from Garrick to Griffith* (New York: Benjamin Blom, 1968). Vardac's thesis was important for alerting film scholars to the prehistory of cinema in theatrical melodrama. However too many scholars have adopted it too literally, ignoring the very real differences between stage craft and film editing.

26 Rick Altman, '*The Lonely Villa* and Griffith's paradigmatic style', *Quarterly Review of Film Studies*, vol. 6, no. 2 (1981), pp. 123–34; see particularly pp. 126–7.

cut line produces an almost masturbatory gesture of ineffectiveness, as he seems to jiggle the phone endlessly, while the cut to his wife performing a similar gesture ironically establishes separation rather than power. The telephone connections and puppet lines have snapped.

The central technological breakdown in this triad, the misfiring revolver, may seem the weakest in terms of modernity, flanked by the stronger examples of the modes of transportation and communication. However, if slightly earlier in invention, the revolver plays a pivotal role in the technological and gendered plot. As a simple form of self-protection, available at the flexing of a trigger finger, the revolver allows an equality of the sexes which permits the husband to leave his wife unprotected (one which, significantly, does not repay his confidence). In Griffith's two later dramas of railway and telegraph, *The Lonedale Operator* (1911) and *A Girl and Her Trust* (1912), it is the woman's ability to create a simulacrum of a revolver that allows her to hold invading burglars at bay until the help summoned by her telegraph can arrive.

The importance of the revolver also indicates that someone at the Biograph company was aware of de Lorde's original. The removal of the bullets by the false messenger from the revolver the husband leaves for protection, as well as the departure of the servants, are details that *The Lonely Villa* shares with *Au téléphone* and which are missing from *The Physician of the Castle*. If not attributable to Griffith, this familiarity might derive from the film's scriptwriter (reputedly Mack Sennett who, in 1912, produced a comic parody of *Au téléphone* at Biograph, *Help, Help*).

If this moment of panic at technological interruption recalls the final effect of de Lorde's play, the contrasts set up by Griffith's version are also revealing. Both patriarchs are rendered hysterical by silence. In de Lorde's play the silence is the signifier of death; in Griffith's film it indicates a dead line. In *Au téléphone* it is the competence of the technological connection that causes horror—the husband can hear the murder as it takes place. In *The Lonely Villa* it is technology's malfunction that causes silence and panic. While Griffith on first sight seems to have generally whitewashed de Lorde's disturbing plot, his portrayal of technological panic may have an equally disturbing dimension.

The panic at the cut phone line parallels a transformation in the experience of technology that Schivelbusch observed in the railway. Initially train travel itself—the sensation of speed and dislocation it entailed—had caused anxiety for travellers. But as familiarity effaced fears, instead of the actual travelling causing anxiety, it was the possibility of the sudden interruption of its functioning that terrified the rail passenger and 'immediately reawakens the memory of the forgotten danger and potential violence; the repressed material returns with a vengeance'.[27] Like de Lorde's particularly modern horror—'the fear of being afraid'—it was the possibility of breakdown, of catastrophic accident, that caused anxiety.

27 Schivelbusch, *The Railway Journey*, p. 132.

Technology appears to play a more beneficial role in Griffith's film than it does in *Au téléphone*. It is, after all, the telephone call that informs the father of his family's danger and allows him to rescue them. However, contained within this fable of the restoration of order is the panic of its interruption. This reveals an essential aspect of modern technology: its inscription of its own interruption as the sign of catastrophe.[28] Just beneath the surface of the smoothly functioning system lies the threat of paralysis and impotence caused by its disruption.

To talk by telephone, *The Lonely Villa* indicates, is to risk being cut off. To travel by car is to risk mechanical breakdown. To rely on a revolver as a means of family protection is to risk having it useless if the bullets are removed. The smooth functioning of technology glides over the abyss of anxiety at its possible sudden failure. Technology functions, as Freud indicated, as a more than mixed blessing; it becomes a system of connections and separations, of distances and proximities, or appearances and disappearances, in fact a sort of titanic game of *fort/da*, by which modernity manages its fear of loss by tying it to a secondary anxiety—that of being cut off.

The climax of *The Lonely Villa* in some sense anticipates the climax of *Intolerance* (1916) in which the race to the rescue is constructed as a race between technologies, pitting racing car against locomotive, telephone against the efficiencies of the modern gallows. The strongest close-up in this sequence from *Intolerance* enlarges the hands of the hangmen with their razors poised over the cords which will release the gallows trap and string up Bobby Harron. Griffith constructs an elaborate system here of the need to make connections (the racing car stopping the train in its tracks, the governor phoning the warden) and the ever-poised terror of cutting them off. The system of *Intolerance* can be described precisely in these terms, as Griffith places long distance calls between millennia and continents, never sure if the circuits will hold. (In fact the great interpreter of modern hieroglyphic civilization, the poet Vachel Lindsay, described the film with a nearly telephonic metaphor: 'In Griffith's *Intolerance* Babylon is shown signalling across the ages to Judea . . .'.[29] Behind the assembling of these shots stands the image of the razor, the cutting implement that precedes the suture. And complexly situated, the spectator is placed to make these connections, a switchboard operator of narrative messages.

In *The Lonely Villa*, parallel cutting portrays a telephone conversation, visually conveying an aural experience. In *Au téléphone* the sound heard over the phone horribly calls us to imagine unseen atrocities. (Before the break-in becomes obvious, Marex had been romantically speaking to his wife saying, 'You are close to me—I hear the slightest inflection of your voice—almost every movement—can very nearly see you—yes, I see you, little wife'.)[30] In the play the new apparatus functions properly, driving the husband and father mad by conveying the fact that there is ultimately nothing more to hear. In the film the panic of interrupted communication galvanizes the head of the

28 Mary Ann Doane's work on the portrayal of disaster on television in a paper delivered to the Columbia Seminar on Cinema, 27 April 1989, entitled 'Information crisis: TV and catastrophe news coverage', stimulated my thinking in this direction.

29 This comment, contained in a 1917 review of Hugo Munster's *The Photoplay: a Psychological Study* in *The New Republic*, is reprinted in George C. Pratt (ed.), *Spellbound in Darkness: A History of the Silent Film* (Greenwich, NY: New York Graphic Society, 1973), pp. 224–7.

30 André de Lorde, 'At the Telephone', in *One Act Plays for Stage and Study*, p. 398.

family into frenzied action, reaching home just in time. But before the restoring action there comes the crucial moment of interruption. De Lorde casts his shadow over this rescue melodrama by revealing at its centre this image of the hysterical father, profoundly cut off.

Interestingly, adaptations of *Au téléphone* did not end with *The Lonely Villa*. Besides Sennett's 1912 parody, I have traced descriptions of a film from the independent Phoenix Company, *The Telephone Call* (1909), as well as versions by other important directors, such as Abel Gance's *Au secours* (1923) with Max Linder, which concludes with a witty send-up of the Grand Guignol standard; a Russian version from 1914 by Yakov Protazanov,[31] and Lois Weber's *Suspense* (1913) which is perhaps the single most original one reeler from the period of transition to features. Further, Griffith's later Biograph films include a large number of technological plots, among them *Death's Marathon* (1912) in which a dissolute father threatens suicide over the telephone and eventually commits it (when a last-minute rescue by friends fails) as his wife listens on the other end of the line.

While the imagery I have invoked from these fables of modernity clearly calls up a series of Freudian concepts, my use of Freud has been somewhat perverse. Following Benjamin's lead in his essay 'Some motifs in Baudelaire', I have tried to use Freudian concepts of castration and the *fort/da* game historically, as images that convey deeper strata of the experience of modernity, rather than as eternal aspects of human nature. Freud himself was often explicit on the role that modern technology played in either causing or revealing the nature of psychic trauma, from the relation between hysteria and the train accident, so important at the beginning of his career, to the wartime traumas that inspired his later speculations on the death drive. While for Freud the technical and historical aspects are ultimately superficial, it may well be that part of the nature of modernity is to call into question the relation between surface and depth, an inversion that Freud was instrumental in initiating, by directing attention to accidental acts of daily life and the nonsense of dreams. In the ongoing investigation of the history of early film Freud may—even unwillingly—provide us with profound insights into the dream world of technology.

---

31 The excellent scholar Yuri Tsivian mistakenly attributes the ending of this film, which returns to de Lorde's original, to Russian melancholia in *Silent Witnesses: Russian Films, 1908–19* (London: British Film Institute, 1989), p. 24.

Appendix: Screen History in *Screen*, 1972–1997

Abel, Richard, 'Scenes from domestic life in early French cinema', vol. 30, no. 3 (1989), 4–28.

Allen, Jeanne, 'Copyright protection in theatre, vaudeville and early cinema', vol. 21, no. 2 (1980), 79–91.

Allen, Robert C., 'From exhibition to reception: reflections on the audience in film history', vol. 31, no. 4 (1990), 347–57.

Balides, Constance, 'Scenarios of exposure in the practice of everyday life: women in the cinema of attractions', vol. 34, no. 1 (1993), 19–37.

Baxter, Peter, 'On the history and ideology of film lighting', vol. 16, no. 3 (1975), 83–106.

Boddy, William, ' "Spread like a monster blanket over the country": CBS and television, 1929–33', vol. 32, no. 2 (1991), 173–83.

Brewster, Ben, 'A scene at the "movies": the development of narrative perspective in early cinema', vol. 23, no. 2 (1982), 4–15.

Burch, Noël, 'Narrative/diegesis: thresholds, limits', vol. 23, no. 2 (1982), 16–33.

Butler, Alison, 'New film histories and the politics of location', vol. 33, no. 4 (1992), 413–26.

Elsaesser, Thomas, 'Lulu and the meter man', vol. 24, no. 4 (1983), 4–36.

Gomery, J. Douglas, 'Writing the history of the American film industry: Warner Bros and sound', vol. 17, no. 1 (1976), 40–53.

Grieveson, Lee, 'Policing the cinema: *Traffic in Souls* at Ellis Island, 1913', vol. 38, no. 2 (1997), 149–71.

Gunning, Tom, 'Heard over the phone: *The Lonely Villa* and the de Lorde tradition of the terrors of technology', vol. 32, no. 2 (1991), 184–96.

Haralovich, Mary Beth, 'The proletarian woman's film of the 1930s: contending with censorship and entertainment', vol. 31, no. 2 (1990), 172–87.

Harper, Sue, and Vincent Porter, 'Moved to tears: weeping in the cinema in postwar Britain', vol. 37, no. 2 (1996), 152–73.

King, Norman, 'The sound of silents', vol. 25, no. 3 (1984), 2–15.

Klinger, Barbara, 'Film history, terminable and interminable: recovering the past in reception studies', vol. 38, no. 2 (1997), 107–28.

Kuhn, Annette, 'The *Married Love* affair', vol. 27, no. 2 (1986), 5–21.

Langer, Mark, 'The Disney–Fleischer dilemma: product differentiation and technological innovation', vol. 33, no. 4 (1992), 343–60.

Lindsey, Shelley Stamp, 'Is any girl safe? female spectators at the white slave films', vol. 37, no. 1 (1996), 1–15.

MacMurraugh-Kavanagh, M. K., ' "Drama" into "news": strategies of intervention in "The Wednesday Play" ', vol. 38, no. 3 (1997), 247–59.

Maltby, Richard, '*Baby Face*, or how Joe Breen made Barbara Stanwyck atone for causing the Wall Street Crash', vol. 27, no. 2 (1986), 22–45.

—— '*King of Kings* and the czar of all the rushes: the propriety of the Christ story', vol. 31, no. 2 (1990), 188–213.

Murphy, Robert, 'A rival to Hollywood?: the British film industry in the thirties', vol. 24, no. 4 (1983), 96–106.

Nowell-Smith, Geoffrey, 'On history and the cinema', vol. 31, no. 2 (1990), 160–71.

Ogle, Patrick L., 'Technological and aesthetic influences upon the development of deep focus cinematography in the United States', vol. 13, no. 1 (1972), 45–72.

Pearson, Roberta E., and Uricchio, William, 'How many times shall Caesar bleed in sport: Shakespeare and the cultural debate about moving pictures', vol. 31, no. 3 (1990), 243–62.

Smoodin, Eric, ' "This business of America": fan mail, film reception and *Meet John Doe*', vol. 37, no. 2 (1996), 111–28.

Spigel, Lynne, 'From the dark ages to the golden age: women's memories and TV reruns', vol. 36, no. 1 (1995), 16–33.

Stacey, Jackie, 'Hollywood memories', vol. 35, no. 4 (1994), 317–35.

Staiger, Janet, 'Individualism versus collectivism: the shift to independent production in the US film industry', vol. 24, no. 4 (1983), 68–79.

Thumim, Janet, 'The "popular", cash and culture in the postwar British cinema industry', vol. 32, no. 3 (1991), 245–71.

—— ' "A live commercial for icing sugar": researching the historical audience—gender and broadcast television in the 1950s', vol. 36, no. 1 (1995), 48–55.

Vincendeau, Ginette, 'New approaches to film history', vol. 26, no. 6 (1985), 70–3.

Zimmermann, Patricia R., 'Trading down: amateur film technology in fifties America', vol. 29, no. 2 (1998), 40–51.

Notes on Contributors

Jeanne Allen is Associate Professor in the Department of Film and Media Arts at Temple University in Philadelphia, USA.

Robert C. Allen is James Logan Godfrey Professor of American Studies, History, and Communication Studies at the University of North Carolina at Chapel Hill. He is the author of *Horrible Prettiness: Burlesque And American Culture* (University of North Carolina Press, 1991) and *Speaking of Soap Operas* (University of North Carolina Press, 1985); he is the co-author with Douglas Gomery of *Film History: Theory and Practice* (McGraw-Hill, 1985); and the editor of *Channels of Discourse* and *Channels of Discourse Reassembled*, both published by the University of North Carolina Press in 1992.

Constance Balides teaches in the Department of Communication at Tulane University, New Orleans. She is completing a book on women and early cinema entitled *Making Dust in the Archives*, to be published by the University of Minnesota Press, and has articles in *Screen* and *Camera Obscura*.

William Boddy is a professor at Baruch College and the Graduate Center of the City University of New York and is the author of *Fifties Television: The Industry and its Critics* (University of Illinois Press, 1990).

Ben Brewster was the editor of *Screen* from 1974 to 1976. He then taught film studies at the University of Kent at Canterbury for fifteen years, and is currently Assistant Director of the Wisconsin Center for Film and Theater Research, Madison, Wisconsin. He is co-author (with Lea Jacobs) of *Theater to Cinema: Stage Pictorialism and the Early Feature Film* (Oxford University Press, 1997), and has contributed articles to such magazines as *Cinema Journal* and *Film History*.

Noël Burch teaches at the Université de Lille III. He has made the following films: *Correction, Please or How We Got into Pictures* (1979), *The Year of the Bodyguard* (1982), *What Do Those Old Films*

Mean (1984–6), *Sentimental Journey: Refuseniks* (1994). He is the author of *Theory of Film Practice* (Secker & Warburg, 1973) and *Life to those Shadows* (British Film Institute, 1990) and, with Geneviève Sellier, *La Drôle de guerre des sexes du cinéma français* (Nathan, 1996).

Douglas Gomery teaches at the University of Maryland, located five miles from the Library of Congress. He has published a number of books including *Shared Pleasures* (University of Wisconsin Press, 1992). His current research and writing concentrates on television and popular music.

Tom Gunning teaches in the Art History Department and Cinema and Media Program at the University of Chicago. He is the author of *D. W. Griffith and the Origins of American Narrative Film* (University of Illinois Press, 1994) and of numerous articles on early cinema. His forthcoming works deal with Fritz Lang (British Film Institute) and with early cinema and modernity (Harvard University Press).

Mary Beth Haralovich teachers film and television in Media Arts at the University of Arizona in Tucson. Her essay on Cold War politics and civil rights in *I Spy* (US, NBC, 1965–8) will appear in a forthcoming collection of feminist essays on US television history, co-edited with Lauren Rabinovitz. Her 1930s Hollywood film project includes research on local film promotion in diverse cities across the USA and analysis of segregated race relations in the films.

Annette Kuhn is Reader in the Institute for Cultural Research at Lancaster University, and an editor of *Screen*. Her publications include: *The Power of the Image: Essays on Representation and Sexuality* (Routledge and Kegan Paul, 1985), *Cinema, Censorship and Sexuality* (Routledge and Kegan Paul, 1988), *Family Secrets: Acts of Memory and Imagination* (Verso, 1995), and, as editor, *Queen of The Bs: Ida Lupino Behind the Camera* (Flicks Books, 1995).

Mark Langer is Associate Professor of Film Studies in the School for Studies in Art and Culture at Carleton University in Ottawa, and has been a guest curator of animation retrospectives for a number of museums, archives, and festivals. His work has appeared in such journals as *Screen, Cinema Journal, Art History, Animation Journal,* and *Wide Angle.*

Richard Maltby is Head of Screen Studies at the Finders University of South Australia. He is the author of *Hollywood Cinema: An Introduction* (Blackwell, 1995) and *Harmless Entertainment: Hollywood And The Ideology Of Consensus* (Scarecrow, 1983). He is currently editing a series of books on Hollywood and its audiences, and completing *Reforming The Movies: Politics, Censorship and the Institutions of the American Cinema, 1908–1939.*

Jackie Stacey is Senior Lecturer in the Department of Sociology at Lancaster University. She is an editor of *Screen*, author of *Star Gazing:*

Hollywood Cinema and Female Spectatorship (Routledge, 1994) and *Teratologies: A Cultural Study of Cancer* (Routledge, 1997); she has also co-edited the following collections: *Off-Centre: Feminism and Cultural Studies* (Routledge, 1991) (with Sarah Franklin and Celia Lury); *Working Out: New Directions for Women's Studies* (Falmer Press, 1992) (with Hilary Hinds and Ann Phoenix); and *Romance Revisited* (Lawrence and Wishart, 1995) (with Lynne Pearce).

Janet Thumim is a senior lecturer in Film and Television at the University of Bristol. Her publications include *Celluloid Sisters* (Macmillan, 1992) and the co-edited collections *You Tarzan* and *Me Jane* (Lawrence and Wishart, 1993 and 1995). She is currently writing a history of early television in Britain for Oxford University Press.